Britain, Germany and the Battle of the Atlantic

Bloomsbury Studies in Military History

Bloomsbury Studies in Military History offers up-to-date, scholarly accounts of war and military history. Unrestricted by period or geography, the series aims to provide free-standing works that are attuned to conceptual and historiographical developments in the field while being based on original scholarship.

Published:
The 56th Infantry Brigade and D-Day, Andrew Holborn (2010)
The RAF's French Foreign Legion, G. H. Bennett (2011)
Empire and Military Revolution in Eastern Europe, Brian Davies (2011)
Reinventing Warfare 1914–1918, Anthony Saunders (2011)
Fratricide in Battle, Charles Kirke (2012)
The Army in British India, Roy Kaushik (2012)
The 1711 Expedition to Quebec, Adam Lyons (2013)

Forthcoming:
The Role of the Royal Navy in South America, Jon Wise (2014)
Reassessing the British Way in Warfare, Keith McLay (2014)
Scotland and the British Army 1700–1750, Victoria Henshaw (2014)
The D-Day Landing on Gold Beach, Andrew Holborn (2014)
Cavalry, Guns and Military Transition in Early Modern Asia, Roy Kaushik (2014)
Australasian Propaganda and the Vietnam War, Caroline Page (2015)

Britain, Germany and the Battle of the Atlantic

A Comparative Study

Dennis Haslop

Bloomsbury Academic
An imprint of Bloomsbury Publishing Plc

B L O O M S B U R Y
LONDON • NEW DELHI • NEW YORK • SYDNEY

Bloomsbury Academic
An imprint of Bloomsbury Publishing Plc

50 Bedford Square   1385 Broadway
London   New York
WC1B 3DP   NY 10018
UK   USA

www.bloomsbury.com

BLOOMSBURY and the Diana logo are trademarks of Bloomsbury Publishing Plc

First published 2013
Paperback edition first published 2015

British Library Cataloguing-in-Publication Data
A catalogue record for this book is available from the British Library.

ISBN: HB: 978-1-4725-0723-5
PB: 978-1-4742-3691-1
ePDF: 978-1-4725-1163-8
ePUB: 978-1-4725-1112-6

Library of Congress Cataloging-in-Publication Data
A catalog record for this book is available from the Library of Congress.

Series: Bloomsbury Studies in Military History

Typeset by Newgen Knowledge Works (P) Ltd., Chennai, India

Contents

List of Illustrations   vi
Acknowledgements   vii
Abbreviations   viii

Introduction   1
1 Elements of German Planning for Convoy Warfare   11
2 Elements of British Planning for Convoy Protection   29
3 New Opportunities for U-boat Bases and Inter-service Rivalry   49
4 The Development of the Western Approaches Command   65
5 U-boat Training to Meet the Requirements of Grey Water Strategy   83
6 Escort Training to Meet the Requirements of Grey Water Strategy   105
7 Learning the Lessons of Training and Procedures:
    ONS-154 – A Case Study from December 1942   125
8 Training to Meet the Requirements of Change   143
9 The Influence of 'OR' on Developments   163
10 The Influence of German 'OR' on U-boat Operations   183
11 The Repulse of the U-boat Atlantic Offensive and Its Consequences   207
12 Return of the U-boat to the North Atlantic and the End Game   231
13 Conclusion   255
Appendix 1   Organization Chart: *Kriegsmarine* 1938   271
Appendix 2   Organization Chart: Naval War Staff   273
Appendix 3   *Lagezimmer* Operations and Staff Support Functions   275

Bibliography   277
Index   301

Illustrations

Charts

Chart 2.1	Organization chart depicting the defence of trade	31
Chart 2.2	Shipping losses by quarter, 1939–45	36
Chart 4.1	Western Approaches Command structure	72
Chart 10.1	Kriegsmarine partial departmental organization chart, effective October 1944	192
Chart 11.1	Track of SC-130	213

Figure

Figure 12.1	Type 'R' diesel/electric submarine 1918	243

Tables

Table 6.1	Training of A/S Officers at Portland, 1935–8	108
Table 11.1	U-boats lost in the North Atlantic – May 1943	222
Table 11.2	U-boats lost in the North Atlantic – March and April 1943	223
Table 12.1	R-Class submarine basic specifications	244
Table 12.2	Front-line U-boat losses (only)	247

Acknowledgements

Copyright material in this work appears by kind permission of:

The Naval Review for the use of a chart showing shipping losses by quarter, 1939–45.

The Royal Naval Submarine Museum, Gosport for the use of a photograph of HMS R3.

Abbreviations

German

Agru-Front	Technical Training Group for Front-line U-boats
Alberich	U-boat Anechoic Tile Covering
Ausbildungsfliegerführer	Aircraft Commander Training
BA-MA	Bundesarchiv-Militärarchiv, National Military Archives
B-Dienst	Beobachtungsdienst, or Surveillance Service
BdU	Befehlshaber der U-boote, Flag Officer U-boats
BdU.org	BdU Organizationsabteilung, Flag Officer U-boat Organization
CPVA	Chemisch-Physikalische Versuchsanstalt, Naval-Physical Chemistry Development Institute
Fähnrich	Junior Midshipman
FdU	Führer der U-boote, U-boat Leader
Feindfahrt	War Patrol
FEP	Forschungs, Erfindungs und Patentwesen, Naval Research Institute
FAT	Flächenabsuchendertorpedo, 'Curly'
Fliegerführer	Flight Leader/Commander
Forschungsabteilung	Research Department
Forschungsaustausch	Exchange of Research Results
Fregattenkapitän	Commander
Führer	Leader
FuMT 1 and 2	Radar Decoys
Geleitzugtorpedos	Convoy Torpedoes
General der Luft	General Air Commanding
Geschwader	Flight [Wing]
Großadmiral	Admiral of the Fleet
HAS	Hauptausschuss Schiffbau, Principal Committee, Shipbuilding

HKU	Höheres Kommando der Unterseebootsausbildung, U-boat High Command Training Centre
Heer	Army
Kapitän Leutnant	Lieutenant Commander
Kapitän zur See	Captain
K-Amt	*Hauptamt für Kriegsschiffbau*, Main Shipbuilding Office
Konteradmiral	Rear Admiral
Korvettenkapitän	Lt Commander (1st Class)
Kriegsmarine	German [War] Navy
Kriegsmarinearbeitsgemeinschaft	Naval Unions
Kriegswissenschaftlicheabteilung	Military Naval Science
KTB	Kriegstagebuch, War Diary
Kurier	Signal Compression, 'Squash'
Küstenfliegerverbände	Coastal Command Units
Lagevorträge	Situation Reports, known in Britain as Führer Conferences
Lagezimmer	Situation Room
Leutnant zur See	Sub-Lieutenant
Li. Bericht	Engineer's Report
Luftflotte	Air Fleet
Luftwaffe	German Air Force
LUT	Lagenunabhängigertorpedo, Position Independent Torpedo
MAP	Militärarchiv, Military Archive Potsdam
MPA	Marine Personalabteilung, Personnel Department *Marineleitung* Naval Command
MKrGesch	Military Science (*Kr*) Division
MND	Marinenachrichtendienst, Communications Division
MRue	Naval Armaments
MWa	*Marinewaffenämte*, Naval Weapons Departments
NVA	Nachrichtenversuchsanstalt/ Communications Development Institute

NVK	Nachrichtenversuchskommando, Communications Development Command
Oberfähnrich	Midshipman
Oberleutnant zur See	Lieutenant
ObdL	Oberbefehlshaber der Luft, Commander in Chief of the Air Force
ObdM	Oberbefehlshaber der Marine, C-in-C of the Navy
ObdW	Oberbefehlshaber der Wehrmacht, C-in-C of the Armed Forces
OKH	Oberkommando des Heers, Army High Command
OKM	Oberkommando der Kriegsmarine, Naval High Command
OKW	Oberkommando der Wehrmacht, Armed Forces High Command
Reichsforschungsrat	Research Council
Reichsmarine	National Navy
Rudeltaktik	Pack Tactics
Seekriegsleitung	Naval War Staff
S-Gerät	ASDIC (SONAR)
Staffel	Squadron
Technische Hochschulen	Technical High Schools
TVA	Torpedoversuchsanstalt, Torpedo Development Institute
TI	Torpedoinspektion, Torpedo Inspection
Torpedoschußmeldung	Torpedo Usage Log
UAS	Unterseebootabwehrschule, U-boat Defence School
UZO	Überwasserzieloptik, Surface Target Optics
Vizeadmiral	Vice Admiral
WFM	Wissenschaftlicherführungsstab der Marine, Naval Scientific Directorate
WO	Wachoffizier, or Watch-keeping Officer
xB-Dienst	Cryptographic Service
Zaunkönig	Wren, Acoustic Torpedo
Zerstörerknacker	Destroyer Killer

British

ACAS	Assistant Chief of Air Staff
ACHQ	Area Combined Headquarters
ACI	Admiralty Convoy Instructions
ACNS	Assistant Chief of Naval Staff
ACNS(UT)	Assistant Chief of Naval Staff (U-boats and Trade)
AOC	Air Officer Commanding
AOC C-in-C	Air Officer Commanding Commander in Chief
A/S	Anti-submarine
AS	Anti-submarine Squadron
ASE	Admiralty Signals Establishment
A/SEE	Anti-submarine Experimental Establishment.
ASDIC	Early British name for Sonar
ASSB	Allied Anti-submarine Survey Board
ASW	Anti-submarine Warfare
ATW	Ahead Throwing Weapon
AUC	Anti-submarine Warfare Committee
AUD	Anti-U-boat Division
BAC	Battle of the Atlantic Committee
C-in-C	Commander-in-Chief
C-in-C WA	Commander-in-Chief, Western Approaches
CAFO	Confidential Admiralty Fleet Orders
CAOR	Chief Advisor on Operational Research
CCDU	Coastal Command Development Unit
CID	Committee for Imperial Defence
CNS	Chief of Naval Staff, First Sea Lord
CVE	Carrier Escort Vessels
DAUD	Director of Anti-U-boat Division
D of Ops	Director of Operations, Air Ministry
DASW	Director of Anti-submarine Warfare Division
DAUD	Director of Anti-U-Boat Division
DAW	Director of Air Warfare
DC	Depth Charge
DCNS	Deputy Chief of Naval Staff
DCOS	Deputy Chief of Staff
DDI	Deputy Director of Intelligence

D/F	Direction Finder
DNC	Director of Naval Construction
DNI	Director of Naval Intelligence
DNOR	Director of Naval Operational Research
DOD	Director of Operations Division
D of P	Director of Plans Division
D of TD	Director of the Tactical Division
DTASW	Director of Torpedo, Anti-submarine and Mine Warfare Division
DTD	Director of Trade Division
DTM	Director of Torpedoes and Mining
EG	Escort Group
FAA	Fleet Air Arm
Foxer	Noise Maker
GAP	Area South of Greenland
GC&CS	Government Code and Cipher School
GNAT	German Naval Acoustic Torpedo, 'Curly'
GRT	Gross Register Tons
HE	Hydrophone Effect
H/F	High Frequency Radio
HF/DF	High Frequency [Radio] Direction Finding
HMS	HM Ship
HMCS	HM Canadian Ship
HQ	Headquarters
HUS	High Underwater Speed U-boats
MAD	Magnetic Anomaly Detector
MAP	Ministry of Aircraft Production
NARA	National Archives, Washington
NCO	Non-commissioned Officer
NCSO	Naval Control Service Officer
NHB	Naval Historical Branch
NID	Naval Intelligence Division
NOR	Naval Operational Research
OIC	Operational Intelligence Centre
OR	Operational Research
ORS	Operational Research Section
POW	Prisoners of War
PPI	Plan Position Indicator
RAE	Royal Aircraft Establishment

RAF	Royal Air Force
RCAF	Royal Canadian Air Force
RCN	Royal Canadian Navy
RN	Royal Navy
RNR	Royal Naval Reserves
RNVR	Royal Naval Volunteer Reserve
RP	Rocket Projectile
SASO	Senior Air Staff Officer, of an RAF Command
SBT	Submarine Bubble Target
S/D	Submarine Detector Branch
S/D I	Submarine Detector Instructor
SOE	Senior Escort Commander Sunday Soviets Free Discussion Groups
TAS	Torpedo and Anti-submarine Warfare
TNA	The National Archives, formerly PRO
TRE	Telecommunications Research Establishment
U-boat	Submarine
USN	United States Navy
VCNS	Vice Chief of Naval Staff
VHF	Very High Frequency (radio)
VLR	Very Long Range
WA	Western Approaches Command
WATU	Western Approaches Tactical Unit

Introduction

The Battle of the Atlantic, although only announced as such by Winston Churchill in March 1941, is generally regarded as beginning on 3 September 1939 with the sinking of the liner *Athenia*.[1] The British surmised that there would be unrestricted submarine warfare[2] and implemented a planned adoption of the Convoy system, albeit only partial, due to a lack of available escorts.

Both Germany and Britain presided over a navy with certain weaknesses, due to prevailing circumstances. The *Kriegsmarine* abandoned its planned long-term strategy of a balanced surface fleet with which to challenge the Royal Navy (RN); had too few U-boats to mount a big offensive; and started out hemmed in by British territory surrounding their naval bases. Attempts were made to secure co-operation with the *Luftwaffe* and had some initial success. In the longer term it could not be sustained, largely because of inter-service rivalries. The British began the war with too few escorts for the provision of adequate convoy protection to operate efficiently, with tactics too basic to be effective,[3] and the provision of air escorts by Coastal Command of the Royal Air Force (RAF) proved to be a challenge,[4] and they suffered from a lack of training. They also had no defined rôle in anti-submarine warfare. Each navy had problems in urgent need of attention, and much to learn. At the outset both were to discover that parts of their organization were ill-equipped to deal with change and in order to learn from past mistakes it was found necessary to modify the existing organization.

On 24 May 1943, Admiral Dönitz (now C-in-C *Kriegsmarine*) called for a temporary withdrawal of U-boat operations from the North Atlantic, due to the heavy losses sustained in the previous three months. This event, together with others in this month, probably signalled the end of the Battle of the Atlantic and has been so cited by numerous historians and by Dönitz, who said, 'We had lost the Battle of the Atlantic'.[5] On that date a part of what he signalled to his U-boat commanders was,

> 'In the meantime we must overcome the situation with the measures already determined and with a temporary change in operational areas . . .'. [6]

Dönitz had much to think about how this situation could have arisen given that the U-boat arm, although slow to start, had reasonable success against convoys for three years,[7] up until three months prior to withdrawal. What could have happened in that short time-span that could explain how things had gone so badly wrong? What were the options left open to him and how could he explain the dilemma to the *Führer*, Adolf Hitler?

The high point of the battle had been reached, but 'historians of the Second World War usually abandon the story of the Atlantic at this stage'.[8] Much has still to be written since the conflict between the U-boat and A/S forces was just beginning to enter a most interesting phase. The main questions, however, linger. To what degree had the two nations prepared for this war; how appropriate were their existing organizations to learn the many lessons of the past; what organizational choices were available to them that could improve their learning capacity; how much training effort and application did they commit to the *guerre de course* (commerce warfare); and how effective were they in translating the feedback of problems into remedies?

Features of the book

This book provides a new insight into how lessons in Convoy Warfare were learned and how they impacted on the Battle of the Atlantic, and is a focused work. There is an examination of organization, training and operational research (OR) and how the feedback and lessons learned were assimilated in these disciplines during this long campaign. In the process it also highlights where some important opportunities were lost. It demonstrates how changing circumstances, that could not have been foreseen prewar, had to be coped with by both navies. What is not discussed is the FAA (Fleet Air Arm), since British CVEs (Carrier Vessel Escorts) did not see service until April/May1943,[9] by which time the Battle of the Atlantic was virtually over; also, from late April 1943, MACs (Merchant Aircraft Carriers) began to replace the CVE.[10]

The *Kriegsmarine* had learnt practically nothing in terms of inter-service co-operation at the front line level with the *Luftwaffe*, and were thus unable to acquire any long-standing agreement on joint sea/air operations that would have simplified detection of convoys and attack procedures. It invested vast sums of time and money into training their fledgling U-boat arm and in the late pursuit of advanced technology, using the medium of inter-service 'OR' – the latter being too late to be of any practical value in the outcome of the Battle of the Atlantic, but percentage gains were in orders of magnitude. They co-operated with the other two services and their departments of research in pursuit of common technology goals by sharing knowledge, and were thus able to learn from each other. Britain too invested heavily in training and was able to show steady progress in anti-submarine warfare measures and tactics. Similar to the Germans the Admiralty also had a degree of inter-service co-operation in OR and the sharing of knowledge of weapons technology but it will be revealed that British 'OR' outcomes were modest and restricted to percentage gains, not orders of magnitude and less in the development of new technology – with the single exception of Radar. In several instances Britain decided to devolve the responsibility for building and supplying items of national interest to the Americans, for example the 'cavity' magnetron, at the heart of centimetric radar development, the 'homing' torpedo,[11] as well as the manufacture of 'bombes' which were at the very core of the GC&CS (Government Code and Cipher School) computer project used in sophisticated decryption techniques; unsurprising when one considers the woeful state of British electrical and electronic manufacture of the time.[12] Thus, several mistakes were made in development strategy; but ultimately some useful improvements to weapons efficiency and convoy strategy were obtained.

This book provides an innovative basis against which to assess the German and British approach to convoy warfare during the Second World War. It contains analyses that highlight some of the deficiencies that both Navies faced and how they attempted to overcome their earlier mistakes, in more subtle and forward-thinking methods than is generally known. Moreover, this book takes the radical approach of making comparisons of the methods used by both sides, something that does not appear to have ever been attempted before.

Several historians start out from a false premise of a U-boat crisis. A good account by Duncan Redford provides the reader with an overview of the 'myth' of the March U-boat crisis in the Battle of the Atlantic of 1943;[13] the 'crisis' scenario was probably started by Stephen Roskill after having viewed the CB 04050 December review of 1943, and drew the conclusion from a viewpoint given by a member of the Naval Staff. Several historians have referred to the crisis, but are incorrect in their interpretation.[14] Redford, a more revisionist historian, is more correct, as may be determined from Roskill's later subtle retraction.[15] Most convoys got through unscathed, but some did not. There are also historians who have availed themselves of the post 1974 'Ultra' secrets and tended to give too much credit of the Atlantic victory to code breaking.[16] However, the more revisionist historian, Milner, for example, tames it down somewhat by suggesting that evasive routing provided by Ultra in 1941 probably saved the Allies about 300 ships.[17]

The typical weakness of many previous accounts of the Battle of the Atlantic is that they tend to concentrate on an apparently continuous succession of convoy battles in 1942–3, almost on a blow-by-blow account, without any discussion on tactical methodology or the training required to implement tactical solutions. Where lessons of tactical or strategic importance were learned they make no distinction about how these lessons learned may have been assimilated through organization, training or 'OR' methods.

Some German historians point to the difficulties faced by a relatively new navy, following the collapse of the last one.[18] The Versailles treaty placed severe restrictions on what assets could be held and it was not until Hitler arrived on the political scene in the early 1930s that they became emboldened in their demands for a stronger navy. But this action presented the administration with a new dilemma. They were not yet organized to present a credible fighting force capable of taking on their arch rival, England (Britain),[19] with whom they were not expected to go to war with for some time.[20] These same historians, however, do not appear to have highlighted many of the lessons which may have been learned from the last war. The German perception of the U-boat war is covered in both primary and secondary sources. German primary material may be found in the captured German documents of the PG (Pinched German) series, which starts with the appointment of Dönitz in 1936.[21] When the *Tambach* collection was microfilmed in Britain after the war, not all documents were included, only those of interest to the Admiralty. The *Bundesarchiv* Freiburg, Germany has the original written documents, including some of those missing from the British collection. The documents relating to the efforts of the *BdU* to work with the *Luftwaffe* provide a good insight into the difficulties faced.[22] Of particular interest in this book are the original documents related to OR conducted on sub-surface rocket technology, the forerunner of the modern sub-surface ballistic missile.[23]

Good information on both British and German assessments may be found in the pages of F. Barley and D. W. Waters's combined versions of the former CB 3304 (1A) and (1B), later BR 1736 (51) A and (51) B, *The Defeat of the Enemy Attack on Shipping 1939–1945: A Study of Policy and Operations*. Of particular note are the explanations of various issues dealt with in this work, and statistical data showing chronological trends in both ship and U-boat losses. The National Archives Kew also has some good evaluations of the U-boat war from a German perspective, and the British response, contained within the ADM and HW series of documents. German organization and training sources come primarily from captured German documents of the PG series and Admiralty appreciations on the subject plus secondary sources, some of which were researched after the war. RN ASW (Anti-submarine Warfare) training is well covered in the ADM series and by good secondary source material, including the ASW tactical school WATU (Western Approaches Tactical Unit).

Although there are several valuable and critical analyses, the delineation of battles against packs of U-boats leads to an exaggeration of their overall historical importance, for in many respects these battles are simply indicative of the general progress made in Convoy and anti U-boat warfare and do not take account of how feedback helped to fashion lessons learned, and how progress was achieved, on both sides.

Of particular interest to readers of naval history is how this book addresses gaps in the existing literature on convoy warfare by first examining the structure of the German and British Navies for the purpose of convoy warfare. It addresses the lacuna of knowledge of how the U-boat arm was organized and how it fitted into the overall structure of the *Kriegsmarine* and the operations department of the *Seekriegsleitung*. It had to build-up the U-boat arm from very modest beginnings in 1936 into a sizeable force by 1943 and interface it with the signals intelligence branch, known as the *B-Dienst,* in order to successfully conduct its operations against allied merchantmen. The literature surrounding the *Kriegsmarine* and the *Seekriegsleitung*, other than in German, is virtually non-existent, except for some pictorial overviews of a non-academic nature that have been written by several authors.

In the prosecution of the commerce warfare the U-boat arm had hoped to secure the co-operation of the *Luftwaffe* but due to intense rivalry between the two heads of the respective services, this became a dismal failure. This work describes the essence of that failure and examines the relationships between the U-boat arm and the *Luftwaffe* and where important lessons could have been learned, which is a subject that historians have barely touched upon. There are two exceptions. One German historian, Horst Boog, provides a good insight into the background of where some of the possible reasons for this dilemma lie, some of which date back to the First World War.[24] Another, Sönke Neitzel, has extensively researched Luftwaffe maritime operations, which fills in part of the gap.[25] That too is discussed in order to obtain a clear understanding of how inter-service rivalry influenced the outcome of what might have proved to be a good symbiotic association. Evidence from other sources is provided in the text that helps to complete the picture, including primary material from the PG series, interspersed with official extracts from the navy's situation reports to Hitler, known as *Lagevorträge*. A German PhD Thesis on the subject of the *Luftwaffe*,[26] and a good book on naval fliers, also provides some input, which adds to this theme. A recent publication, *The Luftwaffe and the War at Sea 1939–1945*, has some limited findings on the Battle of the Atlantic, based on a US Navy post war report. Its signal weakness lies in the lack of much editorial introduction, or comment as to accuracy, and no footnotes to assist the reader.[27]

A good source of material for U-boat training may be found in the pages of the commissioned volumes of the GC&CS series on the Germany Navy. A report commissioned by the Admiralty on the interrogation of enemy prisoners also serves the subject well; as does new unpublished material found at the U-boat archives in Altenbruch, Germany. The new material in Altenbruch deals with the early days of *UAS U-bootabwehrschule,* a cover name used for U-boat training prior to the outbreak of war; *UAS* was the forerunner of the main U-boat training schools, but then continued as a separate entity for specialized training up to the end of the war; a point overlooked by other historians.

The means of communicating the current German situation of the war on convoys was through the medium of regular discussions with the leadership and is another gap in historical knowledge that needs to be filled. Situation reports (*Lagevorträge*) were a feature of the Second World War when the *Kriegsmarine* presented its findings to Hitler on a regular basis. While the anglicized 'Führer Conferences' of the *Lagevorträge*, more correctly translated as Situation Reports, have been published by Brassey the German version is preferred by the author.[28] In the writer's view, the sentiments presented in German are more notionally correct than the English version. The Anglicized Führer Conferences suffer further in that many of the meetings have been abridged, and therefore miss some important aspects. Furthermore, having read some of the English translation version it was felt that some of the nuances, often missed in translation, appeared to occasionally distort matters. For instance, a more definitive account of the failure of the *Luftwaffe* may be read in the various pages of reports given to Hitler by the *ObdM* of the *Kriegsmarine* in his regular meetings, or in his absence by his Chief of Staff. These are guarded comments but emphasize the degree of co-operation, or lack thereof. Such an example is given on page 197 of the *Lagevorträge*, but there were many more.

This book has a section devoted to a brief review of the Admiralty and some interwar considerations. It recounts the early events in the war, describing two committees that were formed in an effort to steer the joint-chiefs of staff in a common approach direction. It discusses the initial assets available to the RN for convoy protection and provides an insight into some of the reasons surrounding the failure of the Admiralty to learn valuable lessons from the First World War. The nub of the RN efforts to provide adequate protection for convoys lay in the structure of WA (Western Approaches Command) and its development as the centre for controlling ship movements, both naval and merchant, as well as air patrols. The book describes the necessity for the physical move from Plymouth to Liverpool in 1941 and the degree of co-operation that existed between the RN and Coastal Command of the RAF. In contrast to the German experience, co-operation with the Coastal Command was one of the success stories of the Battle of the Atlantic and the vein of information is used for comparison purposes with the German experience; and this can be seen in good primary sources of the ADM and AIR series, plus secondary material. Supporting the efforts of WA (Western Approaches Command) was the OIC (Operational Intelligence Centre), the origins of which are briefly described. Also discussed is the training provided to the ASW branch of the RN from its earliest days until the main practical training effort was centred on the WA, which also initiated a tactical school. Tactical doctrine is covered, where applicable.

A necessary part of improving weapons and methods in convoy warfare was achieved through 'OR', a subject never before compared. British OR is quite well documented, but still needs to be put into context of what was meant. A comprehensive body of literature may be found in both primary and secondary sources, thus providing an in-depth interpretation of its origins and what was achieved, by both. German OR is poorly understood and several historians have claimed that it either did not exist, or was only exercised at a 'local' level. Since German OR, as a subject, has never previously been identified and quantified, either in English or German, this work presents a great deal of hitherto unseen material in the subject area.

Evidence of German OR comes principally from captured German documents that fell into British hands in 1945, but a mention should be made about the restrictions of availability. While much survived, having been captured at 'Tambach' Castle in Germany, many of the documents that could have been an invaluable source for several of the subjects discussed in this monograph, were either deliberately destroyed, on orders, or subject to loss by severe bombing raids in and around Berlin in November 1943. Of particular interest, and relevant to the subject of 'OR' in this work, are those lost documents that were housed in the Department of *OKM/FEP* – in the Shell building, Berlin. The loss would probably add little to the definition of German OR but it does limit our documentary knowledge of the extent, and effect, that OR had on new designs, current weapons and countermeasure applications. That said there is ample evidence on the subject for definition purposes.

The subject of OR is dealt with thoroughly in this book so that the difference in approach, by each side, may be better understood. It describes how the RN and the *Kriegsmarine* addressed their specific needs for more efficient weapons systems and notes that both relied heavily on feedback from the front; largely through the use of end of patrol reports, but also through open discussion meetings – often on a one-to-one basis. The contributions made by OR to the outcome of the Battle of the Atlantic are difficult, if not impossible, to measure. In general, British OR gains in terms of achievements were modest, except in the case of radar. The greatest contribution of OR during the war was achieved by TRE (Telecommunications Research Establishment), a civilian body; followed by the ORS (Operational Research Section) group of Coastal Command. German OR, while contributing to better applications in torpedo technology and early sub surface rocket technology, suffered because many of the projects undertaken were either abandoned through lack of funds, developed technology and materials, or were too late to have any impact on operations. Post-war advances made by the Allies in many of the areas of development, involving the projects started by German OR, demonstrate that the *Kriegsmarine* was on the right track.

This book has a thematic approach and much of the chapter contents are entwined, so much so that it is difficult to separate the threads entirely without risking the loss of interconnectivity. In order to preserve any dislocation of the themes they are presented as a chronological analysis interspersed with factual, and sometimes conceptual, presentation.

Notes

1 Günter Hessler, *The U-boat War in the Atlantic 1939–45*, Vols I–III. (1989), 41.

2 TNA CAB 4/26, CID 1323-B, *Review of Imperial Defence by the Chiefs of Staff*, May 1937, 7: TNA FO 371/21692, C 250/250/18, British Naval Attaché, Berlin, to F.O., 10 January 1938.

3 Arnold Hague, *The Allied Convoy System 1939–1945* (2000), 55; Patrick Beesly, *Very special Intelligence 1939–1945* (1977), 25.

4 George Franklin, *Britain's Anti-submarine Capability 1919–1939* (2003), 165–71; John Buckley, 'The Development of RAF Coastal Command Trade Defence Strategy, Policy and Doctrine 1919–1945' (University of Lancaster, 1991), 203–48.

5 Karl Dönitz, *Memoirs* (1959), 34; TNA ADM 199/2060: CB 04050/43 (12), monthly anti-submarine report.

6 NHB PG 30324, BdU KTB, part entry on 24 May 1943.

7 Vice Admiral P. Gretton, 'Why Don't We Learn From History?', *The Naval Review*, 46 (January 1958), 13–25, 18.

8 Marc Milner, *The Battle of the Atlantic* (Ontario, 2003), 155.

9 Hague, *The Allied Convoy System*, 57.

10 David Hobbs, 'Ship-borne Air Anti-Submarine Warfare' in *The Battle of the Atlantic 1939–1945: The 50th Anniversary International Naval Conference* (1994), 388–407, 393.

11 TNA ADM 116/4585, Memo from director of scientific research dated 7 December 1942.

12 TNA AVIA 10/338, Report to the minister of production on the utilization of labour in the radio industry, 31 March 1943.

13 Duncan Redford, 'The March 1943 Crisis in the Battle of the Atlantic: Myth and Reality', *The Historical Association*, 92 (305) (2007), 64–83, 66.

14 TNA ADM 199/2060, monthly anti-submarine report, December 1943, 3; Donald McLachlan, *Room 39* (1968).

15 Stephen W. Roskill, *The Navy at War 1939–1945* (Ware, 1998), 451.

16 F. W. Winterbotham, *The Ultra Secret* (1974); Ronald Lewin, *Ultra Goes to War* (1978).

17 Marc Milner, *Battle of the Atlantic*, 79.

18 F. O. Busch, *Das Buch von der Kriegsmarine* (Berlin, 1939); Michael Salewski et al., 'Wehrmacht und Nationalsozialismus 1933–1939', in *Handbuch der deutschen Militärgeschichte 1648–1938*, 6 volumes (Freiburg, 1964–79).

19 Germans always refer to Britain as England.

20 Joseph A. Maiolo, *The Royal Navy and Nazi Germany 1933–39* (1998), 72; David Syrett, 'The Battle of the Atlantic: 1943, the Year of Decision', *American Neptune*, (45) I (1985), 46–64, 48.

21 NHB PG 31044, Personalakte Dönitz.

22 BA-MA RM 7/171, 'Atlantikplanung einer gewünschten Zusammenarbeit'.

23 BA-MA A/MA, Msg 2/5200 Raketenschießversuche 1944.

24 Horst Boog, 'Luftwaffe Support of the German Navy', in *The Battle of the Atlantic 1939–1945* (1994), 302–22; 'Das Problem der Selbständigkeit der Luftstreitkräfte in Deutschland 1908–1945', *Militärgeschichtliche Mitteilungen*, 1 (1988), 31–60.

25 Sönke Neitzel, 'Zum strategischen Misserfolg verdammt?: Die deutsche Luftwaffe in beiden Weltkriegen', in *Erster Weltkrieg-Zweiter Weltkrieg: ein Vergleich*, ed. Bruno Thoß und Hans-Erich Volkmann (Paderborn, 2002), 167–92; 'Kriegsmarine and Luftwaffe Co-operation in the War against Britain 1939–1945', *War in History*, 10 (2003), 448–63.

26 Ernst Stilla, 'Die Luftwaffe im Kampf um die Luftherrschaft' (unpublished doctoral thesis, Rheinischen Friedrich–Wilhelms–Universität, Bonn, 2005).

27 D. C. Isby, *The Luftwaffe and the War at Sea 1939–1945* (2005).

28 *The Führer Conferences on Naval Affairs,* Brasseys Naval Annual (1990).

1

Elements of German Planning for Convoy Warfare

The German Navy was reconstituted after the First World War and U-boats were far from its first priority, which still believed in a Mahanian battle-fleet philosophy. At the start of the war, they had neither a strong surface fleet nor a large U-boat arm, and the U-boats were not radically different from those of the last war.[1]

Naval problems and Hitler's style of leadership

In the years between 1933 and 1939 under National Socialist leadership, while Germany was moving ahead with her rearmament programme, the *Kriegsmarine* made little headway in the struggle to secure recognition in the nation's Defence Council.[2] Unlike the RN, the *Kriegsmarine* was not the senior service but the lowest and most junior of the services.[3] Hitler had planned for a European war that largely consisted of using the *Heer* in conjunction with the *Luftwaffe*. The Navy's potential contribution to the early phases of the programme for continental expansion was at first viewed as little more than a series of supporting manoeuvres to decisive battles on land, or possibly in the air, by protecting vessels carrying materials to a particular destination, or protecting harbours. Hitler's view was that in expanding his military aims the force required an emphasis be placed upon the expansion of the *Heer*, not the *Kriegsmarine*.[4]

The Navy had been denied its strategic aims in building by the prohibitions of the Treaty of Versailles, especially a ban on submarines.[5] In May 1935, the *Reichsmarine* became the *Kriegsmarine* and achieved, at least superficially, a greater degree of recognition within the War Ministry, and a five-year construction plan that was initially based on the treaty.[6] Some naval appointments were made to the War Ministry as a means of obtaining an increased presence along with a substantial authorized increase in the departmental staffs of the Naval Command, as the *Marineleitung* was then known, and the *ObdM, General Admiral* (later *Großadmiral*) Raeder, was admitted to the Defence Council.[7] However, in spite of these additions the Navy's influence was not perceptibly strengthened, nor was Hitler's view of its responsibilities in time of war in any sense modified.

In 1938, Hitler created the *OKW* with General Wilhelm Keitel at the head of the organization to help him command the German *Wehrmacht*.[8] The *OKW* was given no authority to give orders on its own.[9] Instead, it was responsible for the issuing of directives from the *Führer* to the three services, the general allocation of resources, military policy and the representation of the *Wehrmacht* in government. In general, the *OKW* was only as powerful as Hitler wanted it to be and its power resulted from his delegation.[10] This point cannot be emphasized enough since he could, and did, issue directives via the *OKW* to the *Seekriegsleitung*. These instructed the *ObdM*, and the more separate command of the *BdU*, to comply with orders to support a given plan of action devised by them. This may seem a curious state of affairs in that the *Seekriegsleitung* was able to bypass the *ObdM*, but this only demonstrates that the *OKW* was acting on behalf of the orders given by Hitler himself. For example a campaign of collaboration with the *Heer* and *Luftwaffe*, required the diversion of U-boats to assist in the invasion of Norway;[11] a Mediterranean support for Rommel's forces;[12] and the defence against 'D' day landings to name just three.[13] To highlight just the first campaign, Norway, on 5 March 1940 all available U-boats, including those used for training, were ordered to concentrate in German harbours in readiness for the attack on Norway.[14] Hitler's method of planning was predicated on his First World War experience as a non-commissioned officer in the army, with no knowledge or experience in naval matters. This alone would lead to a lack of understanding of direction in the sea war on commerce.[15] His method of decision-making was also solipsistic, making genuine communication with others impossible. Hitler's early successes covered many weaknesses but his failure to coordinate government departments that were concerned with a given problem would help to cause its ultimate failure. Dönitz later wrote in his memoirs contrasting the British system with that in Germany.[16] 'The *OKW* just did the paper work, with Hitler as the final arbiter in any inter-service quarrel.'[17]

While the British armed services had their 'Battle of the Atlantic' and Anti-submarine Warfare Committees, the German armed services had their '*Führer* Conferences', or *Lagevorträge*. However, none of the new Navy's higher officers, who had grown up in the 'Großeur' (Largesse) of the Imperial Navy system, could be comfortable socially with the domineering Austrian ex-corporal whose conferences were essentially self-centred monologues, and at his briefings rejected proposals that did not suit his preconceptions. In his time as *ObdM*, *Großadmiral* Raeder visited Hitler every three to four weeks to discuss naval issues on strategy and to keep him abreast of how both the surface fleet and the U-boat arm were performing in the war at sea, not to provide feedback on how matters could be improved.

In theory, the conferences constituted an ideal forum to conduct an appraisal of the war situation and recommend a given course of action. However, Hitler kept the services largely ignorant of the ideas of others, rarely admitted to mistakes in his planning or judgement, and was never to benefit from lessons that could have been learned.[18]

Naval organization and its changing relationships during the war

Großadmiral Dr Erich Raeder remained at the head of the *Kriegsmarine* until 31 January 1943. In the judgement of one historian 'Admiral Raeder was a stiff disciplinarian, an intense worker and an extremely practical thinker.'[19] He 'applied himself vigorously to the development of the Navy, and saw that task together with the building of a competent officer corps and well-trained and disciplined crews as his main responsibilities.'[20] It was in his new and independent rôle as *ObdM* that he was able to exercise a range of military and budgetary powers that in Britain were invested in the Board of Admiralty.[21] In a similar manner to the First Sea Lord he directed the Navy's war effort, determined its strategies and through his materiel departments provided the means to execute them, subject to the constraints of Hitler and the *OKW*.[22] A chart in Appendix 1 provides an overview of the organization showing the lines of responsibility.

Admiral Raeder's military responsibilities were discharged through a COS supported by staff directorates known collectively as the *Seekriegsleitung*, equivalent to VCNS (Vice Chief of Naval Staff) in the British Admiralty. Originally modelled on the earlier General Staff, the *Skl* underwent a succession of reforms during the course of the war to meet unforeseen needs and to relieve its head of duties less immediately connected with the conduct of operations.[23] It kept independent departmental war diaries.[24] In contrast the RN, generally, did not. Raeder had always insisted that Hitler should be advised by the *OKM* on maritime questions and was determined to create a more significant rôle for the Navy in Hitler's rearmament plans and to support the *Führer's* expansionist ideology.[25] To this end he presented his ideas to Hitler and other senior political and military leaders on 3 February 1937. In his carefully prepared talk, he provided a detailed explanation of the principles of naval warfare and proposed a build-up of naval assets complete with an air-arm, thus advocating the Navy's rôle as the key player in time of war.[26] One German historian argues that Raeder was merely voicing the sentiments of another, Wolfgang Wegener. Wegener rejected the narrow definition advocated by Tirpitz, which called for a blanket command of the seas, and thus trade.[27]

The initial intention was to build a balanced fleet using the U-boat in a supporting rôle to the main fleet for his intention was to attack British merchant shipping, as predicted by the British.[28] The problem with his ambitious proposals was that the *Kriegsmarine* in fact aroused the jealousy of its rivals and weakened its own position in the war group. When the more powerful *OKW* was created a year later he was unable to get support for the *Kriegsmarine* to go against Herman Göring, Head of the *Luftwaffe*, with whom Raeder had many differences on the conduct of the war;[29] and whom he was never able to best. When war came the German Navy was not as well prepared as the *Luftwaffe*.[30] The result, when war began, damaged Raeder's relations with Hitler. When he had a meeting with Hitler at his Head Quarters on 29 June 1942 the subject of a modification to the current fleet construction programme was discussed. Hitler declared himself against all the planned changes and argued that in view of the encouraging results obtained in the U-boat arm all resources should be used in a U-boat building programme.[31] He had lost all confidence in the surface ships given that *Scharnhorst* had been seriously damaged by air-laid mines on 13 February, as she reached German waters; *Prinz Eugen* had been torpedoed by the British submarine *Trident* on route to Trondheim on 23 February and *Gneisenau* had suffered two direct hits in a Bomber Command attack on Kiel on 26/27 February 1942.[32] Although Hitler did not yet know it the *Scharnhorst* would be sunk on 26 December 1943. Uppermost in his mind may have been the *Bismarck*, thought to be unsinkable, which went down ignominiously in May 1942. Furthermore, at the end of December there was the failure of operation *Regenbogen* (Rainbow) in the Barents Sea against convoy JW51-B.[33] Thus by the end of the year Hitler wanted the surface fleet programme scrapped and berated the combat efforts of ship commanders. Many subsequent differences of opinion with Raeder were to follow. Following severe disagreements with Hitler in December 1942, he resigned his position as *ObdM*, effective 31 January 1943.[34] His position was then taken over by Admiral Karl Dönitz, until then Flag Officer U-boats, a move regarded by Britain's NID (Naval Intelligence Division) as being 'to the great disadvantage of the junior service'.[35] Raeder had a preference for his Admiral of the Fleet, Admiral Rolf Carls, who had vastly more experience in both strategy and tactics, and whom he regarded as a more suitable candidate.[36] Hitler probably made a serious misjudgement based more on what the U-boat had achieved over the surface fleet but without considering his own part in its decline; this is another demonstration of Hitler's incapacity for logic. While Dönitz was without doubt a good tactician, he could in no way be compared to Admiral Carls in terms of a balanced approach to strategy and tactics, taking all assets and variants into account. Since Hitler was not one to be taught he would never learn the lesson.

From 1 February 1943 Dönitz succeeded Raeder but in order to maintain control of the U-boat arm he transferred his staff from Paris to Berlin.[37] It was the start of when things for the U-boat arm began to go seriously wrong; although not completely the fault of Admiral Dönitz it demonstrated a lack of judgement on the part of Hitler. That was followed by an error of judgement on the part of Dönitz too in that he did not plan to delegate more control of the U-boat arm and was to become grossly overstretched, and was to remain so for the rest of the war.[38]

Naval War Staff and U-boat Command

Prior to the outbreak of war the *OKM* had its own Naval Staff, more akin to that of the RN, which performed activities in the fields of control of operations, logistical methods and administration.[39] However, in 1938 the Navy was put onto a war footing and the Naval Staff, once called '*Stab der Marine*', moved to a different format similar to that set-up by Admiral Scheer at the end of the First World War, the *Skl*.[40] The new *Skl* retained its original three divisions of Naval Command, Operations and Fleet Organization and Communications, and all were subordinated to a new Vice Chief of Naval War Staff, Admiral Otto Schniewind, who also served as the COS of the *Kriegsmarine*.[41] One omission in the *Skl* organization, to be rectified in 1939, was a special *Skl* section for the U-boat arm. This was formed on 12 September1939 and catered for their needs and became known as *Skl*/U – U for U-boats. The departmental group *Amtsgruppe Skl*/U dealt with U-boat organization, training and development, and with anti-U-boat measures, more of which is discussed in a later chapter.[42]

1/*Skl* was the operational staff representing the *ObdM* and primarily responsible for initiating all 'purely' naval operations and planning aspects for any combined operations that might arise in terms of strategic and operational concepts, in a manner similar to the Admiralty's Plans and Operations Divisions. It co-ordinated Fleet and Flotilla dispositions, mine warfare, aviation – and initially the U-boat Arm – and acted as an interface in matters relating to merchant shipping, economic warfare and inter-service relations;[43] in this latter rôle they were only marginally successful.

A rich source of British merchant ship movement information came from the *B-Dienst*, and the *xB-Dienst* (decryption service) who were able to decipher much of the encrypted Allied radio communications for a long period of the war, to the great benefit of the U-boat arm. Initially, from 1939 until the end of 1940 they were able to decipher most of the low-level Intel, which caused the RN problems for warship movements. But they were only partially successful in reading of code for Atlantic Merchant-ship traffic. The turn-around in fortune came after the full introduction of the British Naval Cipher No. 3 in February 1942, when the cipher system actually became easier for *B-Dienst* to read. This was the start of when convoy information was more speedily passed on to U-boat command, sometimes within hours of transmission.[44] Such SigInt became the U-boat arm's richest source of information on convoy movements and dispositions, the organizational control of which was in the hands of the *MND*.[45]

The Head of the *MND* (communications division) had under him three subordinated *Generalreferate* (advisory offices) *MND* 1, 2 and 3 that were responsible for the administration of:

> *MND* 1. Central section of communications liaison with axis navies, radar, personnel training and communications security. For example when it was thought that ENIGMA was compromised this section was heavily involved in the steps to trace the source. This included the use of the services of the two other sections in the group.[46]
>
> *MND* 2. Dealt with W/T services, ciphers, visual signals, tele-printers and telephone lines, as well as the manning of the *OKM*'s own W/T and land line service.

MND 3. Formerly known as 'Signals Intelligence Control' became *Funkaufklärung*, with specific responsibility for the interception of foreign W/T transmissions and cryptanalysis,[47] which included the *B-Dienst* – which after 1940 was probably the single most relied on source for U-boat arm intelligence.[48]

It was *B-Dienst* that provided assessments of the enemy situation, foreign navies and their merchant shipping and, among other things, an evaluation of intelligence information that was received from the *xB-Dienst* and *B-Dienst* de-coding centres for use against allied convoys. Equally important was their rôle in the processing of U-boat reports of enemy ships sunk, and these are referred to later when dealing with the functional 'OR' activities of the *Kriegsmarine* and U-boat arm.[49] In this connection it should also be noted that a division of the Naval War Staff, *Skl* (*KA*) (Appendix 2, item 3 *Kriegswissenschaftlicheabteilung*), included the *Skl* (*MKrGesch*), the 'Military Science' (*Kr*) Division, which was involved in connection with 'OR' as well as helping to form the basis of feedback to other divisions.[50] The *Kr* Division exchanged important feedback with the naval institutes engaged in weapons development, and is discussed later in Chapter 10. The whole *MND* system might appear to be complex, due to its frequent use of alpha numeric titles, but it did have an interlocking system that when analyzed, made sense.

The re-birth of the U-boat arm

Without question it is the U-boat arm that has been the focus of attention for many historians since the end of the First and Second World Wars, and was the most effective naval weapon in both. Its effectiveness in World War Two was in no small way attributable to Karl Dönitz, leader and *BdU*. Dönitz had been a submariner of no great distinction in the First World War but had an enthusiasm and drive that made him instantly recognizable to the *ObdM*, Admiral Dr Erich Raeder. In one of the official assessments it was noted in a personnel file that Dönitz was a 'smart', 'industrious', ambitious officer and possessed an excellent professional knowledge, as well as displaying good military and technical competence;[51] there was no mention of his ability in naval strategy. Karl Dönitz was a good choice as commander of the new U-boat arm. He had gained general naval experience on an international scale but it was his service on U-boats during the Great War that had determined his future.

By the end of 1932, the *Reichsmarine* had already considered the construction of U-boats. To them it was a momentous occasion and would be the first time since World War I that construction of U-boats had taken place on German soil. Under the Peace Treaty of Versailles there had been a ban on possession or production of U-boats, but to circumvent this proscription U-boats were handled by 'dummy firms', and financed by the Navy. The *Reichsmarine* (as it was then) used *Ingenieurskantoor voor Scheepsbouw* (IvS), which was a construction office in Holland and where former U-boat designers (mostly from Germaniawerft, Kiel) were able to evaluate and extend their experience of U-boat construction.[52]

Dönitz was head of the U-boat arm during its three stages of development.[53] His big opportunity came during the first stage when he became senior officer of the 1st U-boat flotilla, after the Anglo-German agreement of the 18 June 1935. He then consolidated his position on 1 January 1936 when the organization created a new post for him known as *FdU* (U-boat Leader). Thoughts could now be given to a construction programme for the new U-boat arm.[54] It might be thought that Hitler's rise to power had a great influence on the reconstruction programme, which aimed mainly at attaining parity with France, but this was not the case – although it did cause a slight setback to U-boat planning, due to his priorities for resource allocations. Nevertheless after some debate it was decided to push ahead with the construction of Type VII and Type IX U-boats. At this stage Dönitz had little influence on the future direction of the U-boat arm and in order to implement changes to the overall organization he would have to wait until 1943.

On the day that 'Total Germany' was declared to all British fleets and stations Admiral Raeder had been visiting Dönitz and his staff at Wilhelmshaven, the main base of U-boat operations and administration.[55] According to Dönitz, after the initial shock of hearing the news of war, Raeder told an assembled audience that Germany now had the ideal weapon with which to strike against England – the U-boat.[56] His declaration had more to do with morale boosting than his total belief in the U-boat. In reality, for Raeder, the war had come too soon[57] and he was forced to discard a former plan put together by his Chief of Staff Commander Heye known as the Z-plan.[58] The original Z-Plan was to consist of a force of 13 Battleships and Battle cruisers, 4 Aircraft carriers, 15 Panzerschiffe, 23 cruisers and 22 large Destroyers.[59] The proposed doctrine was for individual high-endurance warships to engage British commerce and compel the RN to disperse in the defence of trade.[60] Meanwhile, two small, but powerful, battle groups each formed around battleships plus a single aircraft carrier, and protected by diesel-powered light cruisers and Destroyers, were to maintain local sea control in the North and Norwegian seas. Such battle groups represented a major departure from conventional naval operational concepts,[61] much of which had been predicted in RN exercises and operations carried out in 1938.[62]

It was Heye who made a comprehensive study, which concluded that attacks from surface and sub-surface, in combination with air support, would produce more effective results than any one type alone.[63] When presented to Hitler he was in agreement with the plan and declared that Raeder had until 1944, at the earliest, to construct his fleet.[64] But Hitler had the continental land war on his mind and disregarded much of what Raeder called for, despite original assurances. Hitler had reneged on his promise of no war with Britain for five years, and so put the German Navy at a severe disadvantage. Raeder therefore decided in favour of building those craft already laid down and increasing the U-boat fleet which, to Raeder, seemed the best of his alternatives achievable in a 'balanced' fleet if there was to be a noticeable immediate contribution to the war effort. The Z-plan had been abandoned, and this marked the start of Raeder losing Hitler's confidence. As one historian noted, Raeder was deeply conscious 'of the failure of his policies ... It presaged too, how little influence he was to have on the conduct of the war'.[65] Other naval historians have been critical of Raeder's leadership, supporting the general view that he was striving to recreate a 'Tirpitzian' battle fleet.[66] While Raeder, like so many other naval leaders, was in favour of battle ships, he also had a firm understanding of a *guerre de course* (commerce warfare) strategy. Historians appear to give little credence to Raeder having received a 'poison chalice' from Hitler at the start of the war, since he had few options open to him. Moreover his 'strategic' conception was sound even if his influence was small, largely due to Hitler needing sycophants around him such as Göring and Keitel. Raeder was no 'yes' man.[67] Hitler never did learn the lesson of naval requirements and for Raeder in particular it meant that naval assets would need to be built up as the situation allowed, given the inter-service rivalry for resources.

On the outbreak of war Germany possessed just 57 U-boats,[68] of which only 26 were suitable and ready for immediate operations in the Atlantic.[69] More would have been built but under the former Z Plan U-boats were to work in conjunction with the surface fleet as scouts, not as front-line boats unless specific opportunities arose.[70]

Andrew Lambert makes a good point when he argues that trade protection was not guaranteed by the provision of a sufficient number of escorts alone, without further the protection of a battle fleet, also noted by Nicholas Rodger.

Escorts would be simply 'swept aside' by heavy units of the *Kriegsmarine*.[71] However, these historians do not appear to have considered the danger the *Kriegsmarine* faced with the few heavy units that they possessed. Only a 'raider' working in total secrecy, taking out single ships, had much chance of survival. Raeder knew that if they tried to engage convoys there was a greater chance of sustaining damage from heavier British units which was the one thing he could ill-afford, since there were no bases for ships to return to, other than in Germany. Therefore that strategy was unworkable.

By 17 October 1939, Dönitz had been put fully in charge of U-boats at Wilhelmshaven and received the title of *FdU* West and had, as already mentioned, become a member of *Skl/U*. As U-boat leader, and later as *BdU*, he had free rein on all aspects of U-boat operations, except in those conditions previously noted, and in matters of discipline. In this case he was subordinated to the C-in-C Fleet, at that time.[72] The second stage of development came in November 1941 when the reporting relationship of the *FdU*, by then *BdU*, was no longer required and he then really did precisely what he wanted, within the confines of resource allocations and *OKW* intervention policy.[73] With his new-found responsibility he was in a good position to dominate the direction of operations and to put in place rigid training routines. But he still did not have sufficient authority to make structural changes. On 21 September 1939 Dönitz received his step to Flag Rank and became *BdU* and *Konteradmiral* in charge, not only operations but also administration and training functions, for which he needed a knowledgeable U-boat man and competent organizer. This job was delegated to (now) *Kapitän zur See* Hans-Georg von Friedeburg (later *Konteradmiral*);[74] to be discussed in a chapter on training.

U-boat arm command and control

On 18 August 1939, the *FdU* was constituted for three different theatres of European war – the Baltic, North Sea and Atlantic. The Baltic U-boats came under the Naval Station Baltic, the North Sea under Naval Station West and the Atlantic was under the control of the *Skl*. As of 18 August Dönitz took control of U-boats for the Baltic and operated as the *Skl/U*, and moved with an operational staff to Swinemünde. It was also around this time, on 28 August, that he had a meeting with Raeder to discuss his memo entitled '*Gedanken über den Ausbau der Ubootwaffe*', 'Thoughts on the build-up of the U-boat Arm', which received Raeder's approval.[75] This document was focused around tactical solutions, not strategy. At the time it was thought that only a war with Poland might occur. However, after the flight of important elements of the Polish fleet to England the Baltic U-boats then centred on the North Sea.[76] Therefore the U-boat organization as it stood became redundant, although *FdU* Baltic remained in a reduced form for a brief period until 19 September 1939.[77]

After the outbreak of war with Britain Dönitz, then at Captain rank and the title *FdU* held a Naval War Staff appointment and therefore mostly controlled all U-boat operations, unless there was intervention from the *OKW/Skl*, or even from Raeder himself through the Chief of the Naval War Staff, Admiral Schniewind, to whom he was initially subordinated.[78] He encountered little interference in the daily running of the command and only in exceptional circumstances when U-boats were needed for combined operations, such as Norway, was the Operations Division 1/*Skl* permitted to intervene in the running of the U-boat war, and then only for a specific purpose. 1/*Skl* was able to maintain its liaison with other divisions of the War Staff by convening a daily conference with those heads of Divisions whose participation was sought in a planned action. By these means Dönitz was forewarned of what was to come, even though he may have been opposed to the disposition of his boats.[79] Convoluted as it seemed the *Skl* organization worked quite well and was never replaced during the war; although some additions and deletions were to be expected, particularly after Dönitz became *ObdM* after 1 February 1943.

The third stage of development came when Dönitz replaced Raeder as *ObdM*, with ultimate authority.[80] This was his opportunity to set about a complete re-organization of the *Skl* and to allocate the U-boat arm its own section with the designation 2/*Skl BdU*-Op. It became his most important change in organization since the start of the war.[81] The re-organization signalled a change in direction and a strengthening of the U-boat arm, its weapons technology and applications. For the first time this was his opportunity to make changes to the organization and implement some of the procedures that he had considered necessary, since he took over in 1935. He could also see benefits to the system introduced by his predecessor Admiral Raeder in creating the *FEP* – a close resemblance to parts of the British OR departments discussed in a later chapter – and involved himself in technical improvements to systems, which were to become the advanced 'Nibelung' system for the Type XX1 U-boat, and a significant advance in sub-sea technology.

As the new *ObdM* and *BdU* he unsurprisingly committed to a hectic U-boat construction schedule, due to the earlier cancellation of the Z plan; this is a clear indication of his inability to think along clear strategic lines.[82] As the new head of *OKM* he was in a strong position to influence Hitler in getting a better balance to the existing fleet and demand closer co-operation with the *Luftwaffe*, rather than to rely solely on U-boats. It was from this position of strength that changes might have been possible. But from the very beginning his predilection was for only one arm of the Navy which was not lost on the assembled officers at *OKM*, when Dönitz addressed them shortly after he took overall charge of the Navy. He made it clear that the 'Sea-war', was a U-boat war, and left little to the imagination.[83] However, his lack of a clear plan was, as one historian puts it, 'compounded by Dönitz's reaction to it, his tendency to emphasize an increase in the number of his boats, rather than in their quality. Thus, more of the existing Types VII and IX boats were constructed, even though they were 'only marginally better than their World War I predecessors',[84] but that position improved slightly with the addition of some new 'true' submersible types. But in order to challenge the growing fighting capabilities of the Allies this was all he had, for the moment.

Furthermore, Dönitz now had more direct contact with Hitler and finally received the authority to turn a large U-boat programme into a reality. Major surface forces were of little interest to him and his background in the surface fleet was minimal. In the original construction schedule planned in October 1939, the programme was to include the auxiliary ships and light naval forces required for protection duties. This programme, set out in April 1943, provided for the annual delivery of about 360 U-boats.[85] The main production thrust was principally targeted at the Types VII and IX U-boats but included some larger types for use in carrying vital supplies to and from Japan, their new ally, following the unexpected attack on Pearl Harbour. It also included the new Type VIIC42 constructed with higher-grade steel to enable diving depths of up to 600 feet to be reached. This construction programme saw for the first time the introduction of the new *Elektro*-boats into a production schedule, of which there were several types, before settling on the Types XXI and XXIII; the test bed of which was the Type XVII.

Conclusions

When the *OKW* was first constituted the *Kriegsmarine* had little influence at HQ since it was considered to be the most junior of the three armed services, and because Raeder had wanted too much control; equally, the *OKW* too had few teeth without Hitler to back them up and was unable to coordinate the three services effectively.

Hitler had promised the *ObdM* that no war with Britain was foreseen for some time and should embark on a programme to build up capital ships by 1944 or 1945, known as the Z-plan. He revoked that plan, leaving the Navy with a few modern warships and a small, but growing U-boat fleet. The fact that the U-boat arm comprised so few U-boats at the outbreak of war was the product of the Z-plan building programme because the *Kriegsmarine* had defined the rôle of U-boats as mainly for reconnaissance, as an addition to the fleet. At this time a sea war was thought to consist largely of fighting with capitals ships for command of the sea and they appeared to have already forgotten their recent history of the U-boat and how effectively they almost brought Britain to its knees in the last war, but for the introduction of the system of convoy. At this stage Dönitz was not a high ranking officer with much influence, but more of a pawn that could be moved around the chess board. Because of his junior status he was unable to make any significant changes to the U-boat arm and construction programme until it was forced on Hitler and the *OKM* by Britain's refusal to surrender in 1940, thus prolonging the war. Surface forces had failed in their attempt to stop ships bringing vital imports from the United States, and that now put the onus on the U-boat arm to continue the fight.

The *Seekriegsleitung* had several functions, one of which allowed them a degree of freedom to instruct the C-in-C of the *Kriegsmarine* to comply with orders to support a given plan of action devised by them – on the orders of *OKW*. In several cases, they were forced to act on a Hitler impulse and unnecessarily divert U-boats from the North Atlantic, when they would have been more useful in the drive against British commercial shipping interests. Regardless of the number of representations made by *ObdM*, and the *BdU*, that a dilution of the U-boat force had a detrimental effect on the commerce warfare, *OKW* remained silent on this issue. Their rôle was a to 'rubber stamp' Hitlers' whims and not designed for learning or processing feedback. Other *Skl* departments operated along functional lines, such as 1/*Skl* that represented the 'operational staff' of the *ObdM* and was primarily for planning naval aspects of any operation, often in an enterprising manner. Signals intelligence, initially quite weak, made great strides in cryptology that proved to be a great challenge to the enemy. One such department *MND* 3, known as *B-Dienst* and *xB-Dienst* respectively, had specific responsibility for the interception of foreign W/T transmissions and cryptanalysis. This was one department that Dönitz relied on for information about Allied ship movements and was constantly trying to maximize efficiency making strenuous efforts to learn from the mistakes of their enemy and stay abreast of events, with some success. The principal error made by *MND* department was not within *B-Dienst* but *xB-Dienst*, the cryptographic section. Throughout they remained convinced of the infallibility of the German Enigma system and advised Dönitz so on several occasions in the course of the war. While some learnt from their errors this department became almost as complacent as the *OKW*, but with more serious consequences that resulted.

After Dönitz became *ObdM* on 1 February 1943, his main focus of attention became the further build-up of the U-boat fleet, with improvements to technology and an eye on a successor to the older Type VIIs and IXs; but the surface fleet was scaled back to perform only those duties where they had the remotest chance of success against a more powerful RN. He appeared to have little understanding in constructing a plan that would embrace the stronger elements of the fleet and in terms of overall strategy had learned few lessons during his time as *BdU*, even though he had regular contact with Raeder; and matters would have included his part in fleet dispositions. He also placed the U-boat arm at a disadvantage since he never learnt the lesson of task delegation as a means of efficiency. But he did learn the lesson of how to get Hitler's attention for an increase in U-boat construction and development, and to speed up the crew training regime, albeit at the cost of cutting corners.

Notes

1   Marc Milner, *Battle of the Atlantic* (Ontario, 2003), 108.

2   GC&CS, 'The German Navy–Organization', 2, December 1945, 23.

3   Ibid., 2, 24.

4   Ibid., 21; see also Appendix 1 for an overview of the Kriegsmarine organization structure; Sönke Neitzel, 'Kriegsmarine and Luftwaffe Co-operation in the War against Britain 1939–1945', *War in History*, 10 (2003), 448–63, 453.

5   TNA ADM 223/696, Essays by Admirals Schniewind and Schuster on conduct of the War at sea, 3.

6   Edward P. von der Porten, *The German Navy in World War Two* (1969), 11.

7   OKM in German meaning Oberkommando der Kriegsmarine, 'Naval High Command'.

8   Hugh Trevor-Roper, *Hitler's War Directives 1939–1945* (Edinburgh, 2004), 20; Keitel was a weak officer and was often irreverently referred to as 'Lackeitel', 'Lackey'.

9   NHB NID 24 GHS/2, Vice Admiral Kurt Assmann, 'Relations between the Supreme Command of the German Armed Forces and the Naval War Staff', 8.

10 Lt. Cdr Andreas Krug, 'Coordination and Command Relationships between Axis Powers in the Naval War in the Mediterranean 1940–1943', Canadian Forces College, CSC 31, 1–91, 71.

11 NHB PG 30259, BdU KTB for 2 March 1940 describes preparations being made to support the Norwegian campaign known as 'Weserübung'; Peter Padfield, *Dönitz* (1984), 210.

12 NHB PG 33352, U-boats to Mediterranean; *Lagevorträge* (München, 1972), 145–46; John Terraine, *Business in Great Waters* (Ware, 1999), 359.

13 NHB PG 30348, BdU KTB entry 6 June 1944. Gruppe 'Landwirt'.

14 Günther Hessler, *The U-boat War in the Atlantic 1939–45*, (1989), I, 17; David Westwood, *The U-boat War* (2005), 279.

15 NHB NID 24/T65/45, Documents on German Navy War Effort.

16 Karl Dönitz, *Memoirs* (1959), 114.

17 Horst Boog, 'Luftwaffe Support of the German Navy', in *The Battle of the Atlantic 1939–1945* (1994), 302–22, 313.

18 TNA ADM 223/694, Kapitän zur See Kupfer's Essay on the War at Sea, 1.

19 von der Porten, *The German Navy in World War Two*, 9.

20 Keith Bird, *Erich Raeder: Admiral of the Reich* (Annapolis, 2006), 123.

21 Graham Rhys-Jones, 'The German System: A Staff Perspective', in *The Battle of the Atlantic 1939–1945* (1994), 138–57, 142.

22 TNA ADM 1/9580, Organization chart of German Naval High Command 1938.

23 P. M. Kennedy, 'The Development of German Naval Operations: Plans against England, 1896–1914', *The English Historical Review*, 89 (350) (January 1974), 48–76.

24 M. Salewski, 'Das Kriegstagebuch der deutschen Seekriegsleitung im zweiten Weltkrieg', *Marine Rundschau*, 64 (3) (Juni 1967), 137–45.

25 Eugene M. Emme, 'Air Power and National Security', *Annals of the American Academy of Political and Social Science*, 299 (May 1955), 12–24, 16.

26 BA-MA RM 6/53, 'Grundsätzliche Gedanken', Vortrag vom Raeder, 3 Februar 1937.

27 C. A. Gemzell, *Raeder, Hitler und Skandinavien* (Lund, 1965), 278–85.

28 TNA CAB 53/6, COS (Chiefs of Staff) 192nd and 194th meetings, 12 and 22 January 1937.

29 Horst Boog, 'Das Problem der Selbständigkeit der Luftstreitkräfte in Deutschland 1908–1945', *Militärgeschichtliche Mitteilungen*, (1) (1988), 31–60, 50.

30 TNA AIR 41/45, Volume One–Atlantic and Home Waters, 35; Stephen W. Roskill, *The War at Sea* (1954), I, 53.

31 *Lagevorträge*, 431–3, Raeder discussion 29 June 1942.

32 Cajus Bekker, *Hitler's Naval War (Verdammte See)* (1974), 234.

33 Bird, *Erich Raeder*, 192.

34 *Lagevorträge*, 355–6.

35 GC&CS, 'The German Navy–Organization', 2, 24.

36 Raeder an Hitler, 4 Januar 1943, zit. bei G. Sandhofer, 'Dokumente zum militärischen Werdegang des Großadmiral Dönitz', in MGM 2/1973, 80.

37 NHB PG 32158, 1/Skl KTB Teil C, entry for 5 February 1943, 76–7; Michael Salewski, *Die deutsche Seekriegsleitung 1942–1945* (München, 1975), II, 225.

38 GC&CS, 'The German Navy–Organization', 2, 24–5.

39 Ibid, 29.

40 'Admiral Scheer's Memoirs', Chapter 18a. in The War Times Journal at www.wtj.com.

41 Appendix 1; Admiral Otto Schniewind held this office from October 1938–June 1941, Walter Lohmann et al., *Die deutsche Kriegsmarine 1939–1945* (Bad Nauheim, 1956), 1 (32), 1.

42 NHB NID 24/T65/45, Documents on 'German Navy War Effort', 71.

43 GC&CS, 'The German Navy–Organization', 2, 35.

44 TNA HW 8/113, January–November 1942; the changeover started October–December 1941, 57.

45 See Appendix 3. MND remained 2/Skl until March 1943, when it was renamed 4/Skl because Dönitz took the designation 2/Skl for this own Operations section after he became ObdM.

46 Author's own comment on the appreciation of functions.

47 GC&CS, 'The German Navy–Organization', 2, 37; the translation given in the English text is incorrect. The correct equivalent term is provided.

48 Dönitz, *Memoirs*, 325.

49 Rhys-Jones, 'The German System: A Staff Perspective', 153.

50 Walter Lohmann et al., *Die deutsche Kriegsmarine*, 1 (32), 4; V.Adm. Kurt Assman (April 1933–June 1943) and then Admiral Karl-Georg Schuster, July 1943–End.

51 NHB PG 31044, Personalakte, Dönitz. The assessment appears to have been by the Fleet Commander of the time, Schniewind.

52 Eberhard Rößler, 'U-boat Development and Building', in *The Battle of the Atlantic 1939–1945* (1994), 118–37, 118.

53 TNA HW 18/55, German Naval Organization 1944–1945, 1.

54 NHB PG 10402, Contains details of Dönitz's progress and promotion.

55 Terraine, *Business in Great Waters*, 214; Padfield, *Dönitz*, 187.

56 Großadmiral Dönitz, *40 Fragen an Karl Dönitz* (München, 1980), 49.

57 NHB PG 32021, 1/Skl KTB Teil A entry for 3 September 1939, 'Gedanken des Oberbefehlshabers der Kriegsmarine zum Kriegsausbruch 3.9.1939'; Michael Salewski, *Die deutsche Seekriegsleitung 1935–1941* (Frankfurt am Main, 1970), I, 22–5.

58 TNA ADM 234/578, Naval staff history: 'The Defeat of the Enemy Attack on Shipping 1939–1945', formerly BR 1736 (51) 1A; Rößler, 'U-boat Development and Building', 125.

59 TNA ADM 1/9729, PD 06476/37, Deputy Chief of the Naval Staff, 18 October 1937; H. T. Lenton, *German Warships of the Second World War* (1975), 22–3; Joseph A. Maiolo, 'The Knockout Blow against the Import System: 1934–9', *Journal of Historical Research*, 72 (178) (June 1999), 201–28, 217–18. The plan was only provisional.

60 Maiolo, 'The Knockout Blow against the Import System', 220.

61 TNA ADM 178/137, German naval strategy and tactics. 'Naval Intelligence Report, Summer 1936, 12; Carl O. Schuster, 'German Naval Warfare in WWII', *Strategy & Tactics*, 226 (January/February 2005), 45–6.

62 ADM 186/159, CB 1769/38, 'Exercises and Operations 1938', (February 1939).

63 Joseph A. Maiolo, *The Royal Navy and Nazi Germany 1933–39* (Basingstoke, 1998), 74; Maiolo took the view that concepts of sea power mattered.

64 *Lagevorträge*, 20. In 1939, the actual proposed schedule of construction had been reduced. For example aircraft carriers numbered just two.

65 Bird, *Erich Raeder*, 128.

66 Holger H. Herwig, 'The Failure of German Sea Power 1914–1945: Mahan, Tirpitz, and Raeder Reconsidered', *International History Review*, 10 (1) (February 1988), 68–105; Tobias Philbin, *The Lure of Neptune* (University of South Carolina Press, 1994), 33–7; Eric C. Rust, *Naval Officers under Hitler* (New York, 1991), 120.

67 NHB NID 24/T 65/45, Report on German Naval War Effort, Para 3, Raeder.

68 TNA ADM 233/84, U-boat appreciations in NID 0714 of 27 February 1941; Sönke Neitzel, 'The Deployment of U-boats', in *The Battle of the Atlantic 1939–1945* (1994), 276–301, 276.

69 Werner Rahn, 'The campaign: The German Perspective', in *The Battle of the Atlantic 1939–1945* (1994), 538–53, 538.

70 *Lagevorträge*, 20. The Z-plan called for approximately 190 U-boats to be ready by 1944; Kurt Assmann, *Deutsche Seestrategie in zwei Weltkriegen* (Heidelberg, 1957), 118.

71 Andrew Lambert, 'Sea Power 1939–1940: Churchill and the Strategic Origins of the Battle of the Atlantic', in *Sea Power: Theory and Practice* (Ilford, 1994), 86–107, (92): Nicolas Rodger, 'The Royal Navy in the era of the World Wars: Was it Fit for Purpose?', *The Mariner's Mirror*, 97 (1) (February 2011), 272–84, 281.

72 NHB PG 32419A, Heft 4–1, BdU Befehle und Absichten, ff. 5; Dönitz, *Memoirs*, 33.

73 NHB PG 15500, Reporting and responsibilities, 355–57; TNA HW 18/55, German Naval Organization, 1.

74 GC&CS, 'The German Navy – The U-boat Arm', 7 December 1945, 10.

75 *Lagevorträge*, 19.

76 TNA ADM 1/9963, confidential message, 1 September 1939; TNA ADM 199/807, C-in-C, Western Approaches to secretary of the Admiralty, 12 September 1939.

77 NHB PG 31013, Notes on U-boat organization and chain of command, folio 10.

78 NHB NID 1/17, Assessment of Godt, paras 25 and 45; Dönitz, *Memoirs,* 49; see also Appendix 2.

79 GC&CS, 'The German Navy–Organization', 2, 36.

80 TNA HW 18/55, German Naval Organization, 1.

81 Salewski, *Die deutsche Seekriegsleitung 1942–1945,* II, 225.

82 This point amplifies the comments made earlier about Dönitz's lack of strategic thought and direction.

83 NHB PG 32158, 1/ Skl KTB Teil A. Entry for 5 February 1943, 14.

84 Geoffrey Till, 'The Battle of the Atlantic as History', in *The Battle of the Atlantic1939–1945* (1994), 584–95, 589.

85 Rößler, 'U-boat Development and Building', 130.

2

Elements of British Planning for
Convoy Protection

Britain could be seen to have been amiss in its responsibilities for planning for a possible war with Germany, up to a point. Had it failed to learn important lessons of the past? This section describes elements of Admiralty pre-war planning and provides a brief account of the setting up of an OIC and the functions of the U-boat tracking centre. Admiralty organization is widely known and not discussed here, other than the WA and divisions related to convoy protection.

Admiralty pre-war planning

The RN's First World War strategy of enforcing a stranglehold on the North Sea and a blockade of German ports contributed to the final collapse four years later of Imperial Germany's bid for continental hegemony.[1] Thus, it was not surprising that the Admiralty should think of the same strategy when a distinct possibility of war with Germany existed. The ink on the Anglo-German naval agreement was barely dry when Germany, and Hitler in particular, felt freed from the naval restrictions of the Treaty of Versailles. It made German possession of U-boats, and naval aviation a pre-condition of the accord, and had severely limited the size of surface fleet. Following the Anglo-German Naval agreement of June 1935 Naval Intelligence soon became aware of a move into U-boat construction and development. As early as 1937 one could not deny the fact that the U-boat arm was growing and represented a very real threat both to the RN and oceanic trade routes.[2] Admiralty's perceived intentions regarding the German Navy were made in a Chiefs of Staff report to the Committee for Imperial Defence (CID) in November, making it plain that 'We must be prepared for unrestricted attack by submarines against our trade, more particularly by Germany.'[3]

Some naval historians who have studied the problem of how the new Germany could have employed its new Navy against Britain have been highly critical of the British Naval Staff's performance. It has been suggested that the Admiralty did not compute a study of war with the Reich in adequate depth, and that when studies were made the analysis was defective. The historians Arthur Marder and Stephen Roskill seem to be in agreement that, to a degree, the Admiralty failed to prepare for the German offensive at sea, suggesting that at the start of the Second World War it appeared obsessed with a decisive showdown between two great fleets. Marder stated that it can be argued that 'where naval training between the wars chiefly failed was in relating a key "lesson learnt" to the setting of the 1914 war', and that 'naval strategy and tactics were largely conditioned by a determination to make the next Jutland a Trafalgar – when a second Jutland was highly improbable.'[4] Corelli Barnett argued that the shortcomings in vessels and equipment emanated from the pre-war Admiralty's 'complacent neglect of the entire problem of convoy protection and anti-submarine warfare'.[5] However, these statements do not relate to facts. Interwar the RN did not face a major threat of a U-boat threat in the Atlantic, primarily because up until 1936 Germany had not embarked on a U-boat construction programme.[6] The Admiralty's top planners had expected that Germany's central maritime objective in war would be to destroy Britain's shipping, as in the last war, and that German naval strategists would adopt all means of attack to achieve this end.[7] On 12 January 1937, the First Sea Lord, Admiral Chatfield (1933–8), discussed this issue with the Chiefs of Staff when considering revisions to the Joint Planning Committee's 1936 appreciation.[8] He shared a naval intelligence assessment with his colleagues about a change in German expectations and articulated the view that its Navy had indeed learnt from the experience of the First World War. His expectation was, therefore, that German Battle Cruisers would be sent out into the Atlantic to attack mercantile trade at the outset and U-boats would conduct an unrestricted U-boat war, just as they had done in the previous war.[9] What was important were the methods available to them to be successful since there were few really novel methods, because what the Reich had to offer was not greatly different from that which they had in the last war; they were technically more advanced, but not radically.[10] But they did have a small battle-fleet, and Lambert and Rodger make the point, (discussed in the previous chapter) that trade protection would not have been guaranteed by the provision of escorts alone, without further the protection of a battle-fleet.[11] However, in reality that was unlikely to have been the scenario, given the number of the battle units available in the *Kriegsmarine*.

Notwithstanding the criticisms, one of the principal problems to be considered was that, for some time, Britain had planned that in the event of a future European war France could be relied upon as a strong partner in an Anglo-French alliance. It was anticipated that Britain, France and Belgium at sea would prove to be stronger than Germany.[12] In the spring of 1939, the French had agreed to the *Force de Raid* (based at Brest) operating in the Atlantic, consisting of two Battleships, an aircraft carrier, three Cruisers and ten Destroyers, as well as committing ten additional Destroyers to the Channel patrol.[13] The Admiralty was no doubt pleased with this arrangement, but in the event, matters took a different course. On 10 May 1940, France was invaded and on 22 June, an Armistice was signed.[14]

OIC and trade

The Admiralty was the body ultimately responsible for all naval activity to do with the defence of trade. The need for staff collaboration between Plans, Intelligence and Operations, and the Admiralty is self-evident and, as Stephen Roskill notes it, 'it is no exaggeration to say that together they formed the "Trinity" on which the execution of maritime strategy chiefly rested.'[15] Chart 2.1 is a convenient organization chart that provides a clear overview of the interrelationships that existed between the Defence of Trade Departments, the Board of Admiralty and various others, including the all-important OIC; and one, which will be referred to on occasions.

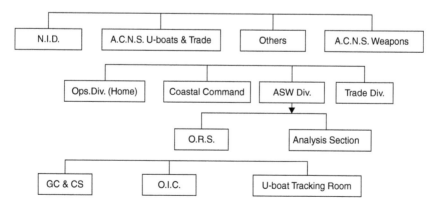

Chart 2.1 Organization chart depicting the defence of trade
Source: Defence of Trade Links.[16]

The sections in the chart are of primary interest in this chapter but other divisions relating to operations, such as the Training and Tactical Development, and the relationship of OR to ASW and Trade, are discussed in later chapters. It is interesting to note that the Admiralty's anti-submarine effort lay within the province of five bodies. The OIC and the U-boat Tracking Room were formed in late 1937; the Trade Division was constituted under ACNS (Assistant Chief of Naval Staff) (Trade) in May. But it was not until October 1939 that the ASW Division was established, again under ACNS (Trade), and it was as part of this Division that ASW analysis and ASW ORSs were formed after August 1940. While late, it does demonstrate how rapidly the Admiralty put in place the sections needed to fight a commerce war, for by 1 January 1939 none of these bodies had actually been constituted; only the Trade Division already existed as part of a section of the Naval Plans Division. Nevertheless, the hard experience gained from the First World War was not lost by forgetting the importance of intelligence, and the late arrival of ASW. It required time to fine-tune this system and to ensure proper liaison between its various parts, but by 1942 a mature routine had been established.[17]

OIC provided vital information concerning ship and U-boat movements. The origins of the OIC may be traced back to the 1914–18 War when the head of Room 40 was 'Blinker' Hall;[18] the section was then effectively disbanded after the war and became moribund. In 1935, by a stroke of good fortune, one man that had been in Hall's team was still in a position to cast a stone into this not quite stagnant pool. Deputy Chief of Naval Staff was Vice-Admiral Sir William James, who had been Deputy Director of Intelligence (DDI) after 1918. In 1936, worried by the Abyssinian crisis and Italian behaviour in the Mediterranean, he sent to the Directors of Plans and Intelligence the question: 'What would happen if war were suddenly declared?' and asked for comments, but he was unconvinced that anyone could shed any light.[19] From other sources, he was also aware that British intelligence had been flawed. 'A recent illustration of effective concealment on Germany's part is to be found in her naval rearmament, on which our Intelligence proved defective.'[20] Other factors became disquieting. The Admiralty had lately been concerned at the time of the Spanish Civil War with the need to identify submarines which had been sinking merchant ships in the Mediterranean.[21] It was discovered that the small 'Movements Section' at the Admiralty, where reports of ship movements were filed, was totally inadequate for the job so the DCNS went on probing and casting a net around to find a solution. In June 1937, it was decided to bring Paymaster Lt-Cdr Norman Denning into NID to determine the kind of organization that would be required for a war-time operational intelligence centre. It did not take long for Denning to realize that the current set-up was defective and that the information coming in fell far short of what the Board wanted.[22] Rear Admiral J. A. G. Troup, Director of Naval Intelligence, wrote an explanatory note on 18 October 1938 to Rushbrooke (later to become the DNI) explaining the progress that had been made to date. The note explained the setting up of a new OIC which was proposed to assist the intelligence branch and 'Defence of Trade Department' to make greater use of enemy intercept signals to track known U-boat movements, all of which was to become valuable information.[23] This is one area where a key lesson of the past was recognized and incorporated as an organization change into the department.[24] By contrast, the U-boat arm had no equivalent and dealt directly with *B-Dienst*, the SigInt surveillance service, in order to get information on merchant convoys. They were not engaged in ASW to the same degree as the RN and had little requirement for a Trade Division. In the early days of the war, up to the end of 1940, it was the *Luftwaffe* which provided sighting information, before *B-Dienst* had broken into Naval Cipher No. 3 with sufficient regularity.[25] In contrast, OIC (the sections within the Division) was in receipt of incoming intelligence and on the basis of major issues made individual recommendations, via their Chiefs of Staff, to the Board relating to action. One section of OIC was wholly devoted to U-boats, for it was correctly estimated that it was the German intention to again use them against merchant shipping in a classic 'commerce war'. The OIC U-boat Tracking Room was well established by February 1939 under the VCNS.[26] It had now acquired its war-time specialized sections dealing with surface warships and disguised raiders, including U-boats, air operations concerning the Navy, merchant shipping and minefields and wireless interception.[27] In August the actual naval code-breaking operations were physically moved to Bletchley Park, an estate 40 miles from London. Although the official designation was 'Station X' it was renamed the Government Code and Cipher School (GC&CS) under the direction of Naval Commander Alastair Denniston, who worked very closely with the OIC,[28] and German intelligence from section 8G – GC&CS was passed to OIC by tele-printer.[29] By the start of the war the operational intelligence section was well placed to assist the Trade Division, supplemented in October 1939 by the ASW Division formed under ACNS (Trade).[30] It was also as part of this Division that ASW analysis and ASW OR (to be discussed in a later chapter) sections were formed after August 1940;[31] indeed it was only after the sinking of the aircraft carrier *Glorious* in 1940 that it finally consolidated its position.[32]

The person largely responsible for setting up OIC was a ghost from the past in the form of Paymaster Captain Thring. Thring had originally worked in 'Room 40' and although over 60, 'possessed a highly sceptical and analytical mind and a stubborn integrity which was not to succumb to browbeating from superiors in the Admiralty or the optimistic blandishments of juniors afloat.'[33] One of the staff engaged to assist Thring was a civilian, Rodger Winn (originally a barrister by trade, later drafted into the RNVR service). Winn was eventually to take over from Thring and develop the 'art' of U-boat tracking into a 'fine art', something undreamt of in the 'Room 40' days of the First World War.[34] Each piece of evidence, from reports of torpedoed merchantmen to the crop of doubtful sightings and unreliable rumours, was carefully vetted and then, based on the findings, might be used as the basis for routeing shipping clear of danger- or for countermeasure action by escort forces. For a re-routeing decision 'it was an officer in the Trade Division who actually ordered a convoy to change course, but it was an officer in operations who sent orders to warships or to the commands.'[35] OIC is referred to in the literature as occupying 'Room 39', but the 'Submarine Tracking Room' was housed in 'Room 41', and Winn disliked anyone to enter unless they had business there.[36] While there are some historians who opine that evasive routeing was of little value when large numbers of U-boats in packs converged on a convoy,[37] there is sufficient evidence from practitioners and other historians which concludes that this tactic was an important element in a defensive/offensive strategy.[38]

The start of the U-boat war, 1939–41

Germany only started the war with 57 U-boats, of which just 26 were ready for ocean duties.[39] However, it was quite evident that they would soon attack British shipping so the key areas needing protection were the transatlantic routes and the 10,000 square miles of water in the South-western approaches of the British Isles, one of the busiest sea-borne trade routes in the world.[40] During the winter of 1940–1 it became obvious that Britain would not be subjected to a German invasion, after the *Luftwaffe's* failure to secure air superiority over southeast England. No German Army could get ashore onto

English soil without air cover and the surface forces based on the east- and south-coasts were fully capable to mount any offensive against landing craft, of any nature. But the German fleet would remain a threat until well into 1941.

The shipping losses to date were ominous.[41] In the first 16 months of war Britain and her allies had lost nearly 1,300 merchant vessels of some 4.7 million Gross Register Tons (GRT), of which the U-boats alone accounted for 585 vessels sunk, or 55 per cent of the losses,[42] largely independents and stragglers, many of which could not be put into convoy due to a lack of escorts.[43] If these numbers were bad, the trend was worse. British shipping losses continued on an upward slope and in January 1941 the combined tanker and non-tanker imports into the Britain fell below 3 million tons for the first time in the war (Chart 2.2). These depressing trends did not bode well for the future and Mr Churchill informed the current CNS (Chief of Naval Staff), Admiral Sir Dudley Pound, that it was incumbent upon all to raise the topic to the highest plane, over everything else. He informed those around him that a special committee of the 'Battle of the Atlantic' (BAC) would be formed.[44] On 6 March 1941 Mr Churchill issued his Battle of the Atlantic Directive, setting out his vision and goals. An organization with cabinet status, it met weekly without fail from March 1941 and included the war cabinet and other ministers.[45] He regarded this battle as being a re-run of the 'Battle of Britain' and anticipated that it would produce a similar clear-cut decision within a fixed period of time. Churchill then issued one of his directives declaring that the next four months should be sufficient to defeat the attempt to strangle food supplies and the nation's connection with the United States.[46] The first monthly meeting was held in Downing Street on 19 March 1941.[47] The last meeting was seven months later on 22 October. What the 'Battle of the Atlantic' Committee actually achieved in its brief life span is difficult to identify though Mr Churchill himself seemed satisfied with its outcome; it certainly was of short duration. During a closed session speech to the House of Commons on 25 June 1941 the Prime Minister declared 'that the steps taken by his government were already producing an improvement in the war at sea';[48] this claim was re-asserted in his war memoirs.[49] Perhaps implicit in that statement was the fact that, prior to the entry of the United States into the war, American material assistance to Britain was increased significantly when, 'on 27 August 1941 the first fourteen Liberty ships were launched and a further 312, representing some 2,200,000 tons, had been ordered.'[50]

The Battle of the Atlantic, and the lack of escorts, had been uppermost in the mind of the new C-in-C WA. As far back as January, it had been suggested by Admiral Noble that the 15-knot upper speed limit of ships for inclusion into convoy should be reinstituted. Over several months the Admiralty considered the matter but it was not until after further pressure from Noble that they finally agreed to his proposal,[51] – as more escorts became available.[52] Then 'the North Atlantic saw an even more important, if not dramatic, decline in sinkings from the end of June.'[53]

The decline was also due, in part, to improvements in control measures used against stragglers and, perhaps more importantly, the introduction at

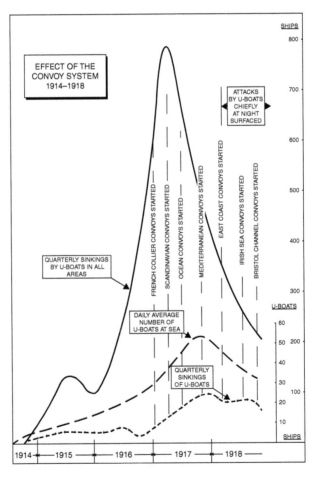

Chart 2.2 Shipping losses by quarter, 1939–45
Source: D. W. Waters, 'The Science of Admiralty VI'.[54]

this time of end-to-end escort protection.[55] The British had known about the vulnerability of independents to U-boat attack from the last war, but were unable to institute full convoy for the reasons discussed. But, with more escorts coming on-stream they were now able to revert to the lesson already learnt in earlier times.

On 4 November 1942, the Prime Minister inaugurated a replacement Committee known as the Anti U-boat Warfare Committee, which had been mooted in June and July on the suggestion of the Representative of the Australian Government, the Right Hon S. M. Bruce. It was his contention that the Committee should be comprised of those best equipped with knowledge and experience, those responsible for policy, those capable of rapidly translating policy into action that would enforce the priorities of the Battle of the Atlantic,[56] for convoys were about to reach their peak.[57] The members comprised a similar mix of experts as the BAC who were rotated according to the subjects under discussion, the objective being to get opinions from the relative experts in their field that would assist in identifying problems and solutions. In the event this Committee had Cabinet status, which enabled decisions to be reached quickly and priorities firmly decided and enforced.[58] It was a good platform for essential feedback from key personnel and helped to identify requirements needed at the front, and became a regular conference that helped shape the course of convoy warfare. In general, historians regard the BAC, and its successor, as useful instruments for discussion, and where some vital decisions were taken from lessons learned.[59]

As mentioned in the previous chapter the enemy too had a method of progress reports, '*Führer* Conferences'/*Lagevorträge*, designed to keep Hitler informed about aspects of how the naval war was developing and discuss specific needs of the Navy, albeit in a less democratic fashion. While the *Lagevorträge* helped to highlight many of the requirements of the Navy, they did not have the forum of a wider interested audience and, in contrast to the improving British Committee, only tended to slow down the rate of progress and development. Neither did it have cabinet status, nor comprise an organization for change. Hitler was difficult to reason with, domineering, and therefore obstructive. Only later in 1943 did he become more malleable, and only then within the restrictions of dwindling resources.

Convoy protection assets – surface vessels

It is claimed that navies, which had studied the lessons of the past, the RN included, were those best equipped to face the future.[60] However, some of the lessons that might have been drawn from earlier wars in British naval history had not been taken to heart by the Admiralty. In particular, the relatively recent experience of the First World War appears not to have alerted the Admiralty, and the government, to the fact that fast vessels of long endurance were needed for convoy escorts against the threat of U-boat attack, and that 'fast vessels needed for escort against submarine attack cannot be improvised'.[61] This point cannot be emphasized enough.[62]

Historians have not unreasonably asked why 'no comprehensive British history of the U-boat and anti-submarine operations in 1914–18 was written after the First World War',[63] and just what the Admiralty was doing in the more than 20 intervening years. They were surely aware that defeat by the U-boat in the First World War was only principally averted through the belated introduction of convoy, using escort warships as a protective shield.[64] From these experiences, the Admiralty might have also determined that a sufficient number of escort vessels with a high turn of speed were needed, in order to close on a detected U-boat. Historians may justly apply some criticism of the Admiralty since it appears not to have learnt the lessons of convoy from past history, dating back to at least the sixteenth century; and the 1914–18 war was almost lost, after many lives and ships had been forfeited.[65] It was indisputably the same failure to provide fast escorts of long endurance,[66] in sufficient numbers, more than any other single factor, which was to lay a heavy burden on Britain's fighting effort to protect its transatlantic lifeline in the Second World War, but why?[67]

In 1923, plans were put forward by the Admiralty for a large Destroyer-building programme to meet the future needs of the country. So much was achieved on paper.

The argument used in Committee was that by 1929, 87 of Britain's 207 Destroyers would be at their age limit and it suggested that Britain would be facing a situation in which it would have only 120 useful Destroyers for use across the whole of the dominions of the British Empire. The Admiralty proposed to build two flotillas, 'each of eight ships and a leader, every year from 1927 to 1931, and thereafter to build one such flotilla every year'.[68] At first, there seemed to be no objection to the proposal but following the collapse of the Baldwin government and MacDonald's institution as the first Labour Prime Minister the whole construction schedule seemed in doubt. When Baldwin's government had a second term of office, the process of the application for fleet replacements was restarted. In July 1925 the Admiralty announced a reduced building programme with the intention of building alternate flotillas with either ASDIC (SONAR) or minesweeping capability. Then in a 1931 paper, the Director of the Tactical Division argued that in the event of a European war a total of seven ASDIC fitted flotillas would be needed. The paper does however propose to add a further three flotillas for 'other operations', of which two should be fitted with the device.[69] By the 12 August 1932 a hand written note from the D of TD, Grace suggested that 'it is very desirable that an early decision of our (Memo) 7285/32 should be obtained'.[70] In the memo it stated that a total of 117 would be insufficient in the case of a European war and particularly in view of the large numbers of submarines likely to be employed by the enemy; this was bearing in mind the abandonment of the ten-year rule in March 1932.[71] Therefore, in a war in which attacks were made on British lines of communications the submarine would prove to be a primary menace.[72]

Interwar, the Admiralty planners had given some thought to the need for long-range escorts, and worked on securing types of escort vessel. Several escort requirements for a potential war were considered and it was decided to build six prototype long-range vessels, in case of war.[73] However, in August 1932 the D of TD had already warned of too few being planned. The financial implications of more would have had little effect on budgets and did not prevent good contingency planning. It was a wise move to have designed and build some prototype long-range ocean-going escorts before the war so that they could be put into production when, and if, needed.[74]

In early 1938 it was slowly becoming clear to all that a war with Germany was a strong possibility. The Director of the Tactical Division calculated the forces required for war and stacked his results against the assets that were actually available, especially for a trade war, that is with U-boats. It was estimated that 100 ocean-going escort vessels would be needed for convoy protection and implicit in the terms of the estimates was an acceptance that no modern Destroyers were to be included in this figure. The actual number of vessels available to WA for defence of Atlantic trade on 3 September 1939 comprised just 21 Destroyers, 6 escort vessels and 3 A/S trawlers, a modest start – and one which would make the task of defending convoys difficult in the extreme. 'A partial convoy system was introduced in 1939 but, given the diversion of assets to other priorities, it was far from complete.'[75] Therefore, the doctrine employed at the start of the war comprised a 'standard escort' consisting of only two escorts, in order to provide protection for the maximum number of convoys possible.[76] The problem of an acute shortage of convoy escort vessels continued and by the middle of 1940 the situation had only marginally improved. Two of the reasons appear to have been due to Churchill's lack of foresight in naval affairs, despite his claims to the contrary. (1) He needed money to fund a 55-division army, an enlarged Air Force and a merchant fleet building programme estimated at 1.5 million tons per year.[77] Escorts were not at the top of the list. (2) His reason for not engaging in this problem was the naval plan for offensive patrolling, a debunked idea from the last war – but which Churchill endorsed. In this instance the Admiralty might have stepped forward and blocked this idea; but the then CNS Admiral Sir Dudley Pound was an administrator, no longer a fighting Admiral, as he once was – even though he must have known that 'this method of hunting submarines was not effective';[78] a point of view shared with other historians.[79] However, in defence of the charge that the Admiralty had ill-prepared at least three historians, Andrew Lambert, Nicholas Rodger and H. P. Wilmott, agree that the interwar RN was not faced with an interwar submarine threat in the Atlantic and, as Rodger puts it, they were 'fit for purpose'.[80] The larger threat came from the Japanese and Italian Navies. The Lambert article concludes that even if sufficient escorts had been available they would not have comprised vessels of long endurance, being mainly planned for regions around Britain, not the Atlantic.[81] But what cannot be in dispute is that the Admiralty was well aware of a possible threat from Germany as late as 1935, if not earlier, and by the outbreak of war little had been achieved in terms of the correct mix of escorts available.[82] The notion that German forces could be confined to areas of the North Sea was a strategic atavism from the First World War, which in the first 6 months was effective; a point of view shared by Maiolo.[83] But in 1940, after Norway and then France collapsed, and U-boats had broken out through the use of newly acquired bases, it became an inappropriate strategy. But, as yet, there was no reserve strategy. There was a naval alliance with France which, while desirable, could never have been a main plank policy. It was an alliance founded on the principle belief that there should be no repeat of the 1914–18 war;[84] the French were mainly relied upon for support in the Western Mediterranean, which allowed the RN to institute 'a secure Channel barrier in 1939'. These set-backs were not foreseeable, and not as a result of Admiralty policy.

With France lost, escorts would need to cover the wide expanse of water occupied by U-boats, and 'the available forces were neither numerous, nor well balanced'.[85] Mining would have taken too long. Furthermore, it should also be noted that 1939 was in the age of aircraft of greater endurance, and would likely force U-boats to operate further out into the Atlantic. In 1917 aircraft performance was not high, but operated into the Atlantic. With patrol bases in Ireland, at Queenstown (Cobh County Cork), Lough Foyle, Wexford and Whiddy Island, the Atlantic would have been on their doorstep, except for the further Wexford.[86] However, Wexford was well placed for the southern approach to Liverpool. In terms of endurance and range in 1918, the RAF's (R.N.A.S.) Blackburn 'Kangaroo', with twin Rolls Royce engines, had a range of approximately 900 miles.[87] By 1939 that had increased twofold, when even the simple Warwick Mk I had a range of 2,000 miles.[88] U-boats had long endurance in the last war. Indeed it is clear from history that in 1918 U-boats operated successfully off the eastern seaboard of North America/Canada, without any French ports under their control. Alone in August 1918 U-boats sank 29 ships.[89] Therefore if U-boats could already reach North American convoy routes in 1918, it seems clear that nothing less could be expected in 1939. All this should have been known to Air Ministry planners. Therefore the notion of air escorts with low endurance was also inappropriate.

Conclusions

It has been suggested that the Admiralty did not sufficiently study the possibility of war with Germany and therefore its analysis was defective. Some historians seem to be in agreement that the Admiralty failed to prepare for a German offensive at sea and appeared obsessed with a plan for a decisive battle fleet showdown, but the evidence clearly points to the fact that several naval departments were aware of shortcomings and were able to get some matters rectified. The Admiralty had learnt an important lesson from the last war and responded to the changing situation with the setting up of key organization elements required in the fight against the U-boat menace, by installing the OIC and ASW sections.

Other problems to contend with manifested themselves due to the disposition of insufficient escort vessels and the unexpected fall of Norway and France. Some incorrectly suggest that the lack of suitable escorts was because of poor Admiralty planning, but it was more due to constraints forced upon Britain brought about through the political developments in Italy and Japan. Japan's expansionist ideology being of greater worry even led to Sir

Dudley Pound's contribution to the 1939 *Fighting Instructions* being 'written with action against the Japanese in mind'.[90] At least, two historians agree that the Admiralty have judged that the new German heavy ships to be the greater threat at the start of the war,[91] and one of those has defended planners at the Admiralty by suggesting that the balance of escorts was right.[92] At best, it might be said that 'Though the Admiralty may have been somewhat complacent the course of the submarine war prior to the fall France suggests that they were not far out.'[93] Nevertheless, it was always escorts with long endurance that would have still been the key to convoy protection, not Cruisers, or Battleships. Fortunately, in the early years of the 'War on Commerce' events moved at a snail's pace and the time served the British well, as new commands and training facilities were set up, but escorts still remained at a premium. Escorts remained a problem until modifications to older vessels were completed and the United States transferred some of their old stock under a lend-lease agreement in 1941. The loss of France as an ally was an unexpected blow that Britain had to overcome, but under the agreement the RN would have still been responsible for the Atlantic sea routes. Initially France was able to provide some assistance but once it had signed an armistice with Germany, Britain was on its own.

Churchill's move to instigate a Battle of the Atlantic Committee started the process of addressing the critical lack of ocean convoy escorts and acute shortages in other areas. In the following year, using the experience gained from this committee, an even more effective Anti U-boat Warfare Committee was set up. The committee addressed many problems including the need to close the 'air gap' in mid-Atlantic, which required about 40 long-range radar-fitted aircraft. By contrast the *Kriegsmarine* only had the *Lagevorträge* in which to air their views but was unable to debate the overall conduct of the war in committee with senior officers from the other services, due to Hitler's autocratic style of leadership. He had learned nothing from the Kaiser's authoritarian style in the First World War.[94]

Notes

1   Joseph A. Maiolo, 'The Knockout Blow against the Import System: Admiralty Expectations of Nazi Germany's Naval Strategy 1934–9', *Journal of Historical Research*, 72 (178) (June 1999), 202–28, 202.

2   TNA CAB 4/26, CID 1368-B, *Protection of Seaborne Trade*, November 1937, 2.

3   Ibid., CID 1323-B, *Review of Imperial Defence by the Chiefs of Staff,* May l937, 7: TNA FO 371/21692, C 250/250/18, British Naval Attaché, Berlin, to F.O., 10 January 1938.

4   Arthur J. Marder, 'The Influence of History on Sea Power: The Royal Navy and the Lessons of 1914–1918', *Pacific Historical Review,* 41 (4) (November 1972), 413–43, 428; Stephen W. Roskill, *Naval Policy between the Wars* (1968–76), I, 534–7, II, 227–8, 332, 430–1.

5   Corelli Barnett, *Engage the Enemy More Closely* (1991), 256.

6   Andrew Lambert, 'Sea Power 1939–1940', in *Sea Power,* (Ilford, 1994), 86–107, 90; Nicolas Rodger, 'The Royal Navy in the Era of the World Wars: Was it Fit For Purpose?', *The Mariner's Mirror,* 97 (1) (February 2011), 272–84, 281.

7   Maiolo, 'The Knockout Blow against the Import System', 210.

8   Admiral E. Chatfield, *The Navy and Defence* (1942), 212–13.

9   TNA CAB 53/6, COS (Chiefs of Staff) 192nd and 194th meetings, 12 and 22 January 1937.

10 Geoffrey Till, 'The Battle of the Atlantic as History', in *The Battle of the Atlantic 1939–1945* (1994), 584–95, 591; Kenneth Hansen, 'Raeder versus Wegener: Conflict in German Naval Strategy', *Naval War College Review,* Newport-Rhode Island, Autumn, 2005, 1.

11 Lambert, 'Sea Power 1939–1940', 92; Werner Rahn, 'German Naval Strategy and Armament 1919–1939', in *Technology and Naval Combat in the Twentieth Century and Beyond* (2001), 109–28; Rodger, 'The Royal Navy in the Era of the World Wars', 281.

12 TNA CAB 24/268, Note by Chatfield, 10; N. H. Gibbs, *Grand Strategy* (1) (1976), 657.

13 P. Auphan and J. Mordal, *The French Navy in World War* (Annapolis, 1959), II, 19–20.

14 Edward P. von der Porten, *The German Navy in World War Two* (1969), 93–5.

15 Stephen S. Roskill, *The War at Sea* (1954), I, 21.

16 Chart constructed by author.

17 H. P. Wilmott, 'The Organizations', in *The Battle of the Atlantic 1939–1945* (1994), 183.

18 TNA ADM 137/3956, 3962, 4057, Room 40 internal; David Ramsay, *'Blinker' Hall* (Stroud, 2008).

19 Donald McLachlan, *Room 39* (1968), 54.

20 TNA CAB 24/259, Committee of Imperial Defence, 12 February 1936, 35.

21 TNA CAB 23/95, 12 September–3 October 1938. Britain's problems in assessing the German threat, 14 September 1938.

22 McLachlan, *Room 39,* 55.

23 TNA ADM 1/10226, 'Admiralty (5): Development of Operational Intelligence Centre at Admiralty', Note dated 18 October 1938.

24 Rodger, 'The Royal Navy in the Era of the World Wars', 283.

25 TNA HW 8/113, January–November 1942; the improvement began in October–December 1941, 57.

26 TNA ADM 1/10226, Development of Operational Intelligence Centre at the Admiralty'.

27 F. H. Hinsley et al., *British Intelligence in the Second World War* (1979), I, 12.

28 Bill Momsen, 'Code Breaking and Secret Weapons in World War II', Chapter II: 1939–41, (Internet) *Nautical Brass* 1993–2007.

29 TNA HW 8/21, 'Naval Miscellaneous Papers 1939', Organization of German Intel to OIC.

30 D. W .Waters, 'The Philosophy and Conduct of Maritime War, Part II, 1918–1945', *JRNSS*, 13 (1958), 183–92, 183.

31 Wilmott, 'The Organizations', 183.

32 C. I. Hamilton, 'The Character and Organization of the Admiralty Operational Intelligence', *War in History* (July 2000), 295–324, 295.

33 Patrick Beesly, *Very special Intelligence* (1977), 21; McLachlan, *Room 39,* 102.

34 TNA ADM 1/10266, NID 004/l1939, 'Development of the Operational Intelligence Centre at the Admiralty'.

35 C. I. Hamilton, 'The Character and Organization of the Admiralty Operational Intelligence', 301.

36 TNA ADM 223/284, Operational intelligence: Special intelligence monographs notes of R.T. Barrett, 'The Use of Special Intelligence'.

37 W. J. R. Gardner, 'The Battle of the Atlantic, 1941–the First Turning Point?', in *Sea Power* (Ilford, 1994), 109–23, 115; Geoffrey Till, 'The Battle of the Atlantic as History', 585.

38 F. Barley et al., *The Defeat of the Enemy Attack on Shipping 1939–1945,*137 (Aldershot, 1997), 108; Hinsley, et al., *British Intelligence in the Second World War* (1981), II, 170; 1984), III, 212.

39 TNA ADM 233/84, U-boat appreciations in NID 0714 of 27 February 1941; Sönke Neitzel, 'The Deployment of U-boats', in *The Battle of the Atlantic 1939–1945* (1994), 276–301, 276; *Official Account of the Battle of the Atlantic* (1946), 7.

40 TNA CAB 66/2, Memo by the DCNS, Rear Admiral Sir Tom Phillips, 18 October 1939.

41 See Chart 2.2, Shipping losses to U-boats 1939–45.

42 John Terraine, *A Time for Courage* (New York, 1985), 244.

43 Vice Admiral P. Gretton, 'Why Don't We Learn from History?', *The Naval Review,* 46 (January 1958), 13–25, 18.

44 Winston S. Churchill, *The Second World War* (1986), III, 106.

45 TNA CAB 86/1, 19 March 1941: First Meeting and Persons Present; Churchill, *The Second World War,* III, 107.

46 TNA PREM 3/60/1, printed with corrections in Churchill, 3:122–6, Battle of the Atlantic.

47 See TNA CAB 86/1/7, 27, for the date convened and participants. Two further ad hoc, supplementary meetings were said to have taken place in February and May of 1942.

48 Max Schoenfeld, 'Winston Churchill as War Manager: The Battle of the Atlantic Committee, 1941', *Military Affairs*, 52 (3) (July 1988), 122–27, 122.

49 Churchill, *The Second World War*, III, 150–5.

50 Holger H. Herwig, 'Prelude to Weltblitzkrieg: Germany's Naval Policy toward the United States of America, 1939–41', *The Journal of Modern History*, 43 (4) (December 1971), 649–68, (665).

51 Roskill, *The War at Sea*, I, 457.

52 Barley et al., *The Defeat of the Enemy Attack on Shipping 1939–1945*, 31, 40.

53 Edward Thomas, in 'Seek and Sink', RAF Bracknell Paper No. 2, A Symposium on the Battle of the Atlantic, 21 October 1991, 38–48, 40.

54 D. W. Waters, 'The Science of Admiralty, VI', *The Naval Review*, 52 (4) (October 1964), 423–437, 431. Reproduced by courtesy of the Naval Review.

55 Barley et al., *The Defeat of the Enemy Attack on Shipping 1939–1945*, 31, 40. Also, see Chart 2.2 for an indication of the decline.

56 John Terraine, *Business in Great Waters* (Ware, 1999), 501.

57 See Chart 2.2, which shows convoy losses of around 60/quarter in this period.

58 Roskill, *The War at Sea* (1956), II, 88.

59 TNA CAB 86/3, AUC Meetings; Karl Dönitz, *Memoirs* (1959), 116; Horst Boog, 'Luftwaffe Support of the German Navy', in *The Battle of the Atlantic 1939–1945*, 302–22, 313.

60 Rodger, 'The Royal Navy in the Era of the World Wars', 274.

61 Barley et al., *The Defeat of the Enemy Attack on Shipping 1939–1945*, 18. Bracketed inserted by author.

62 Vice Admiral P. Gretton, 'Why Don't We Learn from History?', *The Naval Review*, 46 (January 1958), 13–25.

63 Barley et al., *The Defeat of the Enemy Attack on Shipping 1939–1945*, Ch 1 3.

64 John Jellicoe, *The Submarine Peril* (1934), 112 and 206–7: Sir Henry Newbolt, *History of the Great War based on Official Documents* (1931), V, 3–4; R. Macgregor Dawson, *Canadian Journal of Economics and Political Science*, 9 (1) (February 1943), 14–15, 25.

65 K. G. B. Dewar, 'War on Shipping 1914–1918'; *The Naval Review*, 47 (1) (January 1959), 3–13; Rear-Admiral R. M. Bellairs, 'Historical Survey of Trade Defence Since 1914', *RUSI* 99, 595 (August 1954), 359–77.

66 Rodger, 'The Royal Navy in the Era of the World Wars', 282.

67 Barley et al., *The Defeat of the Enemy Attack on Shipping 1939–1945*, 18.

68 George Franklin, *Britain's Anti-Submarine Capability 1919–1939* (2003), 88.

69 TNA ADM 116/3603, D of T.D. December 1931, the paper arguing for several flotillas but three flotillas for escort work, approximately 24 ships.

70 TNA ADM 116/3603, Note appended to Minute Sheet 1, CW 7012/32.

71 TNA CAB 23/70, Conclusions of Cabinet Meeting, 23 March 1932. Details of the final Cabinet discussion on the matter of the ten-year rule.

72 TNA ADM 116/3603, D of TD December 1931, the paper argues for several flotillas for more than a European war.

73 Franklin, *Britain's Anti-Submarine Capability 1919–1939,* 92.

74 David K. Brown, *Nelson to Vanguard: Warship Design and Development 1923–1945* (2006), 136; Joseph A. Maiolo, *The Royal Navy and Nazi Germany 1933–39* (1998), 121. There appears to be a significant difference of opinion on this point in Franklin's book, (92).

75 Eric J. Grove, *The Future of Sea Power* (1990), 17.

76 Franklin, *Britain's Anti-Submarine Capability 1919–1939,* 147.

77 TNA ADM 205/5, New construction of ships Acteon net defence Economic warfare, etcLetter to the Chancellor of the Exchequer, 21 January 1940.

78 Admiral William V. Pratt, 'Warfare in the Atlantic', *Foreign Affairs,* 19 (4) (July 1941), 729–36, 731.

79 Roskill, *Naval Policy between the Wars,* II, 428; Terraine, *Business in Great Waters,* 244–5; David K. Brown, *Atlantic Escorts* (Barnsley, 2007), 88–9.

80 Lambert, 'Sea Power 1939–1940', 90; Rodger, 'The Royal Navy in the Era of the World Wars', 281: Wilmott, 'The Organizations', 184–5.

81 Lambert, 'Sea Power 1939–1940, 94.

82 Rodger, 'The Royal Navy in the Era of the World Wars', 282.

83 Maiolo, *The Royal Navy and Nazi Germany 1933–39,* 121.

84 M. Howard, *The Continental Commitment* (1972), 96–120.

85 Lambert, 'Sea Power 1939–1940', 100.

86 John Abbatiello, 'British Naval Aviation in the Anti-submarine Campaign 1917–18' University of London, King's College, 2004, 150.

87 TNA AIR 1/ 6A/4/46, Aeroplanes – Statistics and summaries of requirements for RFC, RNAS and RAF; J. M. Bruce, *British Aeroplanes, 1914–18* (1957), 96; R. D. Layman, *Naval Aviation in the First World War* (Annapolis, 1996), 83.

88 Abbatiello, 'British Naval Aviation in the Anti-submarine Campaign 1917–18', 238.

89 Sir Henry Newbolt, *History of the Great War based on Official Documents,* V, Plan 31. This plan shows significant numbers of merchant ships sunk off the East Coast of North America up to Newfoundland, May – October 1918.

90 Jon Sumida, 'The Best Laid Plans: The Development of British Battle-fleet Tactics, 1919–42', *International History Review,* XIV (1992), 681–700, 695.

91 Rodger, 'The Royal Navy in the Era of the World Wars', 281: Andrew Lambert, 'Sea Power 1939–1940', 92.

92 Lambert, 'Sea Power 1939–1940', 94.

93 Brown, *Nelson to Vanguard,* 127.

94 Carl Axel Gemzell, *Organization, Conflict and Innovation* (Lund, 1973), 39; Bird, *Erich Raeder*, 16.

3

New Opportunities for U-boat Bases and Inter-service Rivalry

From March to mid-May1940 the commerce war against British merchant shipping virtually came to a halt, due to the dispersal of U-boats to Norwegian waters in preparation for the invasion of that country; this was one of the incidences that Dönitz had to comply with. U-boat support had been demanded by the *OKW* and tasked with intercepting enemy warships, a mission that they singularly failed to achieve, due to a combination of the high rate of torpedo failures and the task of transport assignments.[1]

With the fall of Norway in March, and France signing an armistice with Germany on 22 June 1940, things changed for the U-boat arm. With France effectively out of the war it essentially left just Britain to fight the war alone.[2] She was about to learn the hard lesson of reliance on a single strategic decision of an Anglo-French alliance that contained no contingency plan, should France not be in a position to participate.[3]

With France under German occupation the door was open for German U-boats to make use of the Biscay ports facilities at Brest, Lorient, St Nazaire, La Pallice and Bordeaux. Lorient (Kernével) served as the main base of operations, where Dönitz set up his central operation in November 1940. Dönitz was already making preparations to move his units into occupied territory during the months of May and June, even while the conquest of France was in progress. He had arranged to have a train standing by loaded with torpedoes and ready to carry all the personnel and material necessary for the maintenance of U-boats. That train was dispatched to the Biscay ports the day after the signing of the armistice.[4]

There was an air of super-confidence abroad, and with good reason. Most of the territory that Helmuth Heye had argued for in his report as necessary for oceanic strategy had now been occupied. The Brittany ports were especially ideal for U-boat operations since they lay so close to the Western Approaches and the English Channel. Heye was a student of Wegener, who in the 1930s, advocated that Germany should deploy her naval power in order to strike at Britain's most vulnerable point, her sea-borne trade and in particular the 'Atlantic'.[5] The new bases contained repair facilities and were quickly made available. This relieved the situation in the German dockyards, making the periods under repair shorter and thus putting more boats at sea. The average number of operational boats available from September 1939 to July 1940 was in the order of 33; the average number at sea was about 14, or approximately 42 per cent of the available boats. From August 1940 to July 1941, the average number available was about 30, of which about 16 or approximately 53 per cent were at sea. Thus in the latter period the proportion of boats at sea was approximately 11 per cent higher. Günter Hessler, an experienced U-boat Commander himself, concluded that with the bases nearer to the enemy, it meant a considerable reduction in the outward and homeward passages, and hence a greater percentage of boats in the operational area.[6] The intention was to push deeper into the Atlantic to meet convoys, and provide a regular fuel supply for their packs.

It was also around this time that Dönitz learnt an important lesson to add to the concept of 'pack' tactics – mobile support groups. While the RN had experience of support groups during the First World War the U-boat arm had not used such a concept. But now U-boats were formed into groups to be stationed at locations, to be called on when needed, and represented an 'almost complete transition in 1941 to a new method of operation'.[7] Thus when groups finished an attack they were dispersed, some returning to base, and others to join a new group ready to do battle again. It worked as a method of rotation. In contrast RN support groups operated in support of a particular convoy escort group, before being dispersed when deemed no longer needed, but remaining as a group to be used for further support missions. U-boat support groups operated only in support of pack operational considerations, reinforcing or creating a new group. It was this key lesson learnt which made a large contribution to U-boat success between mid 1941 to the end of 1942. The *BdU*, *Konteradmiral* Dönitz, had proved himself to be a first-class innovative tactician, not so much strategist, and had quickly gained the initiative from the start; unsurprising, given the parlous state of Britain's convoy defences, at the time. Dönitz had found the soft spots and successfully applied the principle of concentrating his forces to strike where the defence was weak.[8] In consequence, the British-led anti-U-boat forces seemed to be a lap behind, at this time.[9] However, one historian mistakenly thought that by the time they had collected sufficient resources to deal with an attack in one area the U-boats had amassed others in another and were sinking merchant ships right and left,[10] but these were usually independents (and stragglers), not convoys. Indeed, as more escorts became available, the Admiralty ensured that more ships were accommodated into convoy,[11] which drastically began to reduce the rates of merchant ship losses.

As far back as April 1917, *Flotillenadmiral* Bauer had foreseen the rôle for long-range boats for which would be needed a 'Milch Cow' (supply ship). The following year some attempts were made to secure supply, with mixed results; but the principle was established.[12] Bauer was also credited with the original idea of *Rudeltaktik* – although Rößler cites a paper delivered by Wassner of the *Wehrabteilung* in 1922 (Defence Department) on U-boats working together in concert;[13] Dönitz went on to improve on the idea.[14] Now the German Navy had learnt four lessons.

1. They had secured the territory needed to fight an effective Atlantic war.
2. They had built on Bauer's original thesis of working in packs.
3. *Rudeltaktik* had been strengthened through the use of Mobile Groups.
4. They implemented the concept of Bauer's regular fuel supply line.

Admiral Dönitz remained at Kernével complete with his staff until March 1942 when he was instructed, under a Hitler directive No. 40 to all coastal commanders, to be aware of the implications of British raids on the coastline. A small part of it read: 'The coastline of Europe will, in the coming months, be exposed to the danger of an enemy landing in force.'[15] After the British raid on St Nazaire 28 March 1942 it was clear that Kernével was too close to be ignored. The day after, Dönitz recorded that a British raiding party attacked St Nazaire.[16] No U-boats were lost but it was obvious that had there been a similar raid on Kernével the British could have captured the entire staff of U-boat Command; had that happened the U-boat war Command and Control would have been wiped out and that would have been more than just a salutary lesson. He therefore accelerated the move to set up his communications centre elsewhere.[17] It maintained its nomadic existence until February 1943.[18] When Dönitz took up the appointment as *ObdM* his staff followed him to Berlin, and became the Second Section of the Naval Staff with the designation of 2/*Skl*; but changes to the operations organization were minimal.

All successful commands need a leader and good support staff. Under Dönitz was a Chief of Staff, *Korvettenkapitän* (later *Konteradmiral*) Eberhard Godt who remained in close touch with the operational flotillas and was in executive charge of the U-boat arm. Godt had control of assistant officers carrying out their functions in the various departments.[19] In addition to the Admiral's first staff officer (A1) to deal with U-boat deployments and availability, he had an intelligence officer (A3) who kept him up-to-date with enemy situation reports. This officer also made an evaluation of U-boat War Diaries and combat experience which he shared with another staff officer (A5), responsible for the statistics used for OR purposes.[20] From November 1941 Dönitz's son-in-law Günter Hessler became the first staff officer, and continued until the end of the war.

It is of particular note that the third staff officer (Intelligence) was responsible for the presentation of the enemy situation in the daily meetings with the staff officers and providing intelligence and reconnaissance data from all sources, U-boat and *Luftwaffe* sighting reports and Radio Intelligence information. He was also an important part of the evaluation of U-boat records and the generation of a body of combat experience in conjunction with A5, the officer in charge of U-boat records, statistics and reports sent back to the *OKM*.[21] Appropriate observations and recommendations were then forwarded to the respective departments concerned with equipment improvements which would make use of the data provided, essential in 'OR matters'. There were additions and deletions to staff over the period of the war but the essential core of Dönitz's organization remained virtually untouched, except for some minor changes in title, until the end of the war. Chief among them were Eberhard Godt, his right hand operations director, and von Friedeburg in charge of the core organizations, including the all important U-boat training divisions. This then was the basic corps of officers that exercised operational and administrative control over the whole U-boat fleet of flotillas, a remarkable effort for such a small group of five or six staff officers, plus support personnel. No specific reason has been found for the low number of staff officers involved in U-boat operations. However, it is safe to assume that it is likely due to the fact that Dönitz was very security minded and made sure that the small group worked in very close proximity, and that their handling of 'Enigma' transmissions to U-boats remained a closely guarded secret. Any breach of security was something that he feared, even though there was a crypto officer on the BdU staff to check outgoing traffic and the Enigma system was, initially, thought to be unassailable.[22] The Naval branch of the *B-Dienst* was cloaked (as it was in Britain) in the greatest secrecy and any leaks were blamed or attributed to treachery. Because of severe restrictions to access any investigations into naval operations and intelligence did not allow any outsiders to take part.[23]

Dönitz's appointment as C-in-C of the *Kriegsmarine* in February 1943 should have created a strengthening of the U-boat offensive. He retained his old post as *BdU*, and could now change the balance of the whole German fleet, transferring due priority of naval effort from the surface fleet, to U-boats. In the British Admiralty's February report to the War Cabinet Anti-U-boat Warfare Committee, it concluded that the enemy was able to concentrate with remarkable singleness of purpose to interrupt supplies from America to Britain.[24] But that is not how it worked out, in fact. Dönitz was overstretched and some believed that his inability to delegate more authority probably contributed a weakness to the U-boat arm, rather than a strength.[25] He was 'an impatient warrior preoccupied with fighting a battle rather than a careful organizer crafting resources to win a war.'[26] This tends to sum Dönitz up rather well and supports the argument that while he might learn lessons in tactics, he was less likely to shine as a strategic planner. For example, his efforts to find softer targets on the US coast in 1942 in operation *Paukenschlag* (Drumbeat), instead of concentrating his forces on convoy routes crossing the Atlantic, could be considered an instance of ill-defined strategic thinking,[27] and it was 'not till the autumn did they seriously resume the search for convoys in the North Atlantic.'[28] By the time they resumed attacks, more 'independents' had been put into convoy;[29] and more than six months' additional preparation had been given to ASW forces; and life for the U-boats would get harder. Raeder had earlier entertained the idea of hitting the United States when he discussed the idea with Hitler on the afternoon of 25 July 1941. At that time, Hitler declined. He was not in favour of dragging the United States prematurely into the war.[30]

The launch of *Paukenschlag* was an undoubted 'Tonnage' success (initially unopposed).[31] But it has been argued that his primary concern might have been to stop oil supplies,[32] rather than convoys carrying supplies such as materials, grain and other foodstuff, from reaching British shores. A major loss of the oil supply could have brought much of the British war effort to a standstill, with catastrophic effect. Dönitz cannot absolve himself from blame for shifting the focus of his attack from the Caribbean oil supplies back to the wolf-pack attacks on convoys in the North Atlantic,[33] because in discussions with his staff he frequently commented, 'It is incomparably more important to sink than to reduce sinkings by making them in a prescribed area.'[34] It is recognized that the Dönitz strategy was based on 'tonnage' sunk but 'While the operational objective of *Paukenschlag* was met with limited resources, an overall lack of U-boats prevented further consolidation of its operational success and the ultimate realisation of the strategic objective.'[35]

U-boat arm successes on the convoy routes of the North Atlantic during this period had been mediocre. An inspection of records shows that in HX convoys from January 1942 to the beginning of October 1942 only one ship was lost.[36] SC Convoys from January to the beginning of August 1942, also only lost one ship.[37] The author therefore suggests that Dönitz was too prone to diverting boats away from the main objective, the Atlantic crossing routes. There were further diversions off to the Freetown area, the central Atlantic and South Africa, long after the real weight of the attack had been transferred back to the Atlantic.

Inter-service co-operation: The missing dimension

The *Luftwaffe* in World War Two was well known for its rôle in supporting the *Blitzkrieg* tactics of the German Army, but another important rôle was the use of the *Luftwaffe* in maritime operations in support of the *Kriegsmarine*.[38] In the First World War the navy controlled not only the surface fleet and U-boats but also the naval air war and (in a similar fashion to the RN) lost control of the air arm to Göring's *Luftwaffe*; but in their case not before 1935.[39] But there is the strong possibility of a corporate, as well as strategic, interpretation as to why both services remained disconnected. Göring identified the *Luftwaffe* with anything that flew, just as the RAF did after the First World War, and in the commercial world key players achieved 'their distinctiveness through corporate identity and identification'.[40] For example, the *Luftwaffe* and the RAF were identified with the planes that flew attack sorties or carried supplies for logistics. The *Kriegsmarine* lost most of their 'air capability' corporate identity at the end of the last war, and completely in 1935, never to get it back – no matter how much they tried.[41] Their influence on strategic airpower was, therefore, minimal.

The *Luftwaffe's* position with Hitler was further reinforced when their staff produced several studies for what they saw as an effective sea–air war against Britain, thereby creating a decisive rôle for aircraft. They included air-mining campaigns, air attacks on British ports and on the supply lines in the Western Approaches, all seen as adequate measures to severely weaken Britain.[42] Egged on by Göring he decided on keeping the *Luftwaffe* as a land-based force for his drive eastwards with little consideration given to the needs of the Navy, both immediately and for the intended subsequent drive westwards, despite the pleadings of Admiral Raeder.[43]

Also common knowledge are the disputes that existed between political and military authorities in Hitler's Germany that led to many military failures, nowhere more so than in the theatre of air war at sea. 'The *Luftwaffe* and the *Kriegsmarine* never planned together, even if major operations were concerned, and the lack of joint conduct of the war proved to be one of the major faults of Germany in its war at sea';[44] and the underlying causes of the argument of the tactical versus the strategic airpower were never addressed. But even with the *Heer* too, despite the *Blitzkrieg*, there is evidence of poor planning. Each service prepared for and fought its own separate war, and each developed its war plan without regard to the other.[45]

> On the other hand at the Air Force leadership level important information concerning the planning with *OKW*, *OKH* and *OKM* was also missing, due to a decline in information exchange between Hitler and Göring. Attempts at strategic co-ordination failed at least eighteen months before the outbreak of war.[46]

From the outset, the *Kriegsmarine* and the *Luftwaffe* leadership attacked one another in endless disputes, which eliminated any serious prospect of planning or meaningful success against the common enemy, Britain. 'Hence the operations of the *Luftwaffe* over the sea never left their infancy'.[47]

Hitler had promised the *Kriegsmarine* aircraft carriers as early as 1935 and the keel was laid down for the carrier *Graf Zeppelin* on 26 December 1936, but then by 1939 completion was stopped, only to be revived in 1942 – to then be finally abandoned, and become a stores ship.[48] Some might say that this was a curious state of affairs, not acquiring some air capability, especially in view of the known hostility between Raeder and Göring. A large measure in the failure of co-operation was due to their personalities that were in constant conflict over the support of maritime operations and the *Luftwaffe* rôles during World War Two. The ongoing conflict over naval air power between them was legendary but it can be said that some common threads ran between the two. Both Göring and Raeder were loyal National Socialist Party members (Nazis) with utmost obedience to Adolf Hitler. Each wanted his service to be the predominant force and gain prominence within the German military power. But, it was the differences that accentuated the sharpness of their quarrels.[49] The problem of co-operation between the *Kriegsmarine* and the *Luftwaffe* was not just the obstructive nature of Reichsmarschall Göring but the inter-service rivalry that went back to the days of the First World War when the Navy experienced the transfer of operational air assets to the *Luftwaffe*, in a manner similar to that experienced by the RN with the transfer of the RNAS to the RAF. During the First World War the German Navy had been very successful in naval aircraft operations, having shot down 270 allied seaplanes, sank four merchant ships and three submarines.[50] In the interwar years, there remained an interest in a naval air arm. However, the *ObdM* at the time, Admiral Zenker, and his successor Raeder (from 1928), were more surface-ship minded and regarded aircraft as being mainly used in a scouting rôle as the eyes and ears of the fleet, not the development of new tactical and strategic doctrines. Opinion in naval circles began to change towards the onset of war, when it was realized that there was a need for aircraft to co-operate with the new U-boat arm in reconnaissance and attack rôles over the sea. In this Raeder hoped to have his demands met. However, the new head of the *Luftwaffe*, Göring, would severely limit co-operation, and his position was unassailable.[51]

On the declaration of the war in 1939, the Navy had a Naval Air Force total of 14 *Staffeln* of coastal reconnaissance planes and one ship-borne *Staffel* (scouting planes on larger ships) under its tactical command, not overall command.[52] The Navy found itself in a similar position to that of the RN in that the *Luftwaffe* had taken over operational command of almost all flying units and the only assets really under the influence of the *Kriegsmarine* were the *Küstenfliegerstaffeln*.[53] Of the remaining forces allotted for co-operation with the Navy at the outbreak of the war these were divided into two commands, known as *FdL West* and *FdL Ost*, comprising in total 15 *Staffeln* under the tactical command of the Navy. Tactical subordination was understood as subordination in all matters concerning operations; everything else stayed under *Luftwaffe* command and control, a situation not so dissimilar to that which existed between the RN and RAF Coastal Command after 1941.[54]

The Navy was very wary of any *Heer–Kriegsmarine* air co-operation in the interwar period because it feared that this might be the first step to losing the naval air arm to a new air force, as a third service.[55] However, the War Minister, General Werner von Blomberg, was inclined towards the attitude of the Navy and its *ObdM* Admiral Raeder.[56] In the event it was Reichsmarschall Hermann Göring that was able to impose his concept of a powerful, homogeneous Air Force, and the Navy lost out, although during the years that followed Raeder did not give up attempts to acquire his own Naval Air Force. As far as Hitler was concerned, Göring was the kind of sycophant with a distinguished war record that he needed to bolster his own image among those in the defence council, giving him endless credibility while in his presence.[57] As a result, Göring was able to get into the enviable position as Reichsminister on the Research Council, giving him added influence on scientific projects;[58] a position that was above his level of competence. Other very senior officers (but not Raeder[59]) were subservient to Hitler because they too knew it was the surest way to keep hold on, and expand, their power base. However, each officer knew that 'Hitler had the power to eliminate him, just by the scratch of a pen'.[60]

Raeder was not interested in what he called a 'combined policy between two sections of the Armed Forces', which was in favour of a single undivided operational offensive by all naval forces (including *Luftwaffe*) under one direction and command.[61] He would have preferred the kind of partnership such as that developed between the staff of Commander-in-Chief Western Approaches and Air Officer Commanding 15 Group, but he was not successful in achieving his aim. From the autumn of 1938 onwards it was Göring who succeeded in reducing, permanently, the influence of the Navy on matters relating to aircraft movements.[62]

In 1940, *Fliegerkorps* X was initially a better source of convoy detection than the *B-Dienst*, albeit sporadic.[63] It was transferred to the Mediterranean front, thereby weakening the striking power of the *Luftwaffe* against enemy shipping in the north even more.[64] The *General der Luft* was aware of the implications of losing units to the *Luftwaffe* quite early on in the war. He reported his thoughts to *ObdM* and stated frankly that the rationale for his position had substantially diminished due to a steady decline in units under his command, now reduced to seven *Staffeln*. He suggested that a too high-ranking officer now occupied his position, especially if he compared it to the Officer in Charge of the Atlantic Command, which had a total of 15 *Staffeln*, and led by a Lieutenant Colonel. His solution was to subordinate all remaining *Küstenfliegerverbände* to the *Luftflotte 2* or the respective area command and dissolve his command, a seemingly worsening situation.[65] The actual combined operations involving the *Luftwaffe* and *Kriegsmarine* were relatively few up to 1942. With the exception of a small number of raids, the naval air force did cooperate during the Norwegian operation *Weserübung*; otherwise no significant combined operations had been conducted.[66]

Dönitz had long said that air support was an important element in the fight against convoys, even if only used to scatter ships due to the threat of bombing, making them an easier target and a headache for any escort. He had originally been promised a *Staffel* of HE-177s but Hitler had decided that the Eastern front was more important.[67] Even at this stage such myopia on Hitler's part is incomprehensible, other than to signify his ignorance on naval matters. Given that he issued a directive Nr 23 on the subject of attacking shipping by all means – including aircraft – he even seems to have failed to follow through on one of his own directives.[68] In any case the point made earlier about the

Luftwaffe and the *Kriegsmarine* having never planned together meant that forward planning for longer-range aircraft, needed for mid-Atlantic operations and beyond, never even reached the development stage. The lesson of forward planning appears not to have been learnt.

Local co-operation

Out in the Atlantic, despite inter-service rivalries, some co-operation between U-boat Command and the *Fliegerflührer Atlantik* developed reasonably well, thanks in large measure to Hessler, who had a similar approach of respect to the *Luftwaffe* as Peyton-Ward had to Coastal Command for during his tenure as first staff officer he tried to maximize *Luftwaffe* support.[69] Initial cooperation was achieved in air attacks on British shipping in the Western Approaches. In 1940/41 most British merchant ships were poorly defended and generally completely defenceless, for the reasons given in the next chapter. With just a half dozen *Focke-Wulfe FW*-200 Condor long-range aircraft, I/KG-40 sank 52 ships (217,464 GRT) from August 1940 until February 1941 for the loss of just four aircraft, considered to be very good returns. Although it would have been possible to support the Condors on their patrols in the Western Approaches with He-111 H-6 medium bombers from Stavanger in Norway to Vannes in France with bomb loads of 1,000 kg, this never came to pass;[70] indeed *BdU* complained in his *KTB* on 1 October 1940.

> The Luftwaffe should fly reconnaissance N, NE, S, and SE of the operational area but lacks sufficient aircraft, in spite of my representations. The boats therefore have to carry out their own reconnaissance, which is not properly their task.[71]

Such co-operation as was achieved between the *Kriegsmarine* and the *Luftwaffe* depended largely on the goodwill established between local commanders. What was missing – and this was far more damaging than any deficiency in local command structures – was unity of purpose at high level and a depth of commitment on the part of the *Luftwaffe* High Command to the Atlantic campaign;[72] and that included a willingness to train aircrews in the way of naval matters. A training group for sea operations was not set up before autumn 1941 and even then it was only of an improvised nature. In a three-week course given in Großenbrode (Northern Germany) aircrew had just 20 practice operations with torpedoes and mines, resulting in insufficient training; and combined training-attacks by torpedo/dive bombers never took place.[73] The effectiveness of the combat training for aircrew in a naval environment can best be judged by comparing it to the training given to the German U-boat arm.

Courses in the *Kriegsmarine* for U-boat crews varied in length of time spent in training but they learned everything that they might need at the front, not only about firing torpedoes but also about how to position themselves for attack on a convoy and the communication skills needed for co-operation between U-boat groups. Nothing comparable existed for the *Luftwaffe's* crews and their training for operations over the sea were abysmal. Towards the end of 1943, a group for the *Ausbildungsfliegerführer* Baltic was set up but in the end it was unable to supply the front line with well-trained personnel.[74] The only result of this organization was a nominal improvement. The aircrews operating at the front often had to pay the price for this striking failure of leadership. Allied aircraft became better equipped to deal with the *Luftwaffe* and when confronted with increasingly hazardous missions' German aircrews had only a small chance of survival. It would be fair to say that the co-operation between the U-boat arm and reconnaissance aircraft was probably one of the most depressing chapters in German naval–air warfare.[75] Clearly no lessons of inter-service co-operation were learned in this respect.

Communications between the *Luftwaffe* and *BdU* Lorient were farcical. Only on occasion was Dönitz able to use convoy sightings reports in the Western Approaches. The receipt of the reports was convoluted: a Condor reported its sighting to Bordeaux-Merignac; then it was submitted to *Fliegerkorps IV*; from there it went to *Luftflotte* 3, Paris and then to *Marinegruppe* (Naval Group) West, also in Paris. Finally it was transmitted to *BdU* in Lorient; and he finally passed the information on to the front-line U-boats. This bureaucratic nightmare frequently meant that a sighting report took more than one day to arrive: out-dated Condor sightings were therefore rarely useful.[76] On another occasion, 5 March 1942, Dönitz lambasted the efforts of the *Luftwaffe* pilot training and wrote in his *KTB* complaining of their coordinates' ability that there was:

1. Insufficient reliability of aircraft positions. There was a deviation of 70 sea miles on 20 February and must be attributed to the D/Fing of U 96. In addition, it was suspected that on this, and the days following, the aircraft positions were incorrect.[77]
2. Using the former method, the aircraft reports only gave one position, and the course given might only have been that steered at the time.[78]

There was a brief spell from January towards the end of February 1941 when Dönitz managed to get some naval aircraft under his control, but Göring soon put a stop to that.[79] Thus closer co-operation with the *FW-200* unit and for improved communications was never achieved, although *BdU* did have some help from the *Luftwaffe* in attacking British anti-U-boat sorties in the Bay of Biscay, sometimes with success. This element of U-boat and *Luftwaffe* co-operation is not discussed here since it relates mainly to action in the Bay of Biscay area. Like Raeder before him, Dönitz would have benefited greatly by having a 'Coastal Command' type arrangement.

Conclusions

With no Z-plan, and no alternative plan, there was the realization that *OKM* must now pin all of its hopes for a successful campaign on the U-boat arm, and this Dönitz emphasized to *OKM* staff on arrival at HQ. On this point he could be said to have sealed his own fate and demonstrated a lack of strategic thinking. Dönitz had worked closely together with Raeder since the beginning of the war. There had been ample time to consult with the *ObdM* while he was in office and help formulate an alternative strategy, but he had deluded himself into believing that the Battle of the Atlantic could be won with U-boats alone. And that was wishful thinking, perhaps brought on by the gulf between his military education and that of Raeder. It was already too late to pen a new plan for a balanced fleet but there was no alternative strategy, not even to push for maximum *Luftwaffe* participation. Following the fall of France in May 1940 the German naval war effort became increasingly dependent on its U-boat arm, the most junior part of the naval organization, and only given separate organizational status on the eve of war. It had to develop its rôle/organization in a hurry and was thereafter playing 'catch-up'. With French bases now opened up to him, Dönitz began to explore new possibilities, not available before. Once the U-boat arm took advantage of the German conquest of French coastal harbours, they were able to enjoy greater freedom of movement and much shorter passage times to their targets. In so doing they had benefited from the lesson propounded by Wegener, and later by Carls.

However, his failure to create a larger staff (largely due to his fixation of secrecy) meant that he, and those around him, were overworked, and may have missed identifying developments. Neither did he push solutions and new technology through firmly and fast enough. Effective administration was at the mercy of internal departmental whims, and inter-service rivalries were still being fought out between the *Kriegsmarine* and the *Luftwaffe* when war broke out.

Initially *Fliegerkorps* X worked in concert with the U-boat arm, providing Intel information on convoy movements, and was a better source of convoy detection than the *B-Dienst*. The *Fliegerkorps* X was also active in bombing Convoys, with some degree of success but in general the *Luftwaffe* provided little support.

To have accepted *Luftwaffe* non-co-operation, given Dönitz's relationship with Hitler, is perplexing. U-boat efforts far exceeded those of the *Luftwaffe* in terms of commerce warfare and it was incumbent upon him to press this point home to Hitler which he did, but was unable establish any firm relationship with Göring. It was probably his biggest mistake of the war, but the significance of his error was never admitted.

Dönitz's good fortune was as a result of Britain's mistake in changing to Naval Cipher No. 3 for much of its convoy communications but even this, as we shall see, was not long-lasting.

Notes

1 Sönke Neitzel, 'The Deployment of U-boats', in *The Battle of the Atlantic 1939–1945*, (1994), 276–301, 277.

2 John Terraine, *Business in Great Waters* (Ware, 1999), 254.

3 Joseph A. Maiolo, *The Royal Navy and Nazi Germany 1933–39* (Basingstoke, 1998), 111–14.

4 Karl Dönitz, *Memoirs* (1959), 111.

5 Wolfgang Wegener, *Die Seestrategie des Weltkrieges* (Berlin, 1929); C. Gemzell, *Raeder, Hitler und Skandinavien* (Lund, 1973), 278–85; Wegener's Atlantic strategy was a return to the old French *guerre de course* but with a difference. Wegener foresaw the need for Atlantic bases, which would extend to beyond the encircling line of British naval forces, something that was not fully exploited in the First World War.

6 Günter Hessler, *The U-boat War in the Atlantic* (1989), (I), 28; V. E. Tarrant, *The U-Boat Offensive 1914–45* (1989), 90.

7 Ibid., (I), 82–3.

8 Hessler, *The U-boat War in the Atlantic*, (I), 28; Tarrant, *The U-Boat Offensive 1914–45*, 90.

9 Dönitz, *Memoirs*, 107.

10 W. S. Chalmers, *Max Horton and the Western Approaches* (1954), 153.

11 David K. Brown, *Atlantic Escorts*, (Barnsley, 2007), 67.

12 Terraine, *Business in Great Waters*, 142.

13 Eberhard Rößler, *The U-Boat* (1981), 121; Robert C. Stern, *Type VII U-boats* (1998), 24; Timothy Mulligan, *Neither Sharks Nor Wolves* (Annapolis, 1999), 58.

14 Bernard Edwards, *Dönitz and the Wolf Packs* (1996), 22; Dwight R. Messimer, *Find and Destroy* (Annapolis, 2001), 155.

15 Hugh Trevor-Roper, *Hitler's War Directives, 1939–1945* (Edinburgh, 2004), 171.

16 BA-MA RM 45 IV/787, 'Operationen und Taktik; der Überfall auf St Nazaire', 27–8 March 1942; NHB PG 18548, This evaluation of the raid was compiled from local reports in St Nazaire and distributed by Skl (Kr) the Kriegswissenschaftlicheabteilung, to be discussed in a later chapter as a contributor to data related to 'Operational Research'.

17 Dönitz, *Memoirs*, 228.

18 Graham Rhys-Jones, 'The German System', in *The Battle of the Atlantic 1939–1945* (1994), 139.

19 See Appendix 3 for details.

20 TNA HW 18/55, German Naval Organization–Naval Section ZIP/NS dated 26/12/1944, 3.

21 TNA HW 18/55, German Naval Organization, 3; the officer in charge was Korvettenkapitän Dr Teufer, an officer of the admin branch.

22 See Appendix 3, staff position A 4.

23 Donald McLachlan, *Room 39* (1968), 90.

24 TNA ADM 234/578, Naval Staff History: 'The Defeat of the Enemy Attack on Shipping 1939–1945'.

25 GC&CS, 'The German Navy – Organization', 2, 24.

26 Mulligan, *Neither Sharks Nor Wolves*, 46.

27 NHB, 'German U-boat Strategy in the War', Appendix XVIII, Report by the Joint Intelligence Sub-Committee, 'Some Weaknesses in German Strategy and Organization 1933–1945', 180–3.

28 F. H. Hinsley et al., *British Intelligence in the Second World War* (1981), II, 228.

29 F. Barley et al., *The Defeat of the Enemy Attack on Shipping 1939–1945*, 137 (Aldershot, 1997), 31, 40.

30 *Lagevorträge* (München, 1972), 'Skl 1b 1321/41 Gkdos Chefs', 271.

31 Ibid., 355–6.

32 Karl M. Hasslinger, 'The U-boat War in the Caribbean: Opportunities Lost', Naval War College, Newport R.I. (March 1996), Abstract.

33 Hasslinger, 'The U-boat War in the Caribbean', 15.

34 Peter Padfield, *Men of War* (New York, 1992), 193.

35 Sean R. Filipowski, 'Operation Paukenschlag: An Operational Analysis', Naval War College, Newport R.I. (June 1994), 29.

36 Arnold Hague, *The Allied Convoy System 1939–1945* (2000), 127–8.

37 Ibid., 134–5.

38 Winston A. Gould, 'Luftwaffe Maritime Operations in World War II', Air Command and Staff College, Air University, April 2005, iii.

39 Gerhard Hümmelchen, *Die deutschen Seeflieger 1935–1945* (München, 1976), 14ff.

40 Professor John M. T. Balmer, 'Comprehending Corporate Identity: Corporate Brand Management and Corporate Marketing', Working Paper No. 06/19, Bradford University, March 2006.

41 Horst Boog, 'Luftwaffe Support of the German Navy', in *The Battle of the Atlantic 1939–1945* (1994), 302–22, 304.

42 BA-MA RM 7/2079, Der Reichsminister der Luftfahrt und Oberbefehlshaber der Luftwaffe, Genst. 1Abt. Nr. 144/38 gKdos (M), 20.5.1938; BA-MA RL 7/42, Luftflottenkommando 2, Führungsabteilung, B.Nr. 7093/39 gKdos Chefs., 13.5.1939, Schlußbesprechung des Planspieles 1939, S. 1.

43 Horst Boog, 'Luftwaffe Support of the German Navy', 302–4.

44 Lt Cdr Andreas Krug, 'Coordination and Command Relationships between Axis Powers in the Naval War in the Mediterranean 1940–1943', 72.

45 H. Herwig, 'Generals versus Admirals: The War Aims of the Imperial German Navy, 1914–1918', *Central European History* V (September 1972), 208–33, 233.

46 Ernst Stilla, 'Die Luftwaffe im Kampf um die Luftherrschaft' (Rheinischen Friedrich-Wilhelms-Universität, Bonn, 2005), 52.

47 Sönke Neitzel, 'Zum strategischen Misserfolg verdammt? Die deutsche Luftwaffe in beiden Weltkriegen', in Bruno Thoß and Hans-Erich Volkmann, *Erster Weltkrieg – Zweiter Weltkrieg* (Paderborn, 2002), 167–92.

48 BA-MA RM 7/260, 'Ständiger Vertreter des Oberbefehlshabers der Kriegsmarine beim Führer an den Oberbefehlshaber der Kriegsmarine und Chef der Seekriegsleitung', 17 January 1943, 55; Siegfried Breyer, *The German Aircraft Carrier Graf Zeppelin* (Atglen, Pennsylvania, 1989), 15.

49 Gould, 'Luftwaffe Maritime Operations in World War II', 9.

50 J. S. Corum, *The Luftwaffe* (Kansas, 1997), 44.

51 Sönke Neitzel, 'Kriegsmarine and Luftwaffe Co-operation in the War against Britain 1939–1945', *War in History*, 10 (2003), 448–63, 450.

52 Hümmelchen, *Die deutschen Seeflieger 1935–1945*, 51–2.

53 Oberstleutnant Marc S. Koestner, 'The Luftwaffe's Support of Naval Operations During World War II 1939–1941', Canadian Forces College, n.d., 10.

54 NARA PG 74948-975, rolls 3350-3, Kriegstagebuch des General der Luftwaffe beim ObdM/O.Qu., September 1939–December 1941: NARA PG 32975, roll 3986 (n.d.) Copy nr. 54, Telegramme from RdL and ObdL dated 8 December 1939, Handakte General der Luftwaffe beim ObdM, February 1939–October 1941.

55 James S. Corum, *Creating the Operational Air War 1918–1940* (Kansas, 1999), 44.

56 A. Kube, *Pour le mérite und Hakenkreuz* (München, 1986), 51.

57 Neitzel, 'Kriegsmarine and Luftwaffe Co-operation in the War against Britain', 457; Air Ministry, *The Rise and Fall of the German Air Force 1933–1945* (1983), 417.

58 TNA ADM 213/611, Scientific research in Germany, 95.

59 NHB NID 24/T65/45, Report on German Naval War Effort, Para 3, Raeder.

60 David Irving, *Göring* (Electronic version 2002), 395.

61 NHB Report to Raeder dated 7 February 1942, cited in NID 0698/46, 10.

62 Neitzel, 'Kriegsmarine and Luftwaffe Co-operation in the War against Britain', 453.

63 TNA HW 8/113, 'The German Navy's Use of Special Intelligence', 38.

64 Air Ministry, *The Rise and Fall of the German Air Force 1933–1945*, 104.

65 BA-MA OKM GE 958, Conference of the General der Luftwaffe beim Oberbefehlshaber der Kriegsmarine 1 Dec. 1941, 295; NARA PG 74896–74944, rolls 3349–50. 07.03.41.

66 Walter Gaul, 'The Part Played by the German Air Force and the Naval Air Force in the Invasion of Norway'. Essays by German Officers and Officials on World War II (Wilmington: Scholarly Resources Inc.), 5.

67 BA-MA RM 7/2869, U-boat Command, Memo No. 3642-Al to *OKM*/Sk1, 3 September 1942; NHB PG 33349, 1/Skl Iu Allgemein, 284; TNA ADM 234/67, The U-boat War in the Atlantic, 2, 46.

68 Trevor-Roper, *Hitler's War Directives 1939–1945*, 103.

69 TNA HW 18/55, German Naval Organization–Naval Section ZIP/NS dated 26/12/1944, 2.

70 Neitzel, 'Kriegsmarine and Luftwaffe Co-operation in the War against Britain', 453.

71 NHB PG 30274, BdU entry for 1 October 1940, concerning air-reconnaissance and U-boat positions; TNA HW 8/113, 'German Navy's Use of Special Intelligence', 34.

72 Rhys-Jones, 'The German System', 141.

73 Neitzel, 'Kriegsmarine and Luftwaffe Co-operation in the War against Britain', 453.

74 BA-MA RL 2 II/161, Training requirements for *Ausbildungsfliegerführer Ostsee* (Baltic).

75 Neitzel, 'Kriegsmarine and Luftwaffe Co-operation in the War against Britain', 454.

76 Sönke Neitzel, *Der Einsatz der deutschen Luftwaffe über dem Atlantik und der Nordsee 1939–1945* (Bonn, 1995), 76–7.

77 NHB PG 30284, entry on 6 March 1941. Subsequent investigation found that actually the radio interception reports were correct.

78 Ibid., dated 5 March 1941. On 6 March he was furious that because of poor cooperation one convoy had been missed, and thus escaped engagement.

79 WF-04/36387 OKM, 1/Skl 3490/41 gKdos v. 27.2.1941 MAP (Militärarchiv Potsdam, now Freiburg).

4

The Development of the Western Approaches Command

Western Approaches 1939–41

At the start of the war Admiral Sir Martin Dunbar-Nasmith, Commander-in-Chief Plymouth and Western Approaches, was the officer responsible for the protection of shipping in the North-western and South-western approaches to the British Isles. Handicapped though he was by a severe shortage of escort vessels and suitable aircraft, he established a practicable convoy system and was successful in keeping it running for six months without serious loss.[1] The Destroyer strength of WA was just 57 ships, of which just 48 were operational. On the basis of a doctrine of two escorts per convoy in the Western Approaches required 44 Destroyers; clearly nowhere near enough, but there were no more. As part of his escort force he was able to call upon Polish Destroyers, two of which 'were not yet fully efficient', that had managed to escape from the Baltic after the fall of Poland.[2] To begin with, these were used for patrols and as escorts for merchant ships in the English Channel, and around the coasts. Although lacking in some equipment they were a very welcome addition to Dunbar-Nasmiths' meagre forces.[3] Later some were to serve with distinction in the North Atlantic. So great was his concern that he detailed the situation to the Admiralty adding the comment:

> It will therefore be necessary to discontinue offensive anti-submarine operations except such as can be carried out by two Destroyers and the 1st A/S Striking Force. Provided that U-Boat activity continues in the Western Approaches I consider that twelve Destroyers should be available for purely offensive operations.[4]

Matters were not helped on the outbreak of war when 'hunting groups' based on an aircraft carrier with accompanying Destroyers were formed to search for and destroy U-boats. While this measure foreshadowed the Support Groups to come it ignored the fact that convoy escort was in fact an offensive operation.[5] The Admiralty and Dunbar-Naismith did not appear to have grasped the fact that searching for U-boats in so vast an ocean was like trying to find the proverbial needle. Alternatively, perhaps they thought that a 'hunt' was appropriate only in home waters, which was where they had primarily operated in the last war, and were equally ineffective.[6] In any case, logic alone should have indicated that U-boats were more likely to be found and engaged closer to convoy routes;[7] the odder since Dunbar-Naismith had been a much-decorated submariner in WW1.

The situation did not improve and there seemed little likelihood that it would, as things stood, and on 18 February 1940 the C-in-C Western Approaches sent a memo of concern to the CNS, Sir Dudley-Pound, entitled 'Proposals for increasing offensive against U-boats in the Western Approaches.'[8] In it, he suggested a greater need for Destroyers of 'long endurance' to cope with U-boats then working their way out further into the Atlantic. He pointed out that some recent D/F bearings acquired on U-boats had demonstrated that they were working further to the Westward. The memo goes on to indicate that it would not be possible to sustain an offensive against U-boats on the West Coast of Ireland given the state of the current old 'V' and 'W' class Destroyers, virtually of World War One design, which (initially) lacked range. However, the Admiralty had anticipated this problem, and these became modified. In a stern chase they did have the speed to catch-up a U-boat on the surface, even after losing a boiler in order to accommodate more fuel and DCs.[9] Of the 100 or so escort vessels required[10] 'some would have to be found from among the 36 over-age "V" and "W" class Destroyers and the various pre-1932 sloops that were being fitted with ASDIC.'[11] At the start of the war three 'V' and 'W's had been converted, and three were near to completion.[12] However, it would still be too few to meet the convoy requirements in 1939.

By the end of May 1940, British escort vessels were able to provide incoming and outgoing Atlantic convoys with anti-submarine escorts only as far as longitude 12–15° West – to a point around 200 nautical miles to the west of Ireland. In July, the dispersal point for outward-bound convoys was moved to 17° West and there it remained until October when it was found possible to extend close escort as far as 19° West. The biggest problem for the escorts was fuel. Refuelling escorts at sea was not introduced until around June 1942, and only slowly 'spread through the convoys owing to the continuing – indeed, increasing – shortage of tankers'.[13] Yet the problem had long been known about and in 1941 Churchill had voiced concerns to the Admiralty for failing to provide an efficient means for refuelling warships at sea, such as the *Kriegsmarine* had already developed.[14] After the escort vessels had left their convoys the outward-bound merchant ships continued to steam in company for about another 24 hours, after which they dispersed to their various destinations. Meanwhile the escorts moved to a new rendezvous point to meet and bring in the next homeward-bound convoy, provided they had sufficient fuel to remain on station. The availability of fuel for the escort force was a lesson that should have been learnt at a much earlier stage and must be put down to poor planning. The blame might be best targeted at both the Plans Division and the Fourth Sea Lord, in charge of Stores and Victualling.

To be fair, U-boats, in general, rarely ventured so far out of British waters during the First World War but escort vessels did face the problem at the start of 1940.[15] Times had changed but prescience of some planners at the Admiralty to provide escorts with a greater range, had not. '. . . it was a major weakness, and a just point of criticism . . . though the fall of France made it a graver weakness than could have been foreseen.'[16]

The Plymouth Command was ideally suited as a naval base and could have continued to play a vital rôle in the defence of the Atlantic trade against U-boats but for the sudden and dramatic turn of events in the land war of continental Europe, which transformed the geographic situation of U-boat bases. First to fall was Norway, in March, and then France in May. By June 1940, therefore, the Admiralty had to face up to the fact that U-boats would soon be operating on the doorstep of Plymouth Command. After the failure of Churchill's Norwegian campaign this new, and unexpected event would require even more convoy escort vessels than were presently available, and they were already disastrously short in number; and the shortage of smaller anti-submarine escort vessels had also now become acute due to losses and damage during the evacuation from Dunkirk. Added to the problem was the diversion of Destroyers for anti-invasion duties in anticipation of a possible German invasion, known by the German code-name 'Seelöwe', or Sea Lion. This placed impossible demands on the Command so that on occasion no more than two escorts were available for a convoy of 40 merchant ships.[17]

The fall of France in May 1940 had opened the Atlantic convoy routes to greatly increased attacks by U-boats operating out of the French ports in – and – around the Biscay area. U-boats had a much easier time, initially, in transiting the routes to a position much further west than hitherto. From June 1940, convoy losses began to increase, 'but greater had been the increase in the independent losses'.[18]

The geographic change in fortune also meant that German aircraft, with a shorter range to targets, would put an even greater demand for protection on the already overstretched British aircraft resources.

While the attacks on coastal shipping remained a concern, it was the U-boat's penetration into the Atlantic that quickly surpassed the importance of the German attacks on coastal shipping, and they soon became the greater part of the struggle shortly to be called the Battle of the Atlantic.[19] Churchill's concern was not misplaced because the Navy had already received intelligence in 1935 that the Germans had been working on the capability to convert a standard Type 1X U-boat for carrying fuel that would permit U-boats to extend their patrol areas, or have extended periods at sea giving them the endurance to menace the British merchant fleet in near and distant waters.[20] While the *Kriegsmarine* had learnt a lesson from the last war, and provided fuel for far-flung U-boat operations, the RN had nothing with which to ameliorate the plight of escort fuel requirements.

On 22 December 1940 the C-in-C Western Approaches Plymouth Command, Admiral Dunbar-Nasmith, wrote to the First Sea Lord again on the subject of 'Protection of Trade in the Western Approaches', in which he provided an analysis of why the Convoy system, which had (belatedly) achieved so much success in the final year of the 1914–18 war, and again during the first half of 1940, was now failing to obtain a similar result.[21] A close inspection of the facts readily revealed that the most obvious factors were the installation of U-boat and *Luftwaffe* bases on the French Atlantic coast, and this required a re-think about a more appropriate base of operations and convoy approach to the British mainland.[22] It meant that Britain had to abandon the Channel and the South-western Approaches as a main convoy route and appropriately shift all transatlantic convoys to the North-western Approaches, which were still termed the Western Approaches. Dunbar-Nasmith's memo on the subject continued with more bleak news. Escorts had been too limited in number and they were ill-equipped to withstand the enemy's new method of attacking on the surface at night, particularly when the convoy had stragglers and the visibility was poor.[23] Transatlantic escort vessels had chiefly operated out of the Plymouth command and this stayed in force until February 1941.

A pivotal lesson learnt by the British was when they adapted to the changed circumstance of the collapse of France by moving their convoy protection assets away from Plymouth to Liverpool. The actual move of maritime traffic from the Southern Approaches to the more Northern Approaches, around Northern Ireland, started to take place in August 1940 forced on them by the enemy occupation of France. U-boats were now able to operate at will out of the French Biscay ports, as well as the newly acquired bases in Norway and, because of the geographic change, German aircraft also came within reach of many convoy routes and Plymouth. Thus it soon became clear to the Admiralty that the WA could no longer continue to function from Plymouth, and that Plymouth Command operations had to take second place to the main task in hand, the protection of transatlantic convoy traffic. It therefore split the duties by appointing two C-in-Cs; one C-in-C Plymouth and one for WA.

The conversion of part of Derby House in Liverpool, as the new WA HQ, was commenced with the new organization becoming operational early in 1941.[24] C-in-C WA was beset with problems. Escort vessels themselves (the Destroyers aside) still lacked the cruising range for trans-Atlantic work and most were incapable of catching a U-boat even if one was sighted; and the latest types being commissioned were even slower than a U-boat's surface design speed, with a maximum speed of 15 knots (though their designed speed was 16.5 knots), a point of sheer frustration for the crews.[25]

The 20 900-ton Type I Hunt class escort Destroyers of the 1938 programme (launched between December 1939 and September 1940) had a good top speed at 26 knots but, unfortunately, they proved to be unsatisfactory for ocean service and were then mostly confined for use in home waters (which was in-line with original expectations).[26] The Admiralty came up with a 'sticking plaster' solution, the Corvette. Prior to war the 137 Flower class 'Sloops' (925 tons; later re-classed as Corvettes), that had been ordered for coastal work, and first came into service during 1940–1, 'but by the end of 1940 the "Flower" class Corvettes had been found to be almost useless as ocean escorts in winter owing to their excessive rolling and lack of manoeuvrability.'[27] They were no more than modified whalers thrown into the battle, due to a lack of suitable escorts available at the time.[28] However, 'Flowers' were less expensive to acquire since the first ones came from existing vessels; and the later vessels were cheap to construct. With modifications they became more seaworthy but were never intended for oceanic escort work and greatly degraded the crews' effectiveness due to fatigue, and very poor living conditions.[29] Nonetheless, so desperate was the need for escort vessels in the RN that this less than ideal ship was to become the workhorse of the Battle of the Atlantic for years to come. Over time the design needed extensive modifications in order to render later ships more habitable, and give them greater firepower and endurance. Improved Corvettes, that is frigates, did not see service until 1942.[30]

In the early part of the war it was generally considered that the main areas of U-boat activity would be off the home coasts where shipping converged and that there would be less requirement for ocean-going Destroyers; whereas even the Germans knew, in the First World War, that a force of ocean-going cruisers was needed to protect German trade, and deter others from commerce-raiding.[31] The situation improved marginally by the end of 1942 at which time the convoy escort doctrine had risen to around 6 escorts, for a 40-ship convoy.[32] At a meeting of the Anti-U-boat Committee the First Lord of the Admiralty announced that the total requirement for escorts amounted to 1,050, of which Britain could only muster 40 per cent of this number. Single- and twin-screw Corvettes comprised 214.[33] At a further AUC (Anti-submarine Warfare Committee) meeting of the 19 January 1943 the number of escorts available had been revised upwards to 600, or 60 per cent of requirements.[34] It seemed as though requirements would never catch up. It would take until 1944 before an improved and largely prefabricated class, the 'Lochs', were introduced.

The problems faced by C-in-C WA were further compounded because of the deficiencies in officers and men of newly commissioned ships who lacked experience, or training, in A/S warfare; not to mention a weakness in the available technology to combat the U-boat, particularly when attacks were made on the surface at night. Dunbar-Nasmith pointed out that ASDIC (SONAR) was quite blind to all but sub-surface contacts.[35] These observations were all very valid points but a negative view that, despite his achievements, may have contributed to his ultimate loss of position as C-in-C of WA. Despite some interwar planning, Britain was simply unprepared for the task in hand. While it would appear that naval planners had foreseen some of the escort problems they were unable to provide sufficient escorts in order to adequately prepare for convoy warfare, which also affected escort group training.[36] It might have been put down to budgetary restrictions at a time when there was an urgent need to expand and modernize the fleet in a hurry in the later 1930s to meet a greater perceived threat from Italy and Japan. Nevertheless, both the Admiralty and government knew that the key to a sea campaign was the protection of convoys, when it was assumed in the late 1930s that Germany might well embark on an unrestricted U-boat campaign.[37] It was originally thought that U-boats would principally operate in the North Sea and the Western Approaches, and this could provide one explanation of why the question of escort endurance might have been low on the agenda. But once U-boat production increased, and France had fallen, *BdU* was able to operate deeper into the Atlantic. Therefore 'the RN's tactical assumptions, based on shallow water warfare, rapidly became obsolete'.[38] While the Admiralty played at catch-up, the men manning the ships would have to accomplish much in the face of severe shortages, partially offset through the acquisition of American 'four stacker' Destroyers (under a Destroyers for bases agreement in September 1940), and some long endurance coastguard cutters under a lend-lease stop-gap solution in 1941.[39]

Western Approaches at Liverpool, 1941–5

The complex in Liverpool was known locally as the 'Citadel', or 'Fortress', due to the extensive reinforced-concrete protection given to the basement, which became WA's Operations Room. It became the home of the RAF Coastal Command and Royal Marines, working jointly.[40] Admiral Sir Martin Dunbar-Nasmith's stay as Commander-in-Chief here was brief and he continued in his post up until the early changeover period from 7–17 February 1941. On 17 February the senior officer-in-charge was Admiral Sir Percy Noble. With him was his RAF colleague Air Marshal J. M. Robb, AOC in control of No. 15 Group Coastal Command. This was to become one of the most rarely seen examples of inter-Service Operations co-operation throughout the rest of the war.[41] From 15 April both Commanders began to work under the single operational control of the Admiralty, with Noble in overall operational command. Liverpool had such a comprehensive set up that it could have taken over the duties of routeing of Atlantic Convoys, but only after telephone contact with Captain G. E. Colpoys (OIC) in London.[42] However, an intervention by the Air Ministry in September 1941 could have had serious consequences for the recent operational control agreement. The Air Ministry decided to place the RAF aircraft operating out of Iceland under the control of Sir Philip Joubert de la Ferté (AOC C-in-C Coastal Command), which was not acceptable to Admiral Noble. The Admiralty soon intervened and was able to rectify this matter.[43]

The Command was split into three sections in order to deal with 'Operations', 'Administration' and 'Material', each controlled by a Chief Staff Officer of Captain rank, all of which were subordinated to a COS, who at that time was Commodore J. M. Mansfield; two COS changes followed over the course of the next four years. The deployment of Escorts Groups was also administered here by a Captain 'D', or a Captain 'D' at one of the other WA locations, for example Londonderry.[44] In addition, Admiral Noble spent a great deal of his effort successfully organizing the set-up of an extensive escort-training programme for over 170 escort vessels and, thanks to Noble's emphasis on training and development of training facilities, a high degree of expertise had been produced,[45] but no 'Tactical School'; that was to come later, instigated by another. Sir Percy Noble held this position until 19 November 1942, when he was sent to relieve Sir Andrew Cunningham, the head of the Washington delegation. Originally Churchill had wanted Admiral Tovey (C-in-C Home Fleet) to take over the Command of the Western Approaches (Chart 4.2) but the CNS, Admiral Pound, vetoed this on the grounds that he was too valuable in his present job to be removed.[46] In the event it was Admiral Sir Max Horton who relieved Admiral Sir Percy Noble, and became C-in-C from 19 November 1942 until Western Approaches Command closed on 15 August 1945, an inspired appointment. Alongside him now was Air Marshal Slatter (now AOC).[47]

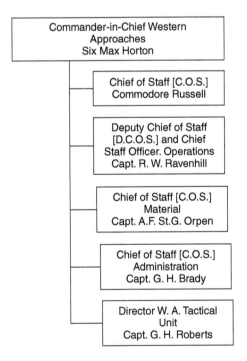

Chart 4.1 Western Approaches Command structure
Source: WA Principal Staff Officers 1943.[48]

The difference between Horton and the former C-in-C was an obsession for the perfect, and his pedigree from First World War actions, demonstrate his aggressive nature;[49] like his counterpart, Dönitz. 'His appointment helped to rekindle the energy and resolve the Prime Minister deemed to be lacking in Atlantic operations.'[50] Twenty years after the war when Dönitz was asked whether he felt, during the Battle of the Atlantic, that he had opposed to him a single commanding mind reading his own he replied, 'not until Horton took over the conduct of the anti-U-boat war at Liverpool in November 1942'.[51] With such a well-defined organization supporting him Horton had the confidence that he could eventually overcome and defeat a competent adversary, a resolute submariner experienced in U-boat warfare. The judgement of the Official War Historian, Captain Stephen Roskill RN, was that 'there was no living officer who better understood the U-boat commander's mind, nor could more surely anticipate what his reactions to our countermeasures would be.'[52]

Air assets and coastal command

At the start of the war the British, unlike the Germans, did have air capability. It was made up of a new fledgling FAA, some pilots of who took part in the Battle of the Atlantic aboard CVEs, and Coastal Command of the RAF. The FAA is not discussed here, because their rôle in the Battle of the Atlantic was small, in general. The bulk of air operations fell to Coastal Command, with further help from the Canadians and Americans.

There appears to have been no official history published devoted to the part played by Coastal Command in the Second World War, although four small volumes on the *Royal Air Force 1939–1945* do provide some references to Coastal Command throughout.[53] RAF Coastal Command grew out of the old Coastal Area organization and was formed on the 14 July 1936, initially at Lee-on-Solent under Air Marshal Sir Arthur M. Longmore. When formed, Coastal Command consisted of three groups. No. 18 Group (Rosyth) based in Scotland, No. 16 in South Eastern England and No. 15 (Plymouth) covering Western England and the Irish Sea.[54]

On 1 December 1937, the Air Ministry stated that the primary rôle of the Coastal Command in war would be trade protection, reconnaissance and co-operation with the RN.[55] It further declared that the aircraft of

Coastal Command would only be employed on other duties when the threat to convoys was deemed insignificant. The primary rôle considered at the time was being a part in 'keeping local sea communications open and preventing destructive seaborne raids on our coastline and ports', but they had no capability for anti-submarine operations.[56] While the Admiralty's appreciation regarding the function of aircraft allocated to naval co-operation was welcome and removed its apprehensions regarding unnecessary diversion of aircraft, it was by no means satisfactory.[57] In the summer of 1939, with a new (from August 1937) AOC C-in-C Sir Frederic W. Bowhill, it moved Coastal Command headquarters to Northwood, Middlesex and was thus in closer proximity to the Admiralty. The Naval Liaison Officer that joined him was Commander (later Captain) D. V. Peyton-Ward RN, an ex-submariner, who would soon play a significant part in the development of Coastal Command's ASW. The rôle of 'Coastal Command' had already been laid down but contained no mention about fighting U-boats. Both Sir Frederick Bowhill and the Senior Air Staff Officer, Air Commodore Geoffrey Bromet, had considered the defence of convoys but they operated in home waters. Defence was expected to have been against surface raiders and aircraft, rather than U-boats. Coastal Command appeared to be compliant and were 'thus following the Admiralty's belief that there would be no threat by U-boats'.[58] That soon changed.

In1939 the U-boat arm's relations with the *Luftwaffe* should have left the *Kriegsmarine* with a Naval Air Force total of 14 squadrons of coastal reconnaissance planes and one ship-borne squadron, had the aircraft carrier *Zeppelin* been completed. However, the *Kriegsmarine* found itself in an analogous position to that of the British Navy in the interwar years in that the *Luftwaffe* had assumed operational command of almost all flying units, with just the *Küstenfliegerstaffeln* used sparingly under the tactical control of the Navy.[59] That situation worsened as discussed in Chapter 1. Meanwhile by comparison, the positive corollary to the developments in anti-submarine warfare to come was that of close co-operation between the RN and Coastal Command, which was to contribute so greatly to the success of convoy strategy, and a lesson well learnt. Probably Peyton-Ward had a lot to do with this relatively harmonious relationship and it was he who, after the war, wrote four volumes on the RAF's Coastal Narrative, *The Royal Air Force in the Maritime War*.[60] These volumes make interesting reading and encapsulate the good progress made in tactics and co-operation with the RN. Terraine commented that 'anyone who reads it (them) will quickly see that here was a "dark blue" officer with a definitely "light blue" mind'.[61]

Coastal Command at war

In 1937, the question of Coastal Command's ability to perform even a General Reconnaissance (GR) was already called into question. Some senior officers had put forward the view that GR aircraft 'should be comparatively slow' as they would otherwise not be able to shadow hostile fleets, or be of much use in protecting convoys which are bound to be slow, or for anti-submarine work.[62] Fortunately, the Senior Air Staff Officer (SASO) did not share the same view. Therefore, in this respect they were saved the necessity of learning this vital lesson.

At the commencement of hostilities in 1939 RAF Coastal Command was quite unqualified to defend convoys against either U-boats or surface raiders even though they possessed about 296 aircraft distributed between 5 Flying-Boats (F/B), 11 GR and 2 Torpedo-Bomber (TB) squadrons based on the British Isles.[63] Unfortunately, the 296 aircraft available for service in 1939 was about double the number which they could put into the air with trained crews, at any one time.[64] Most of Coastal Command's aircraft were assigned to North Sea patrol duties and the bulk of the aircraft numbering more than half the available force, the Avro Anson, was only able to cover short distances due to inadequate endurance. More importantly Coastal Command, still under the total control of the RAF at this stage, was not expected to engage U-boats to any great extent because the Admiralty was still of the view that the submarine menace could be controlled by the combined judicial use of ASDIC and convoy;[65] they were to find out the hard way that this was not the case, and the organization needed change. The Germans correctly assumed that on the outbreak of war Britain's 'forces and air patrols would be small and inexperienced'.[66]

The naval liaison officer, Commander Peyton-Ward, was unhappy with the bleak prospect facing Bowhill and his whole Command in the early days of the war and knew that great strides needed to be made if 'Coastal Command' was to make a serious contribution to the maritime protection effort, stating that:

> Apart from reconnaissance, the striking power of Coastal Command against enemy surface units was almost non-existent and action against U-boats had hardly been considered, other than reporting their presence to naval anti-submarine craft. [67]

The Admiralty and Coastal Command were in continuous battle with the Air Ministry over the primacy of the trade defence war in relation to the bomber effort against mainland Germany; a strategic tussle which could have cost Britain the Battle of the Atlantic.[68] The Air Staff and Bomber Command had the backing of the Prime Minister in this matter while the maritime trade war struggled to receive the necessary recognition.[69] That this state of affairs had been allowed to develop is a matter beyond the scope of this work, but it is true to say that in 1939 Coastal Command had no dedicated anti-submarine detection systems, unsuitable aircraft for the job, ineffective weaponry and no ability to fly night-time missions.[70] In short, there was no considered doctrine or strategy for meeting the challenge of the German U-boats;[71] and unfit for purpose. There was clearly a need for land-based aircraft to cover the South-western Approaches and, significantly, a memo of 25 October 1938 to the Chief of Air Staff Sir Charles Portal refers to having Newquay (St Eval) laid out to take two squadrons.[72] Towards the end of 1939 it was Coastal Command's hope, or intention, to operate one aircraft over each convoy during the day, so long as the convoy was within the range of the Command's airfields. The problem was that there were too few aircraft available to meet the demands made on them.[73]

In terms of ordnance things were no better. They started off with an inadequate Mark III bomb that came into service in 1934 and no proper bombsight, not to mention the low endurance of aircraft. The Mark III was still under test but it was decided to build up bomb reserves of it in three sizes: 100 lb, 250 lb and 500 lb, all of which turned out to be 'quite useless' with repeated and apparently in-eradicable fuze failures, and 'unpredictable under-water travel' characteristics.[74] Neither were they lethal. The 100-lb anti-submarine bomb carried by Ansons proved to be ineffective and on one mistaken direct hit at the base of a conning tower (a British one) in December 1939 HMS *Snapper* was none the worse for wear – except for four light bulbs, although they were surprised when their attacker turned out to be the RAF.[75] The news was not better with the 250-lb bomb version used by the flying-boats. These had to explode within six feet of the U-boat's pressure hull if there was to be any serious harm done, and even the 500-lb bomb had to be placed no more than eight feet away. It was all very depressing for the hard-driven pilots and crews of Coastal Command. Peyton-Ward reflected, 'the result was that attacks on U-boats developing out of intelligent design of anti-U-boat patrols and sweeps came to nought as regards inflicting any serious damage. All we could do was to harass and frighten.'[76] To put things into perspective, between September 1939 and May 1940 Coastal Command conducted 85 attacks against U-boats, but sank only one, and in the whole of 1941 witnessed only two more U-boat kills.[77] It took no great leap of imagination to realize that improved weapons and new detection systems were needed if aircraft were to perform with any greater chance of success. It was not until the technical problem of the detection of U-boats by RADAR had been solved that aircraft played a really decisive killing rôle in the campaign of the Atlantic.[78]

Coastal Command still had a lot to learn. Air Chief Marshal Bowhill quickly realized the ineffectiveness of the ASW bombs in use in his Command, and made strenuous efforts to correct these problems.[79] His efforts were not made easier by the wrangling that went on between the Air Ministry and the Admiralty,[80] with the RAF too pre-occupied with the importance of its strategic bombing campaign, its cultural identity and its feeling of security to control the future rôle of the service. Coastal Command Air assets for convoy protection finally, largely, came under RN operational, not administrative, control from 15 February 1941.[81] It remained 'culturally' identified with the RAF. As Redford explained, 'if it were to fail those advocating the break-up of the RAF would have been handed a powerful weapon'.[82] However, collectively, Britain had not yet learnt to put aside 'corporate' identity in the interest of the state, and some tensions were always present. Corporate identity is somewhat different to cultural identity in that the 'identity' part is what the service is identified with. It comes into being when there is a common ownership of an organization's philosophy that is manifest in a distinct corporate culture, and describes what they do. Corporate identity is also the means by which organizations are recognized and distinguished from each other. *Ergo* air-power over the sea should be identified with the Navy. If the government of the day had linked air assets for sea warfare as residing with the Navy it would have identified it as such. Rumblings of the Navy taking complete control of Coastal Command were heard in November 1940, but in all probability it was the strong RAF lobby on Churchill which reduced the identity down to tactical control only.[83]

Joining aircrews were trained in their particular aircrew categories, pilot, navigator (observer), wireless operator, etc., and all would have had some training in gunnery. An ex-Coastal Command Aircrew man observed that 'notably lacking was training in ASW, although some specialist training was later to be given in ASV/Radar, either before or when on a squadron.'[84] This statement appears to be in contradiction to that contained in Admiralty papers. Shortly before the war started, the Director of the Naval Air Division noted that:

> The training of the RAF in A/S tactics in conjunction with the A/S School at Portland is proceeding better than heretofore, but much remains to be done. It is hoped that it may be possible to arrange later in the year for FAA aircraft to co-operate with the A/S School in the investigation of A/S tactics.[85]

That is not to say that it was a satisfactory performance but the Navy was engaged in their A/S training, and there was still much to accomplish.

Conclusions

Operational Destroyer strength in 1939 was just 48 ships, too few for the Convoys envisaged, and using the debunked idea of 'hunting groups' from the last war made matters worse. Using old ships from the last war and, those supplied by the United States, enabled more convoy coverage as far as 19° West by the end of 1940.

Britain had not learnt, or discovered, the limitations of ASDIC's effectiveness in the interwar years. In the early years of the war Britain's naval effort made slow progress in ASW, but over time did make adjustments grounded on the lessons of experience. Neither had they learnt much about refuelling of escorts at sea which was not introduced until nearly three years after the war started, whereas the U-boat arm had already learnt the lesson, as far back as 1917/1918, that for long-range missions one needed a fuel supply. Without a good fuel supply escorts were always going to be limited in range.

Suitable aircraft and ordnance for Coastal Command and a common doctrine also required serious attention, since in the first two years of operation only three U-boats had been sunk. After the fall of France WA was forced to move their base of operations to Liverpool, where they introduced a new tactical school, and developed a meaningful inter-service co-operation with Coastal Command. Of particular note was the progress made in air co-operation, due to a better understanding of requirements and the lessons learned combating U-boats. Whereas the British gradually built up goodwill with Coastal Command and the Air Ministry, the *Kriegsmarine* was unable to foster any agreement for closer ties with the Luftwaffe. Further lessons were learned in the use of air tactics, but it would take until early 1943 before sufficient numbers became available for the combined escort fighting force to mount a very strong offensive against the U-boat.

Notes

1 TNA ADM 186/799, Naval Staff History, Home waters and Atlantic, September 1939–April 1940; W. S. Chalmers, *Max Horton* (1954), 148.

2 Ian Warwick Skinner, 'British Maritime Strategy and Operations in the Western Channel and South West Approaches 1939–1945', (Exeter University, 1991), 27.

3 TNA ADM 1/9963, Anti-U-boat warfare: policy and information, confidential message, 1 September 1939; TNA ADM 199/807, C-in-C, Western Approaches, Admiral Dunbar-Nasmith, to Secretary of the Admiralty, 12 September 1939.

4 TNA ADM 199/124, Commander-in-Chief Western Approaches, to Admiralty, 23 September 1939.

5 Arnold Hague, *The Allied Convoy System 1939–1945* (2000), 55.

6 F. Barley et al., *The Defeat of the Enemy Attack on Shipping 1939–1945*, (Aldershot, 1997), 55.

7 TNA ADM 205/1, First Sea Lord's records, report of Admiral Binney's committee on war problems 1939–40; John Terraine, *Business in Great Waters* (Ware, 1999), 245.

8 TNA ADM 199/124, Admiral Dunbar-Nasmith memo to CNS dated 18 February 1940.

9 See Antony Preston, *'V' & 'W' Class Destroyers 1917–45* (1971) for full specifications and WW2 modifications.

10 TNA CAB 23/70, Conclusions of Cabinet meeting, 23 March 1932. Details of the final Cabinet discussion on the matter of the ten-year rule.

11 George Franklin, *Britain's Anti-Submarine Capability 1919–1939* (2003), 89.

12 Preston, *'V' & 'W' Class Destroyers 1917–45*, 197.

13 Terraine, *Business in Great Waters*, 533.

14 TNA ADM 205/7, Document NID 0747/35 indicates that in November 1935 technical intelligence of German refuelling capability had been noted; Terraine, *Business in Great Waters*, 142.

15 Sir Henry Newbolt, *History of the Great War Based on Official Documents*, (1931), V, Plan 31. This plan shows significant numbers of merchant ships sunk off the East Coast of North America up to Newfoundland, May–October 1918.

16 Nicolas Rodger, 'The Royal Navy in the Era of the World Wars: Was it Fit for Purpose?', *The Mariner's Mirror*, 97 (1) (February 2011), 272–84, 282.

17 *Official Account of the Battle of the Atlantic* (1946), 19.

18 D. W. Waters, 'The Science of Admiralty, VI', *The Naval Review*, 52 (4) (October 1964), 423–37, 433. Also, see Chart 2.2.

19 Roskill, *The War at Sea* (1954), I, 343.

20 TNA ADM 205/7, NID 0747/35, In November 1935 technical intelligence reached N.I.D. about possible refuelling at sea for U-boats via submersible oil tankers; Marc Milner, *The Battle of the Atlantic* (Ontario, 2003), 151.

21 TNA ADM 205/7, folio 7, Correspondence with First Sea Lord Sir Dudley Pound.

22 Günther Hessler, *The U-boat War in the Atlantic 1939–45*, I, (1989), 28; V. E. Tarrant, *The U-boat Offensive 1914–45* (1989), 90.

23 TNA ADM 205/7, folio 7, Correspondence with First Sea Lord Sir Dudley Pound.

24 Hague, *The Allied Convoy System*, 56.

25 TNA ADM 199/1101, In November 1940 consideration was given to converting some of the 3/4 stacker 'Town' class Destroyers for long-range escort work.

26 Corelli Barnett, *Engage the Enemy More Closely* (1991), 255.

27 Barley et al., *The Defeat of the Enemy Attack on Shipping 1939–1945*, 19.

28 TNA ADM 229/20, Director of Naval Construction: DNCs Reports; Chalmers, *Max Horton*, 179; Franklin, *Britain's Anti-Submarine Capability 1919–1939*, 99.

29 Hague, *The Allied Convoy System*, 61.

30 *Official Account of the Battle of the Atlantic*, 25.

31 Peter Padfield, *The Great Naval Race* (Edinburgh, 2005), 37.

32 Hague, *The Allied Convoy System*, 59; Hessler, *The U-boat War in the Atlantic 1939 –1945*, II, 67.

33 TNA CAB 86/3, Provision of escort vessels; 23 November 1942, 58.

34 TNA CAB 86/2, Note from Minister of Production, Anti-U-boat Warfare Committee, 140.

35 TNA ADM 205/7, 'Correspondence with First Sea Lord Sir Dudley Pound and Dunbar-Nasmith', folio 7; Barnett, *Engage the Enemy More Closely*, 254.

36 James Goldrick, 'Work-up', in *The Battle of the Atlantic 1939–1945* (1994), 220–39, 226.

37 Franklin, *Britain's Anti-Submarine Capability 1919–1939*, 142.

38 George Franklin, 'A Breakdown in Communication: ASDIC in the 1930's', *The Mariner's Mirror*, 84 (2) (May 1998), 204–14, 211.

39 David K. Brown, *Atlantic Escorts* (Barnsley, 2007), 68; Barley et al., *The Defeat of the Enemy Attack on Shipping 1939–1945*, 71–2; Hague, *The Allied Convoy System*, 62.

40 www.liverpoolmuseum.org.uk, Liverpool Museum description.

41 Terraine, *Business in Great Waters*, 305.

42 TNA ADM 223/88, Officer in Charge, Operations Intelligence Centre, 13ff.

43 TNA ADM 205/7, Letter from Admiral Noble to secretary of the Admiralty, 14 September 1941.

44 Chalmers, *Max Horton*, Appendix XI; Ronald Seth, *The Fiercest Battle*, (1961), 67.

45 Terraine, *Business in Great Waters*, 501.

46 Stephen W. Roskill, *Churchill and the Admirals* (Barnsley, 2004), 142.

47 Chalmers, *Max Horton,* 152.

48 Chart constructed by author.

49 Special cable to the New York Times, dated Thursday, 22 July 1915, describing the sinking of the Battleship Pommern, and cruisers.

50 Andrew Williams, *Battle of the Atlantic* (2002), 242.

51 Patrick Beesly, *Very special Intelligence* (1977), xv.

52 Roskill, *The War at Sea,* II, 217.

53 Denis Richards et al., *Royal Air Force 1939–1945,* 3 (1953, 1954).

54 Roskill, *The War at Sea,* I, 36.

55 TNA AIR 41/73, 'The RAF in Maritime War – Atlantic and Home Waters; II, the Defensive Phase, September 1939–June 1941, Coastal Command's ASW file, 42.

56 TNA AIR 15/66, 'The Rôle of Coastal Command in War', November 1937–March 1939, Memo 1.10.1937; Barley et al., *The Defeat of the Enemy Attack on Shipping 1939–1945,* 22.

57 Roskill, *The War at Sea,* I, 30.

58 Andrew Hendrie, *The Cinderella Service* (Barnsley, 2005), 126.

59 Oberstleutnant Marc S. Koestner, 'The Luftwaffe's Support of Naval Operations During World War II 1939–1941' Canadian Forces College, n.d., 10.

60 TNA AIR 41/47–48, 'The RAF in Maritime War – The Atlantic and Home Waters: III, July 1941–February 1943', and AHB II/117.

61 Terraine, *Business in Great Waters,* 248.

62 TNA AIR 15/3, Minute sheet 9/9066/1, November 1937.

63 John Buckley, 'Airpower and the Battle of the Atlantic 1939–45', *Journal of Contemporary History,* 28, 1 (January 1993), 143–61, 144.

64 Barley et al, *The Defeat of the Enemy Attack on Shipping 1939–1945,* 21.

65 D. Henry, 'British Submarine Policy 1918–1939', in *Technical Change and British Naval Policy 1860–1939* (London, 1977), 93.

66 Hessler, *The U-boat War in the Atlantic 1939–1945,* I, 7.

67 TNA AIR 41/73, AHB II/117/3, The RAF in the maritime war, (B), 1.

68 TNA AIR 15/284, Government white paper, Battle of the Atlantic, paras 1–2.

69 Air Marshal Sir Edward Chilton, RAF Bracknell Paper No. 2, A symposium on the Battle of the Atlantic, 21 October 1991, 70; Roskill, *The War at Sea,* II, 371.

70 TNA AIR 15/284, Government white paper, Battle of the Atlantic, paras 1–2.

71 John Buckley, 'Airpower and the Battle of the Atlantic 1939–45', 144.

72 TNA AIR 15/3, Coastal Commands war plan, memorandum 25 October 1938.

73 TNA AIR 41/47, Chapter 1, The expansion and re-equipment of Coastal Command, f. 13, 1.

74 Terraine, *Business in Great Waters,* 248.

75 Richards et al., *The Royal Air Force 1939–1945,* 1 (1953), 61.

76 TNA AIR 41/73, AHB II/117/3, (B) The RAF in the maritime war, 48.

77   John Terraine, *The Right of the Line* (1985), 233, 456.

78   Barley et al., *The Defeat of the Enemy Attack on Shipping 1939–1945*, 23.

79   Alfred Price, *Aircraft versus Submarine* (Barnsley, 2004), 47–8.

80   John Buckley, 'The Development of RAF Coastal Command Trade Defence Strategy, Policy and Doctrine 1919–1945', University of Lancaster, 1991, 213–17.

81   TNA AIR 41/73, RAF in maritime war. Volume II: September 1939–June 1941, 285.

82   Duncan Redford, 'Inter- and Intraservice Rivalries in the Battle of the Atlantic', *Journal of Strategic Studies,* 32 (6) (December 2009), 899–928, 921.

83   John Buckley, 'The Development of RAF Coastal Command Trade Defence Strategy', 214.

84   Andrew Hendrie, *The Cinderella Service,* 63.

85   TNA ADM 1/12141, Armaments (11): Memorandum on Anti-submarine Striking Forces, DNAD (Director of Naval Air Defence), 15 May 1939.

5

U-boat Training to Meet the Requirements of Grey Water Strategy

This chapter discusses the training given to the U-boat arm to meet the needs of a Grey Water Strategy in the North Atlantic and investigates the requirements of the manpower needed to man the U-boat arm of a virtual navy within a navy.[1]

Manpower requirements and training of the U-boat arm, 1933–43

Given that the new U-boat arm only started in earnest after the Anglo-German Naval Agreement of 1935, assembling the manpower needed became one of the first priorities. This job fell to a key naval officer in the U-boat arm organization, Hans-Georg von Friedeburg, about whom little in this work has been said so far. He was reputed to be a particularly gifted organizer and a man endowed with an exceptional capacity for work.[2] Born at Straßburg, in the Alsace in July 1895, he entered the German Navy in 1914 becoming a *Fähnrich* (Junior Midshipman).[3] After serving some time on surface vessels he entered the submarine service and became involved in training courses between December 1917 and June 1918 when he became a first Watch Officer (*1WO*), until the end of the war. On 25 September 1939 he became head of the U–boat Organization Department and in October 1939 it was to him that Karl Dönitz, now *BdU*, entrusted all the organization functions of the U-boat arm.[4] At this time he was made up to a full Captain, *Kapitän zur See*, as well as *BdU* (org) Organization. On 1 September 1941 he was made up to *Konteradmiral*.[5]

As the Chief Administrator of the U-boat arm he was ultimately responsible for all aspects of administration and training.[6] Initially designated as *Organizationsabteilung /BdU.org* in October 1941 his position was renamed *2. Admiral der Unterseeboote*. He was also charged with all questions related to U-boat manning levels and the conduct of official correspondence in matters relating to armaments, organization, technical administration and personnel.[7] Originally von Friedeburg was given total responsibility for both School and Front-line Flotillas but during the course of the war an individual *FdU* was involved in day-to-day running of their flotilla,[8] and a new post was revived, *FdU Baltic*, responsible for the administration and movements of pre-operational boats.[9]

Dönitz estimated that he needed 300 U-boats to achieve his purpose of successfully interdicting Allied Shipping in the British sea lines; in the event he had approaching 800.[10] With such plans for U-boat production the most important duty von Friedeburg faced was to provide the crews needed for all newly commissioned U-boats; which he did with thorough, well thought-out programmes that were the hallmark of this efficient officer. *BdU* (org) was responsible for all matters pertaining to U-boat flotillas, other than operations – which were in the hands of Captain Eberhard Godt, Chief of Staff to Admiral Dönitz.

Personnel requirements for operating Type VIIC and Type IXC U-boats

The training programme discussed for officers and men in this work is based on the need for crews to man the Type VII and Type IX U-boats. Training for 'Coastal' boat Type II was similar, but not considered here in detail.

The work-horse in the North Atlantic was the 67-m long Type VIIC, of 761 tons surface displacement.[11] In basic form she was armed with one 88-mm deck gun, one 20-mm flak gun and five 21-inch torpedo tubes. Torpedo firing systems were probably better than all others and the *UZO U-bootzieloptik* (U-boat Target Optics), like the periscope, had as its primary purpose to enable torpedo attacks. Located on the bridge the *UZO* was only available while the U-boat was surfaced, and most often used in low light conditions (night attacks). Diving time was in the order of 25 seconds +, dependent on sea and weather conditions, but apart from improvements to some of the on-board equipment, and construction methods, the range of U-boats in service differed little to those of the 1914–18 First World War vessels; hence an earlier statement in Chapter 1 about the systems not being radically different.[12]

At the commencement of hostilities U-boats were equipped with a mediocre active ASDIC (*S-Gerät*) set but it had a superb listening hydrophone, known as the Atlas-Werke GHG set, used in boat Types VII and IX. Hydrophone sensitivity was far greater than the systems they used in the First World War and could pick up a surface ship about ten miles off, and a moderate-sized convoy could be detected at an even greater distance.[13] The capability of this unit was first acknowledged in August 1941 when *U-570* (HMS *Graph*) was captured intact. In the passive mode it was far superior to RN ASDIC in the listening mode.[14]

Typically the crew of a Type VII consisted of:

Commander
Engineer Officer
2 Watch-keeping Officers
15 Subordinate Officers
23 Ratings
Total: 42 (48 for the VIIC)[15]

The Type IX was a larger boat, displacing 1,120 tons surfaced and 1,232 tons submerged and had a surface speed of around 18 knots and 7 knots submerged. Diving time was about 10 seconds + slower, and less manoeuvrable than the Type VIIC. Admiral Raeder had a preference for the larger boat but for the Atlantic Dönitz preferred the smaller, more agile boat, Type VIIC. He was of the view that in the event of a depth charge attack it would stand a better chance of survival due to its shorter diving time and greater manoeuvrability; the crew, however, were not as comfortable in its cramped confines. The Type IX's biggest advantages were more crew comfort and the range; 13,850 miles at 10 knots and an ideal choice for overseas missions such as the African and American and Latin-American coasts, as well as being able to carry more torpedoes. Therefore, one modernist historian is incorrect in stating that Dönitz was wedded to U-boats 'which were too small to exploit the easy open access to the open Atlantic'.[16]

Typically the crew of a Type IXC consisted of:

Commander
Engineering Officer (LI)
2/3 Watch-keeping Officers
17/18 Subordinate Officers
28/30 Ratings
Total: 50/53 [17]

Nominal endurance of the Type VII U-boat was determined by its fuel capacity stowage, which was about 8,500 miles at ten knots for the VIIC using about 100 tons oil, and 13,850 miles at ten knots for Type IXC on 200 tons oil. Endurance was not only dependent on fuel but that of the stamina and dedication of the crew, about which there was little doubt.[18] Both types of boat had one thing in common, the need for a systemized approach to U-boat and tactical training doctrine, for survival was often conditioned on what had been learnt.

U-boat training

Some of the lessons of the First World War were applied in the first regular course for future commanders started on 3 January 1933, even before the signing of the Anglo-German Naval Agreement.[19] At that time training was a sensitive political matter and the first school set up was known by a 'cover' name as the *U-bootabwehrschule* (*UAS*), or 'U-boat Defence School'. It was a useful cover-name in the period when Germany was not even permitted to have U-boats. More importantly the school not only primarily concerned itself with listening for surface vessels but also for the detection of other submarines. In order for the boat to listen it would have to maintain complete silence, something that is very difficult to achieve since once a submarine loses all way-on it can become unstable due to the ineffectiveness of its hydroplanes.[20]

Throughout most of 1935, the level of new training became subject to the uneven rate of U-boat production and often had to use improvised surface vessels in place of U-boats for training purposes,[21] not dissimilar to *Osprey's* problems.[22] The level of numbers and training was then stepped up in anticipation of an expected influx of new boats. Following the Anglo-German Agreement the name of the school disappeared until 25 September 1939 when it reappeared, and was no longer shrouded in secrecy.[23] In 1940 it became *Skl U.III*, but still separate from U-boat schools.[24] The *UAS* status was now quite unique within the *Kriegsmarine* and meant that officer and rating training in U-boat defence was centralized and had no other responsibility other than instruction in a given subject. Other schools gave training in preparation for front-line boats, but both schools worked together harmoniously.[25] As a specialized school it was ideally placed as an advisory body on ASDIC techniques.[26]

Staff officer training at *UAS* was only of short duration, consisting of around five days to cover the basics of ASDIC and hydrophones, but hydrophone and ASDIC courses for more specialized operators lasted up to two months.[27] As with standard U-boat training, to be discussed, courses included communications and countermeasure techniques.

For U-boat defence the following is a rough guide to courses provided.[28]

1. Hydrophone basics	Ratings ashore	8 weeks
2. Hydrophone basics	Ratings on U-boats	10 weeks
3. Hydrophone refresher course	Qualified ratings	12 days
4. Hydrophone basics	Leading rates	8 weeks
5. Hydrophone refresher and search gear maintenance	Leading rates	12 days
6. Hydrophone basics	Executive Officers	5 days

The superior quality of the hydrophone equipment however does not signify that U-boats were never sunk by this method. Curiously it was on 9 February 1945 that a British submarine, HMS *Venturer*, became the first submarine to sink a U-boat, *U-864*, when both were submerged; it was the only known incident in naval warfare at this time.[29]

Standard U-boat training courses

As U-boat numbers increased several U-boat training schools were formed culminating in a single authority, the *HKU-Höheres Kommando der Unterseebootsausbildung* (U-boat High Command Training Centre) based at Kiel.[30] It was responsible for teacher training in several divisions and flotillas in all aspects of submarine warfare, including both material and personnel.[31] Practical U-boat training in the working-up phase also came under the *HKU*, later. The purpose was to provide a common doctrine and learn everything about the boat, as a whole, with the premise of developing it into a powerful combat-ready weapon to be put into the hands of a purposeful commanding officer.[32] Normally, a non-specialized training course for seamen was completed in six months, later reduced to three months and then eight weeks, as attrition rates rose; some specialized training time was decreased to only five weeks. It consisted of theory and tactics with further special training in the working of the gyro-compass, underwater sound location (hydrophones) and escape apparatus, all based on systems that had been in development and intended to be used once U-boat production got underway. But the variations of time allotted to standard ratings' training suggests that, as with U-boat commanding officers, personal evaluations, based on feedback of an individual's capabilities, determined the amount of training he received. A fixed training period was not the norm.[33] While the maximum number of passes was desirable, the organization was adaptable enough to accommodate the differences in the ability to learn. Demand for places on programmes was generally high and only the five highest-rated trainees from the seamen ratings 'earned' the privilege of initial sea training aboard a U-boat at sea. The rest had to make do with exercises on minesweepers and quick evening visits aboard berthed boats in port in order to gain some familiarity with the surroundings.[34]

The severest procedures were underwater escape exercises carried out with and without an artificial lung (*Dräger*) using a diving tank filled with about 30 feet of water, similar to exercises performed by RN submariners at *Dolphin*. A small percentage of the trainees in these exercises suffered severe middle ear injuries, including a ruptured ear drum, leading to a reduction in the number of tests.[35] However, in the area to which the U-boats were mainly confined the depths encountered rendered many of these exercises academic, but still the *Dräger* apparatus would save lives from several U-boats and provide the deepest known recorded escapes of the war. One was at 230 feet by a survivor on *U-767* off the Isle of Wight in June 1944, and 240 feet in the English Channel in January 1945.

It had long been the practice of Dönitz to fashion the U-boat training programme around his experiences of the First World War and the thorough training he had helped to develop with Werner Fürbringer and others of that period.[36] He was undaunted in his task and claimed that since ASDIC had not lived up to expectations he would not be put off by British disclosures on its effectiveness.[37] At this stage Dönitz tried to include as many of the lessons he had learned when in command of *UB 68* in the last war, which included better attack methods against convoys using more than one U-boat; and to improve methods of night attacks.[38] Typically from 1940 to 1941 the U-boat school consisted of the 21st and 22nd flotillas and U-boat practical training was carried out by the 24th flotilla based at Kiel, and from May 1940 also by the 26th flotilla. But by the end of 1941, with the rapid expansion of the U-boat fleet, it seriously stretched the resources of the training program. The number of U-boats available for operations went from 45 in November 1939 to 116 by November 1941 and, significantly, the total of training boats increased from 8 in 1939 to 81 in April 1941. The degree of increase in front-line boats was two-and-a-half fold, but the increase of training boats went up by tenfold, a clear indication of how serious training measures were being taken, and met.[39] By providing a greater number of boats available for pack tactics Dönitz's claim, to have applied the lesson learnt from previous experience in the U-boat training programme in the First World War, appears to have been demonstrated.[40]

Training for commissioned rank

The periods into which training for commissioned rank were divided may be roughly expressed as follows:

New entry training
Initial sea time
General naval training course
Second sea time.

New entry training

An officer recruit selected for the executive branch usually joined at the age of 18 at Stralsund and many potential officers were first subjected to psychological assessments to check for suitability, which they probably copied from the early American model at the end of the last war.[41] As a seaman, he generally underwent a six months' seamanship course. After six months' basic training at Stralsund, the new entrant typically served about three months aboard a full-masted training bark (usually the *Gorch Fock*), followed up by a 14-month term aboard a Cruiser and a one-year classroom instruction at the naval school *Marineschule Mürwik* in Flensburg. Thereafter it depended on the career path as to further instruction. Superiors continually evaluated an individual's performance gaining insight into competence, and feedback. The officers aboard his final warship assignment actually elected him by majority vote to his commission as *Leutnant zur See*.[42] Officers were expected to care for the men under them and as such were charged with their welfare, and leadership,[43] many qualities that stem from the Prussian influence.[44] During training the recruit held the rank of *Seekadett* (Officer Cadet) and the unit managed approximately 1,000 such cadets at a time producing around 2,000 potential officers annually. The source for new entrants could come from several places: high schools;[45] naval pilots who had transferred to the *Luftwaffe* in the 1930s proved a rich source of U-boat officers, some also direct from the *Luftwaffe*; many naval personnel came voluntarily to the U-boat service, but one group simply received orders in mid-December 1940 to report for U-boat training. Mass transfers were not uncommon and continued even after Dönitz's promotion to Commander-in-Chief of the Navy on 1 February 1943. For example, 125 officers and midshipmen training as pilots for the nascent Naval Air Service suddenly found themselves transferred to U-boat duty; there was no debate.[46]

Initial sea time

Cadets having completed their course at Stralsund were then sent to sea for a year, usually in smaller types of craft to gain sea experience. After six months they were then promoted to *Fähnrich* (Junior Midshipman). In the initial phase of gaining sea time they never served in U-boats, irrespective of whether or not they had applied to join this branch of the service.

General naval training course

After completion of initial training at sea the Midshipman was sent on a comprehensive training course to Flensburg-Mürwik. During the latter part of this course, he was able to specialize in subjects that were likely to determine the class of ship in which he would to serve, U-boat or surface vessel.

Second sea time

As soon as the period of training at Flensburg-Mürwik was completed, the Midshipman then went to sea again, probably in a U-boat. This stage of training lasted for nine months, after which the trainee would normally be promoted to *Oberfähnrich* (Senior Midshipman). At the end of the second sea term, and given the right conditions, the trainee received his commission as *Leutnant zur See* (Sub-lieutenant). In order to meet the demands for new-line officers it was vital to keep up the numbers of *Oberfähnrich* and *Leutnant zur See* passing out and by the end of April 1943 the organization was adapted in order to increase the pass rate to 45 per month.[47]

The method of training the *WO/Wachoffizier*, or Watch-keeping Officer, throughout the war was to make him follow a normal executive officer training programme until allowed to opt for U-boats. In the same manner as described in the 'second sea time' he too went to sea in a U-boat as a *Fähnrich* and after a period of about nine months' service would receive his commission as a

Leutnant zur See. After a further eight weeks at the U-boat school he was likely to be drafted to a U-boat as the second WO. Engineering officers received similar training followed by 12 weeks specialized training in U-boats at the U-boat school, also attaining the rank of *Fähnrich.*[48] The lessons learned here were tested during the working-up phase, and before dispersal to front-line boats.

U-boat commander training

Dönitz laid great store by the U-boat Commander. He wrote, 'Such operations can only be carried out with Commanding Officers and crews who are thoroughly trained for them',[49] and in recognition of this he held to no fixed formula by which an officer automatically qualified for command.[50] But in general terms an officer who had completed at least one year as a First Lieutenant, or one of the senior WO officers in a U-boat, became eligible for training as a U-boat Commanding Officer. There was no firm distinction. However, several naval officers who were seconded to the *Luftwaffe* during the large-scale attacks of 1940 were returned to the Navy for consideration; these officers appear to have received a degree of preference in the training and distribution to U-boat commands.[51] Officers selected would normally go directly to the Commanders' school but if not directly then to either the first or second instructional division in order to receive instruction on a school boat.[52]

Commanders were issued with a U-boat operational manual in which they were able to review many of the procedures that had been covered in basic training.[53] The contents of the manual had many features of U-boat characteristics to be observed, such as 'maintaining invisibility', 'listening' and 'D/F location'; underwater torpedo attacks, forward shots, angles, stern torpedo shots etc. The section between 310–339 in the manual, deals with 'Conduct on Convoys';[54] that section was regularly updated following the supplementary debriefings after returning from war patrols. Günter Hessler, *BdU's* first staff officer from November 1941, conducted over 4,500 de-briefings, which became one of the rich veins for OR. It was during this period that much of the feedback received from returning patrols was forwarded to the training schools and weapons inspectorates.[55] The de-briefing details accompanied the patrol logs and distributed internally, an example which may be found in PG 30130.[56]

An ingenious, complex system, was devised for commanders, the Convoy Attack Teacher. It was a trainer for officers undergoing courses destined for U-boat command, known as the *F-Gerät* (Patrol Gear). It comprised a complete

U-boat conning tower mock-up suspended above a sheet of water with the periscope looking down upon it. On the sheet of water were placed miniature ships on metal rods.

> They form convoys which move about at varying speeds and courses, directed by a civilian named 'Barkow'. A variety of weather conditions and visibility can be simulated. The conning tower could be turned and speeds up to 18 knots simulated by moving the ships towards or away from the periscope; every prospective U-boat CO must make fifteen successful attacks on the convoy. Nearly every commanding officer has taken this course and refers to it by saying he has patrolled with 'Barkow'.[57]

In May 1940, the 1st and 2nd U-boat training flotillas were formed out of the original U-boat training flotilla, which had been responsible for training U-boat commanders. At this time, the 2nd training flotilla also provided pre-operational training. In July 1940, the training units became numbered: the 2nd U-boat training flotilla became the 25th U-boat flotilla, and the U-boat front-line tactical training flotilla the 27th; the 25th appeared to concentrate very much on the same type of training as the 27th. An inspection of the orders of the 25th flotilla for 24 July 1941 provides some idea of what training was carried out. It included tactical exercises, torpedo firing and convoy attack exercises. U-boats that had been commissioned during the previous two or three months proceeded to sea together with the escort vessels attached to the flotilla, which then acted as the convoy to be attacked. During torpedo-firing exercises they then acted as recovery vessels.[58] Normally, the senior officer of the flotilla, together with the instructors, followed the exercises from aboard the flotilla Depot-ship and discussed with commanders afterwards. Although the 25th and the 27th flotillas were tactical training flotillas, neither of them apparently specialized in any way; each supervised the training of groups of U-boats of all types and in all parts of tactical training. However, in 1941 front-line practical training was set up in the Baltic, at Hela.[59] It was typically carried out by the 25th, 26th and 27th flotillas, but throughout the war many separate flotillas were used at each stage of the training programme. The 25th and 27th flotillas appear to have concentrated very much on the same type of training and the daily orders for 24 July 1941 indicate that it included tactical exercises, torpedo firing and convoy attack.[60] Once an officer was considered to be proficient and capable of taking command his name was forwarded to the Admiral U-boats (von Friedburg) for appointment to one of the flotillas, front-line or otherwise.[61]

In 1937 Dönitz had proposed a three-year training period for the U-boat arm, in which the first year would be devoted to individual training, the second to collective training and manoeuvres, while the third year would be spent at an overseas station.[62] However, the problem of replacements arose as the attrition rate increased between 1940–3. In support of a proposed expansion on personnel requirement Dönitz projected the establishment of a second U-boat training school at Gotenhafen in July 1940.[63]

In July 1942, when the U-boat arm began to reach its maximum strength, the preference was for career officers over reservists. The ratio in front-line flotillas stood at 80:20. Among U-boats under training, or in the U-boat training establishments, the ratio was even higher at 87:13. Whereas the *Wehrmacht*, in general, depended heavily on its reserve officers, the U-boat arm did not.[64]

By 1942 it became plain that the training period for commanders needed to be drastically reduced, due to losses and a still growing fleet, thus the new training flotilla was shelved and part of the existing 26th flotilla was used as a third tactical training unit.[65] By the end of 1943 some commanders were reduced to between four and ten weeks training only, a sharp contrast to that originally planned.[66]

Ratings' training, general

Ratings went through an initial training period in the 'Ships Manning Division' and then either volunteered or were selected for U-boat training, according to their pass grades.[67] Initially U-boat School training lasted six months; but it was later reduced to three months, and then eight weeks; radio (telegraphists) and torpedomen (equivalent TAS (Torpedo and Anti-submarine Warfare) branch in the RN) found their specialized training time decreased to only five weeks. As was the case with officers, the number of personnel available for front-line duty increased proportionately as training was cut back.[68] Clearly the demand for more manpower meant that the degree of training given suffered. If there was a criticism of manpower planning it would be a lack of sufficient numbers.

Shortage in all ranks

Ratings and NCOs (Non-commissioned Officers) were getting short in supply. Dönitz produced a report in August 1940 indicating that the first year of the campaign had been at great cost, in men and materials. Of the 61 operational U-boats 28 had been lost, representing 46 per cent of the total. Crew losses were at a similar level. The original U-boat force started out with approximately 3,000 selected volunteers, officers and men. The average age of the commanding officer was 29.5 years of age, and the greater majority of crew members were aged 21 to 25. The loss in the first year of what has been described as the *Scheinkrieg* (phoney war),[69] still claimed 79 officers and 685 NCOs and ratings and a further 33 officers and 394 other ranks captured – in total a loss of nearly 1,200 men, or 40 per cent of those that began the war.[70] Heavy losses indeed even at that stage of the war. Actually, 'so far as the Royal Navy and Coastal Command were concerned, there had never been a "phoney" war'.[71]

U-boat losses were also relatively high. On 23 October 1939, Dönitz announced in his war diary that five, possibly six U-boats had been lost, mainly he thought by gunfire since there were many survivors. He went on further to report that 'The present losses are actually very high. They exceed supplies of new boats and must therefore lead to a hindrance of U-boat warfare if no means can be found of keeping them lower'.[72] Given Dönitz's earlier comment that 'ASDIC had not lived up to expectations he would not be put off by British disclosures on its effectiveness' he must have had second thoughts.[73]

Replacing the lost U-boats alone proved to be a difficult process. From 1 September to 1 June 1939, German shipyards built an average of no more than two U-boats per month, and just 13 out of the 20 boats were capable of Atlantic operations.[74] Replacing the men was even more difficult. So dire was the dilemma that by the end of 1941 all German Destroyers with the luxury of three engineering officers had the 'Thirds' all removed and assigned to U-boats,[75] and plans were then made to increase the number of recruits for training to make up losses.[76] Ratings and NCOs were particularly difficult to replace. In June 1941 the *Kriegsmarine* had 370,000 ratings and POs, 50 per cent of the conscripts with bodily defects.[77] This is stark contrast to statements made by some historians that there was no shortage of volunteers.[78] Nevertheless, von Friedeburg executed his job well and on 17 December 1943 *Großadmiral* Dönitz expressed his satisfaction by stating that 'in the last few months, with a view to expansion of the offensive arm of our Navy, we have increased our strength by 100,000 men'.[79] He hoped that this additional number of men would suffice to cover his needs. By 1943 the RN too suffered manpower shortages not only in the seaman's branch.[80] Britain had on order a new large class of Corvette armed with a new A/S weapon, the Squid. The manpower shortage was so acute that the RCN (Royal Canadian Navy) was asked to assist in manning some of the new ships.[81] In the Merchant Navy there were also acute shortages of skilled men.[82]

Even more illuminating for the *BdU* was the stress of patrol operations beginning to show on the physical and mental state of his commanders. Just one month after the war began he noted the need to relieve two captains immediately, with the probability of several others soon to follow. His *FdU* (West) Hans-Rudolf Rösing noted in his *KTB*, copied to *BdU*, that some commanders had shown signs of exhaustion leading to a lack of success in sinking's.[83] The most common problem appeared to be the transition from several years' experience aboard the smaller coastal Type II boats to a few weeks' patrol duty on a larger Type VII, or IX, which seemed almost overwhelming. As a result Dönitz had to rearrange Commanders and commands, relieving some entirely, and moving others to smaller or larger boats according to their abilities to cope with the new requirements of war. During the first months of the war no less than 20 U-boat commanders had been replaced. Such rapid and extensive turnover among its captains further impaired U-boat performance in the early days of war.[84]

Average time in training

There is little evidence available to indicate precise lengths of time that a given newly manned U-boat spent with training flotillas, but on average it used to be in the order of five months-later drastically reduced in time for the reasons stated. In a command account given by *Kapitän zur See* Viktor Schütze, Captain of (U-boat) training, it would appear that three months was dedicated to the task of pre-operational training of U-boat complements who spent the following number of days on tasks:[85]

14 days	Flak School VII	Flak training
6 days	19th U-boat flotilla	Harbour training
25–35 days	Front-line training group	Technical training
10 days	20th U-boat flotilla	Pre-tactical training
14–16 days	25th or 26th U-boat flotilla	Torpedo firing
10 days	27th U-boat flotilla	Tactical training

That made a total of between 79 and 91 days, but not all the above training was carried out in one location; there were different locations dependent on the type of training given.[86] From March 1943 Schütze's close contacts with the new 2/Skl[87] meant that he was able to have them provide up-to-date combat experience to pass onto trainees.[88] Tactical training was provided to U-boat officers and some specialized ratings in accordance with plans drawn up in co-operation with *BdU* (org), section A3.[89] During theoretical tactical training the same principles of learning from others, and feedback, applied. The instructor, usually someone with good combat experience, attempted to instil knowledge and confidence in the participants of the course.

Working-up training

Every two weeks, or so – unless ports were frozen over in winter – newly commissioned U-boats which had completed their technical and weapons training would proceed to sea together with a group of escort vessels in the company of six or more merchant ships deployed in the form of a convoy; together with an anti-submarine screen of three auxiliary vessels.[90] The objective was to configure a good simulation of a convoy likely to be encountered in the Atlantic. Later, to make the conditions more realistic, the convoy was further protected by a squadron of aircraft acting as a combat air patrol. Ideally working-up training should have taken place in an area with good depths and a wide expanse of water. The Baltic was not one of them. 'Compared with the convoy scenario in the Atlantic, the training attack operations in the Baltic took place in a relatively small area. Several cases of damage and the loss of two boats occurred in five years of tactical training.'[91] The operational zone was between the Danish island of Bornholm and the Swedish island of Gotland, where they proceeded with attack procedures on a (simulated) convoy. Senior officers and instructors in the flotilla observed and followed the exercises from aboard the U-boat depot ship and would later discuss results of the exercise with U-boat commanders, and escort executive officers. Dönitz remarked that this was vital since the new commanders' three weeks of tactical training had not allowed them to learn all the things which had earlier been learned by others over several years. At the working-up phase two-way feedback was being practiced and any suggestions for improvement were forwarded to Captain (U/B) for consideration, just as the British Sunday Soviets attempted.[92]

The final step was in the Technical Training Group for Front-line U-boats (*Technische Ausbildungsgruppe für Front-U-Boote*), abbreviated *Agru-Front*, first established in the autumn of 1941which developed highly realistic tests of submariners 'skills and mettle'. Originally conceived as a two-week course it slowly extended to five weeks of gruelling, and often exhausting, tests of endurance in simulated emergency circumstances in deep waters. These were then interspersed periodically with additional classroom instruction. Often feedback on these tests was supplemented by a training officer with extensive combat experience who would proceed to sea with a front-line crew and set up a series of complications during manoeuvres. The complications set ranged from disabling controls during a crash dive, to requiring the crew to repair simulated damages under emergency lighting, or torchlight, while he set off a smoke bomb. Such exercises were intended to test the crew's ability to cope with all emergencies without panicking, and prepare them for the realities of Atlantic warfare. From the evidence collected from a survey conducted among ex U-boat men one experienced U-boat chief engineer, Lt Commander Suhren, himself had to regain control of a plunging *U-512* in order to avoid destruction during an April 1942 test.[93] Real-life exercises demonstrate that learning through practical experience can never be replaced by classroom simulators, and this demonstration was a good example of practical feedback for those on which lives could depend. From the beginning to the conclusion of U-boat training both Commanders and crew were subjected to questioning by the teachers with the purpose of identifying any routine that could be improved, in order to learn from earlier mistakes. At the completion of training, front-line boat working-up Commanders and senior technical officers and ratings were given, and asked for, feedback. Also during working-up, as well as during refits, experts were on hand to interact with Commanders and crew alike so that they fully understood the functions of any new equipment fitted. By this means the U-boat arm was able to add any additional comments in a report that would be forwarded to the relevant technical section for consideration in new designs, a feature that becomes important when discussing 'OR' in a later chapter.

At Kernevél-Lorient, the main base in France for front-line boats, Dönitz's resolve on training matters did not slacken and although he was unable to provide follow-up training for U-boat crews following a patrol, there was a regular 'tactical' school session for U-boat crews. These were often attended by outside instructors, some from the *UAS*.[94] Some U-boat commanders were probably aware of this flaw in follow-up training.

However, if an area had been set aside for this purpose, such as the British had done around Scotland and the Irish Coast, it is likely that U-boat tactics could have been improved. The classroom is fine for initial instruction but nothing compares to 'live' practice. Of the areas open to Dönitz in Europe for follow-up training only the Baltic could have been protected, not areas around the Bay of Biscay, the Mediterranean or Norway. Establishing training areas further afield may not have been practical and even if whole crews could have been transported to the training area, they would not have been in their own boats. Using similar equipment is not the same as using one's own. In theory everything should have performed in the same manner but users get used to the knowledge of any foibles that it might contain.

Conclusions

Dönitz had learnt several lessons from the First World War and was intent on implementing them. The *Kriegsmarine* trained its men of the U-boat arm to work in closely confined environments on patrols that could last for at least two months in more or less self-sufficiency. Practical U-boat training was given to officer and rating new entries, as well as would-be commanders, before they were sent to front-line boats ready for war patrols. Courses lasted six months in the early stages of the war and then later reduced to three months, in some cases eight weeks. They practiced convoy attack procedures, especially night attacks, often receiving (and giving) feedback from experienced U-boat commanders or Engineering Officers who had been rotated. It was von Friedeburg that was primarily responsible for ensuring that operational U-boat crews were rotated back to the U-boat school in order to provide feedback for newly trained recruits as well as crews in the working-up phase of their training.

The strength of the U-boat arm was in its ability to provide very well trained crews and much of their front-line experience was documented for feedback, using training reports and war diaries from the Command and U-boat. As applicable these were sent to weapons research and construction departments, which helped with their efforts to find more effective weapons and methods.[95]

The weakness of the U-boat arm lay in three major areas. The first was poor strategic planning. In order to fight a commerce war they basically only possessed two standard types of U-boat, Type VII and IX, with the emphasis put on the Type VII due to its better diving times and manoeuvrability, but there was no reserve strategy. The second weakness arose out of a 'strength'. The strength, noted above, was to rotate some commanders and senior engineering officers back to the U-boat training schools to pass on acquired knowledge, and minimize some of the 'burn' out effect. However, the aces of 1940 to late 1942 period were rotated before the onslaught that was to follow. Therefore, those who taught classes in the training flotillas could offer little advice on the conditions they had not experienced. The system was further weakened inasmuch as when boats were sunk *BdU* command was unable to interview those that did not survive and therefore lacked the essential information required to improve any training methods available to them. The third weakness lay in the organization of training follow-up procedures. There was no mechanism in place to provide practical follow-up U-boat tactical training once crews had returned to base, largely because they had no surface ships in the area with which to practice tactical procedures. The experience gained on patrol – provided they were fortunate enough to survive – proved a far more effective teacher than anything in the *HKU* curriculum did, but they were unable to share practical experiences with others. It is true that tactics were discussed at the drawing board level using some experienced instructors and ex U-boat Commanders, but the facility that they had for follow-up training, in comparison with Western Approaches, looked distinctly pedestrian. While it may be said that many lessons were learned in terms of attack procedures and tactical ASW countermeasures when at the front, they were unable to translate these gains through combined exercises back at base. On this point the U-boat arm had clearly not yet even considered it to be a mistake, but they would still learn. The German training system started out strongly producing competent Commanders and crew, but such a standard could not be sustained and as time went by they were unable to keep up with countering the degree of allied sophistication in mobile assets and tactics as they developed.

Notes

1   George Franklin, 'A Breakdown in Communication: ASDIC in the 1930s', *The Mariners Mirror*, 84 (2) (May 1998), 204–14, 213; The same sentiment applied to the submarine arm of the RN which was seen as a private navy within the navy, and little contact to other branches.

2   Karl Dönitz, *Memoirs* (1959), 120.

3   Alsace had long been a dual language region of French and German.

4   GC&CS, 'The German Navy – The U-boat Arm', 7 (December 1945), 10; Walter Lohmann et al., *Die deutsche Kriegsmarine 1939–1945* (Bad Nauheim, 1956–64), 2 (72), 7.

5   Lohmann et al., *Die deutsche Kriegsmarine*, 2 (72), 7.

6   John Terraine, *Business in Great Waters* (Ware, 1999), 213.

7   NHB PG 15500, Documents detailing the responsibilities of von Friedeburg, 355–7.

8   NHB PG 31020, Three new authorities were created to deal with various aspects of training and working-up, 58 and 74.

9   GC&CS, 'The German Navy – The U-boat Arm', 7, 60.

10   F. Barley et al., *The Defeat of the Enemy Attack on Shipping 1939–1945*, 137
(Aldershot, 1997), Plan 7; Patrick Beesly, *Very Special Intelligence* (1977), 35; Marc
Milner, *Battle of the Atlantic* (Ontario, 2003), 16.

11   Robert Stern, *Type VII U-boats* (1998), 18.

12   John Terraine, *The Right of the Line* (1985), 237; V. E. Tarrant, *U-Boat Offensive
1914–45* (1989), 169–76.

13   TNA ADM 186/389, CB 1328, WW1 German Hydrophones; TNA HW 18/200,
GHG hydrophone; this version consisted of 24–12, on either bow, 15.

14   David K. Brown, *Atlantic Escorts* (Barnsley, 2007), 29.

15   TNA ADM 186/ 809: CB 04051 (103), Interrogation of U-boat survivors describing
training methods, 8.

16   Nicolas Rodger, 'The Royal Navy in the Era of the World Wars': Was it Fit for
Purpose?', *The Mariner's Mirror*, 97 (1) (February 2011), 272–84, 281.

17   TNA ADM 186/ 809: CB 04051 (103), interrogation of U-boat survivors describing
training methods, 11.

18   Brown, *Atlantic Escorts*, 29.

19   Dönitz, *Memoirs*, 4.

20   Authors comment.

21   Kapitän Herbert Wilde, 'UAS, die Unterseebootabwehrschule 1933–1945', an
appraisal of events 1963–4, 5.

22   Osprey had similar problems, see next chapter.

23   NHB PG 15508, paper 17, details of the school, 2.

24   GC&CS, 'The German Navy – Organization' (1945), 2, 40.

25   Ibid., 5, 160–1.

26   At least two historians have not fully understood the function of the UAS, Mulligan
and Westwood.

27   GC&CS, 'The German Navy – Organization', 5, 162.

28   Ibid., Appendix T, 166.

29   A documentary film has been made of this incident and details of the action can be
found on www.Uboat.net.

30   TNA HW 11/20, The German Navy – U-boat Arm, 7, Chapter 2, 1; David
Westwood, *The U-boat War* (2005), 280.

31   Erich Topp, 'Manning and Training the U-boat Fleet', in *The Battle of the Atlantic
1939–1945* (1994), 214–19.

32   Topp, Ibid., 214; Timothy Mulligan, *Neither Sharks Nor Wolves* (Annapolis, 1999), 14.

33   GC&CS, 'The German Navy – The U-boat Arm', 7, 97–102.

34   Mulligan, *Neither Sharks Nor Wolves*, 142.

35   Mulligan, *Neither Sharks Nor Wolves*, 141; The RN developed similar exercises for
the submarine service at HMS *Dolphin*.

36 NHB PG 33390, 'Denkschrift: Welche Entwicklungsaufgaben und welche operativen Vorbereitungen müssen heute zur Führung eines U-boots-Handelskrieges gegen England in alle erste Linie gestellt werden', signed Fürbringer, 17 May 1939.

37 Dönitz, *Memoirs*, 18.

38 Ibid., 4.

39 Günter Hessler, *The U-boat War in the Atlantic 1939–1945* (1989), Appendix II, 112; David Westwood, *The U-boat War*, 73.

40 NHB PG 33390, Denkschrift: 'Welche Entwicklungsaufgaben und welche operativen Vorbereitungen müssen heute zur Führung eines U-boots-Handelskrieges gegen England in alle erste Linie gestellt werden'.

41 *Nauticus: Jahrbuch für Deutschlands Seeinteressen* (Berlin, 1938), 182; Karl Dönitz, *40 Fragen an Karl Dönitz* (München, 1980), 9. Dönitz himself was brought up with Prussian principles of obedience and the philosophy of Kant, who was an empiricist and believed that 'knowledge' is acquired through experience alone; K. E. Gardener, 'Selection, Training and Career Development of Naval Officers: A Long-term Follow-up, Using Multivariate Techniques' 1, Graduate Business Centre, City University, 1971.

42 Dirk Richhardt, 'Auswahl und Ausbildung Junger Offiziere 1930–1945: zur sozialen Genese des deutschen Offizierkorps' (Universität Marburg, 2002), 290.

43 Konteradmiral Siegfried Sorge, *Der Marineoffizier als Führer und Erzieher* (Berlin, 1943), 32–8.

44 Werner Rahn, 'Ausbildung zum Marineoffizier zwischen den Weltkriegen', in *Marine Schule Mürwick* (Herford, 1989), 121–31; Carl von Clausewitz, *On War* (Ware, 1997), xv.

45 BA-MA RH 53-7, Chef HL PA gKdos Nr. 664/34, v. 17.3.1934, 88ff. Utmost secrecy was impressed on all pupils that had been spoken to.

46 Fähnrich Z. S. Wolfgang Jacobsen *(U-305)*, quoted in Martin Middlebrook, *Convoy* (1976), 60–1.

47 NHB PG 32119, 1/Skl KTB Teil B Heft V, Januar–Juni 1943, 'Niederschrift über die Sitzung am 8.4.43 beim Chef MPA', 14 April 1943.

48 TNA ADM 186/ 809: CB 04051 (103), Interrogation of U-boat survivors describing training methods, 54.

49 NHB PG 30275, BdU Entry, Conclusions for the day 20 October 1940.

50 Mulligan, *Neither Sharks Nor Wolves*, 158.

51 TNA ADM 186/ 809: CB 04051 (103), Interrogation of U-boat survivors describing training methods, 54.

52 NHB PG 24098, Deals with officer selection criteria.

53 NHB U-boat Commanders Handbook.

54 Ibid., 4.

55 TNA ADM 186/ 809: CB 04051 (103), Interrogation of U-boat survivors describing training methods, 37; Mulligan, *Neither Sharks nor Wolves*, 50–1.

56 NHB PG 30130, KTB Log of the Type IXC, U-130, Routeing Sheet.

57 TNA ADM 186/ 809: CB 04051 (103), Interrogation of U-boat survivors describing training methods, 55; Mulligan, *Neither Sharks nor Wolves*, 132.

58 GC&CS, 'The German Navy – The U-boat Arm', 7, 72.

59 NHB PG 33945, Setting up of a Front-line training unit.

60 GC&CS, 'The German Navy – The U-boat Arm', 7, 72.

61 NHB PG 24098, Report on Officers training for Command.

62 Dönitz, *Memoirs*, 32.

63 NHB PG 33541, BdU memo to Kommando der Marinenstation der Ostsee Personal Bedarf, 13 November 1939.

64 Karl Dönitz, *Die U-Bootwaffe* (Berlin, 1939), 27.

65 NHB PG 32173, 1/Skl KTB Teil C Heft IV; Proposal to create 28th flotilla as expansion to training facilities.

66 NHB PG 29399, Microfiche various training programmes, 6; TNA CAB /66/32/38, Naval Situation, folio 147.

67 GC&CS, 'The German Navy – The U-boat Arm', 7, 92.

68 Mulligan, *Neither Sharks Nor Wolves*, 142.

69 *Lagevorträge* (München, 1972), The 'Phoney War' was referred to in German as 'der Scheinkrieg', 21.

70 NHB PG 32011, 1/Skl KTB Teil C Heft IV, BdU/Operationsabteilung an OKM/M, 'Ein Jahr U-Bootkriegsfuhrung', 24 August 1940.

71 *Official Account of the Battle of the Atlantic* (1946), 18; Stephen W Roskill, *The Navy at War* (Ware, 1998), 40.

72 NHB PG 30250, KTB entry for 23 October 1939.

73 Dönitz, *Memoirs*, 4.

74 R. Busch et al., *U-bootbau auf deutschen Werften* (Cuxhaven, 1994), 6–7.

75 *Oblt. (I)* Walter Lorch, cited in Martin Middlebrook, *Convoy* (1976), 59–60; Timothy Mulligan, *Lone Wolf* (Connecticut, 1993), 42–3; Peter Padfield, *Dönitz* (1984), 209.

76 NHB PG 32119, 1/Skl KTB Teil B Heft V, Januar–Juni 1943, 28 Mai 1943. 'Vortragsnotiz über eine notwendige vermehrte Rekrutenzuteilung für die Kriegsmarine'.

77 NHB NID 24/T65/45, Report on German Naval War Effort, Part IV: Mobilisation of Manpower, 146.

78 Topp, 'Manning and Training the U-boat Fleet', 216; Mulligan, *Neither Sharks Nor Wolves*, 123; Alfred Price, *Aircraft versus Submarine* (Barnsley, 2004), 153.

79 NHB PG 10058, Großadmiral Dönitz statement on personnel.

80 William Glover, 'Manning and Training Allied Navies', in *The Battle of the Atlantic 1939–1945* (1994), 188–213, 192.

81 Arnold Hague, *The Allied Convoy System 1939–1945* (2000), 69.

82 Thomas A. Adams, 'The Control of British Merchant Shipping', in *The Battle of the Atlantic 1939–1945*, 158–78, 169.

83 NHB PG 30902, FdU KTB entry dated 2 October 1939.

84 Mulligan, *Neither Sharks Nor Wolves*, 74.

85 Lohmann et al., *Die deutsche Kriegsmarine 1939–1945*, 2 (74), 5. FdU Ausbildung (Leader U-boat Training) March 1943 until end of war.

86 NHB PG 29399, Excerpt from U-boat training log.

87 After Dönitz became ObdM in 1943 he claimed the designator 2/Skl, BdU.op (Unterseebootsführungsabteilung) and made the former 2/Skl (MND) into 3/Skl.

88 Eberhard Rößler, 'Die deutsche U-bootausbildung und ihre Vorbereitung 1925–1945', *Marine Rundschau*, 68 (8) (1971), 453–66, 462.

89 TNA HW 18/55, German Naval Organization–Naval Section ZIP/NS dated 26/12/1944, 5.

90 TNA HW 18/200, Short courses in theory and tactics would be given ashore while iced up, 21.

91 Topp, 'Manning and Training the U-boat Fleet', 214.

92 W. P. Cunningham et al., 'Of Radar and Operations Research', *Operations Research*, 32 (4) (July–August 1984), 958–67, 963; Mulligan, *Neither Sharks Nor Wolves*, 144.

93 Mulligan, *Neither Sharks Nor Wolves*, 14.

94 Kapitän Herbert Wilde, 'UAS, die Unterseebootabwehrschule 1933–1945', 17.

95 Training and operational reports are discussed in chapters under 'Operational Research'.

6

Escort Training to Meet the Requirements of Grey Water Strategy

This chapter reviews the setting up of British ASW training, working-up and what was perhaps one of the most important functions in the RN from the point of view of the defeat of the U-boat menace in the North Atlantic, the ASW tactical training given to escorts for the many types of surface vessel employed.

Developments in ASW training, 1930–43

ASW training was one of the major determinants of success in the Battle of the Atlantic. A great majority of officers and ratings were 'Hostilities Only', reservists, or RNVR, and many with little if any seagoing experience. Many of the men, particularly Canadian, had never seen the sea. The *Wehrmacht*, too, depended heavily on its reserve officers but the U-boat arm preference was for career officers over reservists.[1]

In the late 1930s it was estimated that 357 escort vessels (200 of which would be trawlers taken up after mobilization) would be required. In the event this figure turned out to be but a small fraction of the total number of ships employed on North Atlantic convoy escort duty.[2] Notwithstanding a lack of suitable vessels in which to deploy them a shortfall in trained Submarine Detection ratings (S/D) was forecast. In a memorandum to the Director of the Tactical Division (D of TD), on 24 October 1936, the Captain A/S *Osprey* stated that the only way that he could see an improvement by 1940 was to annually increase the number of A/S courses given.[3] Similarly, in a memorandum on anti-submarine policy dated 31 March 1937, he predicted that some 1,337 S/D ratings were thought to be necessary after mobilization.[4] By November 1938 numbers had again improved and nearly double this number was available in 1939, but it still proved abysmally inadequate.[5]

At the start of the war ASW began to be taken more seriously (where it had been considered to be a 'Cinderella' service, with little prospect of advancement)[6] and progress was made through the early diffusion of what had been learnt in this field. Nonetheless the situation regarding the degree of tactical training given over the past year was of concern. Commitments overseas contributed to a diminution in the number of tactical exercises carried out and thus the standard attained was not high.[7] In the years leading up to the war, from 1931–9, exercises carried out in submarine detection rates fluctuated but overall detection rates appeared to have improved with levels of around 70 per cent claimed.[8] But it should be remembered that approximate areas occupied by British submarines were known in advance, and thus operators were expecting to make contact. In a real-life scenario such luxury would not be forthcoming.[9] In 1939 the number of exercises fell further, due to war conditions, but the level of acquisition rates rose to around 80 per cent claimed at around 1,500 yards; a marginal improvement.[10] It was less than perfect but a doctrine was established which embraced a wide range of Destroyer attacks, from individual units, to massed attacks by several flotillas.[11]

The interwar RN had been ill-placed to develop a body of ASW doctrine, mainly because it had very few officers from whom to draw for the development of its professional knowledge.[12] However, that improved over time and by early 1940 the Admiralty decided that more needed to be done to collectively improve techniques. It was decided that a base should be set up to train whole ships' crews in the latest practice in ASW, provide refresher courses and a common doctrine. The original site chosen was (ironically) Lorient as a joint RN/FN (French Navy) base, but little had been achieved by the time of the fall of France – except for the appointment of Vice Admiral (retired) Gilbert Stephenson with the rank of Commodore. Stephenson had a good First World War and interwar track record. In the First World War he had served in the Mediterranean, was engaged in ASW work and employed dealing with Reserve-manned small craft. From 1917–18 he was head of the Otranto Barrage operations against German and Austrian submarines and had some 230 small ships (trawlers and drifters) under his command. His knowledge of the subject was further consolidated during his interwar years spent as Director of the Anti-submarine Division at the Admiralty.[13]

HMS *Western Isles* Tobermory in Scotland was selected as the adjunct to *Osprey*.[14] Given the nature of this problem the first aspect of training considered here was that of manpower levels and branch needs.[15] How many men, and with what levels of qualifications, would be needed? Were the facilities and instructors in place to provide it? In what condition were the RN A/S establishments and planning mechanisms? Staff officers were assigned from each major specialization to cover specific ships and remained their 'tutors' for the duration of the work-up, and ensured consistency of doctrine.[16] This was followed soon after by a further development in January 1941 when the Anti-submarine School transferred from Portland to Dunoon, Argyllshire, in Scotland, primarily due to the invasion of France and the now close proximity of new German Air force bases.[17] Meanwhile, ASDIC development moved to Fairlie, Ayrshire.

Officer selection and training

Training for officers in A/S was first implemented through a fleet order and started in March 1923, the first qualifying course being completed by just five officers. This course lasted one-and-a-half academic terms and included instruction in mathematics, physics, applied electricity and mechanics as well as the more practical maintenance and operation of anti-submarine equipment.[18] The duties for officer instructors were laid down in the instructions, and covered the analysis of technical exercises to developments in tactics, reports and writing up manuals.[19] It also implied a duty of responsibility for others and their actions, as similarly noted under the German officer training section. During the Second World War the British War Office came to recognize the importance of developments in applied psychology when faced with the significant war-time expansion of selection, allocation and training for officer recruits; the German Navy started its development of psychological testing during the reconstitution of their armed forces after 1927.[20] In 1942 the War Office began using a more up-to-date and scientific method of selecting officers and called it the War Office Selection Board (WOSB);[21] but the Admiralty did not hold with new-fangled ideas. The Navy stuck to its traditional way of officer selection with the selection procedure spread over three days, allowing observation of the candidates in a variety of activities. For the RN, which in peacetime had been a relatively small regular force, the problems of selection and allocation of wartime officers were severe.[22] The Admiralty did make a change in 1944 but the Board only approved a limited trial in the autumn, and then a more extensive experiment period,[23] by which time the war was over.

The degree of importance which the Admiralty attached to A/S (Anti-submarine) Officer training may be surmised from the table (Table 6.1).

Table 6.1 Training of A/S Officers at Portland, 1935–8.

	1935	1936	1937	1938
Destroyer CO	13	15	14	
Destroyer 1st Lt.	15	21	9	
Destroyer Control Officer	19	47	59	
Submarine CO	10	15	5	
Submarine Officers	29	28	37	
A/S Long Course	8	6	10	1

Source: Portland Annual Reports for 1935–8.[24]

Apart from Destroyer Control Officers only Submarine Officers appear to have been the other beneficiaries. Given the size of the fleet it is hardly surprising that by the outbreak of war so few officers and ratings had any A/S experience at all: and all that from an Admiralty that professed to have the answer to combating the U-boat. Even if it were correct the above numbers were woefully short of trained personnel, perhaps a sign of overconfidence such as existed in parts of the German U-boat training programme. Fortunately for the Navy, by the outbreak of war, there were a number of trained and experienced A/S officers in critical posts who were able to provide expert advice to sea-going commanders. What seems surprising however is that there was only one specialist on the Naval Staff and none at all in the operational shore staff.[25]

For RNVR officers coming into the service at the outbreak of war training was not as rigid, but those with a degree of aptitude did receive A/S specialist training. An introductory 10-week course provided instruction in 'navigation (52 hours), pilotage (20 hours), gunnery (29 hours), seamanship (38 hours), field training (22 hours), general lectures (23 hours), signals (34 hours) and torpedo (13 hours).[26] After that most had to 'learn on the job'. RNVR Officers serving in Western Approaches – perhaps as few as 10 per cent of the *King Alfred* graduates – then went on to HMS *Osprey* for an anti-submarine course.[27] Around 48,000 served during the war, some went on to command Destroyers and submarines.[28]

A/S ratings training

The 'ratings' organization was known as the submarine detector branch (SD), with the first set of qualified ratings appearing in 1920. Qualified ratings would become a Submarine Detector 2nd Class, or S/D 2nd Class, and would be able to operate ASDIC equipment. Intake into this division mainly came from the seamen's branch and the general rule was that any intelligent man with good hearing could be trained, but non-liability to seasickness was considered to be an additional attribute.[29] As with any selection procedure not everyone could be accepted. Only those with a certain degree of aptitude were passed out. Unsuccessful ratings were normally returned to their ship, if feasible – or drafted into others.

In 1938 SD courses for RNR (Royal Naval Reserve) personnel lasted just 14 days. If one compares the training given to naval reservists compared to 39 days available to regular servicemen respectively, for the same qualification, it is not hard to comprehend the limitations inherent in the reservists.[30] Compared to the length of time spent by the trainees in detection work in the U-boat arm, the time taken was similar, ten weeks, roughly the time spent training by regular service personnel. By 1939 the anti-submarine branch consisted of 757 S/D ratings, 375 Higher Submarine Detector rates and 73 Submarine Detector Instructors. By 1945 the SDIs had nearly tripled in number, to 204; the HSDs had quadrupled, to 1,492; and the S/D rates had multiplied nearly eight times, to 5,911.[31]

Planning for war

A fundamental question that arose concerning the A/S branch was how to prepare for A/S requirements in time of war. In the event of war the Admiralty's firm conviction was that the best means of defence is attack and as early as the winter of 1932–33 a report on anti-submarine measures had been written in which it was stated that an

> early success against enemy U-boats is likely to militate heavily against the value of his subsequent operations. It is, therefore, of great importance that organization and training should be such as will allow of the full development of offensive A/S measures immediately on the outbreak of war.[32]

In the last war, up to 1917, approximately half the successful U-boat attacks on merchant ships were made on the surface at night and in the latter part of 1918 that figure rose to two-thirds, and was clearly a most important tactic in need of a countermeasure. However, in the 1930s when plans for a possible war were being prepared, it is claimed that some of the lessons of the last war were ignored. 'Even the publication in 1939 of a book by Dönitz in which he asserted that night attack on the surface by U-boats was the most effective method, aroused no interest or action.'[33] The book in question went into some detail about the U-boat arm and its tactics.[34] And a statement by Gardner, too, appears to fly in the face of actual pre-war exercises. He contends that when U-boats attacked 'this was to be carried out at night with the hull awash, negating the effect of ASDIC-fitted escorts.'[35] Both statements, by Gretton and Gardner, have little validity since they ignore the fact that the RN had already practiced night attacks by submarines, using their own. Franklin points out that an April 1939 report provides clear evidence that in two trials against submarines detection ranges were found to be between 1,000 and 2,500 yards, and that they had been detected on ASDIC long before they had been sighted.[36] If, as an expert, Franklin is correct, it is highly unlikely that many U-boats could have approached the convoy so closely, unless they were extremely lucky. First because the echo obtainable from a U-boat awash, and not fully on the surface, would have returned an echo, unless the sea conditions had thermal layers near the surface – in which case conditions would have been more difficult, but not necessarily impossible. Secondly, since a shadowing vessel kept in regular contact with others escorts it would certainly have been aware of a U-boat approximate location by HF/DF (High Frequency [Radio] Direction Finding) means, and would have been expecting them. By the period in question HF/DF was in wide use for tracking enemy transmissions. Further support to the argument that the RN had not forgotten some of the important experience gained in the last war came from Marder who stated that, interwar, 'It may rightly be claimed that British naval successes in the Second War can be attributed in part to these studies and exercises.'[37] Maiolo too is of a similar opinion.[38] These revelations are most significant in that it does appear to demonstrate that the RN had indeed been working on such problems prior to the war, a point that seems to have been widely overlooked by historians – even Gretton and Gardner.

The RN was a great believer in learning on the hoof so, in theory, provided sufficient men were already indoctrinated into the use and application of the equipment it should only require that ships and equipment be immediately available. Even so, the main problem was that ASDIC equipment was technically more advanced than most ratings could be taught without ongoing training. In order to competently operate the equipment effectively a great deal of practice was required before they could develop an intuitive 'feel' for the device. In such circumstances efficient operators could not be trained overnight. In the event of war older, more developed, branches of the service could call up retired officers and ratings, or those who had left the service prior to retirement, to provide a ready pool of expertise in wartime; indeed that is exactly what was done in 1939. But in 1939 neither the ASDIC equipment nor the SD branch had been in existence long enough to develop such long-standing skills. This made the probability of passing on valuable feedback acquired through experience initially very slim.

Working up

In the early days, before A/S training was expanded to other bases in Scotland and Northern Ireland, the training of ships' teams at Portland appears to have been shared between the tactical and instructional departments. The RN even installed mobile Attack Teachers in converted buses so that they could be used by smaller bases.[39] Early A/S training for the RAF was also accommodated at Portland, even before coming under RN operational control in 1941.[40] Practice was done in the ships of 1 AS (Anti-submarine Squadron), and reading their logs one finds weeks upon weeks of repetitive training exercises. Every weekday the ships put to sea to conduct A/S practice in the waters around the Portland peninsula, before returning later in the day to base. Regrettably, after 1939 all attempts made to obtain real submarines to work with in the sea-going phase were unsuccessful, although they had been promised in 1938.[41] Instead, practicing ships had to make do with a cheap alternative by using surface ships as targets instead of submarines, as was German practice noted in the last chapter. As may well be imagined this did not work well because the return signal given by the hull of a surface ship was much weaker than that given by a submerged submarine, due to its reduced draught; even so it was known that detection of surface vessels by ASDIC was a possibility.[42] A note of this problem at *Osprey* was pointed out in correspondence between the First Sea Lord and Admiral Cunningham stating that the essential problem facing simulated exercises was that of differentiating between submarine and non-submarine ASDIC echoes.

> It is very much harder to distinguish between two notes of the same pitch played by different instruments, than to appreciate that a note is being struck.[43]

Ships of both 1 AS and the fleets went to Portland for 'working-up' during which the whole ship's team was taken through a series of exercises designed to develop their anti-submarine capabilities. No less than 29 standard exercises were prescribed that ranged in complexity from the A/S operator maintaining contact with a passing submarine on exercise while the school ship was stationary, to conducting convoy defence and area search patrol.[44] The exercises were, nevertheless, quite dated (1928) but many were brought up-to-date as the war evolved and equipment improved.[45] Some of the more interesting exercises undertaken after ships had proved competent in a number of 'set piece' hunting and screening exercises were:

1. Screening and counter-attack. Ships formed a screen around a notional main body and were attacked by a submarine. The ship which detected the submarine counter attacked and was then joined by one other ship from the screen to hunt the submarine and press home deliberate attacks. The submarine was allowed complete freedom of movement.
2. Search for a submarine sighted by A/S vessels. The submarine positioned itself on the surface as if conducting a transit. When the surface vessels sighted it they flashed lights to simulate gunfire, the submarine dived and a hunt was initiated.
3. Convoy exercise. Exercise in air and sea co-operation to protect convoy and prosecute U-boats detected while attempting to attack.
4. Shipping patrol exercise. Air/sea striking force defending shipping: in the vicinity of a notional base.[46]

However, not all newly appointed ship captains, or SOEs (Senior Officer Escorts), underwent training. They had to rely on the experience of others to help them through, gaining their own hands-on experience.[47]

The depth charge and attack training

At the start of the First World War there was no ASW technique to speak of, and no weapons designed specifically to attack U-boats existed in the naval arsenal, so one cannot speak of early training in this field. The first line of defence was passive, in the form of mine barrages.[48] The depth charge came much later in the war.

Initially the only other available A/S weapon was the deck gun. But loading and training guns was a notoriously slow process and shells, if a hit was achieved, could sometimes bounce off the round bilge of the U-boat.[49] Weapons was an area in great need of overhaul and ship-borne radar had still to be fully developed.

Depth charges, or DCs, were amazingly simple in design and not much different from those that had first been proposed as early as 1911, but not introduced until January 1917; and then only two per ship and no thrower.[50] In the Second World War the main anti-submarine weapon in use on surface vessels remained the 400-lb depth-charge with its 290-lb charge of amatol. To launch them required knowledge of their use. Initially they were rolled off the stern of the attacking vessel and made to explode when they reached a pre-set depth but later they were also fired off in patterns using a depth-charge thrower, able to lay charges with some lateral displacement.[51] DCs could be set to detonate at depths of between 50 and 500 feet, and some included several charges of a heavier type which sank more quickly. Charges were at first used in patterns of five, three dropped in line from the racks and one ejected from each thrower to produce a diamond-shaped pattern.[52] The fitting of two throwers on each beam of the ship, and the introduction of a 'heavy charge (iron weights added) produced a more rapid rate of sinking. Thus through selective application of light and heavy charges using different depth settings, and two patterns of ten charges, it was possible to straddle a U-boat.[53] A special thrower, the Mk V was developed for the heavy charge. Their explosions were synchronized with that of the shallower-set charges and thus gave greater coverage in depth. While the depth charge may be simple in design shock waves are complex, involving factors such as the speed of the explosion and the density of the medium, all playing a part.[54] Officers' and ratings' training in depth-charge attacks included some basic instruction on the device itself and it is notable that the most successful commanders insisted in spending considerable time when in harbour practicing the basic tasks, such as reloading depth-charge throwers.[55] Escort groups based in Liverpool were known to make use of the facilities there to brush up on techniques. Later, much of the depth-charge training was given in Londonderry.[56]

During the tactical training period the ship's captain and control officer could be instructed in the most appropriate depth settings and firing patterns under different conditions. These exercises were the result of studied reports of depth-charge attacks carried out by escorts, and represented a valuable exchange of localized 'OR', to be discussed in a separate chapter. The benefit of plenty of such practice loadings made it a little less difficult to load at night in a ship rolling and heaving while covered in spray, if not green seas. From time to time the Admiralty also issued updates on types and applications in CAFOs (Confidential Admiralty Fleet Orders).[57]

Western Approaches tactical unit

Convoy escort groups came under the jurisdiction of the WA. When the Command transferred from Plymouth to Liverpool in February 1941, the new C-in-C Admiral Noble was apparently not aware that something was missing from the Liverpool training organization, something needed in addition to the already existing programme – a 'Tactical Unit'.[58] All aspects of ASW at the beginning of the war came under ACNS (T) and by December 1942 the position was renamed ACNS (UT (U-boats and Trade)) to reflect responsibilities for trade and ASW, only to finally come under ACNS (W). The influence of ACNS (UT) in matters related to technical advances and associated weapons in U-boat warfare was of paramount importance.[59] However, the essential doctrine for combating the U-boats could not be thought through by individuals involved in the daily stress and fatigue of dealing with convoy matters. 'That could only be done by people dedicated to the task.'[60] To assist ACNS (UT) Vice Admiral C. V. Usborne was appointed as an Additional Naval Assistant. He came out of retirement in 1941 to become Naval Adviser to the First Sea Lord on ASW, and an aide to Churchill.[61] His service career was as a gunnery officer and lecturer on tactics, but in the early 1930s became Director of Naval Intelligence.[62]

In December 1941, following a visit to WA Liverpool, he came up with the idea of an addition to the training organization, a tactical table for use in ASW problems. When Usborne reported back to Churchill he urged the formation at Liverpool of a tactical unit in order to evolve anti-U-boat tactics and to train escort commanders. The man he had in mind to set up this new group was Gilbert Roberts, an officer on the retired list, but now re-instated.[63] During the first week of 1942 Commander Roberts was informed that the 2nd Sea Lord, Sir Charles Little, urgently wanted to see him in London; he was to be briefed for a new job. At the Admiralty Sir Charles was joined by Admiral Usborne. Their discussions and briefings were very illuminating. It was made clear that unless something was done to sway the Battle of the Atlantic in the Allies favour the war would be lost simply because vital food and war supplies were not surviving the Atlantic crossing; that ships were being sunk far faster than replacements could be built; that thousands of trained seamen were being lost – in short the survival of Britain and her Allies was in doubt. Following the meeting Usborne took Roberts to see the Prime Minister. 'Find out what is happening in the Atlantic, find ways of getting the convoys through and sink the U-boats', Churchill is reported to have said.[64] Churchill was extremely anxious about the Atlantic situation and several issues worried him. His conversation with Roberts covered some of these worries; such as whether the ASDIC was any good;[65] what do the escorts do when their convoy is attacked and how effective was the depth charge?[66] Here is a case of the Prime Minister getting involved in military situations in a way similar to that of Hitler, except that he did use a degree of delegation to get at the facts. Hitler did not extend the same degree of involvement to his senior officers and had no advisers to provide input on naval matters.[67]

Roberts reported for duty in February 1942[68] and found that Admiral Noble was indifferent to the idea of setting up yet another training organization; indeed his initial enthusiasm was, at best, lukewarm. The appointment was soon accepted by C-in-C Western Approaches, but there were some objections in the Admiralty Directorate of ASW, then Captain G. E. Creasy. Creasy was singularly critical of Usborne's proposition, but reluctantly decided to give it a trial period. Creasy, later made up to Flag Officer submarines, became a convert and was responsible for many of the field trials connected with high underwater speed (HUS) U-boats.[69]

The use of a tactical table was not a novel idea since Roberts was already familiar with its use. Roberts had originally been trained as a gunnery officer and his considered tactical floor was modelled closely on a similar layout that he had worked with at HMS *Excellent,* the RN gunnery school at Whale Island where he had learnt his trade.[70] In his early work with the 'Tactical Unit' at 'Whaley' (Whale Island) Roberts frequently mentioned commerce warfare to the senior staff officers there but, as the new boy, was not listened to.[71] Already in 1935 there were rumblings of war in Europe yet the tactical courses being set were lectures, problems and tactical games with the British Battle Fleet, using as a model the Battle of Jutland. U-boats were rarely ever considered, let alone convoys, or attacks on them by sea or air. At this point the Admiralty seems not to have connected Hitler's rise to power in Europe with the possibility of another *guerre de course* (commerce warfare), but with nearly double the number of U-boats to contend with.[72] When discussing fleet action tactics with 'Carriers' Roberts suggested studying 'actions with dissimilar forces', 'inshore operations', 'night fighting' and 'shadowing' – a foretaste of what Roberts would ultimately set up in Liverpool in the fight against U-boats.[73] The uniqueness lay in the fact that it represented the first real 'Operational A/S Analysis' facility that the RN had;[74] indeed it was to be copied by the USN (United States Navy).[75] Later other tactical tables were set up in Londonderry and Greenwich.

Prior to WATU being in operation each SOE had devised his own tactics and some were noticeably similar, all being based on common experience and training, but no common tactical doctrine. Nevertheless these individual tactics were each known by a code name devised by the originator and this caused confusion within mixed escorts. So it was a necessary step to standardize them.[76] To achieve this objective Roberts knew that it was essential to work with the different commanders so he could reach a consensus on the tactics and terminology that could be used. He also needed a great deal of front-line feedback if he was to advance the state of anti U-boat tactics; feedback from users of the systems became an essential part of the course,[77] and instill a commonality of purpose.

One of the early tasks that Roberts undertook with a returning escort commander was an analysis of convoys such as HG76, which had been escorted by Portland trained ASW Captain 'Johnny' Walker RN, in charge of the 36th escort group. Convoy HG 76 left from Gibraltar for Britain on 14 December 1941, seven days after the attack on Pearl Harbour, and was so configured that the ships sailed in five columns, totalling 32 ships. In the early hours of 19 December, U-574 sighted one of the escorts, HMS *Stanley*, while she was turning to make an attack. Soon after *Stanley* was hit by torpedo and sank. As this action got under way Walker signalled his team to commence a pre-arranged search plan known as 'Buttercup'.[78] In this operation the escorts turned as one away from the convoy firing star shell for 20 minutes, forcing U-534 to dive. HMS *Stork* picked up an echo on ASDIC.[79] Walker maintained his contact and then used a ten-charge pattern of DCs, forcing the U-boat to the surface. After initial ineffective gunfire *Stork* advanced and rammed the U-boat (a practice frowned upon by the Admiralty – for obvious reasons).[80] *Stork* continued around the stricken U-boat and followed up with a shallow depth charge attack. Five of U-534 survived and were brought aboard along with 25 members of the *Stanley* crew.

At WATU, Roberts considered the case related to him from all the angles he could think of. He was now trying to think like a U-boat captain who had torpedoed a merchantman and was in the middle of a convoy. How would he best make his escape? Dive deeper of course – but where to, at submerged speed? The U-boat captain would know that he could not out-run an escort if detected by ASDIC, so he would probably go deep and shut down; let the convoy pass over him and 'KEEP SILENT'.[81] Roberts considered, not just the above event, but all battles fought by Walker using his 'Operation Buttercup' and in the calm of simulation Roberts realized that on occasion U-boats were firing their torpedoes from *inside* the convoy; but Walker confirmed had imagined that the U-boat must be a mile or so *outside* the perimeter of the convoy ships.[82] The discussions with Walker continued and more lessons were learned, all proving the value of feedback which may be considered to be local 'operational' data; and useful in 'OR'.[83] A check and double check on calculations was made in the tactical school using the U-boat model that the staff had used on the convoy. His U-boat model emerged behind the convoy and theoretically made off to safety. The counter measure seemed logically simple. If a U-boat managed to get inside the convoy and loose off a torpedo with effect, on a word of command the escorts, with the exception of the one leading the convoy, would turn at full speed and line up abreast at the rear of the convoy a couple of miles or so astern and then begin an ASDIC sweep forwards. 'The escorts' speed would be reduced to that of the convoy and, like a giant "trawl" behind a fishing vessel, "sweep" everything in front into the "trawl" and they would have the U-boat.' It felt right. 'The method of counter attacking U-boats operating *inside* the convoy area was for the escorts to "double" back as fast as possible, past the "stricken" vessel and return into the convoy columns carrying out a "search" for the U-boat.'[84]

After providing an explanation of his findings Roberts suggested that the counter-attack manoeuvre be called 'Raspberry', in deference to Jean Laidlaw the Wren who had done all the statistics – she had named it as a 'Raspberry' to Hitler. Noble who was at first frosty in his approach to Roberts at the outset informed him that:

> I am signalling the Admiralty that the first investigations of your tactical school show a cardinal error in our anti-submarine thinking and that a new immediate and concentrated counter-attack would be signalled to the fleet in twenty-four hours.[85]

Shortly after Noble's statement Roberts was made up to Captain.[86]

Robert's early experience of receiving feedback from the front was such a success that he introduced tests into the training regime in order to determine what had been learnt; they became standard practice after training sessions, and progress towards a common tactical doctrine was made.[87] What had been learnt was a good example of how an experienced commander might pass on sufficient information that allowed the 'trainer' to reach a positive conclusion to a tactical training session. The reader will also note the similar cross exchange of views and experience in the training of the adversaries.

The effect of having a strengthened escort group with new anti-submarine offensive tactics was not lost on Dönitz who wrote in his log of the 23 December 1941.

> I consider it necessary to investigate whether the operations ordered by the Naval War Staff, by U-boats West of Gibraltar are still appropriate.[88]

He also noted the consequences suffered by the U-boats during the attacks on HG 76.

In an entry of the same date he uncharacteristically wrote:

Actually, I am not in agreement with attacking HG convoys as they are strongly escorted and the ships are small. They have been attacked before only when U-boats had been operating against a South-bound convoy or were coming out of the South Atlantic, and were compelled to be in the Gibraltar area.[89]

In essence he acknowledged how well the convoy escorts had performed, while the U-boats had fared badly in this exchange.

Finally, to sum up this brief review of tactics, Roberts shortly followed the move up by devising a search plan for a submerged U-boat which had been sighted and was believed to be shadowing a convoy. This plan he named a 'Beta Search', which also worked well. The 'Beta Search' was then tried at sea and on one occasion the hunted U-boat was sunk with the first depth charge pattern.[90]

An analysis of this nature has been favourably compared to the 'OR' work done in Coastal Command on air search patterns, giving a new level of sophistication to the evolution of A/S tactical doctrine.[91] After the introduction of the tactical table and subsequent analyses A/S tactics improved dramatically, and proved both decisive and flexible.[92] The British had been quite innovative in their approach to A/S tactics, involving people with solid past experience to implement solutions, and had learnt their lessons well. *BdU* Command and the U-boat schools had no such equivalent organization and this was later confirmed by Admiral Godt, who had no idea that the British were using such a technique.[93]

Conclusions

Britain trained its surface fleet men to defend convoys, initially lacking sound tactics, but was then later able to adopt a more offensive stance with better tactical methods, often with the help of a support group. ASW Training Policy had to be developed on the hoof to overcome a stagnant operation, because the RN had been in a state of flux since the end of the First World War. In the early stages of the Second World War it appeared that little had changed over decades and beyond. Indeed two experts in this field opined that the RN had become too complacent about ASDIC as a sea-war winning weapon.[94] The sets were over-rated, though they did improve as, with experience, did their operators.[95]

In many respects, in spite of a frugal Admiralty ASW training steadily improved throughout the war and grew when the Anti-submarine School transferred from Portland to Dunoon; and used Tobermory, under Stephenson, as a 'Working-up' base. Ever the strict disciplinarian that Stephenson was, the time allowed for an escort to attain an acceptable battle-ready standard of efficiency was set to a maximum of three weeks, 35 hours of which had to be live ASW training.[96] The initial weakness of the WA command lay in a poor understanding of tactics and that was not redressed until late 1942 when it set up a 'Tactical' Unit.

At WATU working-up training continued and later involved Coastal Command participation and the newly introduced CVEs and MACs, in a co-ordinated approach to ASW, followed up with refresher courses. Its strength came from the development of tactical exercises introduced by the WATU technical director Commander Gilbert Roberts, who led by 'forward thinking'. Roberts developed a 'feedback' system in which he was able to translate front-line experiences into tactical solutions. The main lessons learned by the RN revolved around improved tactical solutions and getting fast reaction times to counter the new U-boat threats by means of a hands-on approach from the Tactical Unit, and direct feedback of those at the front. They were lessons they would never forget; they even continued with tactical training effort after they had returned to port.

Notes

1   Karl Dönitz, *Die U-Bootwaffe* (Berlin, 1939), 27.
2   William Glover, 'Manning and Training Allied Navies' in *The Battle of the Atlantic 1939–1945* (1994), 189.
3   TNA ADM 116/3603, Memo 53/6/D.3877, dated 24 October 1936 to the D of TD.
4   TNA ADM 1/12140, 'Memorandum on Anti-submarine Policy Regarding the Use of ASDICS', TD1/38, anticipated 1940 mobilization active service S/D rating estimate by Director of Tactical Division, 31 March 1937, 5.
5   TNA ADM 1/10092, A/S Training, Note by D of TD, 24 November 1938 in Strategy and Tactics (82).
6   D. A. Raynor, *Escort* (1955), 78–80.
7   TNA ADM 186/551, Progress in Torpedo, Mining and Anti-Submarine Warfare 1938, 34.
8   TNA ADM 186/551, Progress in Torpedo, Mining and Anti-Submarine Warfare 1938, Plate 1.
9   TNA ADM 116/3872, Summer Cruise Exercise 1934; TNA ADM 186/499, 'Instructions for Submarine Operations' 1933–6; TNA CAB 53/28, COS 488 (JP) Joint Planning Committee Memorandum, 2 July 1936.

10 TNA ADM 239/141, Progress in Torpedo, Mining and Anti-Submarine Warfare 1939, p, 40.

11 TNA ADM 186/461, Progress in Torpedo, Mining and Anti-Submarine Warfare, 1928; ADM 186/522, Progress in Torpedo, Mining and Anti-Submarine Warfare 1935; ADM 239/261, Fighting Instructions, Sections 286 and 322.

12 H. P. Wilmott, 'The Organizations', in *The Battle of the Atlantic 1939–1945* (1994), 189.

13 TNA ADM 239/248, 'Anti-submarine Warfare – Volume IV – A/S Training', 14; Richard Baker, *The Terror of Tobermory* (1972), 68.

14 James Goldrick, 'Work-up', in *The Battle of the Atlantic 1939–1945* (1994), 220–39, 232.

15 TNA ADM 239/248, 'Anti-submarine Warfare', Volume IV – A/S Training, Appendix 1, Anti-submarine warfare: Admiralty, and Ministry of Defence, Navy Department: Confidential Reference Books (CB 3212D) Technical Staff Monographs 1939–45, 14. This was part of the Anglo-French naval agreement referred to earlier.

16 Goldrick, 'Work-up', 222.

17 TNA ADM 239/248, 'Anti-submarine Warfare – Volume IV – A/S Training', Dispersal of A/S Establishments, 1.

18 George Franklin, *Britain's Anti-Submarine Capability 1919–1939* (2003), 35.

19 TNA ADM 116/2410, 'Anti-submarine Depot at Portland', 1924–8.

20 B. S. Morris, 'Officer Selection in the British Army 1942–1945', *Occupational Psychology*, XXIII, 4, 219–34; in April 1942 the War office introduced the WOSB's, loosely modelled on the German system.

21 K. E. Gardener, 'Selection, Training and Career Development of Naval Officers: A Long-Term Follow-up, Using Multivariate Techniques', 6.

22 TNA ADM 199/2057/2060: CB 04050 /40 and/43, CAFO. Admiralty Fleet Orders No. 276/1940 and 1163/1943 for selection of officers based on a superior level of education.

23 S. A. S., 'Officer Selection 1945', *The Naval Review,* 78 (3) (July 1990), 259–60.

24 TNA ADM 186/519, 527, 536, 547, 'Personnel Training', Portland Annual Reports for 1935–8.

25 Franklin, *Britain's Anti-Submarine Capability 1919–1939*, 41.

26 Glover, 'Manning and Training Allied Navies', 194.

27 Ibid., 209.

28 Stephen Roskill, *The Navy at War 1939–1945* (Ware, 1998), 21.

29 TNA ADM 1/12140, Naval Training (54): Anti-submarine policy, training of anti-submarine personnel, operations, etc., A/S Policy 1938.

30 Franklin, *Britain's Anti-Submarine Capability 1919–1939*, 44.

31 TNA ADM 239/248 (CB 3212D), Anti-submarine warfare, Volume IV – A/S Training, Appendix 1, Anti-submarine warfare: Admiralty, and Ministry of

Defence, Navy Department: Confidential Reference Books Technical Staff Monographs 1939–1945 Date: 1950.

32 TNA ADM 186/500 (CB 3002/32), Progress in Torpedo, Mining, Anti-Submarine Measures, and Chemical Warfare Defence 1932, 34.

33 Vice Admiral P. Gretton, 'Why Don't We Learn from History?', *The Naval Review*, 46 (January 1958), 13–25, 21.

34 Karl Dönitz, *Die U-Bootwaffe* (Berlin, 1939).

35 W. J. R. Gardner, 'The Battle of the Atlantic, 1941 – The First Turning Point?', in *Sea Power* (Ilford, 1994), 109–23, 114.

36 George Franklin, 'The Origins of the Royal Navy's Vulnerability to Surfaced Night U-boat Attack 1939–40', *The Mariner's Mirror*, 90 (1) (February 2004), 73–84, 78; Nicolas Rodger, 'The Royal Navy in the Era of the World Wars: Was it Fit for Purpose?', *The Mariner's Mirror*, 97 (1) (February 2011), 272–84, 281.

37 Arthur Marder, 'The Influence of History on Sea Power: The Royal Navy and the Lessons of 1914–1918', *Pacific Historical Review*, 41 (4) (November 1972), 413–43, 417.

38 Joseph A. Maiolo, *The Royal Navy and Nazi Germany 1933–39* (1998), 120.

39 Corelli Barnett, *Engage the Enemy More Closely* (1991), 589.

40 TNA ADM 1/12141, ARMAMENTS (11): Memorandum on anti-submarine striking forces,Minute DNAD (Director of Naval Air Defence), 15 May 1939.

41 TNA ADM 1/10092, 'Anti-submarine Training 1939', report on conference on trainingCrews of Auxiliary A/S & M/S Trawlers, 15 December 1938.

42 TNA ADM 1/9942, 'Anti-submarine Exercises in Mediterranean', report dated 18 April 1939.

43 TNA ADM 205/3, 'Anti-submarine Training', note provided by Admiral Pound, First Sea Lord to Admiral A. B. Cunningham, Commander-in-Chief, Mediterranean in June 1939.

44 Franklin, *Britain's Anti-Submarine Capability 1919–1939*, 50.

45 TNA ADM 116/2410, 'Anti-submarine Depot, Portland', Admiralty: Record Office: 1924–8.

46 TNA ADM 186/140, CB 1868/1931, 'Anti-submarine Practice Memoranda'.

47 Michael Whitby, 'The Strain of the Bridge: The Second World War Diaries of Commander A. F. C. Layard, DSO, DSC, RN', in *The Face of Naval Battle*, by John Reeve et al. (Crows Nest NSW, 2003), 200–18, 205–8.

48 Robert Stern, *Battle Beneath the Waves* (1999), 64.

49 TNA ADM 239/298, 'Conduct of Anti-U-boat Operations – Shelling U-boats'.

50 David K. Brown, 'Atlantic Escorts 1939–45', in *The Battle of the Atlantic 1939–1945* (1994), 452–75, 460.

51 TNA ADM 189/175, 'Technical History of Anti-submarine Weapons, Depth Charge Throwers'.

52 TNA ADM 186/140, 'Torpedo and Anti-Submarine School, Depth Charge Patterns'.

53 Arnold Hague, *The Allied Convoy System 1939–1945* (2000), 65.

54 Stern, *Battle beneath the Waves*, 66; *Official Account of the 'Battle of the Atlantic* (1946), 16.

55 Brown, *Atlantic Escorts*, 60.

56 TNA ADM 239/248, 'Anti-submarine Warfare Volume IV – A/S Training', 18.

57 TNA ADM 199/2060: CB 04050/43 (1) Monthly Anti-submarine reports, Section 6, 33; TNA ADM 199/2061: CB 04050/44 (2), Monthly Anti-submarine reports, Section 8, 26.

58 TNA ADM 239/248, 'Dispersal of A/S Establishments', 1.

59 TNA ADM 1/10463, ADMIRALTY (5): Assistant Chiefs of Naval Staff: Redistribution of responsibilities.

60 Glover, 'Manning and Training Allied Navies', 203.

61 Mark Williams, *Captain Gilbert Roberts R.N.* (1979), 85.

62 TNA ADM 205/21, Reports to First Sea Lord by members of the Board of Naval Staff, January–December 1942.

63 Goldrick, 'Work-up', 227.

64 Williams, *Captain Gilbert Roberts R.N.*, 86.

65 TNA ADM 205/13, 'Churchill to First Lord and First Sea Lord', 14 November 1941.

66 Williams, *Captain Gilbert Roberts R.N.,* 86.

67 See Chapter 1, 'Naval Problems and Hitler's Style of Leadership'.

68 TNA ADM 1/17557, 'Western Approaches Tactical Unit, Annual Report 1944', 1.

69 E. Terrell, *Admiralty Brief* (1958), 149–50.

70 Glover, 'Manning and Training Allied Navies', 202.

71 Williams, *Captain Gilbert Roberts R.N.*, 71.

72 F. Barley et al., *The Defeat of the Enemy Attack on Shipping 1939–1945*, 137 (Aldershot, 1997), Plan 1, Plan 7.

73 TNA ADM 1/17557, 'Western Approaches Tactical Unit, Annual Report 1944', 2.

74 TNA ADM 239/248, 'WATU ASW Training', 19.

75 It was noted earlier that the German U-boat Command was at a severe disadvantage by not having anything remotely similar.

76 Hague, *The Allied Convoy System 1939–1945*, 58.

77 TNA ADM 239/248, 'WATU ASW Training', 19.

78 NHB PG 30301, BdU KTB entry for 18 December 1941, reporting contact with HG 76. The entry of the 19 December concludes that U-574 must have been lost.

79 Williams, *Captain Gilbert Roberts R.N.*, 87.

80 Author's emphasis.

81 Williams, *Captain Gilbert Roberts R.N.*, 93.

82 Glover, 'Manning and Training Allied Navies', 202.

83 TNA ADM 199/2059: CB 04050/42 (11) 1942, Yearly Review of Monthly Anti-submarine Report.

84 Williams, *Captain Gilbert Roberts R.N.,* 93.

85 Ibid., 95.

86 Ibid.

87 TNA ADM 239/248, ASAT's, 'Anti-submarine Attack Tests', 18.

88 NHB PG 30301, BdU KTB entry 23 December, 1941.

89 Ibid.

90 David Owen, *Anti-Submarine Warfare* (Barnsley, 2007), 132.

91 TNA ADM 199/1336, SC/HX convoys: Reports, 1943–1944, *Duncan* 'Mamba Searches', 3 [f. 12].

92 Rodger, 'The Royal Navy in the Era of the World Wars', 281.

93 TNA ADM 1/17561, Captain G. H. Roberts, 30 May 1945, Interview with Admiral Godt.

94 Willem Hackmann, *Seek and Strike* (1984), 134; David K. Brown, *Nelson to Vanguard* (2006), 127.

95 Franklin, 'A Breakdown in Communication: ASDIC in the 1930s', 212.

96 TNA ADM 239/248, 'Anti-submarine Warfare, Volume IV – A/S Training', 15 and 35.

Learning the Lessons of Training and Procedures: ONS-154 – A Case Study from December 1942

This is an account of one of the worst planned, and executed, convoys of the war – ONS-154. It highlights where there are strengths but the focus is more on weaknesses, which demonstrate the need for more ASW training and convoy preparation procedures.

Introduction

On the basis of their own assessment of progress in the war against allied shipping the *BdU* felt confident that it had addressed the main issues that would give them an advantage over their adversaries and that the *Rudeltaktik* was working well. At this stage of the war it may be said that the German U-boat arm was a potent force and that it might well have felt that the bulk of tactics used had produced a satisfactory result, thus far.

In the summer of 1942 the RN may have thought that it had the measure of the U-boats but that was somewhat of an illusion, even though the tactical training given to Escorts had made good progress in the almost one year of its existence.[1] Following *Paukenschlag*, from August to December 1942, German U-boats had some success in sinking allied merchant shipping on the North Atlantic run and the worst fears of Winston Churchill had become a reality; it may have contributed to him writing, 'The only thing that ever really frightened me during the war was the U-boat peril.'[2]

SigInt intercepts had been very helpful in the early days of 1942 for identifying areas of U-boat activity, sometimes enabling the re-routeing of convoys around a danger zone, but in February the Germans introduced a fourth 'Rotor' (Shark) into their Enigma ciphering equipment and Bletchley, the home of the British decryption service, was then practically blind to U-boat information. The work-around solution thus had to rely on a more 'intuitive' technique of deduction, which often did not work. However, on 13 December the code was finally cracked.[3] The blackout had lasted ten months but however good the news was it was to be of little value to the fate of this convoy. On the basis of communications intelligence information obtained from German sources, and decoded at the time while ONS-154 was making its way towards the south-west, it was estimated that there were about 30 U-boats stationed in the North Atlantic north of N45° and between W25° and 40°. At this stage such information might, at best, be worth watching.[4] There were some delays in de-ciphering some information and that meant some diversionary tactics that might have been used by ONS-154 were not implemented before it had been detected on Christmas Day.

Normally a slow convoy could make about 240 miles in 24 hours, whereas a U-boat could cover between 320 and 370 miles over the same period. A decryption delay of as much as three days to discover that U-boats had been ordered to move to new positions could therefore mean that the intelligence received was too late to be of use for convoy diversion.[5] Furthermore, it became increasingly less likely that diversion would be an effective means of evasion at this time because there was a steady increase from 212 to 240 in the total number of operational U-boats in the Atlantic, and because the proportion of those operating on the northern convoy routes rose even greater.[6] With such a large number of U-boats in theatre, it would have been almost impossible for convoys to have gone undetected, and not attacked, even if the Germans were not reading British naval ciphers – which they were.

In November 1942 a number of U-boats in the North Atlantic had been diverted when they were called away to attend other duties, and the number of merchant ships sunk in November fell slightly. *BdU* reluctantly ordered that several U-boats should move to concentrate off Gibraltar in order to counteract measures being undertaken by the allies in the Mediterranean.[7] The offensive against the transatlantic convoy routes was therefore reduced for the time being and by 8 December, many of the boats normally operating in the North Atlantic were in the Gibraltar area.[8] Not for the first time was Dönitz compelled to comply with what he regarded as a futile mission and as previously reported in earlier Chapters *OKW* was only constituted as a rubber stamp for Hitler, not for learning from experience.

The following *BdU* Log entry for 7 November 1942 read:

U-boat situation 7 November:

Transfer of more boats to the Mediterranean: The effect of English activities in the Mediterranean is easily noticeable in the Atlantic. Defences of the convoys most recently attacked were much weaker than before, evidently because of greater escort power in the Mediterranean. Numerous slow ships sailing alone, lead us to believe that this is the case ... In considering the transfer of more boats to the Mediterranean, the past situation must be regarded and prospects of small successes in the Mediterranean must be weighed against the more favourable chances in the N. Atlantic, keeping in mind the overall situation ...[9]

The diversion of U-boats from the Atlantic did not last long. On 1 December 1942 the number of U-boats available was:

In Commission on 1 November 1942:	368 (not all at sea)
In Commission on 23 November:	391 (not all at sea)
Lost in November:	15
Temporarily under repair:	1
Total available	375 [10]

From this number Dönitz chose to establish two groups.

The control of the U-boat Command over the U-boats when deciding which boats to engage the enemy in attacking convoys was complete. On the basis of a SigInt assessment, and logistic requirements, it ordered the formation, or re-formation, of patrol lines between specified geographical positions at regular intervals, addressing each U-boat Commander by name; or who was to take a place in a line and giving him his precise position in it.[11] They regrouped into two lines and went back into action in the Atlantic where, towards the end of December 1942, convoy ONS-154 recorded one of the highest number of merchant ships lost. Dönitz gave the Groups the code names of Spitz (Tip, or Barbed) and Ungestüm (Daring, or Impetuous).[12] *BdU* was also greatly helped by the simple manner in which the enemy rarely departed from its convoy routeing plan. In September, *BdU* noted:

It is amazing how in the last few months the English have consistently plied the routes immediately north and south of the Great Circle despite several large-scale attacks by U-boats. For several weeks boats have been disposed in the same area each time to pick up westbound convoys. Nevertheless, the 'English' have stuck to their old route and this time they were picked up in exactly the position plotted by dead reckoning.[13]

Perhaps the Admiralty was blissfully unaware that *BdU* Command could work out such details;[14] the latter had learnt a lesson, but the Admiralty had not. *BdU* even reported this fact during one of the regular Hitler meetings.[15] It was at this point, almost at the end of 1942, that the Battle of the Atlantic then entered a critical stage where the Germans attempted, by means of larger U-boat pack formations, to increase the severity in disruption of convoy routes between North America and Britain.

The Battle for Convoy ONS-154

This particular battle was between some hard-core, well organized, submariners of the *Kriegsmarine* and a weakly defended Convoy ONS-154. The subsequent review of the attack on convoy ONS-154 identified three major causes for concern:

- How the U-boats had the upper hand when a convoy was outside the range of air cover.
- The weakness and inefficiency of this particular Convoy escort.
- The poor planning and control that went into this particular convoy.

In this attack 11 U-boats of the patrol groups (18) *Spitz* and *Ungestüm*, between them, sank 13 ships, damaged one, and lost only one of their number doing so.[16]

Convoy ONS-154 – North America (slow) consisted of 46 merchantmen, some loaded with export cargo and spares needed overseas, and some sailing in ballast – that is unloaded. Either way the Germans made no distinction between ships loaded or in ballast, inbound or outbound. The U-boat Flag Officer had just one thing in mind; sink the means to transport cargo tonnage, full or otherwise.

The convoy set sail from the western entrance of the North Channel for North America on 19 December 1942 and would later meet up with its escort, comprising five RCN Corvettes and a Destroyer. HMCS *Battleford*, *Chilliwack*, *Kenogami*, *Napanee*, *Shediac* and the Destroyer *St Laurent* formed a group known as EG C-1, with Lieutenant Commander Guy Stanley Windeyer – the SOE in *St Laurent*.[17] Also in company was *Fidelity*, a disguised – or 'Q' – ship used as a decoy to lure a U-boat to strike. *Fidelity* was said to have even carried an aircraft as well as ASDIC (SONAR), which Lt Commander Windeyer apparently did not know about.[18]

This escort group was fraught with problems and inconsistencies from the outset. It started out with the fact that HMS *Burwell*, which should have been in the group, did not sail with it because she had, yet again, experienced problems and needed to put in for repairs. The loss of the Destroyer *Burwell* was significant because, although old, she was capable of speeds of over 30 knots and would have added greater tactical flexibility to the group. The inconsistencies were of an organizational and procedural character. The SOE had been recently appointed and, due to complacency, conducted no pre-sailing briefings to discuss tactics in the event of attack and matters such as communications, something a more experienced SOE would have done. Furthermore, the ships of EG C-1 had never exercised together due to a new SOE being appointed, and were therefore unused to each other's ways,[19] although most had probably passed through Tobermory. In addition, due to poor procedural skills, Windeyer appears not to have checked that all ships' captains had been issued with a standard set of 'Admiralty Convoy Instructions' (ACI),[20] especially the Vice Commodore of the convoy group. Some of that blame could have been laid at the door of the Vice Commodore himself who must have been aware of the procedure, and done nothing to rectify it. Three ships were therefore without these instructions and in the event orders were made up as they went along, and passed out at sea. This lack of procedure was redolent of a missing cipher key in June 1941, aboard *Wetaskiwin*, discussed later.

On the technical front matters were just as blasé. ONS-154 sailed without having a good operating HF/DF system in place. *St Laurent* left minus its HF/DF officer[21] and to make matters worse the equipment on board had not been calibrated, making it virtually useless for tracking a U-boat. Having a rescue ship was a lesson from the First World War.[22] The rescue ship assigned in this case was *Toward* and did have a functioning HF/DF set aboard, but possessed no working gyrocompass with which to lay-off more accurate bearings and this too would add to detection problems. By this stage of the war all the warships had been fitted with the Type 271 radar and that should have at least added to the ability to detect U-boats on the surface; unfortunately the operators aboard were relatively unfamiliar with the equipment, with the result that 'plots' would, at best, be full of errors.[23] All these shortcomings tend to suggest that there were many procedural and training lessons still to be learnt.

After reaching the North Atlantic ONS-154 shaped a course to the south-west making for North America by way of the southern Great Circle. This specific route was selected so that 18 merchantmen heading for the South Atlantic could be detached from the convoy at the appropriate time, which turned out to be fatal. The error was, in part, caused by the 'Working Fiction' of the Tracking Room, which did not report the forming up of U-boat positions towards the Azores, across the convoy's planned track.[24] The route was also believed to have offered a more favourable weather pattern than the northern route, and shorten the length of the voyage.[25]

The problem with this course however was that it would require the convoy to cross at its widest point into a sector of the North Atlantic where it could not receive shore-based A/S aircraft support; and CVE's had not yet been introduced. On Christmas Day the SOE was advised that a U-boat had been tracked by shore-based HF/DF making a transmission within 100 miles of the convoy's location and warned him to be aware of its presence. The first inkling of imminent attack by U-boats came when the lead escort HMCS *Shediac* sighted a U-boat and pressed home an unsuccessful attack.[26] The *Spitz* group of U-boats had worked themselves into a patrol line which ran from N54°09' W24°45' to N52°27' W21°55', and the eight *Ungestüm* boats deployed into a patrol line from N50°21' W32°15' to N48°09' W29°55'.[27]

Weather conditions had deteriorated and they could not be certain of their position and found difficulty in obtaining contact with their quarry. U-boat HQ thought that it had indeed been delayed by bad weather.[28]

The *BdU* report for 26 December noted the possibility of delay:

Convoy No. 72: (ONS-154)[29]

The expected 'ON' convoy was detected during the afternoon of 26 December. This delay may have been caused by its late departure from port as well as by the bad weather encountered . . . The convoy operation is being continued.[30]

The lead U-boat Commander had timed it right. On 26 December the convoy had passed beyond the range of allied shore-based A/S aircraft, and ONS-154 was now on its own as it entered the 'Black Pit' (an area of the Atlantic Ocean between Iceland and the Azores beyond the protection of aircraft).[31] The first attack on the convoy was in the early hours of Sunday, 27 December, when four ships were torpedoed by *U-356*, under the command of *Oberleutnant* Günther Ruppelt, on his first and only patrol.[32] *Empire Union*, *Melrose Abbey* and *King Edward* were all sunk, and Soekaboemi damaged.

The SOE in *St Laurent*, Lieutenant Commander Guy Windeyer, had experience as 'skipper' having previously commanded a Corvette before taking over the RCN *St Laurent*, but lacked the degree of competence for escort work that flows from continuous on-the-job training with others. At some time he broke down, exhausted, and the first lieutenant took control; so great were the demands that he was unable to cope.[33] In response to the sudden attacks the *St Laurent* and the Corvettes *Chilliwack*, *Battleford* and *Napanee* all fired off depth charges at the *U-356*. Three attacks were made on the U-boat, and sank it at 0431 on 27 December. The entire U-boat crew of 46, including the Commander *Oberleutnant* Ruppelt went down with the boat, the only boat sunk throughout the whole operation. At the time of the third attack Windeyer was left with the impression that the U-boat might have escaped the last attack. It did not.[34] The remaining U-boats were driven off and lost contact with the convoy. This attack demonstrated that despite the problems being experienced sinking U-boats was achievable. It is what happened next that demonstrates how singularly unprepared this escort group was to meet the challenges ahead.

It was the night of 28 December which turned out to be a night of unparalleled slaughter with all 18 U-boats (in 2 wolf packs) attacking the convoy. A further nine merchant ships were torpedoed in the space of just two-and-a-half hours.

Successes:

	Sunk		Torpedoed
1) U 260	2 Ships	9,000 GRT	1 Ship 4,000 GRT
2) U 225	3 Ships	9,000 GRT	3 Ship 12,000 GRT
	1 Ship	7,000 GRT	
3) U 591	1 Damaged	5,000 GRT	1 Ship 5,000 GRT
	Sinking not observed because of defences		
4) U 435	1 Destroyer		
5) U 628	1 Damaged Ship 5,000 GRT		
	1 Corvette		
6) U 406	2 Ships 11,000 GRT		1 Ship
	1 Ship sinking 6,889 GRT		
7) U 123	1 Damaged Ship 5,000 GRT	1 Ship 9,419 GRT	
			Torpedoed by U 435 (later sunk by another boat by gunfire)

Some survivors were lucky enough to be picked up by other vessels, only to be torpedoed again.

It is interesting to note that U-boat Commanders continued to be overoptimistic in their assessments of vessels sunk. In this case they refer to sinking a Corvette, and later a Destroyer too. In fact no escort vessels were sunk except for the 'Q' ship *Fidelity*, which was part of the convoy, not escort; and she might have avoided being sunk were it not for engine trouble.

Both *St Laurent* and *Kenogami* conducted an A/S sweep about midnight of 28/29 December, which extended to ten miles astern of the convoy. At 0520 hours, in an attempt to help matters, Gibraltar ordered the Destroyers HMS *Viceroy* and *St Francis* to leave convoy KMS-4 and proceed some 450 miles to aid in the search for survivors, refuelling at Azores if necessary. The SOE received various signals regarding reinforcements informing him that HMS *Fame* had been ordered to leave convoy ON 155 and proceed to join ONS-154 in support.[35]

On 31 December the U-boats lost contact with the convoy and since only five boats still had sufficient fuel to continue operations the hunt was broken off at dusk, and they received orders to withdraw. *BdU* was also aware of activity in motion to support the convoy, and thus it was prudent to cease operations.[36] U-boats had performed well and demonstrated that, in this convoy at least, they had the upper hand, outside the range of air cover.[37]

Conclusions

The WA had singularly failed to provide adequate protection for this convoy and had much to answer for. It may have appeared to have been a routine exercise for naval staff in the selection of the escort group and the course chosen for the crossing but the results were disastrous, and gave the impression of inadequate preparation. On the other hand U-boats had performed well on this occasion, and had exceeded expectations in its own losses to tonnage sunk. Dönitz's prime objective was to achieve the highest tonnage sunk per U-boat day at sea. His ideal tonnage sunk/day at sea was now in excess of 1 million tons per day, but he must have realized that this was no longer achievable.[38] Nevertheless, on balance, this assigned group had a creditable success against this convoy with approximately 70,000 tons sunk and 60,000 tons damaged.

No sooner had the surviving ships in ONS-154 arrived in port than the recriminations began to pour in, from all sides. In his report the SOE Windeyer described attacking U-boats with gun-fire and complained that the cordite used blinded the ships company and they were unable to train their eyes on surfaced U-boats, or their wake/wash; a tell-tale sign of U-boat position. In reply it was pointed out to him that 'flash-less' cordite had been available for some considerable time at Londonderry and it was up to the SOE to have made sure that it was carried,[39] and that is more a procedural than a training weakness. Windeyer went on to say that if he had known that *Fidelity* had ASDIC he would have reformed the escort group to take account of an extra escort vessel. But *Fidelity* at 9 knots was far too slow; had a mixed bag of seamen of different nationalities that had never before worked together; were almost all non-RN; had no Radar or HF/DF; but did have some D/C capacity. In short, in her best configuration she could have helped in the rear, but no more. No evidence was found that she carried any form of ASDIC.

Any experienced SOE knew what his responsibilities were without having to be instructed, and would have checked out what was available. It would certainly have come up in a 'captains' briefing session, had there been one. The general rule for convoys was that before the ships sailed all Masters of merchant vessels were called to a conference with the NCSO of the port, as well as a representative of No. 15 Coastal Command Group, so that it could plan the arrangements to provide air cover for the convoy for as much of its route across the Atlantic that was within range. At the conference the Commodore of the convoy would be present and the chair was occasionally taken by the C-in-C Western Approaches himself; more often it would have been his Chief of Staff, or the NCSO, that would assume the rôle but would have been briefed beforehand.[40] Before coming to the conference each Master would have been provided with written orders regarding the formation and departure of the convoy together a set of the necessary signals instructions, and typically the Commodore would explain what his intentions were, should any emergency arise.[41] None of the aforementioned appears to have taken place, which again points to a failure in procedure.

The choice of Escort groups to provide convoy protection was made by WA, possibly the COS and Captain 'D' in charge of Escort Administration, in consultation with the Admiralty. Ships had been organized into Escort groups by the WA and once a group had been formed 'every endeavour was made to prevent it being broken up'.[42] The ideal size was about eight ships but only rarely could a group work at its full strength; the normal operating strength of a group was, perhaps, two-thirds of its full numbers, due to wear and tear or battle damage.[43] Generally an experienced escort group would be allocated according to availability and in the case of ONS-154 the group chosen was the Canadian group EG C-1 consisting of just six ships. General training was carried out in Canada, but initially the Canadians did not have their own tactical division and thus tactics would have been covered by the WA – some at Portland/Tobermory and the rest in Liverpool, or Londonderry. In Liverpool captains and crews would have practiced several of the current anti-U-boat tactics devised by Captains Roberts and ships would have been given the opportunity to work together in surrounding waters, or around the waters of Northern Ireland. However, while they were under British tactical control they were administratively answerable to Canadian authorities, therefore it is not known to what extent they were assessed.

That said, the first mistake was due to Captain Ravenhill's (DCOS at WA) team's lack of knowledge about the make-up and quality of the group, given that the Canadians appear to have been trained at Tobermory, or Dunoon, with tactical training in Liverpool; and as Gretton once said, 'we were a well-trained group and never missed an opportunity to drill or to exercise'.[44] Had their knowledge been incomplete it seems illogical to have assigned this group to such an important task, especially since there were already serious doubts about the general ability of RCN escort groups. The doubts in 1942, later confirmed, show that 'in the last six months of 1942, with only 4 of the 11 escort groups in the Mid-Ocean Escort Force Canadian, RCN convoys lost 60 of the 80 vessels sunk by U-boats'.[45] Windeyer's naval credentials as a first-class Escort Commander were highly suspect. He was first commissioned in the RN in 1922 as a junior lieutenant and retired from the navy as a Commander in 1930, with eight years of peacetime service. At the start of World War Two he entered the RCN with a rank as Lt Commander. Eight years as a junior officer in the peacetime RN could not provide him with the degree of professionalism that was required to command an escort group in 1942 against a wolf pack in the North Atlantic, with junior officers who were typically thrown into battle with little experience and only basic training.[46] But this was not his first wartime command. He had been SOE of a Canadian group in *Wetaskiwin* detailed off by Admiral Noble to find and assist OB 366, a westbound convoy. On 23 June 1941 Noble ordered Windeyer to detach two Corvettes to support HX 133, which he promptly did; except that he realized that the cipher he needed for many of the signals he was receiving was not aboard, and that suggests bad procedural staff work.[47] Evidence that training had taken place was clear from some of the manoeuvres carried out during U-boat attacks therefore the principal problem appears to have been with the poor organizational ability of the SOE.

The second mistake made by the planners of this particular convoy was to track ONS-154 to North America via the southern Great Circle, due to a Tracking Room error.[48] In 1942 they had fundamentally two choices of route – the northern or southern Great Circle. In general terms a convoy following the northern route would be able to obtain air cover from squadrons based out of Newfoundland, Iceland and Northern Ireland, but would be without such support in the area south of Greenland in the area known as the 'Gap'. However, as stated earlier, a convoy on the southern Great Circle track would have to navigate a much greater distance without air protection into the area known as the 'Black Pit'. ONS-154's route along the southern Great Circle passed out of the range of allied A/S aircraft just as the U-boats started their attack on 26 December. The convoy's escort, already weak in quality and numbers, thus had to take on U-boats without any air support.[49] It is true that they would have come under attack at some time, anyway, but it is difficult to comprehend why the longer route was chosen; even allowing for the dispersal of some vessels to other destinations as the convoy moved further west. Given the experience gained over three years of war in the North Atlantic and given that it was common knowledge that air support was essential to the defence of a convoy under attack by groups of U-boats, the shorter route should have been chosen. Alternatively a support group should have been on hand to provide extra backup while the 'Black Pit' area was cleared.

Dönitz must have been surprised at the ease with which the British allowed this poor air cover track to take place. As early as 3 September 1942 Dönitz had concerns that the day was coming when in all areas of the North Atlantic – the U-boats' principal battleground – the situation in the air would be just as bad around the convoys, an indication of what he had already experienced in better prepared convoys, but not this one.[50]

In a report by the Director of ASW in March 1943 it was pointed out that the faults criticized by Windeyer, in what was termed an 'unhappy lack of organization', were largely of his own making. DASW (Director of Anti-submarine Warfare Division) was aware that Lt Commander Windeyer had since been relieved of duty but concluded that 'the main lesson to be learnt from this encounter is the very real necessity of delegating the control of operations of this magnitude and importance should only be given to officers whose experience and ability are proportionate to the task.'[51] This appears not to have been done and is a reflection on whoever made the choice of Escort group for this convoy.

Intelligence had already made known to the Admiralty that:

> All experience of convoy engagements with U-boat packs indicates with increasing emphasis . . . that heavily concerted attacks by considerable numbers of U-boats can be and usually have been prevented if aircraft are in company with the convoy . . .[52]

Perhaps this lesson had been forgotten, or ignored, but if the earlier lessons of SC-104 in October 1942 had been adopted beforehand, losses on this scale might not have happened. SC-104 lost eight ships and two escorts sustained damage, even with the late arrival of air cover.[53] But two U-boats were sunk in the process. ONS-154 fared much worse. For ONS-154 to have been routed into an area where there was no means of air support, and unsupported into a known concentration of U-boats was a British tactical mistake of the first order, over which SOE Windeyer had no control.

During the most crucial part of the Battle of the Atlantic, Canadian training for ships, far less groups, was virtually non-existent, except for that provided by the RN, quite a lot of which was at Tobermory.[54] Group training exercises had been arranged but some were cancelled owing to the weather and the breakdown of the submarine. Three ships had been diverted to have Type 271 radar fitted and these did not arrive back at Moville until 16/18 December.[55] The ships sailed on the 19th. It is therefore unsurprising that the crew had little experience with the more sophisticated Radar. Someone was responsible for that error, and the group already sailed from a point of weakness, with no common doctrine in A/S techniques.

However, regardless of the training and technology provided so much depended on the individual Commander and his decisions, demonstrating that lessons can be learned at the institutional and personal level. In spite of the efforts of 22 years service with the RN, Cmdr J. D. Prentice, the Canadian-born SOCC (Senior Officer, Canadian Corvettes), was unable to achieve a balanced organization and was replaced in 1944.[56]

It would be simple to suggest that the disaster might have been mitigated if Escort Group C-1 had been more professional and effective. While it is true that C-1, as with some other Canadian EGs during 1942 lacked the training, experience and professionalism necessary to conduct and fight a major convoy battle, the WA convoy organizers might have taken a hand in enforcing correct pre-convoy sailing procedures; and it might have been better to have routed the convoy further north in order to extend the range of air cover. For example, there appears not to have been any convoy procedural management in place to ensure that no EG could leave without having briefed escort and merchant captains beforehand. And neither was any procedure in place to ensure that all escort vessels had the optimum degree of working equipment on board complete with operator, to ensure that in the absence of air cover they could give a good account of themselves (a further admission of inadequate preparation).[57] Furthermore, by the time the Admiralty finally woke up to the unfolding catastrophe it was already too late to mitigate the horrendous losses that transpired. The earlier statement by DASW about SOE's having sufficient 'experience and ability proportionate to the task' would have been better to have put into practice earlier, not after the event.[58] By the time vessels had been detailed off to come to the aid of ONS-154 the only thing achieved was to alert the U-boat HQ that strong reinforcements were on the way. At which point they sensibly withdrew.

There were lessons to be learned. The first could be to plug the gaps of WA procedure in the way they permitted this convoy to proceed to sea without any regard for matters of security for the merchantmen that were in their charge. The second lesson to be learnt from this experience was to ensure that Admiralty planners route ships in convoy along the northern Great Circle route, where greater air cover was present; although by no means perfect at this time. It would have meant that a long detour would have been necessary for those ships departing to destinations other than North America but at least they would have been outside of the main body of U-boats stationed in the 'Air Gap', and fuel would not have been a problem. How much tightening of procedure was implemented is not known but this problem was never to be repeated again; and the COS Mansfield at WA was promoted to Rear Admiral and sent off to help solve the training and procedures problem.[59] Was this a tacit admission of blame? To move someone with such a high profile, at the peak his activity, must be rare.

It is clear that the Canadian EG's lacked group training and first-rate professional leadership on which to build; that would come later. Perhaps Macintyre was correct stating that 'It would have been wise if the Canadians had pocketed their pride and sailed their ships with experienced escort groups until they were themselves battle-worthy.'[60] C-1 in particular, like some of the other Canadian EGs, needed the leadership of officers who had sufficient operational experience and understood the requirements of battle and who could adapt the changing situations to fit the demands of combat, like those of Escort Commanders Johnny Walker of *Starling* and Peter Gretton of *Duncan* fame. Regrettably, Lt Commander Windeyer was not such an officer and the mistakes committed by this SOE Commander of C-1 were manifest. He failed to brief his own fellow Commanders of the EG and the convoy captains before sailing, giving such reasons as bad weather and lack of a ship's boat to make the crossing for a meeting in mitigation. On the organization front, he failed to comply with the procedure that the officers of C-1 and ONS-154 captains received proper written instructions before sailing, so that each knew who did what. He may also not have regularly consulted CB 04050, which kept

Commanders abreast of tactics and encouraged them to take the lead.[61] In the instance of being off-station shortly before U-boats attacked he demonstrated a distinct lack of judgement. On the technical deficiency side C-1 sailed without an HF/DF officer, or a correctly functioning HF/DF set.[62] Normally, an experienced commander would have addressed that anomaly at once, for everyone's safety, and that lack of appreciation was an especially critical mistake. Furthermore, Windeyer failed to inform one of his own escorts that the convoy would alter course at some point with the result that *Battleford* was absent from the escort screen during the night of 28 December, the night of severe U-boat attacks. His lack of attention to procedure led to a serious error of tactical judgement when he in HMCS *St Laurent,* the most powerful ship in the EG, left the convoy screen just as ONS-154 was about to be attacked. Understandably following the Battle for ONS-154 Windeyer, was relieved by his first lieutenant, after suffering from nervous exhaustion. On 1 January 1943 *St Laurent* departed for St John's due to shortage of fuel,[63] and the SOE was passed to *Fame.*[64]

The third lesson learnt was the need for a wholesale re-training of Canadian Escorts. The aftermath and consequences of the battle for ONS-154, and some earlier convoys escorted by Canadian groups, had far-reaching effects, much of which caused consternation within the nascent RCN. Even before ONS-154 sailed, on 17 December, Churchill had petitioned the Canadian government to stand down its escorts from the mid-ocean, citing the problem on the RCN's too rapid expansion and resulting lack of efficiency.[65] For several months the Canadian mid-ocean escort groups that had borne much of the brunt of escort duty in the North Atlantic were now withdrawn for retraining; loosely termed 'other duties' by the Naval Staff in the Monthly A/S report of January 1943.[66] In this same report Canadian escorts came in for severe criticism for the manner in which they reacted to U-boat attacks; no doubt the Canadians were demoralized by the whole episode. The reality was that both Horton and the CNS were concerned at losses incurred with the earlier SC-107, not to mention this latest catastrophe.[67] In those following few months Canadians were rapidly retrained in all matters dealing with escort efficiencies and communications techniques and later proved to be equally as professional and battle-hardened as their British and American counterparts.[68]

There would be other defeats and several near disasters in the North Atlantic, particularly in the second half of March 1943, before the lesson finally sunk in completely. It is not that the RN was unaware of the problem. It was more that there was insufficient conviction on the part of Churchill, the RAF and US C-in-C

Navy to recognize the importance of the Battle of the Atlantic in the allocation of suitable VLR aircraft for Coastal Command. In the forthcoming months, it took the Allies some time to get the required number of well-equipped escorts and the degree of air support needed for convoys in mid-Atlantic and it would not be until this materialized that the U-boat menace would ultimately face its own major defeats, and become the hunted.

Notes

1 Robert Fisher, 'Group Wotan and the Battle for SC 104', *The Mariner's Mirror*, 84 (1) (February 1998), 64–75, 73.

2 Winston S. Churchill, *The Second World War II* (1954), 455; Francis L. Loewenheim et al., *Roosevelt and Churchill* (New York, 1975), 262.

3 F. H. Hinsley et al., *British Intelligence in the Second World War* (1981), II, 233.

4 TNA ADM 199/2060: CB 04050/43 (1), Monthly Anti-submarine Reports, Section 2, 7. The number of U-boats quoted from 28 December to 3 January 1943 was 36.

5 TNA ADM 223/96, Intelligence Reports and Papers, OIC SI 478 of 4 January 1943; TNA ADM 223/97, Intelligence Reports and Papers, OIC SI 559 of 5 April 1943; Stephen W. Roskill, *The War at Sea* 1956), II, 475.

6 NHB PG 30314, BdU KTB entry for 1 December 1942; TNA ADM 223/96, OIC SI 463 of 14 December, SI 468 of 21 December 1942.

7 TNA ADM 223/95, OIC SI No. 394 of 12 October 1942; TNA CAB 66/32/46; the number of operational boats was thought to be more like 90, 3.

8 This move was one of those interventions forced on the BdU by OKW, seen by the Flag Officer U-boats as a fruitless exercise.

9 NHB PG 30313, Excerpt from BdU KTB 7 November 1942, setting up orders to remove U-boats from the North Atlantic.

10 NHB PG 30314, BdU KTB entry for 1 December 1942; ADM 223/97, OIC SI 504 of 1 February 1943; TNA ADM 223/107, NID 01730/15, March 1943. These documents suggest a level similar to that recorded by the Flag Officer U-boats on 1 December 1942.

11 Hinsley et al., *British Intelligence in the Second World War,* II, 550.

12 Some of the meanings of names given to the U-boat groups will have only truly been known to Dönitz. Others like Donau or Moselle are obvious.

13 NHB PG 30311, BdU entry for 9 September 1942 about British convoy routes.

14 TNA ADM 234/67, U-boat War in the Atlantic, 2, 50. The Admiralty quote the reason for not deviating from the routes was because of the acute fuelling problems of escorts from the winter of 1941 to the spring of 1942.

15 BA-MA RM 7/846, 1/Skl KTB Teil C Heft IV, Niederschriften Raeder an Hitler, 236–48; NHB PG 32174, 1/Skl KTB Teil C Heft IV, Minutes of meeting between Raeder and Hitler.

16 TNA ADM 234/578, Naval staff history: 'The Defeat of the Enemy Attack on Shipping 1939–1945', an account of ONS 154; Hinsley, et al., *British Intelligence in the Second World War,* II, 233.

17 TNA ADM 199/356, ONS, ON and HX convoys: Report of attack on ONS-154, f. 276.

18 NHB PG 30314B, BdU KTB entry 30 December 1942, stating that the 'Q' ship (Fidelity) sunk in quadrant CE 3178 carried a 'seaplane', was heavily armed and had depth charge throwers; Günter Hessler, *The U-Boat War in the Atlantic 1939–1945* (1989), II, 70; TNA ADM 199/356. ONS, ON and HX convoys: Report of attack on ONS-154, f. 281.

19 TNA ADM 199/356, Captain (D) Newfoundland report, folio 281; David Syrett, 'The Battle for Convoy ONS-154, 26–31 December 1942', *Northern Mariner,* 7 (2) April 1997, 41.

20 TNA ADM 199/356, ONS, ON and HX convoys: Report of attack on ONS-154. FO Newfoundland Force Report, 23 January 1943. ACI (Admiralty Convoy Instructions) handed to officer of HMCS *St. Laurent*; TNA ADM 239/344, ACI – CB 04234, 1942–4.

21 The HF/DF officer had gone ashore on an errand, and the ship sailed without him.

22 F. Barley et al., *The Defeat of the Enemy Attack on Shipping 1939–1945,* 137 (Aldershot, 1997), 45.

23 TNA ADM 199/356, ONS, ON and HX convoys: report of attack on ONS-154, f. 276; David Syrett, 'The Battle for Convoy ONS-154, 26–31 December 1942', 41.

24 TNA ADM 199/356, Report of attack on ONS 154, Captain 'D', folio 275, 13 January 1943.

25 TNA ADM 199/356, Attacks on ONS-154, memo-FO Newfoundland, 13 January 1943, 3; Terraine, *Business in Great Waters,* 510.

26 TNA ADM 199/356, ONS, ON and HX convoys: Reports 1942–1943, 282–96.

27 Hessler, *The U-Boat War in the Atlantic 1939–1945,* II, 69–70.

28 TNA CAB 86/4, Memorandum of First Sea Lord, 30 March 1943, A.U. (43) 103, bad weather conditions over the winter of 1942–3.

29 BdU had a different convoy recognition numbering system for convoys, but sometimes used the British original.

30 NHB PG 30314, entries dated 26 December 1942.

31 TNA AIR 41/47, 'The RAF in Maritime War – The Atlantic and Home Waters: III, The Preparative Phase July 1941–February 1943', 517.

32 Ruppelt's U-356 was the only U-boat lost in this action.

33 Commander Tony German, 'Preserving the Atlantic Lifeline', *Legion Magazine,* 1 May 1998, no page numbers given.

34   TNA ADM 199/356, The official account suggests doubt about the sinking of U-356. It was considered that the U-boat was possibly damaged, 276–7; Axel Niestlé, *German U-boat Losses During World War II* (Annapolis, 1998), 57.

35   TNA ADM 199/356, ONS-154 convoy reports.

36   NHB PG 30314B, BDU KTB entry date 31 December 1942.

37   Hinsley, et al., *British Intelligence in the Second World War,* II, 233.

38   NHB PG 32174, 1/Skl KTB Teil C Heft IV, 'Einfluss der Schiffsversenkungen', Abt. F. H. B Nr. 85/42 gKdos Chefs: 9 September, 1942, 4.

39   TNA ADM 199/356, ONS, ON and HX convoys: Report of attack on ONS-154, f. 276.

40   Richard Woodman, *The Real Cruel Sea* (2004), Illustration 3, the pre-departure conference.

41   TNA ADM 116/3128, Operational policy of the Naval Control Service; Ronald Seth, *The Fiercest Battle* (1961), 67; in the foreword by Vice Admiral Gretton it was stated that Ronald Seth's account was authentic.

42   Stephen W. Roskill, *The War Sea* (1954), I, 359.

43   Ibid.

44   Seth, *The Fiercest Battle,* 13.

45   Marc Milner, 'The Battle of the Atlantic', *Journal of Strategic Studies,* 13 (1) (1990), 45–66. Citation by Milner on the Journal website.

46   Michael Whitby, 'The Strain of the Bridge: The Second World War Diaries of Commander A. F. C. Layard, DSO, DSC, RN', in *The Face of Naval Battle,* (Crows Nest NSW, 2003), 200–18, 209.

47   Terraine, *Business in Great Waters,* 349.

48   David Syrett, *The Battle of the Atlantic and Signals Intelligence,* 139 (Aldershot, 1998), 111–12; Terraine, *Business in Great Waters,* 510.

49   David Syrett, 'The Battle for Convoy ONS-154, 26–31 December 1942', *The Northern Mariner,* 7 (2) (April 1997), 41–50, 46.

50   BA-MA RM 7/2869, U-boat command, memo No. 3642-Al to OKM/Sk1, 3 September 1942.

51   TNA ADM 199/356, 29 March 1943 report by the Director of ASW.

52   TNA ADM 223/17, U-boat trends, 9 September 1942 to 1 September 1943.

53   TNA ADM 199/2011, 'ASW Analysis of U-boat Operations in the Vicinity of SC 104, 11–16 October 1942'; Donald Macintyre, *The Battle of the Atlantic* (1961), 146–50.

54   Arnold Hague, *The Allied Convoy System 1939–1945* (2000). Referring to Tobermory he said 'Indeed not a few RCN and Allied escorts also passed through his hands', 28.

55   TNA ADM 199/356, WA.797/RP.65/11 Letter to the secretary of the Admiralty, 8 March 1943.

56 W. J. R. Gardner, 'An Allied Perspective', in *The Battle of the Atlantic 1939–1945* (1994), 516–37, (522).

57 TNA ADM 199/356, Director of signals department acknowledged the need to extend calibration facilities in the United Kingdom and overseas, and hoped that such an incident would never happen again, 19 May 1943.

58 TNA ADM 199/356, 29 March 1943 report by the Director of ASW.

59 William Glover, 'Officer Training and the Quest for Operational Efficiency in the Royal Canadian Navy 1939–1945', (University of London, 1998), 247–8.

60 Donald Macintyre, *U-Boat Killer* (1956), 78–82.

61 TNA ADM 199/2059: CB 04050/42 (11), 'Mistakes and Lessons Learned', section 3, 14.

62 TNA ADM 199/356, 'Memorandum to DTD', Re: Attacks on ONS-154, 276–8.

63 TNA ADM 199/356, 'Proceedings of RCNS St. Laurent', 3 January 1943, 6.

64 Ibid., folio 388.

65 TNA PREM 3/331/8, Memo from CNS to Churchill related to training of Canadian manned escorts: Marc Milner, *The Battle of the Atlantic* (Ontario, 2003), 140.

66 TNA ADM 199/2060: CB 04050/43 (1), Monthly Anti-submarine reports, section 2, 9.

67 NAC RG 24, Vol. 6796, 8375–4: Memo from Admiralty to CNS Canada, 1 339A/18/12/42. Reference retraining of Canadian manned escorts.

68 Marc Milner, *North Atlantic Run* (Toronto, 1985), 210–13.

8

Training to Meet the Requirements
of Change

This chapter covers the period from 1943 until 1945 when both sides responded to events in the Battle of the Atlantic with changes to the organization of training and tactics to meet a new set of requirements. For the Germans, matters had already come to a head in May 1943, with the temporary withdrawal from operations in the North Atlantic. It was time to review the prospects of the U-boat arm in the light of allied advances in weapons technology and tactics, to address the issue of replacing men lost between July 1942 and July 1943, and to plan for the training required in anticipation of the new *Elektro*-type U-boats. The British, too, still had lessons to learn about tactics with the introduction of a new German weapon, the acoustic torpedo. Each side modified, or added to, the organizations needed to improve methods of training and tactics.

Part one: Germany 1943–5 recruitment

As the war entered its fourth year, recruitment to the service became one of the problems to be solved by Admiral von Friedeburg. As Admiral U-boats he administered the requirement for U-boat officers and ratings in every particular, including their selection from other services, or other parts of the navy, for the U-boat arm.[1] To man an expanding fleet of U-boats required more than a mere relaxation of pre-war standards and strains were already beginning to show. In the period from June 1943 to September 1944 the *Kriegsmarine* estimated that 335,000 officers and men would be needed. A total of 60,000 men were needed for the U-boat arm in order to man the projected increase of more than 600 new U-boats and new training flotillas, new escort vessels and target ships for a new co-ordinated approach to training.[2] The plan also required that specific categories of technical personnel (e.g. 3,538 petty officers, 6,220 ratings from engineering, nearly 3,900 telegraphists, and around 3,000 torpedo mechanics) reached numbers that precluded confidence in the appropriate numbers of qualified volunteers coming forward. In the officer ranks engineering was one of the categories where the lack of capacity was acutely felt;[3] and the number of non-specialized officers and ratings in the seaman's branch were also in short supply. The complement of a Type VIIC U-boat carried about a third from the seaman's branch alone.[4]

According to one U-boat Commander, Eric Topp, 'very few people had to be drafted into submarines: many of the crews and practically all of the officers were recruited as volunteers.'[5] Eric Topp was one of those commanders who wore his political beliefs on his sleeve and declared that the new batch of young submariners coming through was shaped decisively by the education and society of the Third Reich – meaning Nazism. 'They were, in other words, conditioned by their upbringing in a totalitarian state to accept as natural a philosophy of all-out war, total war.' His view was not that shared by the *Kriegsmarine* hierarchy, at least not before 1943.[6]

Recruitment to the service was not a simple matter but the advertising put out by the authorities painted a good picture.[7] In fact, the picture was quite different. So dire was the dilemma of personnel shortages that by the end of 1941 all German Destroyers with the luxury of three engineering officers had the 'Thirds' all removed and assigned to U-boats;[8] this is in stark contrast to statements made by some historians that there was no shortage of volunteers.[9] The reality is perhaps best summed up by the following statement. 'Many *Freiwillige* (volunteers) for submarine service did so unwillingly or with little choice.'[10]

Nevertheless von Friedeburg executed his job of acquiring sufficient personnel well and on 17 December 1943 Dönitz expressed his satisfaction by stating that 'in the last few months, with a view to expansion of the offensive arm of our Navy, we have increased our strength by 100,000 men.'[11] He hoped that this additional number of men would suffice to cover his needs as U-boat production increased, and that he might extend the length of training given to crews and Commanders. This proved to be the case and he was also able to get a good number of younger men into the service for after 1943 the average age of U-boat crews dropped to 21; and commanding officers were then usually in the order of 23 years old. By 1 June 1944 naval strength had risen to 819,932 officers and men, from which they could choose suitable U-boat crews.[12]

However, the question of crew preparation and experience masks the more general conclusion of vulnerability of U-boats to new Allied technology and weapons during the second half of the war. Loss rates of only 3.9 per cent from January to June 1942 rose to 39.3 per cent in July 1943, but the problem was less attributable to any training programme than with its capacity to keep pace with developments in the Battle of the Atlantic. Doubtless influenced by the heavy casualties to his forces in 1939–40 Dönitz himself believed that training could not substitute for combat experience, as noted in his war diary on 25 July 1942 when he stated,

> Under difficult conditions it was again only the experienced that managed a successful attack . . . The fact remains that the difficult school of convoy attack cannot be exercised at home, but only when in direct contact with the enemy.[13]

U-boat Commander training had suffered by being made shorter and this began to have a marked effect on the ability of Commanders to gain sufficient experience before undertaking a combat patrol. As an indication and confirmation of how the Commander's training had been shortened, a brief extract from an account by the German historian Jochen Brennecke from his book *Haie im Paradies* is given. In it he talks of a command change-over of *U-181* in November 1943 from Kommandant Lüth (a U-boat Ace) to Kommandant Freiwald.

> It is without doubt difficult for a new Commander to take over a long serving crew . . . In comparison to Lüth, he might have had good peacetime training but in time of war he could barely show a brief three month U-boat training period.[14]

The account shows how much a Commander training period of three months, or less, had changed from earlier times of at least six months.

Specialized working-up authorities

The new allied technical developments in weapons and superior aircraft, which forced the U-boats away from the convoy routes after May 1943, brought about a rapid reaction in the sphere of pre-operational training. At a meeting with Hitler, Dönitz vigorously presented his views on the current state of the Battle of the Atlantic and berated the efforts put in by the *Luftwaffe*, claiming that more could have been achieved in joint operations. But to be of any use now it would require sending better aircrews that just *Zuckerbäcker*, 'Confectioners', 'those that dress the icing on a cake', a derogatory term implying little skill required, unlike the U-boat arm with a 4–5-month training programme. The *Luftwaffe* too needed to learn about astronavigation, drift, DF techniques and working with U-boats, in order to get a feeling for convoy work. Hitler entirely agreed.[15] It was probably through Hitler's admiration for Dönitz's hard line that Göring became more approachable, up to a point. Dönitz had learnt a most important lesson in May. The first evidence came in June 1943 when the 20th U-boat flotilla was created at Pillau, specifically for a new tactical approach to U-boats training with aircraft. It was his attempt to create a new working relationship that he hoped would help stem the current losses of boats and men.[16]

It was noted in Chapter 5 that part of the existing 26th flotilla was used as a third tactical training unit,[17] but by the end of 1943 some Commanders were reduced to between four and ten weeks of training only, due to high attrition rates.[18] Both Dönitz and *BdU org.* were to implement the new lesson by adding another level of training in anticipation of new front-line Commanders having to face an allied convoy defence, now replete with air cover. A more sophisticated, co-ordinated, form of training in group exercises and convoy attacks was now offered with the 20th U-boat flotilla, usually conducted off Pillau, East Prussia or Danzig (Poland); similar group exercises were also practiced by the British at HMS *Philante*, in their consolidated approach to training.[19] Lasting typically 10 to14 days U-boats remained at sea and worked with their instructors in simulated combat operations in day and night exercises. The latest experienced instructors were used to teach U-boat crews best procedures to follow in shadowing a convoy while pack groups assembled; the optimum course track to follow in pursuing, approaching and attacking targets; boat manoeuvres to evade attack by convoy escorts; and the use of effective Flak defence against aircraft attack. Throughout the training sessions feedback was sought, and given. Refuelling operations (using water instead of oil) were also practiced. Methods were rigorous and could involve six to nine U-boats in simulated attacks against convoys, made up of three or four target ships with escorts, while the *Luftwaffe* provided air cover. *Luftwaffe* co-operation for the exercises was achieved in consultation with the local *FdL* (*Fliegerführer Atlantik*). *FdL* was in charge of air operations over the North Sea between latitude 52°–58° North and over the approaches to the Baltic, as well as with U-boat protection as far west as Cherbourg.[20] These exercises were intended to give both services the opportunity to develop an understanding of each other's tactics and to iron out previous poor communications between U-boats and *Luftwaffe* aircraft.

Exercises were designed to simulate combat conditions as closely as possible to reality, although it is not known whether dummy *Flak* rounds were used against aircraft.[21] At the end of the exercises discussions were held and it was determined that some advances in procedures and doctrine had been made. In future, the lessons learned would be used in practice for closer co-operation between the *Luftwaffe* and operational U-boats, in particular for when sufficient number of the Type XXI could become operational.[22] This was a belated attempt to redress some errors of the past. Once Commanders and crew had finished all their training they were then ready to be deployed which marked the next stage in their learning process, and they began the harsh lessons of combat – with no prospect of returning for a refresher course. In sharp contrast to the British WATU, no system existed for further follow-up training once the boats arrived at their front-line bases; and co-operation with the *Luftwaffe* never reached an acceptable level before capitulation.

By September 1943 there was a need for a further extension to the working-up of a U-boat that was brought about by the development of *Schnorchel*, the use of which is discussed in a later chapter. In the early days of *Schnorchel* fitting, most U-boats carried out operational training at their final fitting-out bases. But it is worth noting here that its development was responsible for the addition of another Front-line Training Group because of an increase in the number being fitted, and the need to train U-boats in its use. In July 1944 a branch of the Front-line Training Group was set up for this purpose at Horten (in Oslofjord) since the waters of the East Baltic were by now very congested, and British mining was still a problem.[23] However, even with the new breathing device some boats leaving, or travelling to Horten, were caught on the surface or 'Snorkelling' just below the surface.[24]

A further technical development which was to engender the setting up of another new unit in May 1944 was the initiation of trials of new location gear with a group of U-boats and *Sultan,* an 'OR' experimental group of U-boats and torpedo experimental vessels operating in the Baltic – a useful platform to test other U-boat requirements for OR purposes and evaluate the training requirements for up-coming *Elektro*-boats.[25] In July a further similar 'OR' unit was identified, known as the *Pascha* group.[26] Both these units were subordinated to Captain (U/B) Training, and their position regularized in October. Together they were known as the U-boat Trials Group, and commanded overall by *Korvettenkapitän* Topp – who was later to be identified with the new *Elektro*-boat evaluations and testing. In May 1944 Topp was authorized by Dönitz to examine, and report on, the new location gear *Nibelung* for Types XXI and

XXIII with recommendations for its use. Full facilities of the specially created 'OR' groups *Sultan* and *Pascha* were made available for testing the new location methods incorporated into the Types XXI and XXIII, first submerged, then on the surface.[27] However, in the meeting that Dönitz held with Hitler from 1–3 January 1945 he voiced the concern that with the Allies now gaining ground after the ground invasion of France, and the Russians advancing along the Baltic coast from the east, it could become impossible to continue with U-boat training if the Baltic became untenable.[28] The Baltic was the only training ground they had and Dönitz had once again demonstrated how poorly thought through a single location for his key training ground was.

As late as January 1945 the 18th Flotilla was set up at Gdynia for the purpose of training U-boat crews and, in particular, those of the new prefabricated U-boats, in location methods and torpedo firing (*Nibelung* ranging).[29] This branch of training had originally been the special province of the 25th U-boat flotilla but by January 1945 had assumed such proportions that it warranted the setting up of a special flotilla. On 29 January the flotilla moved to Eckernförde (Western Baltic).[30]

Completed 'Elektro' type U-boats and training

As is so often the case when new vessels and machinery are being run during trials the need for numerous modifications on completed boats become necessary, and this further delayed the bulk of boats from being accepted for front-line operations until well into 1945; added to which were the effects of allied strategic bombing raids on the main shipbuilding centres. Also, because of the 'unorthodox' methods used in the construction of these boats it produced an inordinate number of defects in the first to commission.[31] That meant frequent interruptions for repair and modifications, which combined, led to a lengthening of the crew-training period from the usual three months to nearly six.[32] Only by the autumn of 1944 had basic testing of experimental *Elektro* U-boats reached the stage where the standard training of crews could commence. As things stood they could not have begun operating as front-line boats before 1945.[33] The first seven completed boats were not fit for combat patrols but used for training and experimental purposes.[34] While not meeting the standards required for front-line service they did serve their purpose in training-up the very first crews so that they were ready to take over an improved version, when available.

The first two Type XXIs to see service of any kind were given to two very experienced U-boat Commanders, Eric Topp (*U-2506*) and Adalbert Schnee (*U-2511*) who, with select crews, began a rigorous training programme initially devised by *BdU* command. *BdU* had kept all the logs of previous commands and made a study of the tactical deployment of the new boats, possibly aided by *Kr* the Naval Science Division. The results of the study were then passed on to new commanders, training, experimental and trials staff for evaluation and improvement. Their job was to trial the new methods and to come up with further suggestions that could be used in training methods for new crews and operational use. Their evaluation formed the first 'OR' report on the new vessels. *Korvettenkapitän* Topp and *Kapitänleutnant* Emmermann, conducted extensive sea trials in the two boats Type XXI and XXIII respectively. From these trials were drafted the next version of the new training curriculum, and a set of Battle Instructions. Also contained in the report was an evaluation of the *Nibelung* 'programmed firing' equipment performance under simulated battle conditions, when operating on the surface or below the convoy; this was made possible by the *Sultan* trials group. Data collected by echo ranging was converted and the unit then automatically set the running pattern of the *LUT* torpedo, discussed in Chapter 10, 'Practical use of Feedback from Meetings'.[35] On paper the combat capability of the XXI was high.

Part Two: The other side of the channel 1943–5

British expansion in ASW training reached its peak in 1944, by which time included the use of the 'Q' attachment and Type 147B teacher for depth determination;[36] Type 147B equipment was also supplied to the US Navy.[37] Basic training for ratings was provided ashore at the base of HMS *Osprey* Dunoon, while junior officers, and S/D rating basic sea-training was given by HMS *Nimrod* at Campbeltown. What did change, for the better, was the availability of British submarines as targets. In January 1943 up to six submarines were available for trainees and that number was improved on after the Italians had surrendered and some of their submarines were available as targets for training purposes in the Mediterranean, particularly around Taranto, thus freeing up some submarines for home use.[38] By late 1944 general ASW training was further helped by the fact that Horton was able to allocate submarines to other areas, for example Campbeltown (5), Tobermory (1), Philante (1), Rockabill (2), Inskip (1), CCDU (Coastal Command Development Unit) (1).[39] In all more than 8,000 officers and men passed through these training facilities, and a further 8,000 came for short, or refresher course.[40]

British ASW training 1943–5

Basic ASW training had not changed substantially up to 1943. At the beginning of 1944 the RN faced some different challenges in detection methods, when U-boats were virtually withdrawn from the North Atlantic and concentrated their efforts more in British coastal waters, some of which were shallow waters. ASW training therefore had to concentrate more on methods of detection in waters with temperature inversions, salinity changes and wrecks, or rocks, on the bottom. These conditions around British coasts all compounded the problem of initial detection making the identification of a rock, wreck or actual U-boat hard to distinguish. During the final period of the campaign, echo sounders became very useful in helping to distinguish bottomed U-boats from wrecks shallow waters.[41] Admiralty charts with recorded depths around Britain, while not up-to-date due to the war, made for good reference points. By February 1944, some escorts had the use of QH, the forerunner of the Decca Navigator/GPS to fix position.[42] While making an ASDIC (SONAR) search for possible U-boats a track was laid down on a plot, compared to local charts and was often of great value in eliminating false ASDIC returns.

> The first impressions gained from these operations was that the efficiency of ASDIC was markedly low in shallow water than it was in ocean warfare . . . but once they had become accustomed to these it was found, by analysis over the period from June 1944 to January 1945, that the chance of a U-boat being sunk in coastal waters was about double that in deep water.[43]

At WATU Admiral Horton involved himself very much with this problem and placed constant emphasis on improving training which was to pay great dividends in the shallow water warfare of 1944–5.[44] Training, tactics and technology do not stand still.

A co-ordinated approach to training

For the last two-thirds of the war the chief organization equipped for the tactical investigation of anti-U-boat problems was the WATU.

After Admiral Max Horton succeeded Admiral Noble as C-in-C WA in November 1942 his own aggressive instincts, and experience, pushed him in the direction of raising the standard of tactical training even further. He had inherited a basic set-up from Admiral Sir Percy Noble but soon got to work seeking methods of improvement. HMS *Western Isles* still continued with basic working-up training but the more experienced escorts received regular tactical training in ASW tactics at WATU. WATU's exercises stressed the need for co-ordinated pre-planned responses to the U-boat, which was an utmost requirement for comprehensive group training. Having learnt a great deal from Robert's work in setting up the 'Tactical Unit' Horton then established an advanced tactical training unit in February 1943 when HMS *Philante* was commissioned with a staff of A/S specialists and a shore Tactical Unit, similar to that first started in Liverpool. Owing to congestion around Londonderry, the original choice, Larne was designated instead.

As an expert submariner himself he adjudged that there were an increasing number of U-boats working in concentrated packs spread out across convoy routes which called for a high degree of understanding and team-work between the ships on escort duty, and accompanying aircraft. Each Escort Group was taken to sea in turn for elaborate and realistic U-boat 'battles' in conjunction with Coastal Command and FAA, using British submarines as targets. 'These large-scale exercises allowed commanding officers to carry out all the necessary complicated manoeuvres and to plan and try out new schemes to combat the constantly changing tactics of the enemy.'[45] By coincidence, or design, the Germans planned to do the same thing in 1943 with their co-ordinated attack procedures, in conjunction with their surface ships and *Luftwaffe* support. WATU planned approximately three days for exercises, dependent on operational requirements. By contrast the U-boat arm had some catching up to do and spent 10 to 14 days exercising at sea. But there was no provision for refresher courses. This point is raised in a later chapter.

Both sides used a similar approach where the excercises were designed to be as close to as 'realistic' as possible and the mix of assets were of the same type used in theatre. The British enhanced their A/S practice to coincide with aircraft firing practice, just as would be experienced by escort crews when operating with aircraft cover. *Philante* acted as the Commodore of a Convoy and using two submarines and/or targets observed Coastal Command, as well as FAA aircraft, make dummy attacks on the targets. Afterwards, question and answer sessions were held back at base. In addition, by housing both RN and Coastal Command staff together after the exercises it not only gave personnel a chance to discuss matters openly but also provided both services with good operational training experience.[46] Admiral Horton was a Commander that led by example and what he did was to disseminate best practice.[47] It is interesting to note that Horton went on to establish another unit at HMS *Osprey* in 1945, indicating that perhaps he, at least, had not forgotten the lessons of experience accumulated to-date.

But one might well be justified to ask why

> . . . the *Philante* Group Training Centre did not start work until mid-1943. It seems that all the lessons were forgotten by the Service between the wars.[48]

Generally this might have been a familiar story of not learning from history, for exercising submarines with surface vessels and FAA units was practiced up to as late as 1939.[49] In retrospect the appointment of Admiral Noble to WA in February 1941 might have been a mistake, despite some early success. Although an excellent administrator, and the organizer of a well-oiled ASW training regime, he did not have the submariner 'killer' instinct of Horton. Neither was he initially keen on the idea of a 'tactical' table. As it was, Horton was not appointed to the post of C-in-C until 19 November 1942 and would have needed time to assess WATU's tactical training and operational efficiency. What he inherited, and discovered, was a weapons training regime that was often ad hoc and early tactical training was by 'trial and error', usually in the face of the enemy at sea. Malcom Llewellyn-Jones referred to these methods as 'Osmosis';[50] a drip-by-drip process.

Horton was influenced in training requirements by the experiences of a number of senior escort captains of the period, including Commander Peter Gretton and Captain Johnny Walker. Gretton has contested the view of some historians

> which still persists in many circles and should know better, that convoy is a purely defensive system. *It is not.* Research into its history shows that convoy from its very nature is inherently offensive, and that this is so because it forces the enemy to play on your own ground on your own terms. . .[51]

Gretton's view has been challenged by one British historian who states that it 'betrays a fundamental misunderstanding of how ASW was viewed by the Admiralty . . . as interdependent and symbiotic parts of A/S strategy, and not as alternative strategies.'[52]

Both views contain valid assumptions but Gretton was stating his preferred tactic of attack whenever possible, but regarded attack as the best means of defence. He clearly did not state that there were no elements of 'defensive' nature in the strategy, and far from misunderstanding RN A/S doctrine he was a SOE who practiced some elements of a defensive strategy, which Llewellyn-Jones has overlooked. Also, an inspection of the records of SC-130 alone shows that Gretton frequently ordered 'ad hoc' changes in convoy course in order to confuse shadowing U-boats, and they were effective.[53] That is a defensive tactic, but it does not preclude a preference for attack. In fact, he was performing precisely the nature of an interdependent strategy[54] by applying tactics as he saw fit which would produce the best outcome if he got them right – which he invariably did. His approach to convoy warfare demonstrated a sound understanding of the principles of strategy by applying the appropriate tactic within the strategy to suit the situation. Moreover, on the subject of evasion techniques, Gardner postulates that a 'greater number of submarines allowed the use of multiple U-boat packs negating to a large extent the gambit of evasion';[55] a point agreed with by Till.[56]

Those who have little confidence in evasive routeing appear to base their conclusions on periods when SigInt was unavailable. But effective evasive routeing goes back a long way to the early sixteenth century when Spanish *Flotas* were in convoy, and used evasive routeing to great effect.[57] They had no Sigint. SOEs too, often changed tack in the middle of the night and were successful in shaking off the shadowing U-boat. It is true that it did not always work but 'it is estimated that the evasive routing provided by Ultra in 1941 saved the Allies about 300 ships . . . It certainly contributed to the sharp decline in the efficiency of the U-boat fleet in the Atlantic . . .'.[58] Along with U-boat casualties in the Atlantic a serious problem to the U-boat Command was the continued successful evasive routeing of convoys but it decided on 10 May that only location by enemy aircraft can be accepted as the cause of our boats being picked up. This also accounts for the detour made by the 'HX and SC convoys'.[59] Even in a post-war analysis of the 1950s, evasive routeing was still considered to be a part of convoy policy.[60] Together with the records of SC-130 and other convoy data it rather tends to nullify the general statement of 'negating to a large extent the gambit of evasion',[61] in practice.

The introduction of the Zaunkönig

U-boats returned to the North Atlantic four months after their temporary withdrawal during which time some new tactics had been worked out. The details of the means and tactics to be used are discussed in Chapter 12, which largely consisted of heavier Flak and the new acoustic torpedo *Zaunkönig*. The British had not yet encountered the introduction of the acoustic torpedo, and

had therefore not trained for it.[62] In September 1943, concurrent with the return
of U-boats to the North Atlantic, two Westbound Convoys ONS-18 and ONS-
202 were advised by Admiral Horton that they should join together for common
protection and sail at six knots, due to a known new U-boat formation in the
vicinity. The convoy size was now 67 ships with good protection. One of the
Escorts, *Itchen*, detected a U-boat and proceeded to make an attack. The U-boat
in question launched one of the newly introduced acoustic torpedoes *Zaunkönig*.
Itchen was struck forward right under her magazine area and blew up, leaving
just two survivors.[63] Other Escorts in the convoy were sunk or badly damaged by
the same type of torpedo, mostly towards the stern where it was designed to hit
home, centred on propeller cavitations.

Feedback of the attack on *Itchen* was at once passed by signal to WATU. In
the Tactical School Roberts studied the problem and came up with a solution.
He called it 'Step-Aside' and had the move tested on the tactical table. On paper,
it worked! Calculating the possibilities, he determined that escorts could avoid
detection (acquisition) by one of four methods:

1. Reducing speed to below ten knots.
2. Using a manoeuvre known as 'step aside'.[64]
3. Through the use of shallow set DC's to counter-mine the torpedo.
4. By the use of noise makers towed astern.[65]

The 'Step-Aside' counter-move was as follows: if an escort detected a U-boat
on Radar, or HF/DF it would turn back, about 150 degrees, and attempt to put
the U-boat 60 degrees on the opposite bow, severely limiting the acquisition
capability of the acoustic torpedo. This course would be held for one mile
(as position three) speed 15 knots. There would then be a turn parallel to
the initial sighting bearing and proceed for another mile (to position four),
at which point there would be a turn towards the U-boat for attack. If the
procedure was conducted correctly, contact should then be gained in two or
three minutes.

Horton was present at the tactical plot of this move and watched as 'Step-
Aside' was demonstrated. After an explanation of the principles, he declared
himself satisfied with the approach and ordered that a signal be prepared for
the Escort Commanders, and got it into fleet orders for immediate dispatch.
Arrangements were also made to include the new tactic into the training
schedule through the use of synthetic tactical teachers, which made it possible
to practice anti-acoustic torpedo tactics, but only on a small scale. Anti-
acoustic torpedo precautions could be accommodated on the simulator, but

only representing one surface ship. A modified device was made to increase the number of ships taking part in an exercise using the 'Cotton' projector, which projected the movements of several ships on to a vertical screen, but this facility was only made available at the Liverpool base.[66]

The details of the anti-acoustic tactic devised at WATU were sent to captains of Escort Groups for future use and later results from this solution proved to be a successful anti-dote to what was feared to be a new phase in weapons warfare.[67] Even so Admiral Horton was never complacent about any advances made in any tactics for he knew that tactics rarely remained static and he still nurtured some concerns that Escort Commanders might not take the current counter-measures seriously enough. As late as 17 January 1944, he wrote of his concerns to Admiral Darke (submarines):

It is a game, this U-boat struggle – the 'gnat' is a nasty snag and delays the approach – all ships hit to date have not completely carried out instructions (careful approach to the U-boat), but in the heat of the moment the offensive spirit of the Escort vessels takes charge, and it is hard to blame them severely.[68]

Commander Hessler at *BdU* HQ expressed disappointment with the performance of the *Zaunkönig,* despite the initial reports of success obtained against Escort ships. The first ships sunk or heavily damaged through the first use of it were encouraging – *Itchen, St Croix, Polyanthus* sunk and *Lagan* badly damaged. A report made on 24 September at *BdU* HQ stated that 24 T5s (*Zaunkönig*) had been fired and Commanders claimed 13 hits, 3 probables' and 7 failures (that accounts for 23, not 24). Nevertheless, Dönitz, at least, appeared to be satisfied with the initial reported successes using the T5 but it was not until 1944 that he realized that U-boat claims submitted for sinking Escorts were highly doubtful.[69]

As more experience was gained, WATU called special attention to SOEs of the dangers of the acoustic torpedo and suggested other scenarios for evading it, including the use of a depth charge if the torpedo approached too close. The lessons learned were then published in the February 1944 CB04050 monthly A/S report as a section on anti 'GNAT' tactics.[70] The WATU team had once more demonstrated the value of 'local' OR. Under Captain Gilbert Roberts WATU staff and students continued to develop tactics against U-boats using the feedback gained from the experiences, and ideas, gained from others like Walker, Macintyre and Gretton – all first rate Commanders. Roberts was pleased with progress and commented that 'If, during three years work, standard game and lecture routeing had been adopted, the Staff would long ago have become tired and stale'. Approximately 4,000 naval officers, ranging from Admirals to Midshipmen, took part in the six-day training courses held at WATU. Some were already battle-hardened campaigners and they brought with them their own experiences;[71] and the results obtained from units operating in the North Atlantic bear witness to WATU's efficacy.

Continuous training 1943–5

The working-up training received by a newly commissioned Escort after it left 'Western Isles' was supplemented first through specialized training received, either at Liverpool, or group training at *Philante*. After return from convoy duty 'continuity' training was given, designed to maintain the efficiency of the ship. Training commenced after a period of leave and was intense – starting with at least five hours of A/S attack teacher training. Groups then put to sea for about two or three days of sea training which enabled S/D operators and A/S COs (A/S Command Officers) to practice classification of echoes, maintaining contact all the time, but discarding false echoes[72] – although these would later be of interest for inshore coastal training in 1944 when U-boats began operating in these areas. Basic group exercises with convoy and accompanying submarines were followed which included HF/DF contacts, inter-ship, ship to air communications and A/S tactics, under the watch of a 'Training Commander'.[73] In order to achieve as much realism as possible, night exercises with submarines were included in which submarines approached a target and then dived, having been detected. By holding the target with ASDIC and observing how British submarines tried their evasion techniques operators were able to enhance their own experience. It was during such exercises that 'some good tactical ideas evolved'.[74] At the end of the training period the Training Commander was to inform the SOE of any group deficiencies. After a report to Captain 'D', and a general consultation, a coordinated training report was then sent to the C-in-C WA.[75] These reports became a written record of how Escort Groups had performed, and might be used for selection purposes.

Conclusions

In 1943 a number of events took place, which changed the face of convoy warfare. As a result of their experiences each side initiated changes to their training organizations to reflect new requirements brought about by developments in tactics and weapons technology. The Germans learnt the lesson that the British had significantly improved U-boat detection methods, both above and below the surface, and had increased the endurance of their long-range aircraft. Furthermore it became clear that advances had been made in the type of depth charges being used, some of which gave no warning of an impending explosion – the 'Hedgehog', followed later by 'Squid'. Initially *BdU* was most concerned about the methods of location, that convoys were now being escorted right across the Atlantic, and that the 'Air Gap' around Iceland had been closed to them. Both these events happened in the first half of 1943, [and] led to a temporary withdrawal of combat patrols from the North Atlantic, following the loss of many U-boats and experienced personnel.

The job of acquiring sufficient personnel as replacements was well underway in June and Dönitz used the period of reflection from June to September to reorganize the training facilities to bring them more up-to-date to meet the new threats facing the U-boat arm. One method of increasing output to man new boats was to cut training time for all ranks, which he did – at the expense of better-trained Commanders and crew. Another was to relax the dependence on volunteers and career men, and take officers and men from other branches within the Navy; and those he could get from other services, particularly the *Luftwaffe*.

With a new understanding of what could be achieved through a co-ordinated approach to training he set about setting up new flotillas for the purpose of an improved training regime for front-line boats. He had learnt a bitter lesson from recent losses and belatedly attempted to remedy a gap in the training regime through co-ordinated combat training with the *Luftwaffe*. His efforts to get more co-operation with the *Luftwaffe* in training exercises should also serve to have better communications between U-boats and aircraft. The weakness in his plan was that he had left it late with no allowance for any kind of follow-up training and no refresher courses, in contrast to the British scheme of continuity training provided by WATU.

In preparation for a return to the North Atlantic theatre several boats were converted to allow for the fitting of a breathing tube for longer underwater endurance and stealth operations, the *Schnorchel*. For the successful deployment of this device extra training would be required for both boats working-up prior to front-line service, and those in theatre. Dönitz organized a new training flotilla for this purpose, and for those U-boats located some distance away *Schnorchel* training was received at their final fitting out location.

In expectation of the arrival of the new *Elektro*-boats another group was established consisting of several U-boats and tenders charged with the task of testing out a new training regime designed by *BdU* Command for the evaluation of systems. By January 1945 the 18th flotilla was fully functional and practicing firing methods, using the new *Nibelung* ranging method. The evaluations carried out formed the basis of the new training curriculum and fighting instructions.

The British also experienced changes in the need for more advanced tactical training. In February 1943 Admiral Horton extended the facilities at Liverpool and created a new section dealing with ASW at Londonderry, the main purpose of which was to establish practical advanced tactical training in a co-ordinated approach with aircraft. Exercises included complicated manouevres using Coastal Command aircraft in as realistic a way as possible, to the extent that live firing practice took place at the same time. WATU continued to be challenged when the *Zaunkönig* was first introduced and quickly came up with a solution. Although the *Zaunkönig* showed initial promise a successful solution to the problem was found.

In September 1943 Britain benefitted from the surrender of Italy. By using some Italian submarines for training purposes in the Mediterannean they were able to release some of their own submarines for British training purposes. Real submarines were of particular help for training both A/S personnel as well as Coastal Command. Rather than use towed targets both surface vessels and aircraft crews were able to practice live location methods. Once submarines had dived A/S methods were able to benefit from the tactics employed by submarines, something that was not possible with benign targets. When U-boats abandoned the North Atlantic theatre in early 1944 to take up inshore combat patrols the use of British submarines in shallow coastal areas helped groups to practice differentiating between bottomed U-boats, wrecks and rocks.

WATU's strength was its versatility in overcoming tactical problems.

Notes

1   GC&CS, 'The German Navy – The U-boat Arm', 7 (December 1945), 90.
2   NHB PG 31747, 2445/43, appendix to 1/Skl KTB – gKdos M-Wehr.
3   NHB PG 33541, BdU/Organizationsabteilung an Kommando der Marinestation Ostsee, 'Personalbedarf der U-Boote auf Grund des Schiffsneubauplanes', 13 November 1939.
4   Timothy Mulligan, *Neither Sharks Nor Wolves* (Annapolis, 1999), 3.

5 Eric Topp, 'Manning and Training the U-boat Fleet', in *The Battle of the Atlantic 1939–1945* (1994), 214–19, 216.

6 *Lagevorträge* (München, 1972), 449; Edward P. von der Porten, *The German Navy in World War Two* (1969), 11.

7 David Westwood, *The U-boat War* (2005), 280; Mulligan, *Neither Sharks nor Wolves*, 118.

8 *Oblt. (I)* Walter Lorch, cited in Martin Middlebrook, *Convoy* (1976), 59–60; Timothy Mulligan, *Lone Wolf* (Connecticut, 1993), 42–3; Peter Padfield, *Dönitz* (1984), 209.

9 Topp, 'Manning and Training the U-boat Fleet', 216; Padfield, *Dönitz*, 318; Alfred Price, *Aircraft versus Submarine* (Barnsley, 2004), 153.

10 Mulligan, *Neither Sharks Nor Wolves*, 135.

11 NHB PG 20537, Großadmiral Dönitz's statement on personnel.

12 NHB NID 24/T65/45, Report on German Naval War Effort, 146.

13 NHB PG 30309B, BdU KTB entry 25 July 1942; Günter Hessler, *The U-boat War in the Atlantic 1939–1945*, (1989), II, 100 and III, 21 – Loss rates.

14 Jochen Brennecke, *Haie im Paradies* (Hamburg, 2002), 125. Translated by author.

15 *Lagevorträge*, 507–10.

16 NHB PG 33945, 1/Skl, 'Erstellung einer vortaktischen Ausbildungseinheit'.

17 NHB PG 32173, 1/Skl KTB Teil C Heft IV, Proposal to create an extra flotilla to training facilities.

18 NHB PG 29399, Various training programmes, 6; TNA CAB /66/32/38, Naval situation, folio 147.

19 TNA ADM 239/248, 'Anti-submarine Warfare', Volume IV, Joint air/sea training, 21.

20 Horst Boog, 'Luftwaffe Support of the German Navy', in *The Battle of the Atlantic 1939–1945*, 302–22, (311).

21 Eberhard Rößler, 'Die deutsche U-Bootausbildung und ihre Vorbereitung 1925–1945', *Marine Rundschau*, 68 (8) (1971), 453–66, 459–60; NHB PG 33945, 1/Skl, 'Erstellung einer vortaktischen Ausbildungseinheit'.

22 NHB PG 33048, 1/Skl /IL KTB, Conference on questions of co-operation with U-boats, 7 September 1944.

23 NHB PG 34398, Operational use of the '*Schnorchel*'in the front-line training group.

24 F. Barley et al., *The Defeat of the Enemy Attack on Shipping 1939–1945*, 137 (Aldershot, 1997), 125.

25 GC&CS, 'The German Navy – Organization', 2, 273.

26 NHB PG 32065, 1/SKl KTB Teil A June 1943, Trials and development boats: NHB PG 34398, Specialized groups for testing and evaluating U-boat developments.

27 NHB NID 24/T13/45, 'Status of Technical Developments of the German Navy in February–March 1944', 2; Axel Niestlé, 'German Technical and Electronic

Development', in *The Battle of the Atlantic 1939–1945,* 430–51, 435; Westwood, *The U-boat War,* 281.

28 NHB NID 24/T65/45, Report on German naval war effort phase V, 42; *Lagevorträge,* 'Zum Problem der Ostsee', 569.

29 Rößler, 'Die deutsche U-bootausbildung und ihre Vorbereitung 1925–1945', 462.

30 GC&CS, ZTPG/329765, 3341824, Intercepts.

31 See Harald Bendert, *Die UB-Boote der Kaiserlichen Marine 1914–1918* (Berlin, 2000). Building U-boats in sections was not a new concept and went back to the First World War.

32 TNA ADM 234/68, U-boat War in the Atlantic, 3, June 1943–May 1945, 85.

33 Eberhard Rößler, 'U-boat Development and Building', in *The Battle of the Atlantic 1939–1945,* 118–37, 133.

34 TNA ADM 234/68, U-boat War in the Atlantic, 3, June 1943–May 1945, 85.

35 NHB PG 31752, 1/Skl KTB Teil C, 'Überlegungen über die Anwendung der neuen Elektroboote'.

36 TNA ADM 239/248, Anti-submarine warfare, Volume IV, 5.

37 TNA ADM 213/341, Report on the use of sonar, 5; Willem Hackmann, *Seek and Strike* (1984), 261.

38 TNA ADM 239/248, Anti-submarine warfare, Volume IV, Provision of targets, 11.

39 TND ADM 199/1732, Memo from C-in-C WA to Admiralty and Western Isles 20.11.1944.

40 TNA ADM 239/248, Anti-submarine warfare, Volume IV, Appendix 1; David K. Brown, *Atlantic Escorts* (Barnsley, 2007), 60.

41 David Zimmerman, 'Technology and Tactics', in *The Battle of the Atlantic 1939–1945,* 476–89, 483.

42 Michael Whitby, 'The Strain of the Bridge: The Second World War Diaries of Commander A. F. C. Layard, DSO, DSC, RN', in *The Face of Naval Battle* (Crows Nest NSW, 2003), 200–18, 214.

43 TNA ADM 239/246, 'Development of the U-boat Campaign', para 79, 20.

44 James Goldrick, 'Work-up', in *The Battle of the Atlantic 1939–1945,* 220–39, 231.

45 TNA ADM 239/248, Anti-submarine warfare, Volume IV, Joint air/sea training, 21; *Official Account of the Battle of the Atlantic,* 56.

46 TNA ADM 239/248, Anti-submarine warfare, Volume IV, Joint air/sea training, 21.

47 TNA ADM 1/17555, WATU, annual report 1944. By December 1944 the courses included mock attacks against TypeXX1 Walter boats, 2; W. S. Chalmers, *Max Horton* (1954), 169.

48 Vice Admiral P. Gretton, 'Why Don't We Learn from History?', *The Naval Review,* 46 (January 1958), 19.

49 TNA ADM 239/141, Progress in Torpedo, Mining and Anti-Submarine Warfare 1939.

50 Malcolm Llewellyn-Jones, 'The Royal Navy on the Threshold of Modern Anti-submarine Warfare, 1944–1949', University of London, King's College, London, 2004, 39.

51 Vice Admiral P. Gretton, 'Why Don't We Learn from History?', 14.

52 Malcolm Llewellyn-Jones, *The Royal Navy and Anti-Submarine Warfare 1917–1949* (Abingdon, 2006), 3.

53 TNA ADM 199/2020, Analysis of Convoy SC 130, 11 July 1943.

54 Llewellyn-Jones, 'The Royal Navy on the Threshold of Modern Anti-submarine Warfare, 1944–1949', 14.

55 W. J. R. Gardner, 'The Battle of the Atlantic, 1941', in *Sea Power* (Ilford, 1994), 109–23, 115.

56 Geoffrey Till, 'The Battle of the Atlantic as History', in *The Battle of the Atlantic 1939–1945*, 584–95, 585.

57 Barley et al., *The Defeat of the Enemy Attack on Shipping 1939–1945*, 41.

58 Marc Milner, *Battle of the Atlantic* (Ontario, 2003), 79.

59 Barley et al., *The Defeat of the Enemy Attack on Shipping 1939–1945*, 41, 72, 92.

60 Eric Grove, 'The Modern Views: The Battle and Post War British Naval Policy', in *The Battle of the Atlantic 1939–1945*, 576–83, 577.

61 W. J. R. Gardner, 'The Battle of the Atlantic, 1941', 109–23, 115; TNA CB 04050, Review of 1943. Naval Staff also got it wrong on occasion.

62 TNA ADM 199/2060: CB 04050/43 (7), Monthly anti-submarine report.

63 TNA ADM 199/2022, Analysis of U-boat operations: Convoys ONS 18 and ONS 202, 19–24 September, 1943; Mark Williams, *Captain Gilbert Roberts R.N.* (1979), 127.

64 TNA ADM 199/2061, Monthly anti-submarine report, June 1944, 27; Arnold Hague, *The Allied Convoy System 1939–1945* (2000), 50.

65 TNA ADM 253/650, 'Acoustic Measurements of Foxers', No. MS 982/44, June 1944.

66 TNA ADM 239/248, Anti-submarine warfare, Volume IV, 20–1.

67 TNA ADM 1/17557, Western Approaches Tactical Unit, annual report 1944, 1; Chalmers, *Max Horton*, 170.

68 Chalmers, *Max Horton*, 211.

69 Hessler, *The U-boat War in the Atlantic 1939–1945*, III, 26–7.

70 TNA ADM 199/2061: CB 04050/44 (2), Monthly anti-submarine report, (f) 'The Anti "gnat" (Acoustic Homing) torpedo', 24.

71 TNA ADM 1/17557, 'Western Approaches Tactical Unit, Annual Report 1944', 1–2; Williams, *Captain Gilbert Roberts R.N.*, 100–1.

72   TNA ADM 239/248, Anti-submarine warfare, Volume IV, Continuity
     Training, 17.
73   TNA ADM 116/4520, WAGO – Western Approaches General Orders, Part 1,
     Section 1, para 106.
74   TNA ADM 239/248, Training programmes and facilities, Section 101, 21.
75   TNA ADM 116/4520, WAGO – Western Approaches General Orders, Part 1,
     Section 1, Para 106/4.

9

The Influence of 'OR' on Developments

The next two chapters demonstrate how 'OR' influenced the shaping of British and German developments in tactics and weapons, not their outcomes. British R&D/OR has been given high praise with the suggestion that much of the success of the Battle of the Atlantic was attributed to it.[1] The linkage between OR and scientific development is considered from a British perspective, where the term originated.

British operational research

The most common form of British OR was that centred around a weapons system, but it could also be a study of weapons systems combined in simple tactical organizations. The distinctive overlying characteristic of OR is that the researcher always looks at whatever element he is considering as a whole and how a specific problem fits into its larger background.[2]

Not much appears to have been accomplished during the interwar years, at least nothing of significance to the history of operations research. Given the progress made in the development of aircraft, submarines, surface vessels, early radar and radio and telephone it does seem surprising that virtually no literature on OR could be found; and yet while the designers led in their field of endeavour, tactics lagged, and effective countermeasures were virtually non-existent.[3]

The basics of British operational research and early results

The British approach to OR was different to the German system, which had a more centralized methodology and was based more generally around emerging technology and methods, whereas the British system was more commonly based around getting the best performance out of existing technology, organically, using practitioners,[4] except in the case of radar development. German OR was important to leading-edge weapons applications, particularly torpedoes, rockets and countermeasures. No comparison of systems has ever been undertaken, and this is the first.

Before embarking on further discussion of this subject it is as well to define the meaning of 'OR' as it applies in this book. OR may be referred to simply as the deployment of scientific methods in the analysis of managed activities. Although in this form it is sometimes regarded as a vague definition it is perhaps one of the most enduring. However, OR has two distinguishing features in modern science:

1. Experimental/empirical science, built on observation.
2. Mathematically articulated theory, maintained by positivism, and its descendants.

Both features constitute scientific knowledge in that they correspond in some canonical way to nature;[5] and 'OR' requires a close personal knowledge of the working conditions in which it is used, and of the people that use it.[6] Much of the work connected with OR is also *a priori*, or a deductive method of determination, in an attempt to find answers to certain problems of relative subjectivity. Patrick Blackett defined *a priori* as an 'attempt to find general solutions to certain rather arbitrarily simplified problems',[7] and it is used as a means, not of defining a problem, but of acquiring results of operational value which may then, afterwards, be quantified; and there are many examples of this in both navies.

Feedback based on operational experience was invariably used to reinforce, or modify a given weapon, or tactic. Both in the British and German case these were derived through data gleaned from operational patrol reports, interviews with key operations crew, open discussions during debriefing meetings and prisoner interrogation reports; all achieved in much the same way.[8] It is, however, worth noting that Germany relied on War Diaries as their key vehicle of analysis. Britain did not.

The emphasis was placed on an 'adjustment and continual re-definition of individual tasks through interaction with others', which is part of the organic form of organization.[9] This then is the simple explanation for the true function of what was established and became known in Britain as 'OR'.

It is the interplay between the OR scientist and the technical/operations staff that could be the key to successful applications. The Navy had its

Signals Establishment, the War Office its Radar Research and Development Establishment, and Signals Research Establishment, but in 1935 the Bawdsey Research Establishment near Felixstowe was specifically set up to research into, and develop, the possibilities of using radio echoes as a means for locating enemy bombers; while the British army was also conducting exercises on a radar system for the detection of aircraft. Interestingly it was postulated that OR in all three services started as a more or less formal occupation in or around the early part of the war.[10] In Britain it would be difficult to state clearly who first started the function, OR, not the term. Professor Blackett is said, with some justification, to have started it in all three services but most would agree that it revolved around the research into Army and Air Force Ground-Radar. In the Navy it was primarily centred on A/S problems, mostly involving radar, HF/DF and problems surrounding convoy protection.[11]

In Britain OR is traceable back to the First World War.[12] The starting date for more serious work in OR was probably after the Anglo-German Naval Agreement of 1935, when the threat of war had started to gather momentum. An example may be found as late as 1939 when torpedo trials were carried out using a magnetic pistol, one of which broke the 'back' of HMS *Bruce* off the Isle of Wight on 22 November 1939.[13] The German system of OR is also traceable back to the First World War to estimate test firings and the results of gunnery practice on targets.[14] Even the early 'Holland' type U-boat of the *Kaiser* era was subject to developmental testing and evaluation done by the *Königliche Versuchsanstalt für Wasserbau und Schiffbau,* producing test results.[15] It was not until later in September 1942 that German OR came under an administrative organization known as the *FEP*, to be discussed later.[16] But while OR came under departmental control, on both sides, many ad hoc solutions were found using local OR, not involving the scientist.[17]

The first use of the term 'Operational Research'

The term 'Operational Research' OR was given by E. J. Williams as a suitable description of this new branch of applied science. At the time he was a Junior Scientific Officer at the Bawdsey Research Station of the Air Ministry. Sir Robert Watson-Watt and A. P. Rowe coined the term operational research section 'to put on the organization chart above our names – simply to distinguish this new kind of work from the normal work of research and development establishment. It was as simple and obvious as that.'[18] Williams later wrote in confirmation of the above statements:

> Military operational research is not new. It did not suddenly begin at Bawdsey in 1937, even though the phrase did . . . But what is new about operational research, I think, is its importance . . . they are: (1) the determination of the operational effectiveness of weapons and equipments; (2) the analysis of the results of operations or (in peace) of exercises to determine the effectiveness of tactics the influence of weapons on tactics and of tactics on weapons; (3) the prediction of the results of future operations; and (4) the analysis of the efficiency of organizations or of methods.[19]

OR in radar development

The year 1940 was a very busy period for radar and OR. In May, Rowe and his research team transferred from Scotland to the south coast of England, to the TRE at Swanage; there to continue their research efforts. At TRE research continued into ways to improve methods and sensitivity of radar detection and it was P. I. Dee who became the driving force behind the search for centimetric radar as a means of solving some of the airborne radar problems. Up until then there had been no equipment working on a wavelength shorter than 25–30 cm and most of the sets in service worked in the 1 to 1.5-m range, but for U-boat detection they were too insensitive and easily detected by U-boat search receivers.

Then the most significant scientific event of that year happened, the imaginative invention of the cavity magnetron. Scientists at Birmingham University and at the General Electric Company had been working on the problem of radar operating at shorter wavelengths, but in 1940 J. T. Randall and H. A. H. Boot, both of Birmingham University, invented and constructed the first cavity magnetron. It enabled the development of a form of radar that significantly reduced the bulk of equipment needed and provide flexible and highly accurate information to the users.[20] In this area alone the Germans had nothing comparable, and were never able to construct a reliable centimetric system.[21]

Sunday soviets

A. P. Rowe, in charge of research into radar, was not just a good scientist and administrator but also understood a great deal about getting the best out of a combination of the military end-user and the civilian scientist. In the early days at Bawdsey he had already discovered the utility of Admirals, Generals and Air Marshals visiting the facility to see for themselves what was being done in their name. When Rowe was made head of station in 1938, he started to stimulate free discussion between these visitors and the Bawdsey scientists with a view that both the visitors and the scientists could interact with suggestions providing feedback and possible solutions to both applications and problems. It was from these early beginnings that the 'Sunday Soviets' developed.[22] Rowe described these meetings as an event which occurred at TRE on Sundays when senior officers of the RAF (sometimes Commanders-in-Chief), junior officers fresh from operations, top headquarters people and scientists came from other establishments; some that were themselves engaged in OR. Discussions were so uninhibited and so regardless of the status of the participants that it became a dictum that anything could be said at the Sunday meeting. Headquarters service and civilian people, many of them possessing great executive authority, returned back to their own working environments to take formal action but few present would deny that the major decisions were made where the scientists worked. After free, uninhibited, discussions between the users and scientists the best solution to a given problem was often usually clear to most concerned.[23] This represents an important step in OR, free discussion at all levels, and one of the most effective forms of feedback. The impact of radar development had its greatest effect later in the war, with the resonant 'cavity magnetron'.[24] It produced a staggering peak-power output of 1 Kw in the 10-cm band.[25] Both ships and aircraft were equipped with this valuable tool of detection against which the U-boat had little in the way of countermeasures.

Two examples of this step help to clarify OR and local OR.

1. 'Sunday Soviets' were intended to provide feedback to the scientists on equipment applications, drawbacks, enhancements and efficacy. Not only were the most senior of officers involved in the discussions but also the users at the front end who relayed their own thoughts and experiences of using equipment, or following a prescribed attack procedure. Their means of direct communication were the regular discussions held but equally important was feedback obtained through the operational 'log' entries which often gave a detailed account of patrol, or engagement activity, in a manner similar to the German method of gathering OR data.

2. Individuals were also known to work on projects quite removed from an OR group but with the same intended outcome – simplification and efficient use of a device, weapon or attack pattern, known as 'local OR'.

Two engaging officers come to mind. One was Squadron Leader Leigh famous for his night-time attack searchlight, used to great effect against U-boats.[26] Leigh had conducted discussions with aircrews and mixed their ideas in with his own. The other was Admiral Max Horton equally famous for his intervention in the application of rocket projectiles modified from a standard RAF product but suitable, he thought, for use in carrier borne aircraft.[27] His modified device was also a mix between his thoughts and those of 'Swordfish' pilots. It seems incredible, but true. Only eight weeks were needed to introduce a new weapon, get the aircraft fitted with it, the crews trained in its use, and get a kill with it in mid-Atlantic. HMS *Archer's* aircraft sank *U-752* on 23 May 1943 'with 3-inch rockets, a new and effective weapon.'[28]

But feedback from the field was a key element to success – illustrated by the 'Sunday Soviets' and group meetings.[29] OR had at its core a balance between the scientists and users. Sharing information, either within a group or sharing information by opening it up to all-comers, was a strong feature of OR.

The point made here is that British scientists alone did not achieve break-throughs in weapons developments, any more than German scientists at the *MWa/FEP* did. In both cases it was a combined effort of scientists and service personnel from all ranks; and it would be naïve to think otherwise.

OR in communications

In the mid-1930s the RAF considered the need for short-wave radio communications to enhance the advantages conferred by the new radar early warning system. Radio development was in the hands of the RAE but until 1937 research on high-frequency techniques was desultory and relations with the radio industry were at a low point. This sorry state of affairs was transformed by the arrival of Squadron Leader Hugh Leedham who took charge of radio development.[30] Working with a team of about 40 young engineers and scientists they were able to apply lessons from the past to develop a VHF (Very High Frequency) set which could accommodate more channels, essential if Fighter Command was to expand. VHF was less susceptible to being jammed by enemy transmitters. Much of the guidance as to what was required on the front line came from the air patrol reports filed by pilots and observers after sorties and training flights. All patrol reports represented a record of 'feedback' of operational value, including those of Coastal Command during the Battle of the Atlantic.[31] Any problems with communications were also noted.

The first VHF trials took place on 30 September 1939 just a few weeks after the declaration of war.[32] The Director of Signals reported to the COAS that there was no doubt that the new Mark I unit opened up a completely new chapter in radio-telephone communications.[33] VHF sets were then provided to the RN for communications with Coastal Command.[34] This is an example of inter-service co-operation, the sharing of 'OR'. The use of VHF in the North Atlantic convoys was one of the success stories for inter-ship and aircraft communications and was vital for co-ordinated attacks against the U-boat.

Coastal Command and naval OR sections

One of the foremost research scientists of the day was Professor Patrick Blackett. Blackett, himself an ex-naval officer, did some good work during the war both for Coastal Command, initially, and then for the Admiralty in the field of OR. In March 1941 he became Scientific Advisor to the AO C-in-C and helped form the Coastal Command ORS.

ORS addressed several problems in the war one of which was to analyze the attacks made by aircraft on U-boats, to date.[35] Blackett's work at ORS then led to his appointment as CAOR (Chief Advisor on Operational Research) and DNOR (Director of Naval Operational Research) at the Admiralty where he worked, principally, on convoys and the anti-U-boat campaign.[36] Interestingly it was in OR, after the United States entered the war, that the Americans set up a similar organization to that of the British OR, ASWORG (Anti-Submarine Warfare Operational Research Group).[37] 'There can be little doubt that the work of ASWORG was influenced by the operational research of Professor Blackett and other scientists in Britain.'[38]

When the depth charge was first deployed by aircraft against U-boats it was found that it killed far fewer U-boats than was expected. Blackett and the ORS staff set out to determine precisely where the weaknesses lay, *a priori*. From an inspection of patrol records kept on all attacks they discovered an error, a mismatch, between the expected and the actual number of successes of U-boat kills. Statistics showed that only around 1 per cent of air attacks on U-boats resulted in the U-boat being destroyed and around 2.5 per cent as being 'probably sunk'.[39] From operational reports and feedback discussions with returning crews it was discovered that depth charges had been set to go off from between 50 to

150 feet. Further analysis of attack reports indicated that in most cases, at the point of attack, the U-boat was so close to the surface that the detonations of DCs could do no more than make life uncomfortable for the U-boat. It was determined that in all probability depth charges had been set to explode far too deep to even come within the range of lethality. What was needed, to be more effective, was a shallower setting of 20 to 25 feet. But the problem was that with the current naval model, whose minimum setting was 50 feet and an optimum depth of detonation was not possible. ORS was then set the task of developing a genuine shallow setting depth charge.[40] After some degree of further experimentation depth charges could be set to explode at depths of between 100 and 150 feet which were calculated to be around the approximate depth reached by a U-boat if it started its dive at an average distance, after it had been sighted. It might seem a simple determination but the answer only emerged after the scientist followed his methodology of *a priori* and set in motion the mechanism to collect the data for the model, which came from operational reports.[41] That was the first of several triumphs by ORS during the war.[42] Once the development was completed the results provided a better kill ratio.

ORS, having decided that the depth settings were optimized for the most promising U-boat targets then turned to the question of attack accuracy. A review of reports statistics revealed a particularly worrying issue with the number of kills achieved, which were substantially less than that expected from the number of straddles reported by the aircrew. Blackett, however, asserted that the first thing to do was to discover the facts and that the best way to do this was to fit rear-facing cameras which would actually photograph the positions of the depth-charge explosions in relation to a U-boat.[43] After discussion with pilots and aircrew it was suggested that better evidence was needed. This led to cameras being fitted to aircraft in order to make a record of the attack.[44]

ORS made an analysis of the first 16 attacks which demonstrated that the suspicion of inaccuracy was in fact the cause.[45] They were able to show that the mean point of impact of the depth-charge stick was not on the U-boat's conning tower as was intended but about 60 yards ahead of it, way outside the zone of lethality. The error was traced back to the current tactical procedures that were meant to compensate for U-boat movement prior to an attack. Thus through the use of 'operational analysis' they were able to study tactical problems and help to develop a common doctrine of attack.[46]

> Its early analyses were often in direct conflict with accepted RAF doctrine and the beliefs of operational staff. There was probably no field of the Command's

activities where a greater dividend was paid by the scientist's insistence on relying of facts rather than opinions.[47]

In 1942 Blackett was to apply his analytical skills further, just at the time that the U-boat menace was being acutely felt. He made a study of convoy operations in order to quantitatively compare the effects that bombing had in the land war versus the contribution that aircraft made in the anti-U-boat campaign. He was able to demonstrate that during its operational life a single aircraft would have a negligible effect on Germany's war machine but if the same aircraft was allocated to Coastal Command it could account for preventing the destruction of up to six cargo laden ships. He also estimated that if one quarter of bomber command were transferred to the Battle of the Atlantic approximately one million tons of shipping a year would be saved, at the current rates. Fortunately, his OR arguments contributed to a change of heart in the Air Ministry because some aircraft were ultimately transferred from Bomber Command to Coastal Command in time to contribute to the successful campaign in March to December 1943.[48] Had the message fallen on deaf ears at the Air Ministry the Battle of the Atlantic may have taken longer to resolve. The official historian of the RN in World War Two went further and concluded that an opposite decision could well have cost the war.[49]

Other OR concerns were addressed in combating the U-boat which are briefly worth considering. Efforts were put into studying the efficiency of aircraft co-operation with surface craft following sightings. AUD's conclusions were that in general, the co-ordination between aircraft and surface vessel was satisfactory but that the ship's chances of contacting a U-boat decreased more rapidly with the time that it took to reach the area in coastal waters, than it did if it were operating in ocean waters. Also a successful hunt depended on the reliability of aircraft reports.[50] The report was brief but gave an indication of the nature of the problems being faced once the U-boats began to operate more in coastal waters in 1944, and what might be expected with the introduction of the new Type XXIII coastal U-boat. Further study was deemed to be of considerable value, but the war ended before it could be started.

Given the degree of activity in OR that characterized several commands of the RAF and Army there was no current impetus of OR activity in the Navy when Blackett moved there from Coastal Command in December 1941.[51] This may be due to the NOR (Naval Operational Research) unit being small by comparison, but it also remained small and centralized throughout the remainder of the war. By contrast German OR gathered momentum after they had established the administrative body *FEP* from which emerged a range of projects to be discussed in the last part of this chapter. The pre-occupation of NOR at the time was in finding ways to improve weapons or systems to combat the threat of U-boats through higher kill ratios as well as countermeasures. About three months before the German Naval Acoustic Torpedo (GNAT) was introduced in 1943 Leon Solomon, an Admiralty scientist, predicted that countermeasures and a change in tactics would be needed in order to counter this threat.[52] The countermeasure applied was the 'Foxer', noise makers, vibrating metal bars towed astern of a warship designed to simulate the sound of high-speed propellers, and thus 'fox' an acoustic torpedo.[53] 'Foxer' may have been found through OR but the tactics were done more at a local level by WATU.

Efficiency became a by-word for the RN and as the war progressed the Admiralty looked for other means to obtain greater efficiencies from current and other weapons delivery platforms. In 1944 DNOR participated in a combined exercise with WA and Flag Officer submarines and training departments to ascertain the current efficiency of training and detecting the new type of U-boat soon expected. HMS *Seraph*, a converted RN submarine, with additional batteries, managed an underwater-speed of up to 12 knots, a good test for existing ASDIC (SONAR),[54] to be discussed later.

Convoy size and escort efficiency

It is generally accepted that the major achievement in naval OR attributable to Blackett and his staff was their analysis of convoys crossing the Atlantic during 1941 and 1942 which concluded that merchant ship losses were, for all practical purposes, independent of the size of the convoy. It was found that if an increase in the average size of convoys was raised from 32 to 54 ships the model showed a corresponding decrease in losses of no less than 56 per cent.[55]

Effective though this positive change in strategy was one is fully justified in asking what the study really achieved that had not been known in earlier times, a point not picked up by most historians. A similar study had been conducted during the last war. Convoy statistics on comparative escort strength from 1917–18 had been analyzed by an acting commander, Rollo Appleyard RNVR. Valuable information in respect of convoy size, gained out of the 1914–18 war, appears to have been disregarded. Appleyard's report stated quite unequivocally, and convincingly, that 'The escort strength requires to be measured, not in terms of the number of vessels in convoy, but in terms of the total area comprised within the boundary formed by lines connecting all outer vessels.' Appleyard went on further to prove mathematically that the ratio of a torpedo attack area around the convoy perimeter to the number of escorts directly watching is 'a more correct numerical measure of the escort strength of a convoy than is the ratio of the number of ships in convoy to the number of close escorts'.[56] How could such a report be buried in the Naval historical archives and remain unseen for so many years? Unfortunately it was a lesson that had not been learnt. Had the printed results of mathematical research been acted upon the Admiralty would have been aware of 'the law of convoy size'. As it was, it was not until 1943 that Blackett and his team produced the similar interesting statistics about ocean convoys. But the last word on this matter should to Sutcliffe who correctly forecasted that by the time the researchers' efforts into this subject were bearing fruit, the allies had already won the Battle. Therefore it does not really matter how dramatic the potential improvement might have been, it would have had little real impact.[57]

A greater benefit to accrue to convoy protection was to look at the effects that escort numbers made to the overall efficiency of a convoy. It was determined that an increase from 6 to 9 escorts per convoy would lead to a reduction in losses of ships of about 25 per cent. If one looks back to the early days of the war it was accepted that the stronger the surface escort the better would be the protection afforded; but the problem was that additional escorts were just not available. Numerically this was correct but the advantage of escort duty size came when convoys passed through known, or anticipated, U-boat areas around convoys. When convoys passed into comparatively safe areas the numbers could then be reduced. An increase in the size of the escorts, where numbers mattered critically, could be of substantial benefit in terms of ship losses.[58] Regrettably this was only made possible after the 'Torch' North African landings had finished at the beginning of 1943, when support groups were formed which could reinforce the escort of threatened convoys. The value of the new support groups lay in their ability to make longer searches which served to increase the total kills of all surface ships by up to 30 per cent.[59] This one strategic move was a welcome development and a lesson well re-learnt from the past war.[60]

A summary of other naval OR

The febrile activity of ASW in naval OR began to ease after Dönitz withdrew most of his U-boats from the North Atlantic in May 1943 with little success to show after this move, and research began to slow down; curiously this was at the time when German OR was in ascendancy. There was an organizational change in June 1944 when the CAOR became the DNOR but of the 105 reports published in 1944 only 35 per cent were ASW-related, and in 1945 only 15 per cent; 'the rest were subjects that included mine warfare, anti-ship warfare, air operations, amphibious operations and several more.'[61] DNOR was also engaged in SigInt OR, not discussed here.

HF/DF

Direction finding research came within the orbit of the ASE (Admiralty Signals Establishment) and was the responsibility of a small team of scientists under Christopher Crampton working in collaboration with a team of skilled operators.[62] Several shore-based HF/DF stations spread around the coasts of the British Isles (even back to the First World War) were able to provide an approximate position of a U-boat by means of comparing cross bearings and working-up a 'cocked hat'. But much greater accuracy could be obtained using HF/DF when mounted on ships. This was however, as Crampton discovered, a tricky technical problem to solve.[63] One of the initial problems was finding the best place on a ship to mount the aerial so that it would not be obstructed by masts, funnels or other sources of possible interference. Good results were found by experimentation, a local form of OR. Next, the HF/DF receiver had to pick up signals that had necessarily been transmitted in as short a time as possible. Initially the signals from the first set, known as FH3, were received aurally (with the operator wearing headphones) but the early results, more often than not, were unsatisfactory. A member of the OR group, S. de Walden, one of the Polish engineers, suggested that a unit providing visual signals would be more effective with a live display than having to intercept rapid transmissions aurally. This was achieved by adapting a cathode ray tube and adding it to the direction-finder, in a similar manner to that used by Watson-Watt for his pre-war ionospheric studies, and also as used on the later Radar PPI units.[64] Although the addition was small it was, technologically, an important step forward.

Another major problem with the ship-borne system was obtaining the range of a detected U-boat transmission since the likelihood of two escorts being in the same area to make cross-bearings could not always be relied on, although it would have simplified matters. This problem was largely solved when radio transmissions were monitored in tests using *U-570* (renamed HMS

Graph, captured intact in August 1941 by Coastal Command). The strength of its radio transmissions was measured which enabled a figure for the range to be determined; generally this was usually around 15 to 20 miles.[65] The use of HF/DF in the Battle of the Atlantic was a great success for the Navy and one which the U-boat Command did not fully realize, at first.[66]

The importance of this device is better judged by a comment by Dönitz, who sometimes referred to his losses as being due to a location device.[67] In an entry of the *BdU* log for the 21 May 1943 situation report he remarked, referring to the enemy,

> He is using various surface and underwater location devices, the physical and technical principles and practical use of which are not completely understood in all instances, and the presence of which can only be confirmed in some cases by their effects.[68]

Even at this late stage he still had no idea about the contribution made by HF/DF.

Escort attack strategies on U-boats

Naval OR carried out research studies into attacks on U-boat by escort vessels, and how best to improve the 'kill' ratio. Calculations of efficiency found that in 40 per cent of the cases the DC was set to explode at a depth too deep to be of any practical value, but the vast majority were set to the ideal depth of lethality – with just a small number being set too shallow.[69] In the majority of cases the U-boat had already dived but even if the U-boat had been sighted beforehand it was impossible to estimate to what depth. It was not until much later in the war that there was a more reliable means to determine both direction and depth of a U-boat, and even then it depended on sea conditions. No serious development work was undertaken from 1934–9 but in 1939 it appears that a failed attempt was made to adapt ASDIC recorders for use with ahead thrown weapons.[70] It would appear that few lessons were learned from these exercises and that Britain had lost an opportunity that would have proven to be of major consequence.

The improvement came with development of the ahead throwing Hedgehog 'Mortar', which gave more accurate control and improved the 'dead time' between losing ASDIC contact and the point of launch of projectiles. The equipment could now launch a 'pattern' of charges making it a more effective 'killer'.[71] The weapon was an advance on the standard depth charge but still only had a limited range of only some 200 yards ahead of the ship and with the fixed beam Type 144 ASDIC in use at the time it meant that Hedgehog, at best, was only accurate down to about 350 feet. Up until the early part of 1944 Hedgehog attacks on deep U-boats had to be made using a stopwatch and firing the weapon manually, which accounts for too much human error.

A report demonstrated that using the standard DC, Hedgehog or Squid, the probability of sinking a U-boat per attack was 8, 27 and 53 per cent respectively, broadly in line with theoretical predictions.[72] By the end of the war it is estimated that about 50 U-boats had been sunk by Hedgehog.[73] Had conventional U-boats remained in the North Atlantic the chances of their losses increasing were raised significantly.[74] This was evidence of how development scientists had used the Navy's operational knowledge to the full.

Early in 1943 Blackett's group was asked by the Anti-U-boat Committee to analyze the marginal values of both escort vessels and aircraft in attacks on U-boats. The group studied the statistics from the previous two years and came to the conclusion that the number of losses inflicted by U-boats on a convoy, in an attack of a given scale and with a given number of escorts, had been roughly dependent on the size of the convoy. Seemingly a convoy size of 40–50 ships suffered no greater losses on average than a convoy comprised of 30 vessels. Their calculations were confirmed by examining several possible variables such as the effect of weather, more efficient escorts or more aircraft patrolling over large convoys. The study also looked at the management of convoys.[75] The OR group was then asked to consider the viability of whether escort support groups were likely to make a difference to the battle between surface escorts and U-boats. It tackled this question by examining the value of each additional escort in terms of the merchant ship sinkings it prevented by its mere presence in the convoy(s) screen. The data demonstrated that from summer 1942 until the end of the year, 210 merchant ships had been lost to U-boat attacks at a time when the average available escort strength was about 100 for the period. A detailed examination of convoy statistics showed that if an increase in the number of escorts present in the convoy screen from six to nine were considered it would reduce losses, all other factors being more or less equal, by a factor of about a quarter. The OR group called it the 'defensive' value of additional escort vessels making it less likely for U-boats to mount successful attacks on more heavily defended convoys.[76] Such a study was a powerful argument for an increased number of support groups.

Conclusions

The origins and achievements in British OR have been described, but their actual utility is harder to define. Certainly great strides were made in this newly created scientific method of converting data into a form that could be subjected to a mathematical model, so that a measure of efficiency could be established. In terms of the efficiencies that were actually achieved, improvements were generally in percentage terms, not orders of magnitude, although some OR projects produced better outcomes than others. When one talks about statistics this, for many of the projects, has little meaning because when statistical models are built they generally only benefit large samples, not the smaller ones that were available for measurement. Further consideration should also take into account the organic growth of the system, or development.

In order to understand British benefits it is worth highlighting the projects where some utility occurred, but not specifically ranked in order of importance. One thread is common to both sides, feedback – either through operational reports, or direct contact with those engaged in operations.

- When a system such as radar was first introduced it was in its early stages of development but like many products they developed over time, often gradually through improvements or new component discoveries – such as the 'cavity magnetron'. The 'Sunday Soviets' were quite unique but only applied to radar developments. The feedback British scientists received led to an impact of technology on Radar development that had its greatest effect later in the war, when the 'cavity magnetron' was fully installed and operational in both aircraft and ships. Up until the beginning of 1944 the U-boat had little defence against centimetric radar.
- Communications too saw developments in the war. When war became a distinct possibility it was already known that the existing system was too limited. Work began on a practical VHF set that could use multiple frequencies, which would permit communications between several aircraft at the same time. Inter-service relations were good, and they 'shared' their experience with sets being provided to the RN so that communications with Coastal Command could be improved. This was an example of co-operation, the sharing of 'OR'.
- Of the two OR groups, the ORS produced the most tangible results of the Battle of the Atlantic. Blackett's group made the discovery of an error between what was expected and actual number of U-boat kills, based on

the number sightings and attacks. Statistics proved only a low percentage of kills.[77] The findings helped to devise new methods of depth charge deployment and depth settings, which increased the zone of lethality. Kill ratios improved and the ORS group could be justly proud of their efforts.

- The Naval OR group made an interesting study of the effect that additional escorts would have in terms of merchant ships saved. The group referred to the effect as the 'defensive' value of additional escort vessels making it less likely for U-boats to mount successful attacks on more heavily defended convoys, and it marked the beginning of the offensive rôle of escorts.

- Perhaps one of the greatest contributions to the Battle of the Atlantic was the 'local' OR provided by WATU. As situations arose Roberts, together with SOEs (Senior Escort Commanders) and the WATU staff, enhanced the ability of Escort Groups to achieve a higher rate of U-boat 'kills' and to make tactical changes in countermeasures, achieved through his system of two way feedback. Commanders could relate their problems for WATU to study, and in so doing often created an almost immediate solution to a tactical problem. In this area the U-boat arm had nothing comparable; although their de-briefings provided detailed feedback on tactics used and weapons settings employed, vital ingredients for an OR study.

Notes

1   J. G. Crowther et al., 'Science at War', *The Naval Review*, 36 (2) (May 1948), 197–200, 198–9; F. H. Hinsley et al., *British Intelligence in the Second World War* (1981), II, 563.

2   Omand Solandt, 'Observation, Experiment, and Measurement in Operations Research', *Operations Research Society of America*, 3 (1) February 1955, 1–14, 2; M. Pidd, 'The Future of OR', *Journal of the Operational Research Society*, 52 (11) (2001), 1181–90.

3   Joseph F. McCloskey, 'The Beginnings of Operations Research: 1934–1941', *Operations Research*, 35 (1) 1987, 143–52, 144.

4   M. Aitken and J. Hage, 'The Organic Organization and Innovation', *Sociology*, 5 (1) (1971), 63–82; T. Burns et al., *The Management of Innovation* (1961), 103–4.

5   J. E. Tiles, 'Experimental Evidence vs. Experimental Practice?', *The British Journal for the Philosophy of Science*, 43 (1) (March 1992), 99–109, 99.

6   Crowther et al., 'Science at War', 197.

7 TNA WO 291/1911, P. M. S. Blackett, 'A Note on Certain Aspects of the Methodology of Operational Research', May 1943, 2; TNA ADM 219/630 'OR' History.

8 TNA ADM 1/ 17561, Interview given by Admiral Godt after the war to Captain Gilbert Roberts; GC&CS, 'The German Navy – The U-boat Arm', 7 (December 1945), 111.

9 Burns et al., *The Management of Innovation*, 105; Dennis Haslop, 'New Product Development and Team Leader Autonomy in Industrial R&D', Brunel University, 1997, 17.

10 TNA CAB 66/27/32, 11 August May 1942, 1. It was suggested that co-operation should exist across all three services in radar and communications equipment; Solandt, 'Observation, Experiment, and Measurement in Operations Research', 1; David Zimmerman, 'Preparations for War', in *Patrick Blackett* (2003), 110–25, 110.

11 TNA WO 291/1911, Blackett, 'A Note on Certain Aspects of the Methodology of Operational Research', 2; C. H. Waddington, *OR in World War II* (1973), 27.

12 F. W. Lanchester, *Aircraft in Warfare* (1916) 31, 99.

13 David K. Brown, *Nelson to Vanguard* (2006), 18–24.

14 BA-MA RM 5/2059, Artillerie Schießversuche und Ergebnisse September 1911–Juni 1914.

15 BA-MA RM 3/22941, Reichsmarineamt, Schleppversuchsergebnisse 'Hollandtyp' mit einem Schiffsmodell aus Paraffin.

16 NHB PG 42238, Document 11214: Organization of the FEP Forschung, Erfindungen und Patentwesen.

17 TNA ADM 213/611, German underwater weapons department.

18 M. Fortun et al., 'Scientists and the Legacy of World War II', *Social Studies of Science*, 23 (4) November 1993, 595–642, 600.

19 E. J. Williams, 'Reflections on Operational Research', *Journal of the Operations Research Society of America,* 2 (4) (November 1954), 441–3, 441–2.

20 John Cornwell, *Hitler's Scientists: Science War and the Devil's Pact* (New York, 2003), 277.

21 W. P. Cunningham et al., 'Of Radar and Operations Research: An Appreciation of A. P. Rowe (1898–1976)', *Operations Research,* 32 (4) (July–August 1984), 958–67, 962; Cornwell, *Hitler's Scientists; Science War and the Devils Pact,* 277.

22 Alfred Price, *Aircraft versus Submarine* (Barnsley, 2004),181; Cunningham et al., 'Of Radar and Operations Research', 962.

23 Cunningham et al., 'Of Radar and Operations Research', 963.

24 Christopher Schumacher, 'Forschung, Rüstung und Krieg: Formen, Ausmaß und Grenzen des Wissenschaftlereinsatzes für den zweiten Weltkrieg im deutschen Reich', Ernst-Moritz-Arndt-Universität, Greifswald, 2004, 99; Corelli Barnett, *The Audit of War,* 180.

25 TNA ADM 239/246, ASV Mk.3 introduction February 1943, 11; Jerome Kraus, 'The British Electron Tube and Semi-conductor Industry 1935–62', *Technology and Culture*, 9 (1) October, 1968, 544–61, 550.

26 Price, *Aircraft versus Submarine*, 579.

27 This chapter also discusses a similar German inter-service co-operation.

28 TNA ADM 239/246, 'Development of the U-boat Campaign', 14; TNA CAB 66/37/24, Naval, Military and Air Situation from 0700, 20 May, to 0700, 27 May, 1943, 2.

29 Cunningham et al., 'Of Radar and Operations Research', 963.

30 E. B. Callick, 'VHF Communications at RAE 1947–1942', Institution of Electrical Engineers International Conference on 100 Years of Radio, September, 1995, 153–60.

31 TNA AIR 15/279, Analyses of reports on anti-submarine operations, October 1942 to August 1943; TNA AIR 27/1105/6, No. 172 Squadron operational records 1942–1945.

32 G. Hartcup, *The Effect of Science on the Second World War* (Basingstoke, 2000), 47.

33 TNA CAB 102/641, History of development production of Radio and Radar, 78.

34 TNA ADM 220/1486, HF/DF in ships.

35 Royal Society Paper, RS-Operational Research (OR) CSAC 63.1.79/D.83-D125, 1940–74.

36 Paul Sutcliffe, 'Operational Research in the Battle of the Atlantic', in *The Battle of the Atlantic 1939–1945* (1994), 418–29, 418.

37 William Glover, 'Manning and Training Allied Navies', in *The Battle of the Atlantic 1939–1945* (1994), 188–213, 206.

38 M. C. Meigs, *Slide Rules and Submarines: American Scientists and Subsurface Warfare in World War II* (Washington, 1990), 51.

39 Alfred Price, 'Development of Equipment and Techniques', in 'Seek and Sink', RAF Bracknell Paper No. 2, 21 October 1991, 51.

40 Royal Society Paper, RS-Operational Research (OR) Correspondence CSAC 63.1.79/D.135, 1942.

41 J. W. Abrams, 'Military Applications of Operational Research', *Operations Research*, 5 (3) (June 1957), 434–40, 436.

42 Price, 'Development of Equipment and Techniques', in 'Seek and Sink', 52.

43 C. H. Waddington et al., 'Lord Blackett', *Operational Research Quarterly*, 25 (4) (December 1974), i–viii, v.

44 C. H. Waddington, *OR in World War II*, 182.

45 TNA AVIA 15/1319, Research and Development: General (Code 45): Establishment and Organization of Operational Research Sections (ORS) liaison with RAF Commands.

46 Glover, 'Manning and Training Allied Navies', 204.

47 Air Ministry, *The Origins and Development of Operational Research in the Royal Air Force*, 76; Paul Sutcliffe, 'Operational Research in the Battle of the Atlantic', 422.

48 TNA ADM 219/16, 'Scientists at the Operational Level', Section 1.

49 Stephen W. Roskill, *The War at Sea 1939–1945* (1957), II, 371.

50 TNA ADM 1/17641, Contains a U-boat study of air/sea communications co-operation.

51 TNA AVIA 15/1319, Confidential Note AFC, dated 18 December 1941.

52 TNA ADM 219/52, 'Some Operational Implications of a Homing Torpedo', L. Solomon, Report 36/43, 1 June 1943.

53 David K. Brown, *Atlantic Escorts* (Barnsley, 2007), 461; Marc Milner, *Battle of the Atlantic* (Ontario, 2003), 176.

54 TNA ADM 173/18701, Admiralty, and Ministry of Defence, Navy Department: Submarine logs, Monthly log of HM Submarine Seraph, month of September 1944.

55 TNA WO 291/1911, size of Convoy, Appendix B, 11; Joseph F. McCloskey, 'British Operational Research in World War II', *Operations Research*, 35 (3) (1987), 453–70, 465.

56 Arthur Marder, 'The Influence of History on Sea Power: The Royal Navy and the Lessons of 1914–1918', *Pacific Historical Review*, 41 (4) (November 1972), 413–43, 425; D. W. Waters, 'The Science of Admiralty', *The Naval Review*, 51 (4) 1963, 395–411, 400.

57 Paul Sutcliffe, 'Operational Research in the Battle of the Atlantic', 427.

58 TNA ADM 219/334, Analysis of hunts on U-boats by surface craft, 1; Vice Admiral P. Gretton, 'Why Don't We Learn from History?', 18.

59 TNA ADM 234/578, Naval Staff History: 'The Defeat of the Enemy Attack on Shipping 1939–1945', 96.

60 F. Barley et al., *The Defeat of the Enemy Attack on Shipping 1939–1945*, 137 (Aldershot, 1997), 47.

61 TNA WO 291/1911, OR air campaign, May 1943, 8; Paul Sutcliffe, 'Operational Research in the Battle of the Atlantic', 420.

62 TNA ADM 220/1486, Crampton on high frequency direction finding (HF/DF) in HM Ships; P. C. Redgment, 'HF/DF in the RN Development of Anti-U-boat Equipment, 1941–45', in *Applications of Radar and Other Electronic Systems in the Royal Navy in World War, 2* (1994), 231–48, 239.

63 D. Howse, *Radar at Sea* (1993), 142–6.

64 TNA ADM 220/1486, Crampton on high frequency direction finding (HF/DF) in HM Ships.

65 TNA ADM 239/258, Report on HMS Graph, ex U-boat U-570: G. Hartcup, *The Effect of Science on the Second World War*, 48.

66 Hinsley et al., *British Intelligence in the Second World War*, II, 550.

67 *Seekriegsleitung*, 1/Skl KTB Teil A, 68 vols. 1939–45, 58 (Bonn, 1989), 774;
    TNA HS 8/767: TNA ADM 186/ 809: CB 04051 (103), Chapter 11,
    'Contact-keepers are Often Forced to Submerge by Aircraft and Ships
    Following up HF/DF Bearings', 40; David Syrett, *The Battle of the Atlantic and
    Signal Intelligence,* 139 (Aldershot, 1998), 2.

68 NHB PG 30324, Enclosure to 2/Skl, Naval War Staff BdU Op. Group Command
    2968 of 21 May 1943.

69 Paul Sutcliffe, 'Operational Research in the Battle of the Atlantic', 424.

70 TNA ADM 186/153, Exercises and Operations 1933.

71 TNA CAB 86/3, Memorandum of the First Lord of the Admiralty on Surface
    Ship Weapons, 24 November 1942, 49.

72 Paul Sutcliffe, 'Operational Research in the Battle of the Atlantic', 424.

73 David Syrett, 'Battle of the Atlantic', *American Neptune,* 45 (1) (Winter 1985),
    46–64, 55.

74 TNA ADM 189/175, Technical history of A/S Weapons, folio 13, 11;
    TNA ADM 239/246, 'Development of the U-boat Campaign', 1, 13.

75 TNA ADM 219/209, Leon Solomon, 'Some Problems of Naval Operational
    Research', 14 September 1945; TNA PREM 3/414/3, Progress of analysis of the
    value of escort vessels and aircraft in the anti-U-boat, February 1943.

76 Barley et al., *The Defeat of the Enemy Attack on Shipping 1939–1945,* 115;
    David Zimmerman, 'Preparations for War', 118.

77 Price, 'Development of Equipment and Techniques', 51.

10

The Influence of German 'OR' on U-boat Operations

The second part of this chapter investigates German OR from its origins up to 1942 and beyond, when OR and scientific research came under one administrative body. It demonstrates that contrary to the beliefs of several historians the *Kriegsmarine* used 'OR' and undertook significant projects.

Operational research and the development of military products with industry

Most historians of OR do not appear to have explored the issue of whether the German military had any form of 'OR' in any great depth. This may be because of a historiographical preoccupation with the significance of scientists' involvement in the military decision-making or it may be because of a language barrier; or even the ready availability of research material. It might also be explained away by historians adopting a technological determinist view of World War Two.[1]

One British historian is of the firm conviction that German OR did not exist, in any form. In an article written for the *Patrick Blackett* book he suggested that in contrast to British OR 'none of the characteristics (of OR) were evident in Germany, either then or indeed at any time during the war'.[2] Allied success has generally been attributed to better training, tactics and technology.[3] Nevertheless, it is useful to consider his view of the German case in greater detail. It is hypothesized to be true that they never developed anything remotely like OR given the general nature of the Third Reich with its compartmentalization, deliberate overlaps and the ability to divert resources to both wasteful redundancy and significant turf fighting; and this alone precluded such developments.[4] Hartcup and Price expressed a similar view.[5]

An American historian, Timothy Mulligan, who made a study of the U-boat arm and its organization used much of the material obtained from the German U-boat archives. He stated about OR that the U-boat Command made no attempt to scientifically analyze military operations, search procedures or weapons effectiveness, as was done by the allies. It is further suggested that operating in such a relative vacuum of information the *BdU* staff believed in their own technology and their U-boat commanders' claims.[6] It would appear that all these statements fail to grasp the reality of what the German military and scientific community actually achieved in this field. None of these historians appear to have produced any evidence to support their arguments.

Pre-1943 examples of *a priori*, OR and positivism

Although 1943 became the year of concerted effort in OR it had in fact begun earlier. Others continued into 1943, and these are presented later under the post 1943 heading. As was the case in British OR the objective was to learn from experience in order to implement new, more effective, solutions to problems. But there was always the odd, unexpected opportunity, which helped solve a problem, not related to OR. For example in 1942, faced with copper shortages, *OKM* was compelled to cutback U-boat production until applying lessons learned from a captured British submarine. Steel started to replace copper in torpedo tubes and propellers.[7]

Torpedo failures

One early example demonstrates the German understanding for the *a priori* technique and its application in OR. The problem of torpedo failures began in the first days of the war. Lt Günther Prien's (*U-40*) attack and sinking of Royal Oak on 13/14 September 1939 in Scapa Flow, demonstrated how serious the defect was.[8] Out of five torpedoes launched only the last two detonated, perceived as an unacceptable failure rate by the commander.[9] In January 1940 Admiral Karl Dönitz noted in his *KTB* that:

> The Director of the Torpedo Inspectorate telephoned me today. Trial shots have been made on the torpedoes in stock, with the result that the Torpedo Inspectorate considers the possibility of torpedoes not firing is proven.[10]

In May, still concerned with the number of torpedo failures that his U-boat arm had suffered since the start of the war he approached 1/*Skl*, the operations department, to enquire into the matter. 1/*Skl* with the support of the *BdU* requested *Kriegswissenschaftlicheabteilung* (*Kr*) to inquire if there were any differences between the percentage number of 'hit' detonations achieved in the First World War with those of the present day. In the reply from the *Kr* to 1/*Skl* of 6 May 1940 they were able to report that in an examination of the 52 discharged torpedoes considered, 10 failed to explode, 13 went astray and 28 were positive detonations. Calculating all instances over a period of time they determined that an average of 53.8 per cent of torpedo firings were failures. Compared to the First World War there was little difference with an average of around 52.9 per cent.[11] These calculations represent 'Positivist' methodology, no longer perceived but quantified,[12] and corresponding in a canonical way to nature.[13]

High underwater-speed U-boats

It may be thought that the development of a HUS U-boat was an event which coincided with the defeat of the conventional U-boat in May 1943. It was not. As early as 1937 Dönitz had learnt from Professor Walter about the possibility of a HUS U-boat using a revolutionary technique, but he found no enthusiasm in the Naval War Staff. By 1940 they began to listen and in July 1942 a contract was issued for 2 small boats of 250 tons.[14] At the end of September 1942 Admiral Raeder and Dönitz called on Hitler. Dönitz outlined to him that the 'most important of all was the demand for underwater-speed, to be accomplished by the new Walter submarine'.[15] It was a gradual creep up to 1943 when the matter became most acute. However, Dönitz began to realize a lesson in the making in that a HUS U-boat would be needed one day. He had defined the problem earlier and now he used the *a priori* method of acquiring results from U-boat *KTBs*' and feedback to reinforce his argument. In fact he waited too long to press his case – and then faced an uphill struggle.

Decoys and camouflage

The decoy primarily used as a countermeasure against ASDIC (SONAR) was first requested by Dönitz in 1941 when he wrote to the head of the

Communications Division (2/*Skl MND*), *Vizeadmiral* Maertens, stating that some form of ASDIC decoy was required; an admission that British ASDIC was more effective than first thought.[16] The idea of a decoy was readily determined from *MND's* inspection of *KTB* patrol logs; logs would have described manoeuvre tactics used to clear the ASDIC area, and dive deep. By so doing, valuable time was wasted trying to regain a favourable attack position. By the autumn of that year a decoy was ready for use. Known as 'Bold', or SBT to the British, it consisted of a round cylinder 15 cm in diameter packed with chemicals which when in contact with water gave off an effervescent stream of gas.[17] By ejecting three, one after the other in succession, the area covered with the gas extended large enough to give off false echoes to the ASDIC.[18] British operators however were soon able to distinguish between the real echoes and those given off by Bold. The decoy effect was soon overcome and became quite ineffectual. 'SBT was a nuisance but never became a menace, thanks to our good knowledge of it.'[19]

Another project of even greater interest was U-boat camouflage known as *Alberich*, named after an 'Elf' in the German legend of the *Nibelungen* who could pull on a helmet and become invisible. Interest was already shown in1938 and directed at the development of sound-absorbing coating, intended to neutralize ASDIC. This research was deemed an 'operational' necessity and undertaken by a team directed by Professor Dr Erwin Meyer of Technical University, at the request of Raeder, using the operational expertise (OR) of U-boat practitioners, and their records.[20] Erwin Meyer was known in Britain as an expert on sound absorption and delivered a series of five lectures at the University of London in October 1937, from which a book was published.[21] *Alberich* progress was further discussed at a meeting with Hitler in September 1942 where *OKM's* head of the Communications Division reported on development in anechoic reflective coatings; on what would now be called 'stealth technology.[22] The work continued into 1943 and beyond, and is discussed more fully in that section where further progress was made.

Weapons and 'Operational Research'

The *MWa* were responsible for all technical matters in relation to the weapons of the *Kriegsmarine* and carried out their work through a series of subordinated departments, including the research institutions mentioned in this work. It was the responsible naval authority that performed its duties through various

Ministries to the Reich's Ministry for Armaments and Munitions, or *MRue*. As a combined unit they carried out the functions of the departments that in Britain reported to the Third Sea Lord (Controller).[23]

Specialist inspectorates within departments were charged with ensuring the quality of the product, which did not always work.

An early example would be the poor pistol firing mechanisms and depth keeping qualities of torpedoes.[24] OR to test and find solutions was carried out by the *TVA* and a special unit know as *Sultan,* which was an 'OR' group of U-boats and torpedo experimental vessels operating in the Baltic, a useful platform to test other U-boat requirements, such as noise reducing propellers, etc.[25] There were other scientifically based calculations of OR made. An example of this may be found in examples given in the *BdU* War diary in December 1942, and again in May 1943.[26] The details provided covered torpedo attacks against Corvettes, Destroyers, cruisers and aircraft carriers. Calculations were based on operational data provided by the *BdU* Organization from the user's perspective, which provided the feedback necessary for analysis. As a result of OR new torpedo depth settings were introduced on 20 March 1943 based on the depth of 'target' ship, some of these results would have also involved trials with the OR group *Sultan.*[27]

By the middle of 1942 it became apparent that the enemy had deployed operationally effective radar systems in surface escorts and in aircraft but the developments achieved by the *MWa*, for both ships and aircraft, looked distinctly pedestrian by comparison.[28] In August the *BdU* had already noted how the balance of technology was shifting in favour of the allies.

BdU War Diary of 21 August 1942.

a) *General*:

Number of enemy aircraft have increased, a great variety of aircraft types have appeared, aircraft are equipped with excellent Radar set against U-boats: all these factors have made the conduct of the U-boat war in the Eastern Atlantic very difficult. Outward and inward-bound boats in the North Sea and Biscay are exposed to grave danger by daily, even hourly, hunts by aircraft . . .[29]

Some put this lack of development down to the effects of State regulation, or due to National Socialism, which in itself often stifled creativity. But the fact that *MWa* had originally designed, produced, and then accepted some products suggested the absence of an effective system appraisal;[30] this same problem is confirmed in the work of Oliver Krauss.[31]

By the late summer of 1942 Raeder would, himself, wonder if the Navy's scientific base was broad enough to meet the needs of war in terms of new weapons development, and further, whether the material departments could compete successfully in the industrial sector.[32] Dönitz shared the same view and had often been at odds with the *ObdM* about developmental issues and the need to address the requirements of his U-boat fleet at the front.[33] On 28 September 1942 Raeder held a meeting of all heads of department to 'openly' discuss development requirements of the Navy and to announce the setting up of a new organization, *FEP*, which was to be instrumental in addressing new developments to meet operational requirements.[34] The new structure should address practical solutions to incremental problems that involved the use of operational data as a major source of data measurement, the essence of OR.[35] Such a meeting was overdue and would lead to more use being made of feedback.

Institutional and local OR

On the day before he withdrew U-boats from the Atlantic, 23 May 1943, he invoked the spirit of discussion by calling a conference of some 200 to 300 scientists.[36] Unhappy with the conflicting advice and continual failures on the part of technical advisers on the subject of radar, he ordered the formation of a Naval Scientific Directorate, known as the *Kriegsmarinearbeitsgemeinschaft*, which became the *Wissenschaftlicherführungsstab der Marine* (*WFM*) in January 1944.[37] According to one American historian, 'Its duties corresponded loosely to those of the Allied operational research teams, which had played a major part in the development of allied weapons and tactics for more than two years.'[38] This quotation is incorrect since it was merely an advisory body.[39] The technical direction for Radar was put in the hands of Professor Küpfmüller of *Siemens Werke*, but not the wider OR for it;[40] Küpfmüller introduced a form of 'Sunday Soviets', free discussions sessions, along the lines of the British.

Before moving on to the main body of evidence of German OR it is instructive to consider the evidence of an important OR source. On the completion of a war patrol U-boat Commanders were required to submit their *KTB* patrol report to U-boat HQ, and Commanders were individually interviewed for content. Remarks by Dönitz, or later by the COS, were sometimes appended to the 'Log'. These logs were then copied and sent via a routeing list to several recipients according to the need perceived by *BdU*.

One, dated 28 May 1942 relates to the 'Log' of *U-130*, which was copied to: M zur Vorlage beim Ob.d.M. – Staff.

1. Iu and Ik, – individual Officers within the command. 'u' signifies U-boats.
2. 1/*Skl*. C/*Skl*. Vorlagen. – Operations Dept, and Chief, submissions.
3. Ia, Iop, Ig, Ib, IE. – Individual Officers in *Skl*.
4. *Chef MND*, – Chief Naval Intelligence Service.
5. 3/*Skl*. – Intelligence Appraisal Division.
6. *NWa*. – Communications Corps.
7. Über 1/*Skl*. an *Kr*. Via 1/*Skl to Kriegswissenschaftlicheabteilung.*

   Source: Routeing Sheet of Log U-130, typical of many logs.[41]

One set of the U-boat logs was sent to *OKM* where they were taken apart in detail, and operational and technical items studied. The interesting recipient is that featured in point 7. – 1/*Skl* to *Kr*. An inspection of the separate *Skl* War diaries, Parts A, B, C and D, indicates that at the end of each month one copy of the respective war diary was signed off by the Ib *Kr* officer responsible for the handling of war diary material. These were used for evaluations – for the improvement of Weapons, tactics and strategy.[42] The 'Logs' served as a 'primary source' linked to scientific inquiry, in keeping with the *a priori* model.[43]

Another source of OR came from the *BdU KTB* who circulated a copy of his war diary, informing several key departments of his activities and thoughts. One example of OR may be found in his *KTB* of December 1942. On 1 December details of boat deployments were given as follows:

Number of boats in the Atlantic in November:[44]

Daily average, at sea	94.9	boats
Of these, in the Op. area	38.2	boats
Of these, outward bound	56.7	boats
Of these, returning to base	24.5	boats

These details would have been included in any model used to calculate U-boat operations efficiency.[45] Many of the technical orders for use at sea were contained in *BdU's* monthly journal and by regular standing orders issued to U-boat commanders on subjects ranging from torpedo depth settings, types of torpedo and pistol, to improvements on tactics. In some ways it corresponds closely to the monthly British Anti-U-boat appreciations CB 04050 containing statistics and operational recommendations. The verbal and written feedback provided to a list of naval departments engaged in weapons development provides clear evidence that, although the route taken may have been different to the British the *Kriegsmarine* was in possession of 'OR' data obtained from the U-boat logs.

One British historian remarked that there were local quantitative methods applied by Dönitz that had all the hallmarks of the OR practitioner.[46] His evidence of an 'assumed' OR probably stems from the knowledge that data analysis was practiced by the section A5.[47] The officer largely responsible for collecting and disseminating this data was *Korvettekapitän* Dr Teufer who was not a front-line but an administrative support officer, with different rank markings to those of his other officer colleagues;[48] in much the same way as that of the RN Paymaster branch.[49] The function of this small group was essentially to analyze data collected during patrol operations in order to assess trends in performance, and their underlying causes.

Considered in this light, the above statements made by historians about the non-existence of German OR do not bear out the facts. In the first case there was a presence of OR in all three German services, including the Navy. In the second case there was a section, A5, within the *BdU* Command organization whose very job it was to collect data, analyze the effectiveness of patrols and submit reports to the *OKM* for further consideration. Thereafter it also involved the *Kriegswissenschaftlicheabteilung*, or *Kr*. *Kr* worked very closely with the *Skl* but was not formally, organizationally, an integral part of the division; although for many purposes attached to it.[50] Thirdly, it is not correct to state that 'none of these characteristics was evident in Germany, either then or indeed at any time during the war'.[51] *FEP's* and *Skl* (*Kr*)'s existence is evidence that OR was practiced, but there will be other hard evidence presented later in this book. Whatever the reasons may be for the gap in this debate there can be little doubt that 'OR' was practiced, and it matched perfectly the concept expressed by E. J. Williams as a suitable description for this new branch of applied science.[52]

The creation of FEP

Until 1942 R&D activity had been guided by the *OKM* and was handled at a local level where they had to request funds and material based on an incomplete survey of requirements; indeed this led to several occasions of duplicated work.

Raeder had shown concerns for the state of German DF and radar technology and stated in his memoirs that,

> It is surely in the nature of things that such developments are best carried out by those who are in daily contact with related questions and are constantly encouraged to evaluate the latest results.[53]

It was therefore deemed logical that the time had approached when a separate and independent departmental group should be formed, rather than a subordinate one.[54] A new departmental/office group was created reporting to the director *MRue* known as *OKM/FEP. FEP*, first created in September 1942 under the guidance of *Konteradmiral* Wilhelm Rhein,[55] became the German administrative arm for 'OR' groups, the common term used in Britain. In the document No. 11214 about the need to set up a body to oversee naval military research and development it stated that:

> The war has brought about the necessity to set up an efficient means of research. For this reason the armed services had to organise their resources based on availability and needs. Since it was found that in the opening years of the war the armed services did not have the necessary facilities it was decided that during the course of 1942 the *OKM* would create a special group to be known as the *FEP*, in order to centralize matters pertaining to research and development in the Navy.[56]

FEP was divided into four sections:

FEP I was referred to as the division for the Conduct of Research, by that it was meant that it was responsible for the planning of scientific work by the Navy in co-operation with other research agencies.

FEP II was assigned a form of intelligence rôle known as the Central Office for the Dissemination of Information, Interpretation and Reports.[57] The main purpose of this department was to collate and interpret the products of German and foreign scientific institutions in order to make recommendations for possible research into military applications. Section *FEP* IIb was responsible for the dissemination of test results in much the same way as British OR sections. Recommendations deemed worthy of further investigation were then passed to.

FEP III was the actual research division for examination and testing.

All new inventions and patented processes then became the responsibility of *FEP* IV, the Division of Inventions and Patents (*Abteilung für Erfindungs und Patentwesen*).

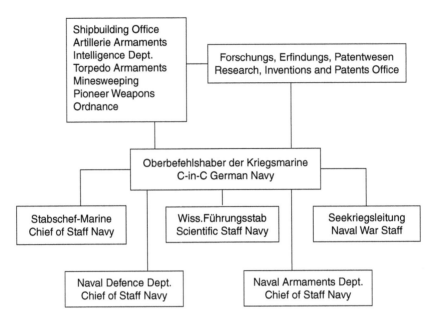

Chart 10.1 Kriegsmarine partial departmental organization chart, effective October 1944
Source: Chart translated and constructed by author.[58]

As may be seen in the organization chart (Chart 10.1) there is an interface between the *MRue* and the *FEP,* both of whom reported to the *ObdM.* Without going further into the structure of the *MRue* it should be noted that around the same time as the creation of the *FEP* the *Wi* (Economics) section *MWa* had been raised to an independent status and was thus able to function as the financial administrator between the Navy and external scientific and industrial institutions. This new arrangement therefore meant that the Navy could now engage in projects that could be of benefit to the Navy in which it was not the only participant.[59] The *OKM* order of 11 September 1942 was then confirmed in a letter of 16 January 1943, and the *FEP* group became responsible for dealing with the whole question of conduct of Research, Development and Patents.[60]

The authority invested in this office in relation to other offices and services of the *Kriegsmarine* was limited to the following tasks:

1. Summary, harmonization and individual handling of all questions in the area of research, inventions and patents that come within the bounds of the *Kriegsmarine.*

2. Bring about broad agreement and unity of purpose in the areas handled by the *Kriegsmarine* in relation to outside interests.

3. Guarantee carrying out individual *Kriegsmarine* procedures according to the President of the *Reichsforschungsrat*, the head of the Armed Services, the Minister of Armaments, and other general authorities and government offices for the Administration of Research, Inventions and Patents, as required by the *ObdM* and *OKM*.

4. Appraisal of research requirements, work and contracts – and agreed principles – with other research groups, in particular those of the Army and Air Force; Determination of urgency and emphasis . . .

9. To be in constant touch, and research exchange, with Research and Development centres of the Navy, other Armed Forces, Science and Industry.[61]

Point 9 was one of *FEP's* most important areas of authority, and crucial to successful implementation of feedback for inter-service OR projects.

The above was part of a 19-point plan developed for the operational authority. Its remit included searching for new methods into best practice procedures, an inspection of operational logs and feedback.[62]

The extent and flow of information on OR as indicated by FEP related documents

An indication of the type of work carried out in R&D, and the information exchanged between departments of the armed forces, can be provided through an analysis of some of the captured German documents relating to *FEP* activities. Each month a list of test results were compiled by *FEP* IIb and sent to the relevant section dealing with research projects at the Army and Air Force research centres in order that such information be shared. The Army and Air Force personnel engaged in their areas of expertise were also required to reciprocate with their findings.

In the test results for June 1943 two items, No. 25 and No. 26 would have been of particular interest to the Navy, but may also have had application in any of the other two services:[63]

Item No. 25 is an interesting development because it investigates a rotating antenna on U-boats and S-boats (E-boats) for the rapid detection and position of HF, presumably for HF/DF.

Item No. 26 is also an appropriate development because it deals with a U-boat, four-section rotational antenna for the detection of radar transmissions in the centimetre band.

Item No. 27 consists of land-based rotating antenna for direction finding of transmissions in the broadband range of 50 cm to 3 m. This may have had Army or Air Force application.

There were many more proposals for research, or development, accepted by the *FEP* on behalf of the Navy over the course of the war, including an infra-red device for sub-sea rockets (discussed later), but the examples above tend to indicate an important direction in the U-boat war to still to come, countermeasures against centimetric radar transmissions.[64]

Also in 1943 another OR project resulted from patrol reports, which concerned the undesirable effect of U-boats being detected by HE (Hydrophone Effect). This led to further OR tests being undertaken with U-boats in an effort to reduce the 'silent running' limit due to propeller cavitations.[65] Practical testing was done with the *Sultan* OR test group in the Baltic.[66] This group also became involved with the latest developments in both active and passive underwater detection systems, for example, the enlarged passive multi-unit hydrophone set with balcony array, and active/passive echo-ranging system *Nibelung* designed for use in the new *Elektro* boats. The system was very advanced and enabled submerged torpedo attacks without the use of the periscope, using instead super-sensitive arrays of receptors connected to a range and distance computing device.[67]

Practical use of feedback from meetings

Good ad hoc contributions to OR came through feedback obtained in face-to-face discussions with operational staff and construction specialists, or from participants at the end of a course of instruction. One such example took place in November 1942. In order to find out when the future *Elektro* U-boat was expected to come into operational service Dönitz called a conference at U-boat headquarters in Paris, attended by Professor Walter and technical experts from the construction branch of *OKM*, Schürer, Bröking and Waas.[68] Admiral Dönitz stated in his memoirs that

> At this conference I learnt to my regret that the Walter U-boat was nowhere near ready for service . . . At this conference in Paris Schürer and Bröking

suggested that by adopting the streamline form of the Walter U-boat, which had been successfully tested, and by doubling the numbers of batteries carried, we might be able to transform the current types of U-boat into vessels of high underwater-speed.[69]

It then became an *Elektro* boat.

First-hand information based on a local study can lead to unexpected positive results, and in this case they did.[70] This was a demonstrably good example of positive feedback due to local OR, and may be favourably compared to that of the meetings held at Bawdsey to discuss radar developments, or at ORS to discuss changes needed in air-launched DCs.[71]

Torpedo developments

TVA had learnt how difficult it had become to approach a convoy too close. When U-boats did it often had disastrous consequences for them. The 'Curly' type of torpedo, called in German *FAT*,[72] first introduced in 1942, had some early degree of success in overcoming this problem.[73] *FAT* was probably only used at night when its track would not be seen; and primarily with the long-range 30-knot setting. Its capability soon became known to British naval intelligence and described as,

> fired with normal gyro angling, and will then run straight to any set range. On reaching this point the torpedo would begin to execute either long or short legs either to the Right or Left, as may have been pre-set.[74]

The *FAT* was therefore best suited for shots from roughly around the beam of a convoy, possibly 'browning' shots, but not for shots from dead ahead.[75] Because of the impact that the centralized research facility *FEP* was having on torpedo developments they were able to step up development of the wandering 'types' of torpedo, which were introduced in 1942–3 in order to have a greater chance of hitting a convoy, or escort vessel. Acoustic torpedoes were regarded as an important escort killer, or *Zerstörerknacker*, and the specifications of operational efficacy were guided by data from evaluations done after the First World War, and on experimental work done in 1937.[76] Scientific and technical staff had studied the results of the standard U-boat *Torpedoschuß*meldungen, and War Diary entries and came to the conclusion that by incorporating an acoustic search device it would serve as an anti-escort counter measure to reduce their own U-boat losses. This was OR in practice.[77] The British felt the impact of this development in September 1943.

Post 1942 OR defensive countermeasures – decoys and camouflage

A study of records from patrol *KTBs* had shown flaws in the U-boat's ability to apply countermeasures against British Radar and ASDIC. What was needed were means to minimize risk of detection above and below sea level. Two types of radar decoy were developed in 1943 and designed to provide a 'false' target to enemy air and surface craft radar. Solutions came from 'Sunday Soviets' type discussions between the U-boat staff at HQ Paris and the new Director of *MND*, *Konteradmiral* Stummel in June 1942. Stummel had been copied with U-boat patrol *KTBs* and concluded that they were probably being detected by aircraft radar while running on the surface, not visually. What *MND* came up with as a short-term measure were two decoys.[78] One was a balloon decoy *FuMT* 1 'Aphrodite IV', introduced in June 1943, and the other a floating buoy *FuMT* 2 'Thetis IIC', first used in January 1944. The problem was that both were designed to reflect radar transmissions in the metric band, but by now the centimetre band was in use. Recovered specimens revealed that there was hardly any response to centimetric radar. It is therefore doubtful if they had much effect on Allied A/S operations.[79] While Stummel had demonstrated how practical feedback was assimilated to generate rapid solutions, Allied technology had moved on.

Other than *Alberich*, alternative forms of camouflage received very little attention until 1943 when U-boats were fitted with *Schnorchel*, a breathing device initially suggested as a stop-gap until the new 'truly' submersible was due to appear.[80] Tests found that if an unprotected *Schnorchel* was extended 1 m above the surface its theoretical detection limit was still about 20–25 per cent of the broadside detection range of a surfaced Type VII-C. What was now needed was to camouflage the *Schnorchel* head itself.[81] In spring 1944 a Professor J. Jaumann, in co-operation with the IG Farben Company, designed an absorbent material against centimetric radar. The design called for a hollow cylinder construction with a 7-cm-thick wall, consisting of seven layers of thin, semi-conducting paper separated by layers, or spacers, about 9-mm thick of cellular polyvinyl chloride (Igelit, US trade name Thermozote). The *Schnorchel* camouflage was an effective absorber in the 3–30 cm radar transmission band. With it one was able to obtain a reflection co-efficient of less than 10 per cent in amplitude for flat plates and a minimum of less than 1 per cent at 9.3 cm, which was the principal wavelength used by Allied centimetric radar.[82] A good camouflage lesson had been learnt.

The second camouflage project still of great interest, discussed under earlier pre-1943 examples, was *Alberich*, which were anechoic tiles fitted to the hull of a U-boat. Initially it was effective when freshly applied, but sea water pressure slowly collapsed the foam structure, degrading its absorbent properties. In some instances the tiles became loose and created unwanted sound.[83] In March 1943 the absorbent coating's operational performance was tested in sea-trials off Arendal in Norway using a coated boat *U-470,* and an uncoated *U-958.*[84] At depths of over 100 m the sound emitted by the coated U-boat barely exceeded background noise, and complete protection was claimed.[85] In theory the *Alberich* coatings, or tiles, provided more security in 'stealth' operations but in reality the problem of adhesive material was never solved in time and thus became another pending problem. Although the lesson had been well learnt it faltered on a bizarre lack of adhesive. Ironically, *U-470's* fate was sealed on its first war patrol on 16 October 1943 when it was caught on the surface by a patrolling British Liberator aircraft, and sunk. There were just two survivors.[86] *Alberich* was only effective below surface.

U-boat rockets

The fact that Germany had rocket-propelled missiles is well documented, and it is well known that the Allies coveted the German ballistic missile technology of the V-2 after the war. Closely related to torpedo matters was the *CPVA* Kiel, which was involved with the design characteristics of planned U-boat Rockets – an offshoot of the Peenemünde 'V' project, whose scientists did the ground-work.[87] *CPVA* activities were described as 'the solution of tasks, and the carrying out of tests in the sphere of physics, chemistry and explosives . . .'[88] *OKM* became aware of the technology in 1942 and the *CPVA* development group was approached to determine how feasible this technology might lend itself as an effective offensive weapon mounted on U-boats.[89] That the Navy should be interested in using technology from another service does not come as a surprise, for their British counterparts had the same idea. ORS examined the use of the naval DC on aircraft and the RN investigated the OR application of the RAF RP. Requirements for U-boat rocket technology were determined, in part, from U-boat patrol logs and staff discussions on tactics.

At *OKM* Dönitz retained his interest in the idea as an anti-escort weapon, but further developments were dependent on a suitable guidance system capable of targeting surface ships, or aircraft.[90] Later in 1944 further practical tests were carried out in conjunction with naval technicians, with an understanding of U-boats, at a facility specially built on an inland lake in Austria at Toplitzsee. The rockets were mounted on a sunken platform down to around 100 m at its deepest point. Trajectory and operational parameters were set up according to advice given by seasoned U-boat practitioners, some of whom were in attendance.[91] Not all the tests were successful. According to the *Marine Rundschau*, one rocket went in the opposite direction to that in which it was supposed to track and landed up in an adjoining lake, Grundlsee.[92]

OKM/FEP had long made a study of reports from the front for requirements to counter Allied Convoy protection supremacy. Research and development contracts in June and July 1943 indicate that the *OKM* was considering some form of heat-seeking infra-red guided weapon system for the smaller U-boat rockets as a partial solution to convoy escorts and patrolling aircraft, against which current U-boat types had suffered so badly in recent times. In a part of two contracts issued in 1943, (to Julius Pintsch, Berlin and Zeiss-Ikon, Optics) may be seen the details of research projects dealing with infra-red devices. These two contracts present a clear indication of investigations into the infra-red-heat-seeking potential of rockets, first placed after operational results using the rockets had been determined. This was OR of the highest order but a target acquisition system was never achieved since the guidance system needed was ahead of its time.[93]

Radar

Before the war the *Kriegsmarine* had developed an early radar set working in the 80-cm band for use on ships.[94] But radar for use on U-boats was not considered to be of great importance. In the early part of the war an 80-cm band became available known as the *Seetakt* – mainly used for gunnery control of the *Panzerschiffe* (Pocket Battleships) such as the *Deutschland* and *Graf Spee*. One OR weakness, never solved, was the development of centimetric radar, even though they did have an early working model of a 'Magnetron'. It was based on a thermionic valve, not a form of semi-conductor. German scientists in the radar field had already attempted to improve on the developments made on a rudimentary form of 'magnetron', originally invented by Albert W. Hull of GEC in the 1920s. This was an unsuccessful venture because it was not possible to obtain a 'steady state' frequency. Some results were obtained in detection up to 20-km distance but only if the magnetron was constantly tuned. In the event development was abandoned in favour of more reliable solutions.[95] Valves (Tubes) produce a lot of heat and become unstable therefore a means of heat compensation to offset frequency drift was never achieved.

Essentially, radar was not a top priority for the German surface fleet and apparently not very high for the U-boat arm. Nevertheless belated research was conducted at the *NVA* and by the end of the war a 3-cm version 'Naxos' originally designed for the *Luftwaffe* was ready, but only about 100 were constructed. If the war had continued they might, and probably would, have been fitted to new U-boats.[96]

Conclusions

British and German historians do not appear to have known that the Germany military also used OR. The reasons for this gap in knowledge remain unclear but it is possible to speculate on some of them. Towards the end of 1943, and certainly in the first quarter of 1944, the Battle of the Atlantic sea war was effectively over. To that extent historians may have been satisfied with the events leading up to that point and not bothered to look any deeper into German records after this time. This applies to both English and German speakers, for there is also a paucity of historical coverage on this subject in German literature. One clear OR link missed by historians was that between the British and German form of *a priori* that led to problem definition and subsequent measurement. A second link missed is that scientists on both sides were 'asked' to investigate a particular problem. Generally, they did not investigate unless asked to do so. Both sets of scientists then used the expertise of practitioners to arrive at a solution.

As the war advanced Raeder, realized that the *Kriegsmarine* pace of development was too slow and needed accelerating, although some OR was in progress. He recognized that if they wanted to get at least one step ahead of their enemy, more central control of research and development was needed, one which could feedback the results from either research or incremental developments. The first serious step was taken in September 1942 when the *FEP* was created. The essence of shared information appeared each month as a list of test results, compiled by *FEP* IIb and distributed to the relevant sections dealing with research, or development projects, including the *Heer* and *Luftwaffe*. The emphasis of new development lay in the advancement of torpedoes, and a 'submersible' of longer endurance. By 1943 construction plans had been agreed for the type XXI and XXIII boats. One of the design features giving problems was the power unit, which used unstable fuel, but an intriguing ad hoc idea became the standard sub-sea power source, making it now the *Elektro*-boat.

In German OR the most tangible results were in incremental torpedo technology, largely because of the headlong rush into trying to do too much with too few resources, in too short a time. Several interesting projects materialized as a result of the *FEP* research group largely based on lessons learned and feedback obtained from front-line boats. They too are summarized here in no particular order of importance.

- Several new torpedoes were introduced of the type known in Britain as the 'Curly' type of torpedo, the first of which was the *Zaunkönig*. This was followed later by the wandering types, *FAT* and *LUT*. Attacks had become dangerous when approaching too close to convoys. The contribution of OR to the efficiency of German torpedoes was not difficult to define, and early results indicates that kill ratios on escorts greatly improved. However, no written records could be found to suggest that kill ratio efficiencies were measured, but their improvements in torpedo technology suggest that they were, when they worked.
- Another torpedo type was being worked on but never came to fruition, the wire-guided system. This was intended more for use in coastal areas than the Atlantic.
- Radar and ASDIC camouflage. Early results in *Schnorchel* camouflage were encouraging but it was only a partial solution to better stealth operations. *Alberich* would have been a major advance but for the adhesive setback, never solved before the end of the war. However, the *Alberich* camouflage was fully developed by the allies after the war.
- An interesting project, regarded as state-of-the-art for the time, was the development of anti-surface escort U-boat rocket design and trials. Had this weapon been introduced it could have transformed the aircraft and escort threat. Both would produce a 'heat' signature. Evidence given above suggests that an 'Infrared homing device' may have been nearing trials and would have meant that an anti-escort, or anti-aircraft strike, weapon was a strong possibility.

So the system appeared to be working in some areas of application, if not all. The intention was to make a leap in technology, but because of inter-service rivalry for resources many of the projects were shelved. However, none of these projects would have advanced as far as they did without the vital evaluative research done into OR by the *Kr* and inter-service feedback in conjunction with *FEP* and local operational feedback.

There is good evidence in this chapter to support the argument that true OR, did exist in the German Navy, but the greater benefits accrued from OR were realized too late for them to have any major impact on the Battle of the Atlantic. The chief lesson learnt by *OKM* was that they should have started the process of streamlining development procedures and 'OR' at a much earlier stage than they did.

Notes

1   George Raudzens, 'War-winning Weapons: The Measurement of Technological Determinism in Military History', *The Journal of Military History*, 54 (4) (October 1990), 403–34, 405.

2   W. J. R. Gardner, 'Blackett and the Black Arts', in *Patrick Blackett* (2003), 126–37, 133.

3   David Zimmerman, 'Tactics and Technology', in *The Battle of the Atlantic 1939–1945* (1994), 476–89, 476; Timothy Mulligan, *Neither Sharks nor Wolves* (Annapolis, 1999), 161.

4   Gardner, 'Blackett and the Black Arts', 133.

5   Guy Hartcup, *The Effect of Science on the Second World War* (Basingstoke, 2000), 5; Alfred Price, *Aircraft versus Submarines* (Barnsley, 2004), 117.

6   Günter Hessler, *The U-boat War in the Atlantic 1939–1945* (1989), II, 12; Mulligan, *Neither Sharks nor Wolves*, 51; he fails to have knowledge of 'local' OR and yet he acknowledges that Hessler conducted over 4,500 debriefings', one of the rich veins for OR, 50.

7   Edward R. Zilbert, *Albert Speer and the Nazi Ministry of Arms* (1981), 149.

8   NHB PG 32107, Contains Torpedo Short Reports, including U-47's Torpedoschußmeldung.

9   BA-MA RM 87/13 and NHB PG 30247, torpedo failures; Cajus Bekker, *Hitler's Naval War* (1974), 119.

10 NHB PG 30256, BdU KTB entry for 21 January 1940.

11 BA-MA RM 7/2432, 224. Letter from Kriegswissenschaftlicheabteilung to 1/Skl; Also in NHB PG 33322, gKdos, Report on Torpedoes 1914/1940 239.

12 BA-MA RM 7/2432, 223f, contains details of statistical calculations of torpedo failures.

13 J. E. Tiles, 'Experimental Evidence vs. Experimental Practice?', *The British Journal for the Philosophy of Science*, 43 (1) (March 1992), 99–109, 99.

14 Hessler, *The U-boat War in the Atlantic 1939–1945*, II, 44.

15 *Lagevorträge*, 'Niederschrift über die Besprechung beim Führer in der Reichskanzlei, 28.9.1942', 420–4.

16 F. Köhl et al., *U-boottyp VII C* (Koblenz, 1989), 35; In general German ASDIC had poor performance and its removal from U-boats was ordered in April 1942.

17 Hessler, *The U-boat War in the Atlantic 1939–1945*, II, 47.

18 TNA ADM 186/ 809: CB 04051 (103), Interrogation of U-boat survivors describing training methods, 52.

19 Donald McLachlan, *Room 39* (1968), 186.

20 Dieter Guicking, *Erwin Meyer – ein bedeutender deutscher Akustiker Biographische Notizen*, Drittes Physikalisches Institut der Universität Göttingen (Januar 2010), 5.

21 Erwin Meyer, *Electro-Acoustics* (1939).

22 *Lagevorträge*, 'Niederschrift über die Besprechung beim Führer in der Reichskanzlei, 28.9.1942', 420–4.

23 Graham Rhys-Jones, 'The German System: A Staff Perspective', in *The Battle of the Atlantic 1939–1945 (1994)*, 138–57, 147.

24 NHB PG 32029, 1/Skl KTB Teil A entry nr 4. 1 May 1940, 'OR' talk given by Professor Cornelius about trials to fix failures in torpedo firing mechanisms and depth-keeping qualities.

25 TNA HW 11/20, GC&CS, 'The German Navy – The U-boat Arm', 7, 342.

26 NHB PG 33324, 'Torpedowesen'. Details of OR torpedo effectiveness were given as 77.6 per cent in the sinking of 406 ships.

27 NHB PG 30323, BdU KTB entry supplement dated 10 May 1943.

28 Rhys-Jones, 'The German System', 148.

29 NHB PG 30310B, BdU KTB entry for 21 August 1942.

30 Rhys-Jones, 'The German System', 147.

31 Oliver Krauss, 'Rüstung und Rüstungserprobung in der deutschen Marinegeschichte unter besonderer Berücksichtigung der Torpedoversuchsanstalt (TVA)', Christian-Albrechts-Universität, Kiel, 2006, Section 4.4.2, 201.

32 NHB PG 42238, Document 11214, objectives of the FEP; NHB PG 33329, 'Chefsache Band 13, Verschiedenes', 91–6.

33 *Lagevorträge*, 'Niederschrift über die Besprechung beim Führer in der Reichskanzlei 28.9.1942', 420–4.

34 FEP had already been put in hand by 11 September 1942.

35 BA-MA RM 7/846, 1/Skl KTB Teil C Heft IV, Niederschriften Raeder an Hitler, September 1942, 236–48 and 251–78; NHB PG 32174, 1/Skl KTB Teil C Heft IV, ObdM and Hitler meetings, September 1942.

36 TNA AVIA 39/4, 'German Academic Scientists and the War', by Major
    I. W. B. Gill.

37 TNA ADM 213/611, 'Underwater Weapons Department of the Admiralty',
    formation of the Kriegsmarinearbeitsgemeinschaft (Naval Unions), later WFM, 91.

38 Price, *Aircraft versus Submarines*, 181.

39 GC&CS, 'The German Navy – Organization', 2, (December 1945), 120.

40 BA-MA RM 7/1240, Entwicklungen, Bericht des Wissenschaftlichen –
    Führungsstabs der *Kriegsmarine*, 1.5.44–17.11.44.

41 NHB PG 30130, KTB Log of the Type IXC, U-130, Routeing Sheet.

42 TNA WO 291/1911, M. S. Blackett, 'A Note on Certain Aspects of the Methodology
    of Operational Research', May 1943, 1.

43 An example would be 1/Skl Teil A, 9 September 1943.

44 NHB PG 30314B, BdU KTB entry, 1 December 1942.

45 Ibid.

46 Paul Sutcliffe, 'Operational Research in the Battle of the Atlantic' (1994), 419.

47 See Appendix 3, Lagezimmer Control Officers.

48 *Rangliste der deutschen Kriegsmarine nach dem Stande vom 1 November 1938*
    (M.Div. Nr.293) (Berlin, 1938).

49 TNA HW 18/55, German Naval Organization, 3; the officer in charge was
    Korvettenkapitän Dr Teufer.

50 GC&CS, 'The German Navy – Organization', 2, 49.

51 Gardner, 'Blackett and the Black Arts', 133.

52 E. J. Williams, 'Reflections on Operational Research', *Journal of the Operations
    Research Society of America*, 2 (4) (November 1954), 441–3, 441.

53 'Es liegt sicherlich im Wesen solcher Entwicklungen, dass sie von denjenigen
    getragen werden, die durch tägliche Beschäftigung mit den damit
    zusammenhängenden Fragen ständig neu angeregt werden und die neuesten
    Ergebnisse verwerten können', cited in Frank Reuter, *Wissenschaftliche
    Abhandlungen der Arbeitsgemeinschaft für Forschung des Landes Nordrhein-
    Westfalen* Bd. 42 (Opladen, 1971), 189.

54 Frank Reuter, 'Funkmeß. Die Entwicklung und der Einsatz des RADAR-Verfahrens
    in Deutschland bis zum Ende des zweiten Weltkrieges', in *Wissenschaftliche
    Abhandlungen der Arbeitsgemeinschaft für Forschung des Landes Nordrhein-
    Westfalen* Bd. 42 (Opladen, 1971), 189.

55 Konter Admiral Rhein was formerly COS (Chief of Staff) MWa, from 18 December
    1939–31 August 1942; and then in charge of FEP until the end of the war.

56 NHB PG 42238, Document 11214, Organization of the FEP Forschung,
    Erfindungen und Patentwesen.

57 Zentralevermittlungsstelle zur Erfassung, Auswertung und Berichtswesen.

58 NHB PG 42238, Original Document on FEP Organization, section redrawn by
    author.

59 GC&CS, 'The German Navy – Organization', 2, 107.
60 BA-MA RM 8/1587, 'Organization anderer Abteilungen, Marine und Armeebehörden', 62–4.
61 BA-MA RM 8/ 1587 Organization anderer Abteilungen, Marine und Armeebehörden, 62–4; Oliver Krauss, 'Rüstung und Rüstungserprobung in der deutschen Marinegeschichte unter besonderer Berücksichtigung der Torpedoversuchsanstalt (TVA)', 147.
62 GC&CS, 'The German Navy – Organization', 2, 49.
63 NHB PG 42238, Document 11214, Organization of the FEP, Issuance of Contracts.
64 NHB PG 14139, Erfahrungsaustausch June 1943, 5; NID 24/T13/45, List 3, 5.
65 NHB NID 24/T13/45, Taken from FEPII List 3, December 1943–February 1944, 5.
66 TNA HW 11/20, GC&CS, 'The German Navy – The U-boat Arm', 7, 342.
67 Axel Niestlé, 'German Technical and Electronic Development', in *The Battle of the Atlantic 1939–1945* (1994), 430–51, 435.
68 Hessler, *The U-boat War in the Atlantic 1939–1945*, III, 6.
69 Karl Dönitz, *Memoirs,* 353.
70 TNA ADM 234/68, U-boat War in the Atlantic, 3, June 1943–May 1945, 6.
71 Air Ministry, *The Origins and Development of Operational Research in the Royal Air Force* (1963), 76.
72 FAT (Flächenabsuchendertorpedo) Area Search Torpedo, also known as GNAT German acoustic torpedo.
73 *Official Account of the Battle of the Atlantic* (HMSO) (1946), 80.
74 TNA ADM 186/ 809: CB 04051 (103), 52.
75 Browning shots are taken outside of the normal shooting range in the hope of hitting a target.
76 NHB PG 33324, Torpedowesen, including appreciations, 203–5.
77 TNA ADM 186/ 809: CB 04051 (103), Interrogation of U-boat survivors describing training methods, 52.
78 Hessler, *The U-boat War in the Atlantic 1939–1945*, II, 26.
79 Niestlé, 'German Technical and Electronic Development', 444.
80 TNA ADM 1/17667, letters from Professor Walter to Admiral Dönitz on necessity for fast U-boat and *Schnorchel*; Professor Walter to ObdM re visit to Dr Fischer, Dir.U-boat construction 19 May 1943.
81 Niestlé, 'German Technical and Electronic Development', 445.
82 Ibid.
83 Bernard Ireland, *Battle of the Atlantic* (Barnsley, 2003), 116.
84 Niestlé, 'German Technical and Electronic Development', 448.
85 Navships publication 900 (164), *Sound Absorption and Sound Absorbers in Water* (2) Department of the Navy (Washington DC, 1947), 6.
86 Axel Niestlé, *German U-boat Losses During World War II* (Annapolis, 1998), 67.

87 Ibid., Appendix D.

88 TNA ADM 213/611, Underwater Weapons Department:1 report undertaken was a study into operational rocket research (OR) for naval applications, 133; Egon Baumann, 'Die Raketenversuchsstation Toplitzsee 1944–1945', *Marine Rundschau,* 5 (1988), 300–2.

89 NHB PG 33416, Files of Iu Chefsache, Allegemeines relating initially to use of rockets; BA-MA RM 7/1239, Raketenschiessversuche auf deutschen U-Booten der 30 Uflottille im Schwarzen Meer-Sommer 1944.

90 www.uboataces.com/articles-rocket-uboat.shtml.

91 BA-MA RM 7/1239, files contain details of personnel involved in tests.

92 Baumann, 'Die Raketenversuchsstation Toplitzsee 1944–1945', 302.

93 NHB PG 43149, Issued contracts: 1943.

94 BA-MA W04–13677, 'Versuchsaufgaben für Kriegsschiffe ab 1936–37'.

95 Harry von Kroge, *GEMA; Birthplace of German Radar and Sonar,* (Bristol, 2000), 43.

96 Christopher Schumacher, 'Forschung, Rüstung und Krieg: Formen, Ausmaß und Grenzen des Wissenschaftlereinsatzes für den zweiten Weltkrieg im deutschen Reich', 100.

11

The Repulse of the U-boat Atlantic Offensive and Its Consequences

This chapter discusses the events leading up to May 1943, a month when the fortunes of Britain in the Battle of the Atlantic experienced a major about turn, for the better. In this month one of the most important Convoys, in which no merchant vessels were lost, was SC-130. Its impact, and subsequent actions in May, signalled the beginning of the end of the Battle of the Atlantic.

Coastal Command from 1942 onwards

On 9 February 1942, the AOC Sir Philip Joubert de la Ferté (who took over in June 1941) wrote a vigorous letter to the Air Ministry complaining that owing to decisions taken by the Air Ministry in recent months the prospect of Coastal Command being able to work at reasonable efficiency appeared to be more and more remote. He was further critical of no agreed future policy for the build up of any long-range forces at home with improved ASV, which itself was a vital factor in the A/S war.[1] A similar combined complaint to the Air Ministry came from the Admiralty and Coastal Command in May.[2] Things then began to steadily improve.

By the middle of October 1942, the Coastal Command organization had grown in strength and was working not only from the Britain but also now from air strips in Iceland. It possessed 44 squadrons of aircraft, 5 squadrons more than a year before, but of the most favoured aircraft, the US Liberator B24, they could only muster two squadrons, well below what they needed for such an important task as an airborne U-boat killer. 'Where there was no air cover, the sinkings were high; where aircraft operated, sinkings were low.'[3]

Acquiring more VLR (very long range) aircraft therefore became a priority. Fortunately, towards the end of 1942 and the beginning of 1943, the numbers were increased by negotiating with the US C-in-C, Admiral Ernie King, who originally earmarked many of the US aircraft output for his 'Pacific' operations.[4] It was this increase in B24 VLR aircraft that began to substantially alter the course of the U-boat war in the Atlantic. The efforts would begin to pay off by March/April 1943.

> The lesson was again learnt that VLR aircraft are a vital need for convoy protection. An HX convoy was intercepted a few hours before it reached the extreme range of aircraft based in Iceland and Ireland, but cover was provided at the earliest possible moment and the development of an effective mass attack was greatly impeded.[5]

In March 1943 Coastal Command came under the leadership of Air Chief Marshal Slessor, 'who gathered the fruits with both hands'.[6] Air cover was also now coming from US forces, following their entry into the alliance in December 1941. But most of the cover was provided by the British and Canadian forces. Also by the summer of 1943 the CVE was beginning to come on stream so that convoys were able to have FAA fighter escort cover in close proximity of the convoys to fight off, or sink, U-boats. Many gaps in convoy defence had now been plugged making it virtually impossible for U-boats to set up meaningful attacks.

In the interim the close co-operation that existed between the Naval and RAF Commands at Derby House enabled arrangements to be made for the aircraft of Coastal Command to combine their essential tactical training in conjunction with Escort Groups. Everyone needed to work with the same signal code and to make reports of enemy positions on a synchronized navigational basis. As a result, shore-based aircraft could become, when necessary, part of the escort force. Under the direction of the Escort Commander, aircraft could carry out planned search patterns, using positions relative to the convoy. It has been claimed that if an escort vessel obtained a bearing of a U-boat by DF Wireless the Escort Commander could have his aircraft homing in on that bearing within minutes.[7] As nice as it sounds this was not always efficient in application and several escort ship commanders had been known to file adverse reports.[8] 'Often the struggle had to be abandoned and at other times a large proportion of the aircraft's time with the convoy was wasted in this unprofitable way when a quick exchange of signals might have put the aircraft on to a submarine known to be shadowing the convoy'.[9]

Later in the campaign things largely did work better to plan and on 25 May 1943 Commander Peter Gretton (in HMS *Duncan*) the senior escort commander filed a report praising overall co-operation and communications with the Iceland and Northern Ireland Liberator Squadrons but commented on the Newfoundland Squadrons as lacking communications experience, and therefore the training required.[10] Overall, this combined land- and sea-based escort facility worked well and co-operated in finding solutions to problems.

Other events leading up to May 1943

A great deal of apprehension prevailed in the Admiralty and the government cabinet office after the losses incurred during 1942, particularly in the final days of December. To address these concerns, and plan for the future strategy of the war, decisions were taken during the Casablanca conference. In January 1943, it was agreed that the defeat of the U-boat must become the Allies' top priority and that there could be no liberation of Europe until the Battle of the Atlantic had been won.

From 1–12 March, British, American and Canadian Naval and Air Force representatives at the Atlantic Convoy Conference in Washington settled upon several initiatives. The principal objectives of this conference were to pool all Allied resources, naval and air, American, British and Canadian, and to standardize procedures. At the top of the list of priorities was the most urgent naval need to plug the vital mid-Atlantic gap some 600 miles south-east of Greenland through the use of VLR shore-based aircraft supplemented with more aircraft working from CVE's, escort carriers.[11] VLR Liberator aircraft were to be supplied to the RCAF (Royal Canadian Air Force) and RAF Coastal Command to begin the closing of the mid-Atlantic air gap but by the middle of May 1943, it had still not reached the desired level.[12] The conference sessions were productive and produced a recommendation for better arrangements for pooling British, Canadian and American naval resources by agreeing that American groups would work in their own strategic zone, while the Canadian Groups would operate under British command in their strategic zone. The outcome of the Atlantic Convoy Conference also helped shape a closer understanding of the air problems and create a subsequent redistribution of available aircraft, mainly American. If the lessons learned that produced such organizational progress in March 1943 could have been taken a year earlier many more ships with their crews, and precious cargoes, might have been saved.

More developments followed. After the concentrated U-boats attacks and huge losses of March 1943, Admiral Horton insisted upon the return of his escorts from other theatres and the provision of extra vessels drawn from the Home Fleet. This radical action combined with a refusal (after a heated debate at the highest level) to upset the Escort Group routine by the speeding up of convoy cycles resulted in a dramatic change in fortune in the A/S war in the North Atlantic in May 1943. It was using experienced Destroyer Groups from the Home Fleet that had trained and operated together that made such a spectacular change in the fortunes of North Atlantic convoys possible.[13]

Almost concurrent with the advances being made at the Atlantic Convoy Conference gloom appeared to be setting in at the Cabinet Office, as may be seen from the following communiqué:

AU (43) 90   War Cabinet   Copy N0 40   MOST SECRET

March 22nd 1943.   ANTI-U-BOAT WARFARE

Memorandum by the First Lord of Admiralty

I circulate herewith a memorandum by the First Sea

Lord on the U-Boat situation with which I agree.

Battle of the Atlantic

Memorandum of the First Sea Lord

The present situation –

a. After allowing for the necessary shipping to bring the minimum imports into this country, there is insufficient shipping to allow us to develop the offensives against the enemy, which have been decided on. Every ship sunk makes the situation worse.

b. Even if we obtain from U.S.A. the shipping necessary to import 27 million tons per annum, we shall not obtain this amount if a large number of ships are sunk on passage.

c. We can no longer rely on evading the U-boat packs and, hence we shall have to fight the convoys through them.

d. We cannot increase the number of escorts with the convoys until the autumn.

e. We are providing V.L.R. aircraft for covering the convoys as rapidly as possible, but we shall not reach sufficient strength for effective counter attack until mid-Summer.

f. Owing to the postponement of the North Russian convoy we shall be able to provide some support groups from Home Fleet but these will have to be withdrawn when the convoys are resumed. There is no certainty that a support group can be brought to the assistance of every convoy that is attacked.

g. Sufficient escorts will not be available until mid summer.[14]

The above statement by the Admiral Pound on 22 March 1943 appeared to effectively seal the British primary intent of the future, to fight their way through the U-boats by the best means available. However, escort commanders had their own ideas and would take evasive re-routeing when appropriate.

Dönitz 's *BdU* /Flag Officer-U-boats war diary entry of 15 January already contradicted what Admiral Pound said in that:

> Two convoys bring the total up to four that have been missed since 31.12. It is assumed that the enemy has left the convoy routes that he has been sailing for nearly 5 months and is again scattering his convoy routes. This development is a great setback to attacks by our boats, but was only to be expected.[15]

However, there was worse to come. On 21 April 1943 Dönitz reported to Hitler that losses were high and that the U-boat war was 'hard'. In February it was 19, in March it was 15 and to-date (21 April) 6 U-boats had been lost.[16] Total = 40 in less than 3 months.

In March, on the other hand, British evasive routeing remained largely ineffective even though the decrypting of Enigma SigInt rarely suffered from serious interruptions. Some of the decrypts made a few successful diversions possible, but the U-boats made contact with a number of convoys and these conditions did not substantially change before the end of May, the month in which the U-boats took several losses of their own – but still claimed 26 ships from convoys before they at last conceded an effective defeat in the North Atlantic.

From the beginning of April, soon after the arrangements agreed at the Washington conference had been put in-place, the reinforcement of the escorts by escort carriers, support groups and some additional VLR aircraft began to make their mark. If the number of ships sunk in convoy dropped to 25 in April from the critical level that it reached in March it did so because the escorts were now forcing U-boats on to the defensive. The tide had already turned.

The British and their Allies fought a series of battles during May 1943 which inflicted such heavy losses on the Germans – 43 U-Boats[17] – that on 24 May Dönitz reluctantly decided to accept defeat in the North Atlantic and to temporarily suspend U-boat attacks on convoys. Losses for February to 21 April had already amounted to 40 and May's figure was 43 in a single month, horrendous losses.

The final straw and deciding factor for this momentous decision was the culmination of one of these battles, the fight for Convoy SC-130, during which the Allies sank four U-boats and suffered no casualties. To understand the rationale behind the decision requires further explanation of the events surrounding SC-130 by means of a case study.

Introduction to case study

In the following case study it will be argued that, as the result of the combined effects of improved battle-ready Assets, Training and Weapons Research, the German U-boat Command HQ could no longer ignore the attrition rate of U-boats, and equally importantly, personnel.

The fight for SC-130

SC-130, consisting of 39 merchant ships, sailed from Halifax on 11 May 1943 and was initially accompanied by Canadian warships as far as N46° 56' W47° 56' which is about 150 miles south-east of Cape Race, Newfoundland. Two left for reasons given later, therefore the number of ships that did arrive numbered 37, plus the escorts.[18]

15 May: Point 1 on chart

At 0600 hours on 15 May the protection responsibility for SC-130 was taken over by Escort Group B7 who relieved the local escort group, detached and returned to their base (Chart 11.1). EG B7 was made up of the Destroyers HMS *Duncan* (SOE) and HMS *Vidette*, the Corvettes HMS *Snowflake*, HMS *Pink*, HMS *Loosestrife*, the frigate HMS *Tay* and HM Trawler *Northern Spray*. The RCN vessel HMCS *Kitchener* was also assigned to the group as an 'extra Corvette' but was later detached. The Corvette HMS *Sunflower* did not sail with the group immediately and was confined to a dock in St John's, Newfoundland to have her bow repaired, damaged after a ramming incident. *Sunflower* joined the escort group after the convoy got underway.

SOE Commander Peter Gretton RN was a very experienced commander with several convoy escorts to his credit and knew that preparation was half the battle. Because of his uneasiness that *Sunflower* was not ready to sail with

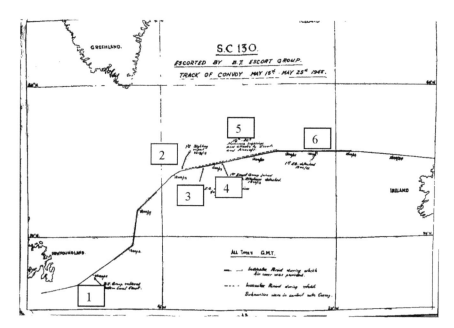

Chart 11.1 Track of SC-130
Source: SC Convoys 1943.[19]

him he signalled the Admiralty on 9 May asking for a 24-hour delay in the sailing; the answer was in the affirmative and the convoy sailed on 11 May.[20] She rejoined the group on 16 May having finished her repairs;[21] it was a wise move to have waited. It may be recalled that earlier in Chapter 7 similar circumstances confronted Lt Commander Windeyer SOE of EG C1 five months earlier when he left the North Western Approaches without *Burwell* in company, with disastrous consequences for ONS-154; although that was only one of his misjudgements.

This SOE had prepared well. *Duncan, Tay* and *Loosestrife* all carried HF/DF and given that *Zamalek* was also fitted with HF/DF the escort's direction finding capabilities were in good order and the SOE rotated the ships on HF/DF duty during the voyage; as he made clear in his reports.[22] Assigned to SC-130 were the oilers *Bente Maersk,* SS E. G. Seubert and SS *Benedick* with a variety of hose sizes aboard, including the American style hose; *Benedick* also carried a reserve of 60 Mark VII depth charges.[23] Both *Duncan* and *Vidette,* being Destroyers, were heavier on consumption than the Corvettes so it was as well that refuelling techniques had improved and that such an experienced 'oiler' was on hand. Both Destroyers were refuelled twice by *Bente Maersk,* as well as *Spey* from EG 1 that joined later.[24]

For the first part of the voyage local aircraft of the RCAF from Newfoundland provided air cover up to 600 miles out and during the cover period no U-boats were detected on the surface.[25] Nevertheless Gretton, a stickler for procedures, was unhappy with the RCAF radio communications and commented on the inexperience of pilots in his post-analysis report as 'not as satisfactory as it might have been'.[26] He was used to all assets under his command being at the top state of readiness.

U-boats were under strict U-boat HQ control while searching for and attacking convoys. It ordered by radio the formation and re-formation of patrol lines between specified geographical positions at regular intervals and passed on to each line of U-boats what to expect in the way of approaching convoys, based on reports received from *B-Dienst*. HQ also transmitted a steady stream of situation reports and general orders. When a convoy was sighted it was U-boat Command that decided on the time, direction and the order of attack. Because of the degree of remote control exercised it meant that in return for its own situation reports it required U-boats in contact with the convoy target to transmit detailed descriptions of the local situation. But there was a price to pay. Given the number of command and control signals transmitted, a lot of radio traffic provided WA and local escort commanders with a rich source for HF/DF location.[27] This became one of the German weaknesses.

The first two days were relatively untroubled but it was not long after that U-boat command discovered the location and course of SC-130, having decrypted an Admiralty U-boat situation report that had been sent to the convoy commodore – copy SOE on *Duncan* on 14 May.[28] In the situation report the Admiralty gave the course, speed and location of the convoy. *B-Dienst* had decrypted this message by 16 May and U-boat command planned the next move.

In May 1943 *B-Dienst* was still able to decipher Naval Cipher No. 3 and knew much about convoy movements. On 17 May *BdU* commented on some of their British intercepts:

> In the same special intercept situation report received mention was made of SC-130. The position of this convoy at 2100 on the 14th May was grid reference BC 4857, course 076°, speed 7.5 knots. In view of earlier experience, it is predicted that this convoy will take the same route as the HX, Groups. 'Donau 1 and 2' will be sent S. to intercept it.[29]

BdU set up two U-boat groups, *Donau* 1 and 2 – consisting of U 640–657–760–636–340–731–304–227–645–952–418–258 and 381 to take up a patrol line at

2000 on 18 May as Group *Donau* 1; and joining it was U 954–92–109–202–664–91–707–413–952–264–378 and 218 designated as *Donau* 2;[30] that gave it a combined strength of 25 U-boats to attack 37 merchantmen, excluding the escort force.

In the meantime GC&CS had decrypted another German signal that indicated knowledge of the SC-130 whereabouts and NID noted that:

The next development will be the establishment of new patrols on an arc between 020° and 140° from Virgin Rocks at a radius of 600 miles from Gander Newfoundland. Twenty or more U-boats are now moving to take these up and the apparent gap through which SC-130 has been routed is rapidly closing: it will be touch and go whether this convoy scrapes through.[31]

But through a serious systems failure this message was not passed on to the Escort Commander. The first inkling of U-boat presence was the first detection by HF/DF.

Being in possession of such a disturbing assessment, and having already decrypted U-boat instructions, it was decided to send out an escort support group to assist. Horton had planned for such events hence putting together his support groups, but this one was without a CVE.[32] First Escort Group, consisted of the frigates HMS *Wear* (Commanding), HMS *Jed*, HMS *Spey* and the ex-US Coast Guard cutter HMS *Sennen* (equipped with HF/DF). All were dispatched from St John's, Newfoundland on 16 May in order to reinforce EG B7 in good time.[33]

The escort group was equipped with 10-cm radar and HF/DF and given that the convoy was provided with land-based air cover the surfaced U-boat's cloak of invisibility was effectively removed.[34] The present situation for SC-130 now meant that there was a combined force of 12 warships to combat 21 U-boats, plus patrolling aircraft from Newfoundland, followed by the Liberator Squadron at Iceland when they came within range. The Air Gap had now been closed.

18 May 1943, Group Donau

BdU Entry 18 May.

At 0043 on the 18th U 304 sighted the expected SC convoy in AK 4675. 21 boats of Group 'Donau' were ordered in to attack the convoy, these being U 640, 657, 760, 636, 340, 731, 304, 227, 645, 952, 418, 258, 381, 954, 92, 109, 202, 664, 91, 707 and 413.[35]

According to a signal sent by *BdU* to all U-boats in the *Donau* group, *Leutnant* Heinz Koch, commander of *U-304*, was assigned lead boat.[36]
BdU continued in his entry on the 18th.

> During the night U 645 and U 952 were in contact the convoy. At 0530 the convoy was in AK 4693 (German Grid Reference). It was proceeding, based on dead reckoning, at about 8 knots . . . The operation is being continued.[37]

18–19 May, Point 2 on chart

First Escort group on its way to join B7 came across a U-boat at 1800 hours on 18 May about 40 miles astern of the convoy and attacked it. There was no indication of success.[38]

For SC-130 the first indication of a U-boat came during the evening of 18 May. At around 2000 hours there had been HF/DF contacts made by the rescue ship *Zamalek* and *Vidette* was despatched to investigate the contact, but found nothing. Other U-boat transmissions were DF'd up to midnight and Gretton was aware that more than one U-boat was in the vicinity, but there was no immediate attack. Early on 19 May both *Duncan* and *Zamalek* picked up good HF/DF fixes on a U-boat about 4 miles ahead of the convoy. *Duncan* made a box search to try to establish contact and dropped a pattern of charges, without success. Gretton reported to the Admiralty that they had about four U-boats in the vicinity and that one of them had been attacked.[39]

As was the procedure U-boats reported that the attack on the convoy had begun giving location, course and estimated speed.[40] *BdU* was also alerted to the fact that the enemy had detected group *Donau*. This information was gleaned from an Admiralty U-boat situation report dated 17 May and decrypted by *B-Dienst*. Again U-boat command asserted that such information probably came from aircraft reports and that their 'Enigma' codes were not the British source of information.[41] As noted earlier this is a lesson that was never learnt.

19 May, Point 3 on chart

During the night Duncan employed one of his 'defensive' tactics and ordered a convoy change of course, which was then resumed back to the old course a few hours later. In the early hours of 19 May the convoy was met by the first of the Liberator Squadron 120, out of Iceland, who reported that he had spotted, and attacked, a U-boat on the surface in a location that the convoy would have occupied had Gretton not ordered a course change during the night, proving the worth of this defensive tactic.[42] In the same report it was told how the aircraft had attacked the U-boat first. The aircraft launched two mark XXIV mines, or US homing torpedoes, dropped in the swirl of the dived U-boat, *U-954*. The pilot reported having seen two explosions close to the entry point of the acoustic torpedoes' and assumed that the U-boat had been sunk. That U-boat was of significance to Dönitz because his younger son Peter was on board serving as a 'watch officer'. *U-954* was indeed sunk, and on that day, but not by the Liberator. She was said to have been sunk later in the day by depth charges of the support group ships HMS *Jed* (Lt Cmdr R. C. Freaker) and HMS *Sennen* (Lt Cmdr F. H. Thornton) acting in concert on 19 May 1943. The revised position in the North Atlantic was southeast of Cape Farewell, Greenland in position N54 54', W34 19'. *U-954* went down with 47 dead, all hands lost. Commander Loewe was on his first war patrol in this boat.[43]

At 0550 in the vicinity of the convoy on the same day *Snowflake* obtained an ASDIC (SONAR) contact ahead of the ninth column and also sighted a periscope off her starboard beam just as her starboard DC thrower fired. Gretton had exercised and trained his team well. *Duncan* continued to hunt the U-boat (using *Snowflake* as well) and launched three 'Hedgehog' attacks one of which appears to have hit the mark for quantities of oil were seen on the surface. Gretton was convinced that the U-boat had been hit and indeed he was correct because both *Snowflake* and *Duncan* were later credited in sinking *U-381*. *Duncan* resumed station 0810 and signalled to the Admiralty 'U-boat sunk by Hedgehog'.[44] No longer did escorts need to blindly eject depth charges when the contact of ASDIC was lost. Now, with an advanced ASDIC system, they were better able to predict both depth and direction and thus calculate the trajectory to be used in firing.[45] Britain was the leader in this field and the United States and Canada introduced the same systems.

The tactics at this point in the battle seem clear. By using a combination of evasion, aircraft and agile-moving escorts in and around the convoy, they were able to keep U-boats from approaching too close, and that soon became known to the Flag Officer U-boats. Those that came within range were subject to an array of lethal weapons systems. One U-boat report received said that 'Several boats reported strong continual air cover over the convoy and the approach of land-based aircraft from low-lying clouds.'[46] *U-92* who had launched a strike attack of two torpedoes, unsuccessfully, made a report to HQ stating that she was 'Continually Forced Under By Catalina (aircraft) from 0750 to 1130'.[47]

Another radio message from U-boat, *U-645*, reported that there was a

Convoy Destroyer in Naval Grid Square AK 5468. Aircraft Attacking Continuously Out Of Low Clouds.[48]

Indeed another Liberator had replaced the first aircraft at around 0915 and was asked by Gretton to conduct a systematic radar search (Mamba) of the area to port of SC-130, during which it sighted a U-boat that immediately dived on observing the approaching aircraft. The aggressive Liberator from 120 Squadron dropped 4 depth charges on the first and forced others in the area to dive.[49]

19 May, Point 4 on chart

A third aircraft soon arrived and carried out several 'Mambas' which produced sightings and attacks on U-boats, while refuelling was in progress.[50] That kind of coolness of command seems to have demonstrated how much in control of the unfolding events that Gretton was. At 1615, while still refuelling, Gretton ordered an emergency turn to port for one hour. He then resumed the convoy's course – still refuelling.[51] These moves again disoriented shadowing U-boats. Also around 1600 hours on 19 May EG1 joined the convoy, having already sunk *U-954* 12 miles astern of the convoy. The SO of *Wear* (Commander Wheeler RNR) was requested to sweep ahead of the convoy until dark and then assume night stations on the extended screen, down moon, ahead and up wind. Since *Sennen* was now on station Gretton was able to detach HMCS *Kitchener* at 1700 and that brought the number of vessels for the screen to seven.

19 to 20 May, Point 5 on chart

During the night there were several passes by Liberators with re-enforcements from Ireland and attacks were carried out at frequent intervals. Operators handled a good deal of HF/DF activity and the fixes obtained resulted in both *Jed* and *Spey* being engaged. There had been a high degree of action during daylight hours and in his report Gretton pointed out that the failure of the U-boat day attacks were due to air cover and the good work put in by the co-operative effort of escorts with aircraft.[52] Several radio intercepts were made by GC&CS which indicated that U-304 was suffering negative buoyancy and that another had electrical problems, all due to depth charging.[53]

20 May

At 0225 on 20 May *Duncan* ordered two emergency turns to port, and the course was resumed at 0330. The tactic had worked for though many U-boats had been sighted by the patrolling aircraft they were not in contact with the convoy. HF/DF activity was also heard, but no attacks came. SC-130 again survived the night 'unscathed'.[54] *Duncan* ordered another emergency turn to port at 1315 in order to avoid contact with a nearby U-boat detected on HF/DF, and returned to the original course after an hour. A short while later at 1530 *Duncan* received a report from an aircraft that a U-boat was circling and unable to dive, so he went in pursuit. However, after 25 minutes the U-boat had indeed dived and *Duncan* returned to his station. His practice of returning to station seldom varied. The sad events of ONS-154 were evidence of an SOE that did not return to station and cover his convoy flank, when he should have.

U-boat Command was following events and was troubled by the lack of progress made by the Donau group. An entry on 20 May in the *BdU* log stated:

> Several boats also reported efficient co-operation between aircraft and escorts, this being confirmed by eight depth charge attacks in succession of which four were particularly heavy. Two boats had to return owing to heavy damage. The loss of *U 954* in the vicinity of the convoy is taken as certain as this boat reported 'contact made' when up to the convoy.[55]

This was news that Dönitz did not want to hear.[56]

The use of a mobile support group was something that the German U-boat command had not counted on and 'whose value cannot be measured in terms of the number of actual encounters they have with the enemy'.[57] Lately, in general, U-boat groups were used to meeting stiff opposition when they attacked a convoy. But to be hunted down when they kept their distance from the convoy, as they had in this case, was likely to have been most disconcerting.

21 May

During the night the same stations were resumed and the convoy had a quiet night of it. By dawn the first air cover of the day arrived in the form of a Sunderland flying boat and constant cover was now being given to the convoy. Their position had now passed W26°. *BdU* log entry for the 21 May 1943 states that: 'The Donau boats withdrawing from Convoy No. 41 (SC-130) to the W will now make for AK 97 and are to operate against the HX 239 convoy.[58] They had effectively been told by *BdU* to move off to the westward, some to engage in the next battle against HX 239, which fared no better – and to add to their problems HX 239 also had a CVE in company.

At 1100 hours on 22 May a signal came in from C-in-C Western Approaches stating:

> If convoy not threatened detach 1st EG to Londonderry now.[59]

The rest of the voyage was uneventful and it arrived in the afternoon of 25 May 1943, each ship now making its way to its final point of destination. It is interesting to note that during the voyage the station keeping of all ships was good and that no less than 20 emergency (evasion) turns were made by the convoy, which helped to keep U-boats at bay. As a result they frequently lost contact.[60]

On one point it is worth reflecting that this battle constituted a naval demonstration of 'Operational Manoeuvre', or *Blitzkrieg*.[61] In terms of the battle for SC-130 it represented a new level of war than had hitherto been adopted by the RN and its allies and may be identified as being between the tactical (the art of battle) and the strategic (the art of war) level. What the U-boat arm experienced in this battle was a 'hostile system', not just an accumulation of menacing forces. The British had, intuitively or by design, deployed their forces and provided an interlocking network of supporting resources, command and control systems, reinforcements and the political will to back it up.

Conclusions

On 24 May 1943, Dönitz withdrew his U-boats from the North Atlantic convoy routes by radioing his Commanders that they would temporarily stand down, until better equipment and more effective countermeasures were available. Dönitz readily acknowledged that Germany had suffered a serious defeat, but was ever confident that the setback need only be a temporary one. To U-boat commanders he sent a long message, part of which was:

> In the meantime we must overcome the situation with the measures already determined and with a temporary change in operational areas. We will, therefore, not allow ourselves to be forced onto the defensive and will not rest but, given an opportunity, continue to strike and fight on with greater fortitude and decision

in order to make ourselves even stronger for the decisive Battle of the North Atlantic . . .'[62]

German ingenuity, he assumed, would soon provide the measures needed to tackle the evident Allied technical advantages – particularly the superior radar with its consequent power of surprise air attack – to which he attributed the recent setbacks.[63] Strangely, at no time did he ever acknowledge his losses due to HF/DF; this was largely attributed to his insistence on reporting procedure. Neither did he doubt that it was imperative to resume the Battle in the North Atlantic if only to stop American men and materials from reaching Europe – for he could now no longer be in any doubt of what would happen next as a result of the withdrawal. From the decrypts of his signals to U-boats the Admiralty was kept reliably informed of the situation but there was also a German broadcast in which he publicly admitted that the U-boats had been 'temporarily thwarted' by 'new Allied defensive measures'.[64]

There was no let up in U-boat production and on 31 May OIC estimated the number in operational service at 240, an increase of 66 since September 1942 despite the losses inflicted on the U-boats in the interval; in June OIC calculated that the number was 226, and almost as many – 208 – were working-up in the Baltic.[65] In September the stage was therefore set for a return, and in some strength. There would be more 'Operational Manoeuvre' exercises to follow. Added to these improvements was a well-run Western Approaches organization led by a C-in-C as determined as his opposite number in the *Kriegsmarine*. The efforts were supported by improvements made in weapons applications, in part made possible by OR analysis leading to improved explosives, variable settings to depth charges and improved tactical efficiency.

On its plus side the *Kriegsmarine* had made substantial improvements to its torpedo technology. It embraced its own form of 'OR' which had a significant effect on the development of special torpedoes and types of target to be acquired but their development programme was unable to give them the leap in technology in new U-boats, thus far. However, missing were the escort countermeasures required to arrest even further progress being made by the enemy. But the predicament confronting the *Kriegsmarine* in May 1943 was faraway more complex than some radically new radar weapon and underwater detection, seek and destroy equipment. The problem stemmed from the limitations of existing U-boat technology because existing U-boats were unable overcome superior Allied weapon systems, intelligence advantages and tactics.[66]

Analysis of the reasons to withdraw

Part of the message that Dönitz transmitted to his U-boat commanders was:

> These decisions signify a temporary departure from the former principles for the
> conduct of U-boat warfare. This is necessary in order not to allow the U-boats to
> be beaten at a time when their weapons are inferior, by unnecessary losses while
> achieving very slight success . . .[67]

First and foremost the U-boats of group Donau did not sink one Allied merchant ship, while four U-boats were lost to the combined force of Allied air and surface escorts. The group leader Commander Koch, in *U-304*, went down on 28 May 1943 South of Iceland, just after the withdrawal of U-boats.[68] Two more U-boats were lost to Allied aircraft in operations related to the Battle for SC-130 but even if the Allies had sunk no U-boats they would have still won the Battle for SC-130, because it arrived safely with no losses.

May was the turning point for the Allies, and the blackest month ever for the U-boat arm. A total of 43 U-boats were sunk worldwide, of which 31 were in the North Atlantic; that equates to 75 per cent of the total sunk in May. Of the total on operations worldwide, 42 boats were in the Atlantic operational area (while 76 were on passage).[69] That too provides an equally staggering statistic of a 75 per cent loss in theatre (Table 11.1).

Of those sunk it may be seen that the percentage sunk by escorts and aircraft is roughly equal, not including CVEs. Two months prior the greater number of U-boats sunk in the North Atlantic were by escorts; the closing of the 'Air Gap' was therefore significant, and Dönitz realized this fact (Table 11.2).

Table 11.1 U-boats lost in the North Atlantic – May 1943

[Acc]cident Land Based [A]ircraft	Escort Aircraft [CVE]	Convoy [E]scort	Convoy [S]hip
Date of Loss			
May 1943	U-boat Number	Assigned U-boat Kill	Type
4	U-439	Acc	VII-C
4	U-659	Acc	VII-C
4	U-109	A	IX-B
5	U-638	E	VII-C
6	U-630	E	VII-C
6	U-192	E	IX-C/40
6	U-125	E	IX-C

continued

Table 11.1 Continued

[Acc]cident Land Based [A]ircraft	Escort Aircraft [CVE]	Convoy [E]scort	Convoy [S]hip
6	U-531	E	IX-C/40
6	U-438	E	VII-C
7	U-447	A	VII-C
7	U-209	A	VII-C
11	U-528	E	IX-C/40
12	U-186	E	IX-C/40
12	U-89	CVE	VII-C
12	U-456	A	VII-C
13	U-753	E+A Shared	VII-C
14	U-640	A	VII-C
15	U-266	A	VII-C
17	U-657	E	VII-C
17	U-646	A	VII-C
19	U-954	E	VII-C
19	U-273	A	VII-C
19	U-381	E ?	VII-C
20	U-258	A	VII-C
22	U-569	CVE	VII-C
23	U-752	CVE	VII-C
25	U-467	A	VII-C
26	U-436	E	VII-C
28	U-304	A	VII-C
31	U-440	A	VII-C
31	U-563	A	VII-C

Acc.=Accident, E.=Escorts, A.=Aircraft, CVE.=Carrier Vessel Escort.

Source: Author Compiled from Niestlé.[70]

Table 11.2 U-boats lost in the North Atlantic – March and April 1943

March 1934	U-boat Number	U-boat Kill and Position	Type
4	U-87	[E] – N41°86′ W13° 31′	VII-B
10	U-633	[S] – N58°51′ W19° 55′	VII-C
11	U-444	[E] – N51°14′ W29° 18′	VII-C
11	U-432	[E] – N51°35′ W28° 20′	VII-C
12	U-130	[E] – N37°10′ W40° 21′	IX-C
13	U-163	[E] – N45°05′ W15° 00′	IX-C

continued

Table 11.2 Continued

March 1934	U-boat Number	U-boat Kill and Position	Type
19	U-384	[A] – N54°18' W26° 15'	VII-C
22	U-665	[A] – N48°04' W10° 26'	VII-C
25	U-469	[A] – N62°12' W14° 52'	VII-C
27	U-169	[A] – N60°54' W15° 25'	IX-C/40
April 1943			
2	U-124	[E] – N41°02' W15° 39'	IX-B
5	U-635	[A] – N58°20' W31° 52'	VII-C
6	U-632	[A] – N58°02' W28° 42'	VII-C
14	U-448	[E] – N46°22' W19° 35'	VII-C
17	U-175	[E] – N47°53' W22° 04'	IX-C
23	U-189	[A] – N59°50' W34° 43'	IX-C/40
23	U-191	[E] – N56°45' W34° 25'	IX-C/40
24	U-174	[A] – N43°35' W07° 35'	IX-C
24	U-710	[A] – N61°25' W19° 48'	VII-C
25	U-203	[CVE] – N55°05' W42° 25'	VII-C

Acc.=Accident, E.=Escorts, A.=Aircraft, CVE.=Carrier Vessel Escort.

Source: Compiled from Niestlé.[71]

Rahn concluded that air power and an increase in the degree of technology available to the allies, coupled with the mobility of support groups with highly trained personnel, were responsible for the heavy toll on crews and boats. Once a U-boat had been detected its slow submerged speed did not allow for drastic evasion manoeuvres.[72] Once detected there was little chance of escape and Dönitz knew that such a rate of attrition was unsustainable.[73]

The tonnage war

Dönitz had set great store by his method of winning the Battle of the Atlantic, the tonnage war. He stated clearly that his aim was to sink as much shipping as possible in the most economical manner and based his calculations on the sinkings per U-boat per day-at-sea, which had to be maintained at the highest possible level.

The peak of ships sunk by U-boat per month was in October 1940. Thereafter it began to fall, for two main reasons:

1. The number of U-boats at sea increased steadily over the next two- and-a-half years but the defenders got better at their job; and SigInt and training of personnel improved.

2. Protection for convoys improved, especially from mid-March 1943 until the end of the war with improved technology becoming available as well as the availability of long-range aircraft. In May 1943 it reached decisive proportions and *BdU* was keenly aware of the impact that it was having on his operations in terms of losses in men and materiel.

The alternative method to achieve his objective instead of the pure 'tonnage war' that he was fighting was the 'supply war' in which attacks would be concentrated on shipping sailing to Britain, or to a particular theatre. The problem was that the more the monthly sinking figure dropped below his required million tons the more the urgency to make the transition from the 'pure tonnage war to the supplies – and freight-war'.[74] He never reconciled the difference; another lesson unlearnt.

Experience of U-boat commanders

Another of his concerns was the diminishing level of service that the average U-boat commander had. In the early days of the war the average time spent in command of a U-boat was upwards of two years before moving to a new post in the service, such as administration support or assisting in the training of new recruits, but by 1943 the picture looked quite different. At the beginning of December 1942 a table showing the months of experience in operational command of all U-boat commanders was issued by OIC. It revealed that the average number of months in operational command was just 8.1 months.[75] But it also shows a worryingly short span of active life that could be expected by the average German submariner at this critical juncture of the war; a point surely noted by the *BdU*. Given his hopes for the future development of the U-boat he needed to retain as many commanders as possible. Looking back over the period of May Dönitz could check his own records of the number of patrols that each of the lost commanders had completed. This too must have been disquieting. The numbers of patrols completed by those commanders of U-boats lost in the month of May shows that with a few exceptions the great majority had been sent out with just one or two patrols to their credit. Just five had seven or eight patrols and one veteran had completed 11 patrols.[76]

Dönitz must have been most concerned that his relatively short experienced skippers were being lost at such a rate. The *Kriegsmarine* had a training programme that was systematic, balanced and thoroughly carried out, up until just prior to the war. Before the end of 1943 the training of some commanders was severeley curtailed to between four and ten weeks training only, a sharp drop due to attrition rates.[77] U-boat commanders and a competent crew cannot be created overnight so senseless losses were anathema to him.

He, alone, would have made the decision to withdraw but he went to great lengths to explain to his U-boat commanders why they had to stand down. From an inspection of his daily *KTB* the degree of anguish that he went through in the issuance of the order was plainly clear, perhaps even to the extent of making excuses for some of the organizational misjudgements that the U-boat arm had perpetrated.

In his address to commanders he wrote:

> I know that operations for you out there at the moment are some of the hardest and most costly in losses, since the enemy's defence at the moment is superior in view of new technical methods. Believe me, I have done everything and will continue to do so, in order to introduce a means to counter this enemy advance.[78]

Things had not gone well for the U-boat arm in the month of May and a major rethink in strategy was clearly needed. He needed to evaluate what lessons could be drawn from the experience and how to counteract the enemy's clear mastery above and below the water. As it was he would have realized that the allies would not sit idly by waiting for events to unfold and would likely step up the deliveries of men and war materiel to Britain. One thing was sure. He was determined to return to the Atlantic hunting grounds at some stage. How successful the U-boat arm would be is another matter, and that is dealt with in the next chapter.

Notes

1 TNA AIR 41/47, Air Narrative, 10.

2 Ibid., 13.

3 Duncan Redford, 'Inter- and Intra-service Rivalries in the Battle of the Atlantic', *Journal of Strategic Studies*, 32 (6) (December 2009), 899–928, 908–9.

4 Stephen W. Roskill, *The War at Sea* (1956), II, 89.

5 TNA ADM 199/2060: CB 040500/43 (1), Monthly anti-submarine report, Section 1; Corelli Barnett, *Engage the Enemy More Closely* (1991), 596.

6 Philip Joubert de la Ferté, *Birds and Fishes* (1960), 211.

7 W. S. Chalmers, *Max Horton* (1954), 173.

8 TNA ADM 237/203, On 12 June 1943 HMS Snowflake's Commander commented on a lack of training in communications procedures.

9 Donald Macintyre, *U-boat Killer* (1999), 95.

10   TNA ADM 237/203, 8; Report on SC-130 convoy.

11   TNA CAB 86/4, War Cabinet: Battle of the Atlantic and anti U-Boat Warfare Committee, Memorandum of First Sea Lord 30 March 1943.

12   TNA CAB 86/4, War Cabinet: Battle of the Atlantic and anti U-Boat Warfare Committee, AU (43) 137, VLR aircraft distribution and strength, 4 May 1943.

13   Arnold Hague, *The Allied Convoy System 1939–1945,* (2000), 58.

14   TNA CAB 86/3, AU (43) 90 Statement by First Sea Lord at the anti U-boat Warfare Committee meeting, 22 March 1943, f. 392.

15   NHB PG 30315, KTB entry for 15 January 1943.

16   *Lagevorträge* (München, 1972), 475.

17   NHB PG 30327, 2/Skl /BdU Op. KTB entry for 7 July, referring to corrections of 1 June 1943, 407 instead of 412 boats.

18   TNA ADM 237/203, Commodores report SC-130, folio 190.

19   TNA ADM 199/1336, SC and HX convoys: reports, 1943–4, SC 130 track. The above chart is quite large. For the purpose of this discussion action points are highlighted and discussed. [Open Government Licence]

20   TNA ADM 237/203, signal dated, 091516Z/5/43 from Cominch C&R, N.S.H.Q., copy C-in-C WA.

21   TNA ADM 199/2020, Analysis of Convoy SC130 11, July 1943.

22   TNA ADM 237/207, Appendix E to report showing HF/DF watches set, 25 May 1943, 1.

23   TNA ADM 237/203, Cable and Wireless signal 12/5/1943.

24   TNA ADM 199/1336, Report on proceedings, 1 [f. 9].

25   TNA ADM 199/2020, Analysis of Convoy SC 130, 11 July 1943, 1; TNA ADM 199/1336, SC and HX convoys: reports, 1943–4, 10.

26   TNA ADM 199/1336, SC and HX convoys: reports, 1943–4, 10; ADM237/203, Remarks on air co-operation, 8.

27   F. H. Hinsley et al., *British Intelligence in the Second World War* (1981), II, 550.

28   Günter Hessler, *The U-boat War in the Atlantic 1939–45* (1989), II, 110.

29   NHB PG 30324, BdU KTB entry for 17 May, under 'Current Operations'.

30   Ibid., this differs somewhat from the account given by David Syrett in 'The Safe and Timely Arrival of Convoy SC-130', 220.

31   TNA ADM 223/15, U-boat situations report No. 1941, report covering dates 20 December 1941 to 28 June 1943, f. 98.

32   F. Barley et al., *The Defeat of the Enemy Attack on Shipping 1939–1945*, 137 (Aldershot, 1997), 47; David K. Brown, *Atlantic Escorts* (Barnsley, 2007), 88.

33   TNA ADM 199/1336, SC and HX convoys: reports 1943–4, EG1 proceedings. HMS *Pelican* was also designated for this group but ran into mechanical problems and returned to St Johns, 2 [f. 46].

34   David Zimmerman, 'Technology and Tactics', in *The Battle of the Atlantic 1939–1945* (1994), 476–89.

35 The boats sunk were U-640 Commander Nagel, on 14 May, and U-657 Commander Göllnitz, on 17 May. See Table 11.2.

36 NBH PG 30324, Signal to all boats in 'Donau' 0836 on 19.5.1943, file copy 545.

37 Ibid.

38 TNA ADM 199/1336, SC and HX convoys: reports, 1943–4, 2 [f. 11].

39 Ibid., 10.

40 NHB PG 30324, BdU KTB entry for 19 May 1943, U-645, 952, and 304 gave their positions as AK49, AK49 and AK46 respectively all very close.

41 Ibid., 1.

42 TNA ADM 199/1336, SC and HX convoys: reports, 1943–4, 11.

43 Axel Niestlé, *German U-boat Losses During World War II* (Annapolis, 1998), 92.

44 TNA ADM 237/203, *Duncan* report, Appendix D, 12. 6. 1943.

45 Willem Hackmann, *Seek and Strike* (1984), 238; Hedgehog had been introduced as early as late 1941.

46 NHB PG 30324, entry 19 May 1943.

47 TNA DEFE 3/718, Intelligence from intercepted German radio communications WWII, 14–22 May 1943, 1129/19/5/43; the Germans were not always able to distinguish aircraft types.

48 Ibid., 1234/19/5/43.

49 TNA ADM 199/1336, SC convoys: reports 1943, 2 [f. 11].

50 Ibid., *Duncan* proceedings, 3 [f. 12]

51 Ibid.

52 Ibid., 1 [f. 9].

53 TNA DEFE 3/718, messages timed at 1637, 1949 and 2018 hours on 19 May, and 0233 hours on 20 May 1943.

54 TNA ADM 199/1336, SC and HX convoys: reports, 1943–4, *Duncan* proceedings, 3 [f. 12].

55 NHB PG 30324, entry 20 May 1943, on air co-operation.

56 The Admiral's younger son was on board this boat.

57 TNA ADM 199/2020, Analysis of the operation of support groups in the North Atlantic, 14 April–11 May 1943, 1.

58 NHB PG 39324, BdU KTB entry 21 May 1943 concerning Danube's boats.

59 TNA ADM 199/1336, Signal to *Duncan* from C-in-C, WA. TOO (time of original) 221158B.

60 TNA ADM 199/2020, Analysis of the operation of support groups in the North Atlantic, 14 April–11 May 1943, 3.

61 Andrew Lambert, 'Sea Power 1939–1940: Churchill and the Strategic Origins of the Battle of the Atlantic', in *Sea Power* (Ilford, 1994), 86–107, 86.

62 NHB PG 30324, BdU KTB entry on 24 May 1943.

63 Hinsley et al., *British Intelligence in the Second World War* (1984), III, 211.

64 Ibid.

65 TNA ADM 223/98, OIC SI 603 of 31 May; 615 of 9 June 5943.

66 'Niederschrift über die Besprechung beim Führer in der Reichskanzlei, 28.9.1942', in *Lagevorträge*, 420–4.

67 NHB PG 30324, BdU KTB part entry on 24 May 1943, signed by Dönitz. For German readers it conveys his depth of anxiety and concern; 'Diese Entscheidungen bedeuten eine vorübergehende Abkehr von den bisherigen Grundsätzen der U-bootkriegsschule. Sie ist notwendig um, nicht in einer Zeit der Unterlegenheit der Waffen durch nutzlose Verluste bei geringen Erfolgen die Unterseebootwaffe zerschlagen zu können. Es besteht aber völlige Klarheit darüber, dass nach wie vor das Hauptkampfgebiet der U-boote im Nordatlantik liegt und dass der Kampf dort mit aller Härte und Entschlossenheit wieder aufgenommen werden muss, sobald den U-booten die dazu nötigen Waffen gegeben sind' . . .

68 Details verified in Axel Niestlé, *German U-boat Losses During World War II*.

69 NHB PG 30325, BdU KTB 'U-boats as of 1 June 1943', Section III, Distribution.

70 Niestlé, *German U-boat Losses during World War II*.

71 Ibid.

72 Werner Rahn, 'The Campaign: The German Perspective', in *The Battle of the Atlantic 1939–1945* (1994), 538–53, 549.

73 TNA HW 18/200, Improved air cover in the Atlantic, 31.

74 Peter Padfield, *Dönitz* (1984), 250.

75 Patrick Beesly, *Very Special Intelligence* (1977), 203: Hessler, *The U-boat War in the Atlantic 1939–45*, II, 100.

76 Rainer Busch et al., *Der U-Bootkrieg 1939–1945* (2) (Berlin 1997); research details are covered in this volume.

77 NHB PG 29399, Various training programmes, 6; TNA CAB/66/32/38, Naval situation, folio 147.

78 PG 30324, BdU KTB entry on 24 May 1943.

12

Return of the U-boat to the North Atlantic and the End Game

This chapter examines the events from May 1943 onwards when Dönitz attempted to renew the battle but which culminated in the final withdrawal of U-boats from the Atlantic. It analyzes the efforts of both protagonists in their efforts to affect the final outcome of the *guerre de course*.

Before moving on to discuss the events from September 1943 onwards it is as well to recall the difficulties experienced by the allies through the use of Naval Cipher No. 3, and how they finally learnt a lesson in faulty communications. The German 'Cryptographic Service', *xB-Dienst*, had earlier solved changes in cipher code and, through *B-Dienst*, provided the *BdU* with much valuable information concerning the movement of ships, one which he came to greatly rely on. However, the allies finally discovered a leak in their own SigInt security. On 28 May 1943 Commander Kenneth Knowles USN, the head of American anti-U-boat intelligence, issued an intelligence summary pointing out that the Germans apparently must have had prior knowledge of the route taken by the freighter *Sydney Star*, proceeding independently from Montevideo to the Clyde. The evidence was based on an Allied decrypted German message stating:

SIDNEY STAR LEFT MONTEVIDEO 12 MAY FOR THE CLYDE VIA NAY. SQ. FK 4391 AND DS 4212: WILL ARRIVE (CLYDE) 1 JUNE. SPEED 14.5.[1]

The phrasing used helped identify the source of the information that reflected the likelihood of it being a message employing Naval Cipher No. 3. Unlike Enigma, Naval Cipher No. 3 was a non-machine cipher and used by the allies working on the protection of the North Atlantic convoys. Once aware that the cipher had been compromised a further investigation revealed that there were several other breaches found in German communications security, indicating that the Germans were indeed reading it.[2] After the war a copy of the same message was found in the *BdU KTB*, dated 19 May 1943.[3]

The Allies began a gradual elimination of Naval Cipher No. 3 on 10 June but because of the system in use the wholesale change over to a different code took some time to complete.[4] From then on *B-Dienst* began to lose its grip.[5]

As the change to codes began to be applied *B-Dienst* did not suffer an immediate blackout, but rather a fade out as the large number of users of the cipher made the conversion to the new system.[6] After the full introduction of the new code some small amount was still read but certainly by 1 January 1944 it became a major obstacle for *B-Dienst* to read intercepts, since *xB-Dienst* was unable to solve the code – and remained so for the rest of the war. The U-boat arm was therefore deprived of one of its primary sources of information.[7] Five years after the war a report estimated that 70 per cent of the convoys intercepted by U-boats between 1 December 1942 and 31 May 1943 were primarily located by intelligence acquired through the deciphering of Naval Cipher No. 3.[8] Indeed, Dönitz was to later admit that during the war the ship movement information provided by *B-Dienst* was 'the only reconnaissance service on which I can rely'.[9]

Learning the lessons in order to return to the North Atlantic Theatre

In preparation for a resumption of operations U-boat Command had equipped some of the boats with improved Flak, such as the *Vierlingen* (Quadruple 20-cm flak guns).[10]

U-boats were also fitted with a new radar search receiver, the *Hagenuk* (or *Wanze*), to replace the rather dated Metox system.[11] At the start of September 1943 when Admiral Dönitz decided that the time was ripe for U-boats to return to his stated *Hauptkampfgebiet* (Principal Battle Area) he instigated a change in tactics in the hope of wresting away the advantage from the Allies. He had taken delivery of the *Zaunkönig* – a new acoustic torpedo known to the British as the GNAT – and was ready to commence the return. One U-boat tactic proposed was to use Flak guns to fight its way out in the event of an aircraft attack. The second was to principally attack the convoy escorts, in preference to the merchantmen themselves, but not exclusively.[12]

Inadequate air support and SigInt blackout

As part of further preparations for the North Atlantic campaign he decided to make a more direct approach to both Göring and Hitler for air support. Negotiations with Göring initially began on 25 February 1943, when Dönitz stressed the need for the earliest provision of twice-daily long-range reconnaissance flights over the Atlantic to aid U-boat efforts.[13] To his surprise Göring promised his full support to this aim maintaining that one *Geschwader* (Wing) would be adequate for the purpose, but VLRs were still not available and none could be realized at this stage of the war.[14] This new co-operation actually came into being because of a meeting that Dönitz had with Hitler on 31 May 1943 at the Berghof, and could explain why Göring had earlier agreed to some co-operation. At that meeting Dönitz explained his plan and reasons stating that,

> We would undoubtedly have been able to sink more with the U-boat arm had we had flying boats in the past year . . . It is still not too late to finally provide an Air Force for the war at sea.
>
> (The Führer wholly concurs with the execution)[15]

Thus with thoughts on how to proceed with renewed attacks on British shipping Dönitz put in place a further attempt to work more closely with the *Luftwaffe* and sought to begin to operate sorties of long-range flying boats, the BV-222 series, in order to locate convoys more accurately as they approached Britain.[16] In order to strengthen what Dönitz hoped would be greater efficiency he had set up the 20th flotilla for the specific purpose of working with aircraft in evasion tactics and attack procedures.[17] One of the most important reasons for this renewed attempt would soon become apparent with the loss of the SigInt previously available through Naval Cipher No. 3 decrypts.

Two east-bound Destroyers were sighted on the northern wing of a convoy and these ships could have been attached to either SC-143 or HX-259, in which case these convoys must have been further east than estimated. SC-143 left Halifax on 28 September 1943 bound for Liverpool. HX-259 was diverted south based on intelligence information, still spasmodically being decoded. A *Luftwaffe* search was started and during the night eight flying boats sighted Destroyers proceeding singly, and in groups, which appeared to be slowly moving in the direction of north-east. From an Enigma message it was assumed that the convoy was nearby, particularly as a decryption of the eighth showed that stragglers of SC-143 had been routed through the area. The search was continued and followed up with air reconnaissance with a BV-222 flying boat aircraft being used for the first time. Signals may have been mixed up, or misunderstood, because the aircraft arrived over the area one-and-a-half hours ahead of the expected time of arrival. On the outward flight it sighted the convoy at once and commenced sending out homing signals, without, however, giving any prior warning to U-boats. Consequently, during the 30 minutes that the aircraft spent in contact with the convoy, none of the U-boats received homing signals. The designated group, *Rossbach*, was ordered to operate in compliance with the aircraft's reconnaissance report but despite good visibility and accurate navigational fixes obtained by the boats they were unable to locate the convoy, and the operation was abandoned on 9 October.[18] The inability of the *Luftwaffe* to navigate correctly was a point made by Dönitz at the 31 May meeting with Hitler. When he referred to *Luftwaffe* crews as *Zuckerbäcker* (derogatory) he was also reminded of the fact that their navigation equipment was of poor quality. To say that HQ was unimpressed would be an understatement. Overall the co-operation between the Navy and the *Luftwaffe* never worked well. Summing up the conclusions of the exercise the Naval Staff contended,

> that most of the past U-boat operations against Atlantic convoys had failed because of a certain lack of training amongst the aircrews and the difficult conditions under which the U-boat were operating.[19]

The response from the *Luftwaffe* was terse

> We cannot accept the view that the failure of most of the past U-boat operations was due to the paucity of *Fliegerführer's* Atlantic forces . . .[20]

Dönitz then tried to ratchet up the U-boat effort even more by placing some *B-Dienst* personnel aboard the boat in order for them to conduct their own exercise in DF in the hope of detecting the direction and, if possible, distance off that a convoy was.[21] How effective these efforts were is unknown but they seemed to be extreme and desperate measures.

Refuelling U-boats at sea

Dönitz then faced a fuel crisis. GC&CS had decrypted a U-boat Command decision emanating from instructions sent to U-boat Commanders, which explained that the dispersion of U-boat groups had been implemented in order to prevent premature detection of large patrols by Allied radar. However, the primary purpose of the dispersal was another attempt to develop a more efficient method of finding convoys, and in this they did not succeed. For various reasons the dispersion policy could not be maintained for long, mainly due to the lack of fuel supply U-boats (*Milchkühe*) – deliberately targeted by the Allies as a tactic, examples of which were the sinking of:

- *U-460* (Type XIV Sunk 4 October, 1943 in the North Atlantic north of the Azores in position N43.13 W28.58, by depth charges from Avenger and Wildcat aircraft (VC-9) of the American CVE, USS Card, 62 dead and 2 survivors)[22]; and
- *U-220* (Type XB Sunk 28 October 1943 in the North Atlantic in position N48.53 W33.30 by depth charges from two Avenger and Wildcat aircraft of the American CVE, USS Block Island, 56 dead (all hands lost)).[23]

Between June and August 1943 American-based carrier planes, aided by decrypts, had sunk five milch cows and reserve tankers. The British abandoned their earlier reservations about using Enigma intelligence in these operations and on 2 October the Admiralty requested that the US Navy send a task force against a refuelling due to take place north of the Azores; US Navy planes found four U-boats on the surface and sank the attending milch cow *U-460*, listed above. A similar request by the Admiralty less than a week later resulted in the sinking on 28 October of the *U-220*, also listed above. The Americans accounted for five Milch Cows and reserve tankers in more or less deliberate hunts between June and August, and equal number were sunk.[24] By the beginning of November the fuel re-supply situation became desperate. Of the U-tankers that Dönitz had in service in the spring of 1943 only one of them now remained intact. The effect was that U-boat operations were now severely compromised. Because re-supply by U-tankers was so dangerous that Dönitz started to avoid having to use them, requiring his U-boats to break off their operations correspondingly early and thus destroying any hope he may have had for a formidable offensive in distant waters, far from Allied air cover. Even at this late stage of the war Dönitz still appeared to have learnt little about the security of his communications.

Abandonment indecision

By the end of November he again abandoned the convoy routes as a theatre of operations, only to return the following month. It was time to learn from the experience thus far. A re-think was needed and U-boat Command came up with a yet more radical change in tactics by abandoning the long patrol line that it had used so frequently in the past. He tried another approach, but it was a retrograde step that harked back to 1939–40; he tried to work with little or no help from the *Luftwaffe* or *B-Dienst*. When a line of U-boats were unsuccessful in finding any ships he split it up into subgroups of U-boats, each in the hope that they would identify targets. It didn't work, any more than it did in 1940. Between mid-December 1943 and the middle of January 1944 his boats sighted not one of the ten convoys that sailed close to them and their total effort resulted in the sinking of one lone merchant ship.[25] It appears that he had learnt nothing, or it could have been more an act of desperation.

Operations in inshore waters

On 7 January 1944 most groups were dissolved and each of the boats were allocated, singly, to attack areas west of the British Isles in an attempt to interrupt the convoys as they began to arrive. This step marked the abandonment of the patrol line and scouting formation for convoy interception unless a provision of air reconnaissance was available.[26] In future individual U-boats would generally have to cope single-handed with the entire convoy escort as they entered coastal waters; and the obvious counter-attack that would surely come, once they were detected.

Schnorchel

Armed with a degree of new invisibility the *Schnorchel* U-boats now began to concentrate on sinking shipping around the British coast-line, and in anticipation of an expected invasion of Western Europe; many of the 40 boats of group *Landwirt*, assigned to operate against allied vessels were equipped with *Schnorchel*.[27]

By late 1944 U-boats were being increasingly fitted with the device which greatly extended their possibilities for stealth and made detection by surface vessels and aircraft much more difficult. Their return to British coastal waters was linked with the realization that detection of a U-boat in (relatively) shallow, wreck strewn, inshore waters would be difficult. Intel had little effect on this move.[28] However, if they did surface there was always a good chance of being detected because Coastal Command had increased air patrols to every half-hour, day or night.[29] Thus the U-boat did not have everything its own way and was often detected, and hunted, sometimes with battery power almost down to zero. In this case they had to resort to starting diesel engines by cartridge.

Neither did escorts have an easy time of it. British escorts that were hunting *Schnorchel* boats recognized the difficulties of using ASDIC (SONAR) detection closer inshore, due to the density layering of water, rocks and sunken wrecks. A November 1942 report declared that the problems of varying echoes had not been solved and some U-boats had escaped destruction.

> Water conditions are never bad enough to warrant abandonment of ASDIC operations in war time. 'Bad' conditions, however, call for greater skill on the part of all concerned, not only from the operator but from the Commanding Officer and i.e. A/S Control Officer.[30]

Nevertheless, despite the advantage in detection now being with conventional U-boats the success that they enjoyed was limited and only amounted to an irritant, not a severe threat.

Allied qualitative/quantitative improvements in weapons and sensors

What was not seen at the time by most of the British and nearly all the Germans in 1943 was that the strategy of convoys, given an appropriate number of escorts with proper weapons and training, could not be defeated by conventional U-boats using existing weapons and tactics.[31] While the Germans concentrated on the advance in design of the 'true' submersible and other new technologies, the allies were busy with more of their own 'OR' and development of new A/S weaponry.

The application of Hedgehog has been discussed and it was seen that while it represented an advance on previous methods of 'depth' charging it still had some significant limitations. A further development of the 'Hedgehog' ahead thrown mortar was 'Squid', which had been in development and went for sea trials in October 1943.

Sea trials was a precursor to further developments by the OR group. The first operational system went into service in December 1943 but did not achieve its first sinking until August 1944, nine months later – although by then no large-scale U-boat 'pack' attacks were in operation since the withdrawal of 'packs' from the Atlantic was now complete.[32] It was the early success of 'Hedgehog' that prompted the Admiralty to have some inclusion of Squid in new ships to be included in the design specifications. In 1944 Squid was incorporated into the first completely integrated ASW weapon system known as the Type 147B ASDIC, with Squid being the A/S mortar component. Squid threw either three, or six projectiles (two separate units), which were detonated by timed fuzes in a triangular pattern carefully designed to maximize the chances of a kill. Squid's computer, for want of a better term, the 147B ASDIC was the only completely new ASDIC set produced during the war. The precise and narrow beam of the 147B became quite effective guiding weaponry after the U-boat had first been located. From August 1944 until the end of the war it is estimated that about 18 U-boats were sunk by this method.[33]

Novel detection methods

Although they were introduced rather late, two other developments demonstrate how the allies were moving forward in sensor design thinking – the Magnetic Anomaly Detector (MAD), and sono-buoys, both originally of British design;[34] and both devolved to the Americans for manufacture. Tizard made the British ideas known to the Americans and they developed MAD; primarily at the Bell Laboratories. Once developed, a limited number of MAD units were fitted in American aircraft and used for locating U-boats which had submerged on sighting, or during patrols over restricted waters such as the Straits of Gibraltar. It was on 24 February 1944 that the first successful contact was made with a U-boat, resulting in it being destroyed off Gibraltar. Its greatest shortcoming was the very short range of detection which never progressed farther than about 600 feet.[35]

The original idea of the sono-buoy was also British. It was Professor Blackett, and his assistant Williams, who proposed that small buoys containing miniature ASDIC sets, or directional hydrophones, could be dropped by low-flying aircraft to detect the HE of U-boats and give a radio warning of those near convoys.[36] At first, the intention was to drop the buoys over the side of a convoy ship. They would then pick up any waterborne sound from a vessel approaching from astern and transmit a radio warning to the convoy. Expendable radio sono-buoys were later used extensively by the Allied air forces.

Coastal command patrols and developments

By June 1943 most of Coastal Command's A/S aircraft had finally been fitted with the new 10-cm ASV radar, against which the U-boats' search receivers were ineffective, except for the later version the 'Naxos'. The AO C-in-C, Air Vice-Marshal Sir John Slessor, took the opportunity given by the withdrawal of the U-boats from operations against the Atlantic convoys to concentrate his aircraft on the northern and southern exit routes of U-boats from bases in the French ports, in an all-out campaign which has come to be called the Bay Offensive.

Another development for Coastal Command came in August 1944. The Mk.VII ASV (Mk.III adapted for 3-cm X Band operation) had undergone trials, but was pronounced by the CCDU to be inferior to the American APS-3 unit. This led on to the APS-15 (ASV Mk.X) which, after being installed in a Liberator, was sent to Angle for tests in August 1944. After the introduction of the *Schnorchel* air-breathing tube for U-boats it resulted in a 'crash' trial by the CCDU using HMS *United,* an *Ursula* class submarine. The British submarine was fitted with a dummy tube and it was proved conclusively that metric ASV Mk II radar was ineffective against such a small target and that the centimetric radars were little better, unless the sea state was anything but calm. This proved to be a wake-up call for the Admiralty.

The way forward

The crisis in the U-boat war was not something that happened overnight and had long been a gradual creep. One of the early attempts to get a high underwater-speed U-boat came in 1934, using a 'steam turbine' with a designed underwater-speed of 28 knots. In 1940 a simpler experimental system achieved 26 knots in trials.[37] In the event, matters had been going quite well with the proven Types VII and IX and it is likely that complacency had set in. If the *Kriegsmarine* leadership had worked more diligently on procuring better U-boats, and defensive weapons, earlier they could have come out of it far better. But there was also the question as to what new countermeasures the enemy themselves might develop, and how they might overcome them.[38]

To achieve this objective Dönitz pinned his hopes on an entirely revolutionary U-boat that had been in the planning stages since as early as mid-1942, and in November termed the 'Elektro' boat. This was to be a U-boat capable of high submerged speed (albeit only for short periods of up to an hour and a half), diving to great depths and armed with the latest weapons and sensors that would permit it to fight, theoretically, without ever having to surface or show a periscope;[39] battery recharging notwithstanding in conditions where the '*Schnorchel*' could not be used.

On 31 May 1943 plans for new boat construction were discussed when Admiral Dönitz presented a new Fleet Building Programme to Hitler at one of his regular meetings. The *ObdM* informed him of the setbacks and high losses currently being suffered in the U-boat war and explained the urgency of his case. When Dönitz was asked how he would remedy the situation, he replied that a monthly delivery of 40 of the new-type *Elektro* U-boats should do it.

> I have already, in agreement with Minister Speer, given the first contract for thirty U-boats per month, and the announced ship building programme, and (now) request the carrying out of the *Führer's* attached order. The *Führer* agrees changes to the number from 30 to 40 U-boats per month, and signs it off.[40]

Unlike his predecessor, Raeder, Dönitz had little difficulty in his relationship with Hitler and without further discussion, the latter agreed.[41] Therefore in June 1943 a new schedule had to be worked out by the *HAS* and K Office (responsible for materials and construction), and the armaments minister Albert Speer in particular. The aim was to make an overall increase in the U-boat production schedule by one third, if possible,[42] to complement the 432 already in service.[43] Dönitz was now in complete command of the *Kriegsmarine* and rejected anything that did not conform to his ideas, in much the same manner that Hitler did – except that he devolved all responsibility for U-boat production to Speer, who would have no truck with Nazi ideology in matters of production.[44] At the beginning of July 1943 he would not accept the plans made by *HAS*; indeed by June he was already sure that he was neither equipped for the large fleet construction programme of 1943, nor the new U-boats construction requirements with the naval authorities under his command.

The design of the *Elektro* U-boat underwent several changes and finally emerged as the Type XX1, for longer range and XXIII, for coastal work. These were now given high priority over all others. What emerged on 6 July 1943 was a plan that meant delivery quotas for 1944 as follows:

VIIC	IXC	IXD	XIV	XX	XXI	XVII	XXII	total	monthly average
225	38	11	5	9	6	90	50	434	36.2

Therefore in August 1943 the existing orders for 180 of the conventional Type VIIC/42 U-boats were cancelled, leaving just enough of the old U-boats to cover the expected losses until the Types XXI and XXIII were ready by mid-1944.[45] Overall, orders were placed for 290 Type XXI U-boats, all of which were to be delivered by the end of February 1945.[46]

Using standard methods of construction the development time required for the Type XXI, from the advancement of the tactical requirement to the delivery of the first production model, would have been in the order of about two-and-a-half years. Given that time-frame the prototype model would have begun trials early in 1946. But Germany was now fighting a life-and-death struggle on all fronts and could not allow such a timescale; and that meant short cuts were to be taken; and those short cuts led to some serious design flaws and construction problems. However, given the urgency, it was decided to forego regular complete trials and equipment testing, although some basic testing was done.[47] It was as though he was waiving any attempt to learn lessons, and this was a mistake from which he could not hope to recover in the time remaining.

From December to March 1943–4, British naval intelligence became aware that the Germans were developing new U-boat types;[48] although their precise nature remained unclear until the spring of 1944 when the Type XXI U-boat was identified.[49] Captain Prichard, DASW, immediately called on existing Admiralty expertise to define the measures necessary to counter this new threat. Prichard soon concluded that such a U-boat, assessed to have an extreme diving depth, long endurance and high underwater-speed, would be able to make long submerged approaches to convoys from any direction. This would make all-round convoy protection necessary, would require extra escorts and improved U-boat detection equipment, none of which were currently available.[50] However, many of the lessons learned over the last five years had been noted and in this field few others had made more progress, if any.

In theory the XXI U-boat had several main operational advantages and may be briefly summarized:

1. Length 245 feet, displacement 1,600 tons;[51] much larger than the Type VII or IX.
2. *Schnorchel*, which in addition to partially solving the problem of running diesels made allied radar and ASDIC detection more difficult, but not impossible.
3. Increased maximum underwater-speed by 250 per cent to 16.5 knots, which permitted a fast attack and withdrawal, for a limited period.

4. Greater submerged endurance due to efficient and silent-running electric motors, reported to be up to 490 nautical miles (at 3 knots).

5. Thicker hull plating, supposedly to go down deeper to over 300 metres. In fact the diving figures were later downgraded.

6. New torpedoes (described in earlier chapters) now coming on stream and rapid reloading times.

7. New active/passive underwater detection with improved 'Nibelung' echo ranging system, enabling attacks to be made without coming to periscope depth.

Not all of these advances applied to the small Type XXIII coastal boat.[52]

Dönitz continued to assert to Hitler that the introduction of the new-type boats would soon be ready for a new offensive and that he expected 40 Type XXIs to be operating in the Atlantic by January/February 1945. At this time in October 1944 he must have known the impossibility of such a claim.[53] He was also sometimes economical with the truth. At a meeting held with Hitler on 12 February 1945, less than three months before the end of the war, Dönitz informed Hitler that in the next few months he could expect a dramatic increase in the number of U-boats for the front. 'At the moment 237 U-boats were being prepared for combat duties consisting of 111 old types, 84 Type XXI and 42 Type XXIII. Together with the current stock they would constitute 450 and represent the highest number of operational U-boats Germany had ever had.'[54] The outcome was quite predictable.

British planned countermeasures and trials

Although the new types of submersible came too late to have any impact on the war's course, their advanced design features were highly prized by the victors at the end of the war and formed the basis for much of post-war submarine development across the world.[55] At the time the Allies were not aware of the impending difficulties faced by the U-boat arm and therefore had to rush through a 'crash' programme of trials in the techniques of detection and countermeasures, in anticipation of the possibility that they were introduced. The sentiment at the time was such that the First Sea Lord was of the opinion that 'The high shipping losses which may occur during the first half of 1945 may well prejudice the maintenance of our forces in Europe.'[56] This threat could have delayed, but not changed, the outcome of the war. The Type XXI was thought to be far superior to any other operational submarine 'and was possessed of exceptional fighting qualities', being designed for long-range patrols in the Atlantic.[57]

Since the Admiralty had received Intelligence information about the characteristics of the Type XXI it realized that with the planned underwater-speed and endurance of the new 'submersibles' the current methods of detection of the time would be inadequate to deal with the menace to shipping.[58] Captain Prichard (DASW) set out to investigate possible solutions to the problem of detection and in a paper dated 14 April 1944 discussed the main findings and proposed work that needed to be done in order to counter the advanced features of this new design, except that an important lesson of the First World War had been overlooked. The most surprising development of that period, which would have assisted ASDIC and HE development, was the British Type 'R' class diesel/electric submarines ordered in December 1917 (Figure 12.1). Type 'R' was capable of under-water speeds of up to 15 knots and a surface speed of 9 knots;[59] not much different to the *Elektro* Type XXIII (Table 12.1). The R class was designed for A/S work, and became the forerunner of the modern hunter-killer submarine. They were delivered to the RN at a time when ASDIC was in its infancy.

After WW1 one of the 'R' class, R4, was transferred to Portland and used by the 6th submarine flotilla as a high underwater-speed target, with poor results but instead of persevering with the ASDIC tests the submarine was scrapped in

Figure 12.1 Type 'R' diesel/electric submarine 1918
Source: HMS R3[60] (painted on bow and conning tower).

Table 12.1 'R' class submarine basic specifications[61]

	R Class
Length overall	163 ft 9 in.
Beam maximum (ex fenders)	15 ft 3 in.
Depth maximum	15 ft 3 in.
Displacement surface tons	410
Displacement submerged tons	503
Reserve of buoyancy	23.5
Speed surface knots	9.5
Speed submerged knot	15
Torpedo tubes bow	Six 18 inch

1934, following a cost-cutting proposal in 1930.[62] It thus begs the question of why it was not used to further advance ASDIC capability to both track at high speed by ASDIC and/or HE, which were needed to counter a 'hunter killer' submarine. From 1918 onwards there was a clear need to address an acquisition system for the fast underwater-speed submarine, if only for improved HE detection. If the RN had thought of a 'Hunter-killer' in 1917 it does not require much imagination to assume that others would hit on the same idea, sooner or later. In 1937 the Germans did, followed in 1939 by the Japanese. Clearly an opportunity was lost in the 16 years from 1918–34, but it is nevertheless important to remember that the two most challenging tasks still facing the ASW team in 1944 – underwater-speed and manoeuvrability – had not been solved.

Equally, it is also worth noting that if Dönitz had been as much of an expert on U-boats, as is widely believed, he would have kept up-to-date on the world-wide submarine developments of Britain, the United States and Japan.[63] If he (or the *Kriegsmarine*) had investigated the Type 'R', say in *Jane's*, it would have immediately become apparent that this was the most advanced submarine of its time, and the forerunner of the types XXI and XXIII. A study made by his experts would have soon determined the utility of following the hull lines and the battery pattern of propulsion, which could have saved them a great deal of development time. It would appear that neither side had paid much attention to history.

In the year 1943 there was an urgent need for a new detection system for ATWs. Both the Hedgehog and Squid suffered from 'time of flight'. In the case of the most powerful mortar, the Squid, time of flight was 7.5 seconds, which when coupled to the 'dead time' of 13.5 seconds – not sinking time – accounted for around half a minute.[64] Tests have shown that if a U-boat was to maintain a speed of five or six knots, the probability of a 'hit' is much greater than if it were to escape at a rate greater than 12 knots.[65] In the latter case both systems would suffer from an appreciable time lag and render any attack close to meaningless. It should be remembered that the design of the current system was based on a slow-moving target, not a fast one. At a depth of 800 feet the typical U-boat had about 30 seconds to take evasive action. If there was no change in depth, or direction, the probability of a hit was good, as high as 60 per cent for some Squids,[66] unless it went even deeper.[67] But the Type XXI could reach 16 knots underwater, not the 12 knots achieved using the British converted submarine HMS *Seraph*. If the U-boat escaped and if contact could still be established it would mean a stern chase for the escort. A report on the Type XXI suggested that unless considerable use was made of HE the chances of gaining an ASDIC contact would be minimal.[68]

The fast underwater-speed boat also brought with it the perennial question of what to do about escorts. If the Germans had been able to deploy the XXI in numbers it was likely touch and go as to whether or not there were sufficient escorts that could achieve continuous speeds in excess of 15 knots, certainly not the 'Flower' class. In a heavy seaway the matters would have been worse, but not for the submerged U-boat.

It would also require very close co-operation of other escort vessels, if available. Type XXI was quiet, manoeuvrable, and every bit of experience in detection methods in the quite zone would be needed for acquisition. The creeping motors used in the XXI were a valuable addition to the propulsion set-up. Not only did they give the desirable effect of quiet operation during evasion tactics, but they also provided valuable surface and submerged propulsion while utilising the diesels for charging batteries. German design characteristics meant that they could be operated on 120 V which provided high propulsion efficiency over the entire speed range, with resultant reduced fuel consumption.[69]

Tactically too, the Admiralty needed to identify what was required in order to equip escorts with sufficient knowledge and equipment to counter the Type XXI if it ventured out into the open Atlantic and again operated in packs. How could escorts maintain contact with a U-boat that had a high underwater-speed and could readily escape, if detected? The problem was given to Captains Roberts at WATU, as well as the tactical table group at Dunoon.[70] The results were encouraging, but they by no means solved the problem. New methods involving the detection of HE, working in conjunction with sono-buoys dropped from aircraft would also need to be studied, and perfected.[71]

No one could state when this would be brought into balance but was likely to take up to five years.[72]

In the event, the new submersible suffered from too many technical deficiencies which they were unable to solve by the close of the war, and the matter of detection required no fixed solution, and was never put to the test.

Type XXI discovered faults

- The hull of the U-boat was prefabricated in 8 separate sections, but in 13 different yards with little in the way of tolerance checks. The first units had been badly rolled and exceeded tolerances. As a result rework became inevitable.
- Some boats arrived at the assembly yards incomplete causing further delays.
- The first boats were launched in an incomplete state and spent many months in dockyard hands, where they tried to rectify problems. Ripping out material already installed often fails to achieve the best results.
- Owing to the new methods of construction many boats were delayed from entering service because of repeated failures on hull pressure tests, diesels, electrics and batteries.[73]

Some of the design faults made the boats less seaworthy than the older, more reliable Type VIIC and IX, and this could account for the lack of success. There were also severe manpower and material shortages, serious shortcomings in design and production problems with the new Type XXI to contend with. Some problems had the potential to render the boat a hazard to the crew, and required significant alterations to structural design. There were also reports of other faults, such as external hydraulics that could render the boat un-manoeuvrable if damaged by depth charge and, as already reported, the diving depth was significantly less than the design specification. Also, the attempt by the Germans to provide a high-powered, small-sized, diesel engine which powered the XXI, and used interchangeable parts from the nine-cylinder MAN engine, proved a failure, which created a serious weakness in the vessel as finally delivered. 'The forced removal of the exhaust gas driven supercharger from the engine decreased the useful output of the engine by nearly half the original designed rating. Furthermore the engine on test, both with and without the supercharger, was limited in output below designed ratings by excessively high exhaust temperatures, which exceed those permitted in US submarine practice by 350° F, have created trouble in all exhaust valves as they are not suitably designed to take this temperature.[74]

The threat from U-boats continued right up to the final days of the war, not only from standard boats fitted with *Schnorchel*, but also from the new boats entering service of the Type XXI and Type XXIII *Elektro*-boats. Experience against *Schnorchel* fitted boats had already been established and thus far they had been well contained, and had not delivered the desired effect. *BdU's* conventional U-boats were still being sunk in numbers and in the first quarter of 1945 the number sunk by A/S forces amounted to 35.[75] However, it is the contrast in losses throughout the war that is striking and reflects both the expanding size of the U-boat arm and the growing expertise of Air/ASW (rapidly increasing ratio of successes of aircraft to warships), and the collapsing expertise of U-boat officers and crews (Table 12.2).

Table 12.2 Front-line U-boat losses (only)[76]

Year	No. of U-boats
1939	6
1940	13
1941	28
1942	69
1943	198
1944	148
1945	63
Total	525

Conclusions

Dönitz's decision to withdraw from operations in the North Atlantic, albeit temporarily, was intended to give him time to regroup and to contemplate the future of U-boat operations. The Admiral was, if nothing else, a very determined fighter and now that he had risen to the heights of *ObdM*, and had a good rapport with the *Führer*, he felt confident in his ability to reverse the misfortunes that had befallen his boats. Dönitz's construction plans for the introduction of the 'revolutionary' U-boats by the start of 1944 had been agreed but he needed to ensure that the enemy was kept well occupied until the renewed offensive could begin. To this end, he quickly arranged for many front-line boats to be brought up-to-date with the latest ideas on defending U-boats while running on the surface.

The Allies meanwhile became aware of Naval Cipher No. 3 being compromised, again, and set in motion the internal mechanisms to ensure that it was phased out as soon as possible, which was completed by the end of 1943. From then on the German *B-Dienst*, via the *xB-Dienst*, would no longer have access to the valuable convoy and ship movement details which had enabled U-boat Command to plan group tactics to the degree that had hitherto been possible.

In September 1943, U-boat Command considered that it was once more in a position to return to North Atlantic operations with their re-equipped boats. The return was marked with early success in attacking escorts, in preference to merchantmen, but once the gloss of early triumphs subsided, losses in U-boats were once again high. Even with partial help from the *Luftwaffe*, the U-boat operations became unsustainable and by the end of the year Dönitz was again compelled to give the order to withdraw. But this time he intended to withdraw completely, once current operations planned and those currently operational had been seen through to a conclusion. There were two compelling reasons to withdraw from the North Atlantic routes. The first was the attrition rate of crews and boats, which was too high to justify a continuation. The second reason was the loss of his re-supply boats, which had been sunk. Allied intercepts were so accurate in detail that they were able to target the U-tankers themselves. With no fuel to re-supply front line U-boats he could not continue with long-distance operations, whether in the North Atlantic or in other far-flung destinations, such as Freetown.

Given the powerful combination of available ASW techniques and total air cover it was now clearly the Allies in the ascendancy. But never one to quit, Dönitz made demands for further requirements in torpedo technology, the *LUT*, and decided on upgrading Type VIIs with a *Schnorchel* breathing tube to extend underwater endurance. In addition he embarked on a risky crash programme of new-type U-boat construction, ignoring the usual procedure of test and development. German engineers produced further torpedo types, and an air-breathing tube for U-boats to remain submerged when charging batteries, while they awaited their revolutionary designed U-boat the Types XXI and XXIII. However, his main error of judgement came in August 1943 when he cancelled all orders for the old-type boats, except those in progress. That meant that when things went wrong, and they did, he had nothing in reserve.

In the relative lull in the Battle of the Atlantic the British and their allies assimilated their own feedback for development purposes and concentrated on improved detection devices, such as the new ASDIC 'Q' device, designed to more accurately track U-boats that had gone 'deep', and radar that worked in the 3-cm band. The new ASDIC had the desired effect and permitted a more accurate placement for the ahead thrown mortars, such as Hedgehog and Squid. Firepower improvements against U-boat hulls were also introduced in the form of 'rocket' propelled small bombs for aircraft and surface vessels. Other, new devices, were being developed which, in time could assist the generic form of ASDIC, the MAD and sono-buoy detectors; it is notable that these too came out of the OR groups efforts, not pure science. While the developments in terms of technology were not as striking as the technology being developed by the Germans the allies were able to improve existing technology; and that improved the killing power of their existing weapons. However, Britain might have achieved technical superiority in ASDIC and HE had the 'R' class submarine been retained and electronics expertise sought in other branches of the RN, or industry.

The next chapter will conclude this book by summing up the efforts made by both sides in the Battle of the Atlantic.

Notes

1   NARA SRMN-037 COMINCH File 066. U-boat Intelligence Summaries, January 1943–May 1945.
2   David Syrett, *The Battle of the Atlantic and Naval Signals Intelligence* (Aldershot, 1998), 411.
3   NHB PG 30324 BdU KTB. The 'Sydney Star' route is also mentioned in an entry for 19 May 1943 under 'Enemy Messages', 18.
4   F. H. Hinsley et al., *British Intelligence in the Second World War* (1981), II, 553–5; David Kahn, *Seizing the Enigma* (New York, 2001), 263.
5   David Syrett, *The Battle of the Atlantic and Signals Intelligence* (Aldershot, 2002), 413.
6   Syrett, *The Battle of the Atlantic and Naval Signals Intelligence,* 413; Kahn, *Seizing the Enigma,* 263.
7   Hessler, *The U-boat War in the Atlantic 1939–45* (1989), III, 25–6.
8   NARA SRH-009, 'Battle of the Atlantic', OEG Report No. 66, 20 August 1951.
9   Cited in Cajus Bekker, *Hitler's Naval War (Verdammte See)* (1974), 314.

10   TNA ADM 234/578, Naval Staff History: '*The Defeat of the Enemy Attack on Shipping 1939–1945*' (Formerly BR 1736 (51) 1A), 97.

11   TNA ADM 234/68, U-boat War in the Atlantic, 3, June 1943 to May 1945, 54.

12   TNA ADM 223/170, OIC SI 745 of 20 October 1943; TNA ADM 234/68, U-boat War in the Atlantic, 3, June 1943–May 1945, 31. See also Chapter 5 for German training details, which appear similar to some of WATU's co-ordinated approach.

13   BA-MA RM 7/847, Besprechung mit Reichsmarschall Göring am 25 Februar 1943.

14   BA-MA RM 7/171, 'Atlantikplanung einer gewünschten Zusammenarbeit', 262–87; NHB PG 32175, 1/Skl KTB Teil C Heft IV, minutes of meeting between C-in-C Kriegsmarine and C-in-C *Luftwaffe*.

15   *Lagevorträge*, (München, 1972), 509.

16   TNA ADM 223/170, OIC SI 726 of 10 October 1943; GAF did not possess long- range aircraft and could only operate up to 800 km, at best.

17   NHB PG 33945, 1/Skl, 'Erstellung einer vortaktischen Ausbildungseinheit'; The proposal was to work closer with the *Luftwaffe* in evasion and attack tactics.

18   TNA HW 18/88, Memo from NS IV.A to Hinsley concerning group Rossbach, 15 October 1943; Hessler, *The U-boat War in the Atlantic 1939–45*, III, 30.

19   NHB PG 32175, 1/Skl KTB Teil C Heft IV, U-boat war, Memo from COS Naval Staff, 7 February 1944.

20   Ibid., Memo from ObdL Füst. IA 1043/44 gKdos, 7 February 1944.

21   TNA HW 18/193, POW Interrogation from U-664. Prisoner had attended 4 weeks U-boat training in Boulogne in the use of DF; TNA ADM 223/384, Ultra signal 1650 /10 August, 1943.

22   HW 18/193, Technical developments concerning U-boats, October 1943–March 1944; Axel Niestlé, *German U-boat Losses During World War II* (Annapolis, 1998), 147.

23   Niestlé, *German U-boat Losses During World War II*, 145.

24   Patrick Beesly, *Very Special Intelligence* (1977), 190.

25   Kahn, *Seizing the Enigma*, 274.

26   Hessler, *The U-boat War in the Atlantic 1939–45*, III, 41.

27   NHB PG 30348, BdU KTB entry for 6 June 1944; Stephen W. Roskill, *The War at Sea* (1960), III (I), 256.

28   Kahn, *Seizing the Enigma*, 274–5.

29   TNA AIR 41/23, The liberation of North West Europe; The administrative preparations, Volume 2.

30   CB 04052/42, November 1942 referring to ASDIC operations around the coasts, 40–1.

31 D. W. Waters, 'The Science of Admiralty', *The Naval Review*, 51 (4) 1963, 395–411, 400; David Syrett, 'The Battle for HG 75, 22–29 October 1941', *The Northern Mariner*, IX (1) (January 1999), 41–51, 49.

32 Arnold Hague, *The Allied Convoy System 1939–1945* (2000), 70.

33 David Syrett, 'Battle of the Atlantic', *American Neptune*, (45) 1 (Winter 1985), 46–64, 55).

34 TNA ADM 1/11741, Admiralty document 134/1942, 'Magnetic Anomaly Detector' (MAD), 1942.

35 John Herrick, 'Sub-surface Warfare', The History of Division 6. NDRC Department of Defense, Research and Development Board, Washington DC, January 1951.

36 TNA ADM 1/15194, Proposed detector buoy suggested by Professor Blackett, 18 May 1941; Willem Hackmann, *Seek and Strike* (1984), 288.

37 Eberhard Rößler, 'U-boat Development and Building', in *The Battle of the Atlantic 1939–1945* (1994), 118–37, 123.

38 Ibid., 132.

39 Marc Milner, *The Battle of the Atlantic* (Ontario, 2003), 171.

40 *Lagevorträge*, 510; 'Ich habe in Übereinstimmung mit Minister Speer das erste Programm für 30 U-Boote und das z.Zt. gemeldete Hilfsschiffsprogramm bereits im Autrag gegeben und ich bitte, anliegenden Führerbefehl zu vollziehen. Der Führer stimmt zu, ändert die Zahl von 30 U-Booten in dem Befehl auf 40 pro Monat und unterschreibt'.

41 Ibid., 509.

42 NHB PG 31747, Appendix to 1/Skl KTB, Dok. 3470/44 November 1943; Rößler, 'U-boat Development and Building', 132.

43 NHB PG 32066, 1/Skl KTB Teil A entry 8.6.1943. Of the 432 boats 239 were front-line, 23 were in acceptance trials, 109 were used for front-line training and 64 for school and research boats.

44 John C. Guse, 'Nazi Technical Thought Revisited', *History and Technology*, 26 (1) (2010), 3–33, 12.

45 NHB PG 33351, 1/Skl KTB Teil C, ,Iu. Allgemeines', U-boat orders and Cancellations, 13 August 1943, 13–14; HW 18/193, Memo, NID Assessment 21 February 1944.

46 NHB PG 31747, 1/Skl KTB Teil C, Appendix Dok. 3470/44 November 1944; TNA ADM 234/68, U-Boat War in the Atlantic, 3, June 1943–May 1945', Section 350, 7; Rößler, 'U-boat Development and Building', 135.

47 Niestlé, 'German Technical and Electronic Development', 434.

48 Hinsley et al., *British Intelligence in the Second World War*, III, 238, 242–5.

49 TNA ADM 186/ 809: CB 04051 (103), Interrogation of U-boat survivors describing training methods, 15.

50 TNA ADM 1/17557, WATU Annual report 1944 submitted by Commander-in-Chief WA, January 1945; M. Llewellyn-Jones, 'British Responses to the U-boat, Winter 1943 to Spring 1945 (University of London, King's College, London, 1997), 7–11.

51 TNA ADM 219/150, DOR/44/68, Type XXI U-boat, a provisional appreciation by E. J. Williams, 4 September 1944; Fritz Köhl, *Vom Original zum Modell* (Bonn, 2003), 10, 55.

52 Niestlé, 'German Technical and Electronic Development', 435.

53 NHB PG 32652, Vortragsprotokoll, Lagevorträge, 13 Oktober 1944.

54 *Lagevorträge*, Meeting with Hitler, 15 February 1945, 653.

55 Niestlé, 'German Technical and Electronic Development', 436.

56 NAC RG 24, Vol.11752, MS 369–2. 'A Forecast of the Results of the U-boat Campaign During 1945'; Roskill, *The War at Sea* (1961), III (II), 662; Corelli Barnett, *Engage the Enemy More Closely* (1991), 854.

57 TNA ADM 234/68, U-Boat War in the Atlantic, 3, June 1943–May 1945, 6.

58 TNA ADM 219/150, Type XXI U-boat, 'A Provisional Appreciation', E. J. Williams, DOR/44/68, 4 September 1944; TNA ADM 199/2061, 'The Type XXI U-boat – A Provisional Appreciation', in Monthly Anti-Submarine Report, 5, August 1944.

59 David K. Brown, 'Revolution Manqé: Technical Change in the Royal Navy at the End of the First World War', in *Warship 1993* (1993), 77–88, 85.

60 Admiralty photo of R3, by kind permission of the Royal Naval Submarine Museum, Gosport.

61 RNSUBMUS BR 3043: Chapter 10, Submarine Specifications.

62 RNSUBMUS, A1929/12/005. Memo from Rear-Admiral (S) dated 28 August 1930. Scrapping of submarines in accordance with the London Naval Treaty, which included a proposal for R4; Robert Hutchinson, *Jane's Submarines 1776 to present day* (2001), 98.

63 Mark Stille, *Imperial Japanese Navy Submarines 1941–45* (Oxford, 2005), 38.

64 TNA ADM 1/17591, ASWD Naval Staff Assessment, 3.

65 TNA ADM 1/17583, DMWD 20/61A Memo, Hedgehog and Squid possibilities, 15 May 1945.

66 TNA ADM 1/17591, ASWD Naval Staff Assessment, 30 June 1945, 2.

67 TNA ADM 1/13698, Memo from CO HMS *Nimrod*, 11 February 1944, folio 28.

68 TNA ADM 219/150, DOR/44/68, Type XXI U-boat, a provisional appreciation by E. J. Williams, 4 September 1944, 1.

69 Design Studies Report 2G-21, 'US Report on Type XXI Design characteristics', S40, Portsmouth Naval Shipyard, Portsmouth, N. H., July 1946, 3.

70 DASW Memo; Calling for problem to be devolved to other Commands, due to complexity of subject not yet resolved, 2 July 1945.

71 TNA ADM 219/160, Notes on trials with a fast submarine, 10–30 October, 1944.

72 TNA ADM 1/17591, ASWD Naval Staff Assessment, 3.

73 TNA ADM 234/68, U-Boat War in the Atlantic, 3, June 1943–May 1945, 84.

74 Design Studies Report 2G-21, 'US Report on Type XXI Design Characteristics', S40, Portsmouth Naval Shipyard, Portsmouth, N. H., July 1946, 5.

75 Milner, *The Battle of the Atlantic,* 226.

76 Calculated from Niestlé, *German U-boat Losses During World War II.*

13

Conclusion

Initially, both the *Kriegsmarine* and the RN were initially ill-equipped for the task of fighting a *guerre de course* with the assets they had, but for different reasons. In Germany, the problems of being ill-equipped for the Second World War are traceable back to the loss of the last one, and the restrictions imposed on them by the Versailles Treaty of 1919. Having lost the core of their navy they needed to rebuild it while at the same time paying attention to the clauses of the treaty, which included a total ban on U-boat construction. From 1933 under National Socialist leadership Germany began to move ahead with her rearmament programme. By 1935, the Versailles Treaty was effectively dead in the water and the rush to re-arm the Navy went ahead. Britain, on the other hand, had just come out of a massive depression and no longer had the capacity for a rapid fleet construction and while their naval armaments capacity suffered a rapid contraction from 1930–5 the world's political situation became much more volatile. For Britain, re-armament was a rushed affair with consequent shortcomings, not least of which was a shortage of suitable escort vessels with adequate range and refuelling opportunity. Air cover too was to remain problematic for some time to come. Not all would agree. Both Lambert and Rodger have argued that in 1939 the RN was 'fit for purpose' and that it had not ignored the lessons of the past.[1] In their view the potential threat came not from Germany, but from Italy and Japan, and put constraints upon Britain's rearmament policy priorities. However, this argument, valid though it is, should be viewed against the backdrop of an inevitable need for convoy with adequate escorts of greater range,[2] and air cover in time of war, regardless of the enemy. A/S preparations on the other hand were ongoing and in this field, the RN had practiced with exercises in the years between 1932 and 1939 to form a common doctrine, although there was still a lack of trained personnel to staff the ships that they had.

The *Kriegsmarine* had an inchoate culture and was a mixture of old Imperial values and the new dictates of National Socialism. While the Prussian Tirpitzian culture had been the dominant force up until the early 1930s the rise of Hitler began to have a marked effect on how *Wehrmacht* policy was influenced, which led to a variety of problems of how to deal with strategy, inter-service communications and exchange of ideas at the leadership level. Within the *Wehrmacht* Office of the War Ministry Hitler shaped the *OKW* to be his personal staff as supreme commander. This new arrangement was strangely inconsistent insofar as the newly created *OKW* was not made senior to the commanders of the three services but equal with them, producing countless rivalries with disastrous consequences in the war. However, it was wholly in accordance with Hitler's principle of creating competing authorities within the same department in order to counteract the influence of individuals, and lend greater weight to his personal decisions. Hitler had not learnt the lesson of the Kaiser period, and was even more dictatorial.

The *Heer, Kriegsmarine* and *Luftwaffe* failed to achieve any real coordination of strategy, acquisition programmes and inter-service co-operation. Interwar naval leaders had learned from the experiences of the 1914–18 War in that during the build up of assets their energy was directed towards acquiring a balanced fleet capable of engaging the old rival, Britain. However, successive service leaders in the inter-war period formulated strategy, just like Tirpitz, without considering national goals, interests, threats or strategies, detached from any grand strategic plan. One American historian described the planning as 'an atrophy of strategic thought.[3] This lack of inter-service planning resulted in the *Kriegsmarine* and the *Luftwaffe* utterly failing to coordinate their efforts in a common objective. By contrast, the British JCOS used the experience gained in the CID (Committee of Imperial Defence) of the last war and met regularly to plan and execute changes in strategy needed to meet the demands of war through the BAC and subsequent AUC Committees. There was no single service dominance in the British committee system and, as an island power, the armed forces had to work together. However, the demands of the RN were not always understood, which led to inter-service wrangling over resources.

When Hitler reneged on his promise of no war with Britain until 1944/45, and cancelled the Z plan, the head of the *Kriegsmarine*, Raeder, was left with a small but growing navy and no hope of building it up in the present circumstances, leaving the *Kriegsmarine* with a wrecked strategy and a dilemma. It had too few capital ships and just a small number of U-boats with which to fight Raeder's preferred commerce war, which initially saw the U-boat as a servant of the surface fleet rather than as the main instrument of war. Capital ships could not afford to sustain damage, which meant that they had to operate alone picking off individual merchantmen. If they operated in strength it was likely that the RN would pick up signal traffic and give battle, the very thing Raeder could ill-afford. The Battle of the Atlantic was therefore fought with U-boats, which although initially adequate, differed little to those of the last war, except for better diving characteristics. Nevertheless, they represented a tried and tested system and, it was presumed, they had little to fear from ASDIC (SONAR).[4] Dönitz therefore started out from a false premise, on both counts.

The Admiralty became pre-occupied with what was happening in the Far East and the Mediterranean, and less on the events unfolding in Germany. Therefore their plans did not include a satisfactory number of convoy escorts with adequate endurance, or refuelling capability required for long-range escort duties.[5] Although a war with Germany was not high on the agenda in the early 1930s, planners had given some thought to the provision, and type, of escort vessels needed for convoy operations in the event of a European war, and the RN had been conducting combined exercises and night-time submarine attacks since the early 1930s – to some effect. However, air power had changed the dynamic and would likely influence the point of U-boat attack, forcing them to operate further out into the Atlantic, even if they had not taken Norway and France, given that U-boat production started to increase from mid-1940. The further out they went the greater the escort endurance required. Therefore, the Admiralty appeared to have forgotten the recent historical reason why Britain was pulled back from the brink of defeat by the U-boat after finally instigating convoys. They also failed to study the available convoy experience as intensively as it did warship experience and yet statistics were available which recommended large convoys, but remained unexamined; a point also overlooked by the distinguished OR practitioner Patrick Blackett. For these, and other matters, planners could have consulted the five volumes of naval history of the Great War by Corbett and Newbolt, which were based on official documents published from 1920–31.[6] In particular Newbolt's Volume IV (last section) and Volume V cover the interesting phase of unrestricted U-boat warfare from 1917–18, the long endurance of U-boats and the early recognition that there were too few escorts available for use, even then; hunting groups too, were found to be ineffective.

In 1939, with U-boat production levels starting to increase, and attacks on convoys imminent, the RN had too few escort vessels, even given the small number of Atlantic U-boats available. Even so, the Admiralty had learnt some of the history of WW1 and had the foresight to build some prototypes of adequate endurance, in case of need. Aircraft protection provided for convoy duties was, however, woefully inadequate, being of the wrong type, lacking both endurance and weaponry for the task in hand. That was an Air Ministry failing, since they had originally determined what rôle Coastal Command should play in the event of hostilities, and had not learnt the lesson of history. The history of aircraft support in the 1914–18 war is well documented and demonstrates that once convoy was implemented in 1917 British aircraft played a significant rôle in keeping U-boats at bay from convoys.[7] In 1917 aircraft performance was not high, yet capable of penetrating the Atlantic – and did. Had British Air Ministry planners read their own history, and the Navy's historical account of air operations assessment of the previous war, it might have made a difference. The Navy praised area patrols in conjunction with convoy escorts describing them as complementary and effective at disrupting U-boat operations. It was also judged that the Germans were forced to change their attack tactics because of the air cover. The report also concludes that 'all evidence points to the sapping of the 'morale' of submarine crews by persistent bomb attacks' and stressed that 'compelling submarines to remain submerged is in itself of great value'.[8] Such evidence might have been a good guide of things to come but it would seem that this part of the history of the past war had been ignored, and an opportunity to establish the early priorities for close inter-service co-operation was missed. This situation only started to be rectified later in February 1941. 'The Second World War results of these oversights and outright blunders were completely predictable.'[9] It would suggest that both the Admiralty and the Air Ministry planners had not paid sufficient attention to their histories. In addition, due to the change in dynamic of aircraft with greater range in 1939, it might have occurred to planners that U-boats would be forced out and away from the Western Approaches, and that U-boats would have to make their main attacks on convoys before they reached the protection of air cover. While it is recognized that achieving balanced needs in ships and aircraft is usually subject to financial considerations, producing the wrong type only compounds the problem.

A counter argument has been that if the U-boats were forced out of the Western Approaches they would find it harder to find convoys and so their threat should have diminished. But in the early days of the war, the *Luftwaffe* co-operated with the *Kriegsmarine* and was the initial source that provided the U-boat arm with convoy information, until *B-Dienst* broke into Naval Cipher No. 3 later in February 1942. Convoy detection therefore became less of a problem.

However, their error committed was not to continue with the level co-operation established, which was to cost them dearly.

As war began to be considered likely, the Admiralty did respond to the changing situation with an organization change with the setting up of departments required for a probable scenario to deal with the U-boat menace. They demonstrated that two key inter-connected lessons had been learned from the experience gained in the First World War by creating two key sections, the OIC[10] and ASW sections both of which served them well – although ASW made slow progress in data analysis and OR to start with. ASW in the last war began late with the appointment of Read Admiral Duff in December 1916, and not in place until early 1917. Nevertheless, there was time to build up experience of dealing with U-boats but some of the knowledge acquired in the period fell into 'disuse' and several lessons were promptly forgotten, such as ineffective hunting groups and closer RAF collaboration.

In the first year of the war not a great deal happened mainly due to the U-boat arm having so few front-line boats to attack convoys, and further U-boat construction was slow in coming. Those that were available made little headway against convoys, with proportionally appreciable losses, but they did have more success against independents. Britain was thus given breathing space to help to revisit the question of the convoy system and to develop ASW tactics, almost unmolested. Then in May 1940 came the fall of France and the beginning of a period of ascendancy for the U-boat arm, particularly against unescorted merchant ships and stragglers, as shown in Chart 2.1. In the interwar years, the Germans had developed a strategy based on a lesson from history by Wolfgang Wegener. His monograph in 1929 entitled *Die Seestrategie des Weltkrieges* (The Naval Strategy of World War) outlined his ideas for defeating Britain's sea power, which included the conquest of some countries in order to acquire overseas bases. The fall of France enabled the *Kriegsmarine* to take over French bases and with these assets now under their control U-boats had easier access to their targets; and the *Luftwaffe* was now just across the Channel ready to attack the RN's Western Approaches ASW base at Plymouth. Through conquest they were able to benefit from Wegener's Atlantic strategy to outflank the British in the North and create a 'gate to the Atlantic', which would enable Germany to undertake a strategic offensive against the vital British trade routes. These new bases gave the U-boat arm an extra boost in that they were complete with repair and maintenance facilities and provided a much-needed local source of labour, which obviated the need for U-boats to make the long journey back to Germany. From this moment on until the end of 1942, the U-boat arm was able to become a greater menace to Allied convoys, equipped as they were with the technique of refuelling learnt in the last war. But while British shipping losses were bad enough in1942 (104 ships) they could have been worse had Dönitz not sometimes engaged in ill-defined strategic thinking. If he had successfully extended operation *Paukenschlag*, oil supplies might have tipped the balance of the war.

On a more positive note, Britain's response to the new U-boat threat was met with a move of WA from Plymouth to Liverpool and in the light of this new challenge, the Admiralty appointed an expert in gunnery tactics to investigate if there was a means of improving A/S tactics. The result was the setting up of one of the Admiralty's success stories of the war, the tactical table for use in ASW. It was a lesson in advanced tactics borrowed from the gunnery branch, well learnt, and used to instil a tactical doctrine used by all. However, the thorny question of air cover remained a problem to be solved. Initially there was obstruction within the Air Ministry to providing more resources for Coastal Command but what started out to be an almost intractable problem was solved through the building up of an excellent relationship between RAF Coastal Command and the Admiralty. It was one of the success stories of inter-service co-operation – without which the Battle of the Atlantic could not have been won. It is also worth noting that the arrangement was a first-class lesson in compromise. The lack of aircraft assets was also addressed and once the War Cabinet began to hold meetings in committee, with the Joint Chiefs of Staff and politicians, a closer understanding of the problems faced became known. However, it took some time to make an impact on the course of the war but by the end of 1942, much had been agreed to alleviate shortages of escorts and the much-needed air cover. By April 1943, much had been implemented, and the lessons finally learned. The same type of vehicle was not used by the Germans. Throughout the war, they relied on the *Lagevorträge*, which was a poor communications vehicle for ideas. Its weakness was that it deprived the Chiefs of Staff of the three services from having a discussion in open forum but with a leader such as Hitler, and his authoritarian style, it would appear that consensus stood little chance of succeeding. Hitler had misunderstood the utility of feedback and missed an excellent opportunity to engage expertise to enhance fighting units.

German and British training regimes have never before been compared and this book has provided a significant contribution to knowledge and understanding. Both sides were heavily engaged in it; German U-boat crews for working-up to front-line status and British escort crews in ASW. Such a comparison of regimes serves to explain the difficulties faced by each side and provides a new interpretation of how differing problems were addressed. At the start of the U-boat war training times were adhered to but as the fleet grew and the manpower losses began to mount training times were cut, sometimes severely. The main dilemma facing the U-boat arm was that when U-boats were sunk the crew was either lost completely, or just a few were saved – generally by the convoy escorts. That created two major problems. First, crew losses needed to be replaced, putting an extra strain on manpower resources and thus training times. Secondly, those that were captured were never to return before the end of the war and were subject to interrogation, which yielded valuable intelligence information to the Allies. Initially, British ASW training was developed on the hoof and slowly moved to more sophisticated tactical training over time, and extending facilities to *Mentor,* Stornoway, in December 1943, rather than curtailing training periods. However, when an escort or merchantman was sunk those surviving the cold waters of the Atlantic could often be hauled aboard a 'rescue' ship and be recycled, thereby helping to maintain training times relatively constant. The rescue ship was a lesson well learnt from the experience of convoy in the First World War, which largely deprived the Germans of their own valuable source of potential intelligence from British POWs (Prisoners of War).

British ASW expertise was shared with its Allies, in particular the Canadians, who set up their own training schemes via the ASSB (Allied Anti-submarine Survey Board), in March 1943.

Once U-boat production had risen in sufficient strength during 1941/2 Dönitz made a new departure from practice and instigated the concept of mobile support groups making it possible to reinforce existing 'packs', or detach U-boats in support of another particular group, or form a new group without having to wait until boats had returned to port. This move proved to be an effective tool to maintain a high degree of operational mobility and was one of the major contributors, along with good training, to U-boat effectiveness up until the end of 1942. Without realizing it the idea of support groups was a most important lesson learnt. WA had the same idea, based on their useful experience of the First World War. So successful was the deployment of escort mobile groups in early 1943, with a common doctrine, that they contributed significantly to the U-boat downfall in May1943. Fortunately the early abandonment of hunting groups at the start of the war, judged as a poor use of resources, was a belated lesson learnt.

Dönitz admitted to temporary defeat in May 1943 after realizing that U-boat losses and the dramatic fall in life expectancy of commanders and crew, was unsustainable. He had been *ObdM* since February and had become grossly overstretched in his duties at a time when the tide had turned and the conventional U-boat was no longer adequate for the task in hand. As *BdU* Dönitz proved to be a good tactician and participated in the evaluation of the patrol reports and debriefing sessions of returning boats gleaning a great amount of operational detail which was useful for OR purposes, but as *ObdM* he could no longer devote time to such matters. However, as a C-in-C that could lead from the front with new ideas on strategy he was found wanting. His new rôle, therefore, had a negative impact on the direction of the U-boat arm.

There was an attempt to address the lessons learned to-date by devising fresh tactics to combat the new Allied ascendancy over the conventional U-boat; and the date for the introduction of a an *Elektro*-boat capable of high underwater-speed was advanced. The first evidence of a change in tactics came in June 1943 when the 20th U-boat flotilla was created at Pillau specifically set up to develop a new doctrine to U-boat tactical training working-up with the *Luftwaffe*. Dönitz noticed that the British had significantly improved U-boat detection methods both above and below the surface, and had increased the endurance of their long-range aircraft. Therefore, there was an urgent need to engage minds to find suitable countermeasures and to work with the *Luftwaffe* on a combined approach to tactical training. The first evaluation seemed to be a step in the right direction but Dönitz knew that more *Luftwaffe* support was needed for operations. However, the combined tactical exercises did not extend to refresher courses for returning U-boat and *Luftwaffe* crews, as they did for British Escort and Coastal Command crews. The RN and Coastal Command had learnt a pivotal lesson in common doctrine, but the *ObdM* and *Luftwaffe* had not.

To be more successful Dönitz needed to level the playing field by using better U-boat tactics and weaponry, and to engage the enemy with aircraft support of their own. The matter was described to Hitler in detail, but there was only a limited amount that he could agree to. Dönitz had negotiated an arrangement with Göring in which he stressed the need for the earliest provision of long-range reconnaissance flights over the Atlantic to aid U-boat efforts. To an extent Göring did provide some support but that was restricted to just one *Geschwader*, which he deemed would be adequate for the purpose; but VLRs (Me-264- range 9,500 miles) were still not available and none were released before the end of the war. Despite his best efforts, Dönitz was unable to achieve meaningful co-operation and the two services remained as much apart as ever. But the antecedents of problems between the two services were traceable back to the First World War and Germany had not learnt the lesson of their Naval Aviation history 1914–18. The close co-operation, which developed between the RN and

Coastal Command, was never a feature that existed between the *Kriegsmarine* and *Luftwaffe* in the Second World War.

Historians have never before compared British and German OR and represent another significant contribution to knowledge. The reason for no work in this area is unclear but is likely due to their limited approach to a campaign requiring a far broader perspective. However, an OR comparison of both sides changes the interpretation of events. 'OR' is subject to history, largely based on previous experience, and can be the catalyst for improvements. The utility of OR in some areas of development was significant, to both sides. For the British the most notable event was the development of centimetric radar, and probably the single most determining factor for success in the Battle of the Atlantic. But it was not the only one. Second of OR importance was probably the outstanding work done by the ORS group while under the guidance of Patrick Blackett. His genius led to the use of statistics in a 'positivist' approach (not always liked by historians) with several lessons being learned in more effective bomb aiming sights, the effective adaptation of the air-launched depth charge and its tactical deployment. He encouraged the ORS staff to set out to determine precisely where the weaknesses of air attacks on U-boats lay, *a priori*. Using operational reports combined with feedback discussions with returning crews it was discovered that in most cases the U-boat was so close to the surface that the detonations of DCs could do no more than make life uncomfortable for the U-boat, not destroy it. Once adjustments had been made, and a new doctrine adopted, the kill ratio improved. The third most likely contributor to OR effectiveness was HF/DF. Used in conjunction with radar it was a powerful method of U-boat detection. Radar and HF/DF practically removed the cloak of the 'night attack', first learnt in the last war.

Blackett's use of OR extended to the analysis of Escort kill ratios. Operating just as support groups to convoy escorts they served to increase the total number of U-boat kills made by surface ships by up to 30 per cent. This one strategic move was a welcome development and a lesson well re-learnt from the last war. In conjunction with aircraft, they demonstrated a marked increase in overall effectiveness. While all of these improvements, with the exception of radar, only accounted for small percentages in increased efficiency, their cumulative effect was greater and represented a holistic approach to warfare. The lessons learned were shared with US Allies who, in March 1942, set up their own (roughly) equivalent 'OR' centre, ASWORG. From the British they had details of the sono-buoy and MAD, while later the United States supplied the British with OR details of aircraft attacks using CVEs.

Synergistic ideas based on the recent experience of history also helped the local OR process. For example, the British had a degree of success with the Shark and ATW (such as the Hedgehog and Squid) but ASDIC developments to accommodate them were slow in coming. In 1939 there was a failed attempt to adapt ASDIC recorders for use with ATW but this failing, too, might have been avoided with the early assistance of the Type 'R' submarine of 1918, which could have helped negate the main advantage of a high underwater-speed U-boat, but which was subsequently sold for scrap in 1934. Given the sentiments of one historian that navies which had studied the lessons of the past, the RN included, were those best equipped to face the future, this omission is a curious oversight. It might have helped ASDIC developments in general between the wars, and they still had to face potential trouble with Italian and Japanese submarines.

Contrary to accepted belief among some historians, German OR was practiced in a manner similar to the British through the use of operational reports and debriefings and open discussion. The *Kriegsmarine* was slow to adopt a more aggressive approach to OR and is probably due to too much compartmentalization of effort. It is not that they had only just discovered it for they had known of its utility as far back as the 1914–18 war. Early evidence of OR during the Second World War may be traced back to the interest in *Alberich* U-boat camouflage in 1938 directed at the development of a sound-absorbing coating intended to neutralize ASDIC, and still one of concern in 1943. Had it not failed, for the want of an adhesive, it could have greatly advanced 'Stealth' capability. Other OR work was started to investigate the torpedo failures of 1939/40 when concerns were raised about the failure of torpedoes to detonate, or keep their depths. But much more sophisticated OR/research was carried out after 1942 when an administrative organization for the control of naval research was established in September of that year. It was the concern of both Raeder and Dönitz that German developments were not meeting the needs of war, which prompted the decision to set up a body known as *FEP* for the control, and administration of all weapons development functions, whether scientific or practical. This was a reorganization of assets lesson belatedly learnt, from which a common approach to development evolved.

Perhaps their most successful development came in the torpedo field with advanced acoustic torpedoes such as the *Zaunkönig* and its variant *LUT*, designed for use against the escorts rather than the merchantman. Initially, in September/October 1943, the U-boat arm scored some success against escorts but WA was soon to introduce a countermeasure, an anti-dote, which practically nullified the *Zaunkönig*'s effectiveness. However, from the German perspective it was seen as a contributor to early success following a return to the North Atlantic theatre. But one weakness which persisted throughout the war was never comprehensively addressed, radar. The *Seetakt* began the war as an adequate 80-cm device for the surface fleet but it would appear that the whole question of radar development for use in both arms of the service was poorly handled. The reasons remain unclear but it is known that U-boat men thought that radar suffered from the danger of emitting radiation, onto which the enemy might home in on. Consequently, some 'German sailors usually left the radar switched off'.[11] No evidence could be found indicating where the drive of any individual, or common doctrine, was present which might have helped to resolve this critical problem; certainly no one person in the *NVA*, and definitely no person associated with the *WFM*, the advisory body specifically set up for this purpose.

Local OR played a significant rôle in the development of *Alberich* U-boat anechoic and *Schnorchel* camouflage as well as radar decoys and increased battery capacity to power the *Elektro* U-boat. The two most promising projects were *Alberich* and *Schnorchel* camouflage. Had both come to fruition, especially with the new Type XXI, it would have made it even more difficult for the British to detect the *Elektro*-boat equipped with new 'Stealth' technology, if at all. On the other hand, the British had had the opportunity to study high-speed submarines in conjunction with ASDIC and HE detection in the early 1920s and 1930s using the Type 'R' submarine and missed a rare opportunity to lead the field in both true submersibles and their detection methods. Therefore both sides lost, but for different reasons.

Not all technology development came as a direct result of OR but some needed a large input in order to come to fruition. In mid-1943, *BdU* Command set up two specialized U-boat 'OR' trials group, *Pascha* and *Sultan*, which were responsible for the development of a sophisticated ranging technique (*Nibelung*) and 'silent running', low HE, propellers, both destined for the new 'true' submersibles. Both owed their design to extensive OR studies under the guidance of *FEP*. Type XXI and XXIII represented the most outstanding German development for a high underwater-speed U-boat originally designed to be powered by an exotic high test peroxide fuel invented by Walter. However, had the *Kriegsmarine* kept themselves abreast of submarine developments during the interwar years outside of Germany their designers might have also benefitted from the features of the British Type 'R' of the First World War (mentioned earlier), but they too do not appear to have paid attention to history. The late introduction of Types XXI and XXIII *Elektro*-boat would not have made a difference to the outcome of the war but had they been successfully introduced, and deployed in numbers, Britain and its Allies would have had great difficulty in containing them, even without 'Stealth' technology. Although countermeasure trials on high underwater-speed U-boats had been instigated as soon as British Intelligence had detected their development no satisfactory method of detection could be found. Other *Kriegsmarine* potential winners may be found in the advanced ideas and OR developments in sub-sea rockets as anti-aircraft and anti-escort devices, but nullified through the lack of a guidance/acquisition system. Nevertheless, through the adopted doctrine of sharing ideas and technology important lessons had been learnt, just as the British had done in their OR programmes.

For some considerable time the Allies had suffered from a compromise in their own SigInt. But by the end of 1943, the Allies had plugged the leak in their security and had finally learnt an expensive lesson, while the *OKM* had not reconciled theirs and were never to admit to the vulnerability of the Enigma system. It is a curious state of affairs that it took the Allies so long to determine that a problem existed. The history of the First World War SigInt has been well documented. Indeed, at the outbreak of war when OIC was first set up several of the officers who helped to establish OIC were ex-intelligence officers from the last war. This is a case of parts of past history being forgotten, or ignored, from the experience gained during 1914–18 War. So effective was Room 40 that they were able to master most of the German decrypts of the time. The new Room 39 and GC&CS must have known how important SigInt security was. It is therefore doubly confusing how the possibility of the Naval Cipher 3 for ship movements was not regularly checked for compromise. Had they done so millions of tons of shipping might have been saved. By comparison, the *xB-Dienst* should have reached the same conclusion by the latest in October 1943 when virtually all U-tankers were lost. According to one U-boat man interviewed, *Oberfunkmaat* Seist, many commanders were aware that their whereabouts could not have come from radar or HF/DF.[12]

Approximately coinciding with the solution to the SigInt problem was the culmination of the Battle of the Atlantic but there is one example of the misuse of history worth mentioning. One historian posited that 'not until 1943 did the combination of escort carriers and radar-equipped long-range aircraft solve the problem of wolf packs and night surface attacks, which were foreseeable in 1918.'[13] While there would be general agreement with this premise the development of radar-equipped VLR, and VLRs themselves, would not have been ready until 1942/43. Furthermore, *Rudeltaktik* (Pack Tactics) was not practiced in the 1914–18 war, except at expected locations and attained little success, with too few boats and inadequate reconnaissance. This practice did not start in earnest until 1941. Therefore, the lesson of history could not have been applied before this date. Once extended joint exercises, comprising Escort Groups with Coastal Command, became a feature in 1943 much was achieved in a co-ordinated approach to U-boat warfare and results of anything new in these exercises were published in the monthly A/S reports CB 04050. Interestingly, Dönitz had implemented combined tactical training sessions with the *Luftwaffe* in June 1943 but by then the Allies had such air and sea superiority it would have already been too late to be effective, even with *Luftwaffe* support.

> Historians of the Second World War will no doubt refer to May 1943 as marking the turning point after which the German U-boat campaign began to collapse under the weight of the combined Allied effort.[14]

Summary

This book has described the organizations, training methods and OR techniques of both combatants. It has taken the radical approach of making comparisons of the systems and methods used and indicated where lessons of history have been learned, forgotten or misused.

In general, it may be said that the successful outcome of the Battle of the Atlantic was largely due to a combination of the ability of the British to implement a number of key lessons learned in the past, and to build on their experiences by adapting their ASW weapons and tactics to the changing environment. They were also instrumental in formalizing individual 'OR' organizations and sensibly shared the results of their findings inter-service, and with their allies. The most notable of OR projects produced superior radar and aircraft attacks on U-boats. A further British advantage was the organizational skill of pushing through remedies with flexibility, which was done more quickly and effectively than by their German opponents. In 1943 Convoy SC-130 marked the start of the end phase, demonstrating that with the powerful combination of continuous ASW training, radar, HF/DF, VLR air cover and mobile escort support groups, the conventional U-boat was attacked in a form of 'operational manoeuvre', or attrition, against which the Germans had no answer. Other accounts of SC-130 have not analyzed the significance of this form of attack, which changes the interpretation of this key battle, and those that followed.

For the Germans, losing the battle was a combination of being saddled with an impetuous autocrat at Armed Forces High Command, and planning disarray caused by inter-service rivalry. With such a command system, they had no ability to reach common objectives and service chiefs had no open forum for discussion in their *Lagevorträge*, in contrast to the British system of a cabinet status committee. They were further disadvantaged by the heads of the *Kriegsmarine* and *Luftwaffe*, who were more interested in their own power base, than reaching a consensus. A myopic strategy of attaching too much importance to one weapons' platform soon developed. Given a 'single' weapons platform strategy, *ObdM* was responsible for not keeping up with the changes required in U-boats and technology, even though it started out promisingly after the fall of France. OR produced many promising projects but most came too late to be of value, and the lesson of a common-based approach to OR should have been implemented much earlier than it was.

Notes

1 Andrew Lambert, 'Sea Power 1939–1940', in *Sea Power* (Ilford, 1994), 86–107, 91; Nicolas Rodger, 'The Royal Navy in the Era of the World Wars: Was it Fit for Purpose?', *The Mariner's Mirror*, 97 (1) (February 2011), 272–84, 281–2.

2 A point of emphasis in Rodger's 'Fit for Purpose' article, 282.

3 Herbert Rosinski, 'German Theories of Sea Warfare', *Brassey's Naval Annual* (1940), 40.

4 NHB PG 30248, FdL KTB, entry for 28 September 1939 concerning Hitler's visit to U-boat headquarters when Donitz told Hitler 'It is not true that England has the technical means which nullifies the U-boat danger; Joseph Maiolo, 'Deception and Intelligence Failure', *The Journal of Strategic Studies*, 22 (4) (December 1999), 55–76, 55. Maiolo's PG reference is incorrect, but the reel number is correct.

5 Rodger, 'The Royal Navy in the Era of the World Wars', 282–3.

6 Sir Julian Corbett and Sir Henry Newbolt, *History of the Great War Based on Official Documents: Naval Operations* 5 Volumes (1920–31).

7 TNA AIR 1/306/15/226/166, Director of Statistics. 'Charts Showing Positions of Merchant Vessels Attacked by Submarines by Day and Night', 17 April 1918.

8 NHB 'The Technical History and Index, Part 4: Aircraft vs. Submarine, Submarine Campaign 1918', Technical History Section (March 1919), 12–19.

9 David Macgregor, 'The Use, Misuse, and Non-use of History', *The Journal of Military History*, 56 (4) (October 1992), 603–16, 606.

10 Rodger, 'The Royal Navy in the Era of the World Wars', 283.

11 Alfred Price, *Aircraft versus Submarine* (Barnsley, 2004), 182.

12 The author attended a U-boat AGM in Altenbruch March 2008 and discussed
matters of interest with various crew members, including *Oberfunkmaat* Seist and
Fähnrich König (U-91).

13 Macgregor, 'The Use, Misuse, and Non-use of History', 606.

14 TNA ADM 234/68, U-Boat War in the Atlantic, 3, June 1943–May 1945, 1; Günter
Hessler, *The U-boat War in the Atlantic 1939–1945* (1989), III, 1.

Organization Chart: *Kriegsmarine* 1938

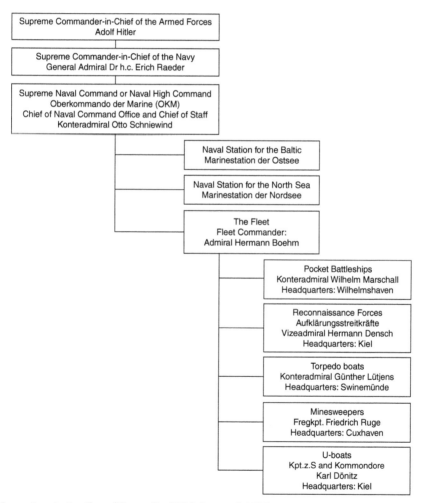

Source: Organization Chart of German Naval High Command, 1938.[1]

The command structure shows *OKW* at the head of the organization and Admiral Raeder with his COS Rear Admiral Schniewind as second in command. In the early months of the war, Dönitz was subordinated was to the Fleet Commander Boehm. On 21 September 1939, matters changed. Dönitz himself was promoted to the Flag Rank of Rear Admiral. He also became *BdU* and this obviated the need for him report to the Fleet Commander Admiral Boehm.

Note

1   TNA ADM 1/9580, Redrawn by author from notes taken from file.

Appendix 2

Organization Chart: Naval War Staff

Within the above structure are three divisions of the Naval War Staff that need clarification, in order to understand their relevance to the U-boat arm. Second only in importance to the Operations Division (item 1) of the *Kriegsmarine* was 2/*Skl*, the Signals Intelligence branch, SigInt. 2/*Skl* was the original section responsible for intelligence communications, *MND* but on 1 January 1940, the original Signals Division 2/*Skl* was reconstituted and split in two. From within its ranks personnel were siphoned off to create a new section of 2/*Skl* and they became responsible for the collection of foreign naval intelligence and political information, and had

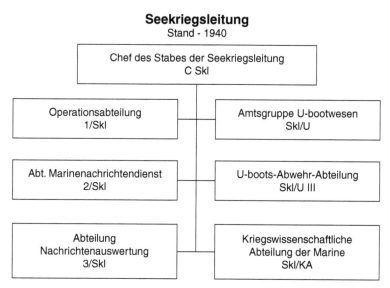

Source: Reconstructed chart.[1]

the discriminant 3/*SKL* (item 2).[2] Within 2/*Skl* was the department *MND* and its III Department, SigInt. The *B-Dienst* (*Beobachtungsdienst*, or surveillance service) and the *xB-Dienst* (decryption service) were able to decypher much of the encrypted Allied radio communications for a long period of the war, to the great benefit of the U-boat arm. *Skl/KA* (*Kriegswissenschaftlicheabteilung*), included the *Skl/MKrGesch*, the 'Military Science' (*Kr*) division[3] that was involved in connection with 'operational research' as well as helping to form the basis of feedback to other divisions. The Military Science Division exchanged important feedback with the naval institutes engaged in weapons development.

Notes

1   Walter Lohmann et al., *Die deutsche Kriegsmarine* (Bad Nauheim, 1964), 1 (32), 9.
2   Ibid., 2.
3   Ibid., 4; V.Adm. Kurt Assman (April 1933–June 1943) and then Adm. Karl-Georg Schuster, July 1943–end.

Appendix 3

Lagezimmer Operations and Staff Support Functions

All successful commands need a leader and good support staff. Under Dönitz was a Chief of Staff, Lt Commander (later Rear Admiral) Eberhard Godt who remained in close touch with the operational flotillas, and overall was in executive charge of the U-boat arm as follows:

First Staff Officer-Operations – A1

Within operations were two assistants, dealing with U-boat deployments and availability, liaison with external headquarters tactics and International Law. All U-boats were subordinated to the operational division at Kernével; but local control at various bases was exercised by the local *FdU* for operational or front line boats. Once dispersed to front-line duties they came under *BdU* operational control. Commander Günter Hessler, Dönitz's son-in-law, was the Admiral's first Staff Officer from November 1941 until the end of the war.[1] During his tenure, he also tried to maximize *Luftwaffe* support.[2]

Second Staff Officer-Organization – A2

Dealt with navigation, arrivals and departures; return routes and anti-submarine operations; minesweeping and harbour defence.

Third Staff Officer-Intelligence – A3

Intelligence, with 1 assistant. Responsible for enemy situation reports, evaluation of U-boat War Diaries, and combat experience. This officer shared information with A5 for statistics and OR (operational research) purposes.[3]

Fourth Staff Officer-Communications – A4

Communications and crypto procedures, evasive and protective measures and enemy location methods.

Fifth Staff Officer-Statistics – A5

Records of sinking's and losses, honours and awards.

Unit Engineer   M1.

Ajutant-Discipline   Z.

   Administrative Office-Administration

   All from *Oberleutnant zur See* to *Fregattenkapitän* rank.[4]

   It is not known how many ratings were on the operational support staff from 1941–4 but from a photograph taken of the operations group in the Berlin HQ 'Koralle' in June 1944 the total number of staff shown was about 150.[5]

Notes

1 Hessler was the author of the official U-boat war account written for the Admiralty immediately after the war, 'The U-boat War in the Atlantic 1939–1945'.

2 TNA HW 18/55, German Naval Organization–Naval Section ZIP/NS dated 26/12/1944, 2.

3 Ibid., 3.

4 GC&CS, 'The German Navy – Organization: The U-boat Arm', 7, 13; Walter Lohmann et al., *Die deutsche Kriegsmarine* 2 (72), 1–2, and are correct in respect of the organization chart for 1 October 1941. COS – Kapt. z. S. Godt (later K. Admiral), A1. K. Kapt. Oehrn, A2. Kapt. Lt. v Eichain, A3. Kapt. Lt. Kuppisch, A4. K. Kapt. Meckel.

5 Michael Salewski, *Die deutsche Seekriegsleitung 1942–1945,* II (München, 1975), no page listed with photo.

Bibliography

Unpublished primary sources

The National Archives: Public Record Office = TNA: PRO

ADM 1: Admiralty and Ministry of Defence correspondence and papers 1660–1976

9580: German Organization Charts 1938.
9729: PD 06476/37, 1937.
9942: Anti-submarine Exercises 1939.
9963: Anti-U-Boat Warfare.
10092: Strategy and Tactics (82)1938–9.
10226: NID 004/l1939, OIC.
10463: ADMIRALTY (5): Redistribution of Responsibilities.
11741: Admiralty Document (MAD) 1942.
12140: Anti-submarine Policy, TD.
12141: Armaments (11)1939.
13698: CAFO, 3 June 1943.
15194: Proposed Detector Buoy.
17555: WATU Annual Report 1944.
17557: Annual Report by Captain Gilbert Roberts.
17561: Report on Interrogation of German Naval Officers.
17583: DMWD 20/61, Hedgehog and Squid Possibilities, May 1945.
17591: Naval Staff Assessment, 30 June 1945.
17641: Containing the U-boat.
17667: Walter to ObdM, 19 May 1943.

ADM 116: Admiralty: Record Office: Cases 1852–1965

2410: Portland 1924–8.
3128: NCS Policy and Procedures 1926.
3603: HMS Osprey and flotillas.
3603: D of TD December 1931.
3872: Exercise 1934.
3956: 3962: 4057: Room 40.
4520: WAGO.
4585: SRE 2140/42, Research 1942.

ADM 173: Admiralty and Ministry of Defence, Navy Department: Submarine Logs 1914–1982

18701: Submarine Logs, 1944.

ADM 178: Admiralty: Naval Courts Martial Cases, Boards of Inquiry Reports and Other Papers (Supplementary Series) 1892–1951

137: NID Report.

ADM 182: Records of the Navy Board and the Board of Admiralty

128: CAFO 1163/1943.

ADM 186: Admiralty: Publications 1827–1970

140: Depth Charge Patterns.
153: Exercises 1933.
159: Exercises 1938.
389: German Hydrophones WW1.
396: German Hydrophones 1917.
461: Progress in 1928.
500: Progress 1932.
519: 527: 536: 547: Reports for 1935–8.
551: Progress 1938.
799: Naval Staff History, 1939–April 1940.
809: Interrogation of U-boat survivors.

ADM 189: Admiralty: Torpedo Instructions School, later Torpedo and Anti-submarine School: Reports 1881–1958

175: Depth Charge Throwers and Squid.

ADM 199: Admiralty: War History Cases and Papers, Second World War 1922–1968

124: A/S 1938.
124: WA to Admiralty 23 September 1939.
356: ONS, ON and HX: Reports 1942–3.
575: Gretton's Account of SC-130.
580: SC Convoys: Reports 1943.
807: WA to Admiralty 12 September 1939.
1101: Operations.
1336: HF/DF Ships in Convoys.

1336: SC and HX Convoys: Reports 1943–4.

1732: WA to Admiralty and Western Isles, 1944.

2011: ASW Analysis 1942.

2020: Analysis of SC-130.

2022: Analysis of U-boat Operations 1943.

2057: Monthly Reports 1939–40.

2059: Yearly Review Report 1942.

2060: Monthly Reports January–December 1943.

2061: Monthly Anti-submarine Reports (5) 1944.

ADM 205: Admiralty: Office of the First Sea Lord, later First Sea Lord and Chief of the Naval Staff: Correspondence and Papers 1937–1968

1: First Sea Lord's Records.

7: File No.7. Correspondence 1940.

7: NID 0747/35.

13: Churchill Memo 14 November 1941.

21: Reports to First Sea Lord.

56: AOC to CNS 17 November 1941.

ADM 213: Admiralty Centre for Scientific Information and Liaison: Reports 1926–1956

341: Use of ASDIC.

611: Research in Germany.

ADM 219: Directorate of Operational Research and predecessors: Reports 1917–1980

16: Scientists Section 1.

52: Homing Torpedo, 1943.

150: Type XXI U-boat, 4 September 1944.

160: Trials with a Fast Under-water Submarine, October 1944.

209: NOR Research 14 September 1945.

334: Analysis of Hunts.

630: OR History.

ADM 220: Admiralty Surface Weapons Establishment and predecessors: Records 1918–1983

1486: HF/DF in HM Ships.

ADM 223: Naval Intelligence Division and Operational Intelligence Centre: Intelligence Reports and Papers 1914–1978

15: U-boat Situations 1943.
17: U-boat Trends, 1943.
88: OIC.
92–101: OIC Summaries 1941–3.
107: Naval Intelligence 01730/15, March 1943.
170–5: OIC Summaries from 1943–4.
184: Ultra signal 1221/25 September 1943.
205: Report, British codes and cyphers:
284: OIC notes of R. T. Barrett.
384: Ultra Signal 1650 /10 August 1943.
690: Essay by Vice Admiral Heye, 1945.
694: Essay by Kapitän zur See Kupfer, 1945.
696: Essays by General Admiral Schniewind and Admiral Schuster, 1945.

ADM 229: Department of the Director of Naval Construction: Directors' Papers 1893–1957

20: DNC's Reports.

ADM 233: Naval Intelligence Division and Government Code and Cypher School: Wireless News 1918–1921

84: U-boat Appreciations of February 1941.

ADM 234: Reference Books (BR Series) 1856–1984

67: U-boat War January 1942–May 1943.
68: U-Boat War Atlantic June 1943–May 1945.
578: Naval Staff History: (1A).
579: Naval Staff History: (1B).

ADM 237: Naval Staff: Operations Division: Convoy Records, Second World War 1940–1945

203: Convoy Records: SC-130.

ADM 239: Confidential Reference Books (CB Series) 1910–1985

141: Progress in Torpedo, Mining and Anti-submarine Warfare 1939.
144: Progress in Tactics 1948.
246: ASW/1.
248: ASW Volume IV, 1939–45.
258: HMS Graph, ex U-boat U-570.

298: Anti-U-boat Operations .
630: ACNS/CAOR 1943–4.

AIR 15: Air Ministry and Admiralty: Registered Files 1930–1974
3: War plans, 1938.
34: Trade Protection, 1939.
66: Coastal Command, 1937–9.
279: ASW Operations, 1942–3.
284: B of A, paras 1–2.

AIR 27: Air Ministry Operations Record Books, Squadrons 1911–1980
911: Operations 1941–3.
1105: 172 Squadron Records 1942–3.
1106: 172 Squadron Records 1944–5.

AIR 41: Air Ministry and Ministry of Defence: Air Historical Branch: Narratives and Monographs 1942–1991
23: Liberation Preparations, 2.
24: Liberation Preparations, 3.
45: Atlantic and Home Waters – 1918–39, 1.
47: RAF in Maritime War – III, 1941–3.
48: RAF in Maritime War – IV, 1943–4.
73: RAF in Maritime War – IV, 1939–June 1941.

AIR 65: Coastal Command Development Unit, later Air Sea Warfare Development Unit: Reports 1942–1970
268: Passive Radio Sono-buoy, March 1950.

AVIA 10: Air Ministry and Ministry of Aircraft Production: Miscellaneous Unregistered Papers
338: Radio Production.
342: War Cabinet Radio Board, August 1943.

AVIA 15: Ministry of Aircraft Production and predecessor and successors: Registered Files 1924–1967
1319: R&D General (Code 45): 1941–3.

AVIA 39: Central Radio Bureau of German Electronic Intelligence
4: 'German Academic Scientists and the War', by Major I. W. B. Gill.

CAB: Records of the Cabinet Office 1863–2009

4/26: The Protection of Sea-borne Trade, May 1937.
23/70: Ten-year rule.
23/95: Assessing German Threat, 14 September 1938.
24/259: CID, Sub-committee Report.
24/268: Chatfield, 1937.
53/6: COS 192 and 194 Meetings 1937.
66/2: DCNS October 1939.
66/27/32: Radar and Communications 1942.
66/32/38: Naval Situation, 147.
66/32/46: Operational Boats Thought to be 90.
66/37/24: Naval, Military and Air Situation 1943.
66/49/39: Need for Scientific Training.
69/4: Defence Committee Papers.
86/1–7: War Cabinet Committees, January 1943.
86/2: Anti U-boat Warfare, 1943.
86/3: Training for U-boat Detection Activity.
86/4: A.U. (43) 103, Memorandum, 30 March 1943.
102/641: History of Radio and Radar.

DEFE 3: Admiralty: Operational Intelligence Centre: Intelligence from Intercepts WWII 1941–1945

718: Intelligence from German intercepts May 1943.

FO 371: Foreign Office: Political Departments: General Correspondence from 1906–1966

21692: Naval Attaché, Berlin, 10 January 1938.

GC&CS: ZTPG Intercepts

ZTPG/329765, 3341824.

HS 8: Ministry of Economic Warfare, Special Operations Executive and Successors

767: CB 04051 (103), Interrogation of U-boat Survivors.

HW 8: Government Code and Cypher School: Working Aids and Correspondence 1914–1946

21: Organization of German Intel to OIC.
113: November 1942; German Navy's Use of Special Intelligence.

HW 11: Government Code and Cypher School: World War II Official Histories 1938–1945

20: The German Navy – U-boat Arm Volume 7.

HW 18: Government Code and Cypher School: Reports of German Navy decrypts 1938–1945

55: German Naval Organization 1944–5.
88: Memo from NS IV.A to Hinsley, 15 October 1943
193: Technical Developments Concerning U-boats, October 1943–March 1944.
200: Information on German U-boats.

PREM 3: Prime Minister's Office: Operational Correspondence and Papers 1937–1946

3/331/8: CNS to Churchill.
414/3: Analysis of the Value of Escort Vessels and Aircraft.

WO 208: War Office: Directorate of Military Operations and Intelligence

3164: German Research and Development.
4566: Undersea Warfare, 8 May to 31 August 1945.

WO 291: Ministry of Supply and War Office: Military Operational Research Unit, Reports and Papers 1941–1982

1911: Research into Size of Convoy, Appendix B.

The National Archives of Canada = NAC

RG 24: Vol. 6796, 8375–4: Memo from Admiralty to CNS Canada.
RG 24: Vol. 11752, MS 369–2. U-boat Campaign.

Royal Naval Submarine Museum

RNSUBMUS: A1929/12/005. Rear-Admiral (S) dated 28 August 1930.
RNSUBMUS: BR 3043: Chapter 10, Submarine Specifications.

RSBP: Royal Society Blackett Papers

RS-Operational Research (OR) CSAC 63.1.79/D.83-D125, 1940–74.
RS-Operational Research (OR) CSAC 63.1.79/D.135, 1942.

Naval historical branch

NHB: CB: Old References: Confidential Reference Books (CB Series)

CB 04050: Warfare Reports Series 1939–45.

Official papers and monographs (by date)

'DASW Memo', 2 July 1945.
'The German Navy – Organization', XIV Volumes December 1945, GC&CS.
'The German Navy War Effort', NID 24/T65/45.
'The German Navy – Organization', NID 24/T13/45, Taken from FEPII List 3, December 1943– February 1944.
'An Assessment of Admiral Godt', NID 1/17, paras 25 and 45.

Naval Historical Center, Washington DC = NARA

PG 32975: roll 3986, 54. February 1939–October 1941.
PG 74896–74944: rolls 3349–50. 07.03.41. Luftwaffe KTBs.
PG 74948–975: rolls 3350–3, Kriegstagebuch des Generals der Luftwaffe 1939– 41.
RG 24: NSS 1271–20 Minutes of the 53rd Meeting January 1944.
SRH-009: OEG Report No. 66, 'Battle of the Atlantic: Analysis.
SRMN-037: COMINCH File 066, U-boat Intelligence Summaries, January 1943–May 1945.
'The Influence of Service on U-boats on the Auditory Organ', Study D II, in Schaefer, ed. *Monograph on Submarine Medicine*, on the *Dräger* apparatus, Dr Jürgen Tonndorf, National Library of Bethesda Md.
'The Naval Aspects of the War', in *Essays by German Officers and Officials on World War II*, roll 3, by Helmuth Heye.

German naval and government publications

Bundesarchiv – Militärarchiv, Freiburg = BA–MA

A/MA: Msg 2/5200 Raketenschießversuche 1944.
OKM GE 958: Konferenz des General der Luftwaffe beim Oberbefehlshaber.
RH 53–7: Chef HL PA gKdos Nr. 664/34, v. 17.3.1934, SS. 88ff.
RL 2 II/161: Ausbildungsforderungen an Ausbildungsfliegerführer Ostsee.
RL 7/29: General z.b.V. Lfl. Kdo 2, Chef des Stabes B.Nr. 100/39 gKdos 12.8.1939.
RM 3/22941: Reichsmarineamt, Schleppversuchsergebnisse 'Hollandtyp' mit einem Schiffsmodell aus Paraffin.
RM 5/2059: Artillerie Schießversuche und Ergebnisse September 1911–Juni 1914.
RM 6/53: 'Grundsätzliche Gedanken', Vortrag Raeders 13 Februar 1937.
RM 7/171: 'Atlantikplanung einer gewünschten Zusammenarbeit'.

RM 7/260: 'Ständiger Vertreter des Oberbefehlshabers der Kriegsmarine beim Führer'.

RM 7/846: 1/Skl KTB Teil C Heft IV, Niederschriften Raeder an Hitler.

RM 7/1239: Raketenschießversuche auf deutschen U-Booten 1944.

RM 7/1240: Entwicklungen: Bericht des Wissenschaftlichen-Führungsstabes der Kriegsmarine: Tätigkeitsbericht der Amtsgruppe FEP; 1.5.44–17.11.44.

RM 7/2079: Reichsminister der Luftfahrt: Genst. 1 Abt. Nr. 144/38 g.K. (M), 20.5.1938.

RM 7/2432: Schreiben von der Kriegswissenschaftlicheabteilug an 1/Skl, 24 Mai 1940.

RM 7/2869: BdU, Denkschrift No. 3642-Al an OKM/Sk1, 3 September 1942.

RM 8/1587: Organisation anderer Abteilungen, Marine und Armeebehörden, SS, 62–4.

RM 24/253: Forschungsaufgaben der Kriegsmarine, Zusammenstellung, Oktober 1944.

RM 24/188: OKM/MWa Id Haushaltsplan der Gesellschaft (GEMA).

RM 45 IV/787: Operationen und Taktik; der Überfall auf St Nazaire, 27–28 März 1942.

RM 48/28: Unterrichtung des Amtschef A am 2.7.1938.

RM 87/13: Torpedo Versager.

W04–13677: 'Versuchsaufgaben für Kriegsschiffe ab 1936–37'.

Unpublished German papers

'Raeder an Hitler' 4 Januar 1943, zit. bei G. Sandhofer, 'Dokumente zum militärischen Werdegang des Großadmiral Dönitz', in MGM 2/1973.

WF-04/36387 OKM, 1/Skl 3490/41 gKdos v. 27.2.1941, MAP (Militärarchiv Potsdam, jetzt Freiburg). Wilde, Kapitän Herbert, 'Die Unterseebootabwehrschule 1933–1945', Einschätzung der UAS (1963/4).

Monographs

Lagevorträge des Oberbefehlshabers der Kriegsmarine vor Hitler 1939–1945 (München, 1972).

Nauticus: Jahrbuch für Deutschlands Seeinteressen (Berlin 1938).

Rangliste der deutschen Kriegsmarine nach dem Stande vom 1 November 1937– 1 November 1938 (M.Div.Nr.293) (Berlin, 1937–8).

Seekriegsleitung, 1/Skl KTB Teil A, 68 vols 1939–45, 58 (Bonn, 1989).

Captured German naval documents

NHB Microfiches = PG series

PG 10058: Großadmiral Dönitz statement on personnel.

PG 10402: Dönitz's progress and promotion.

PG 14139: FEP – from September 1942.

PG 15500: Documents of von Friedeburg, 355–7.

PG 15508: Paper 17, UAS school.

PG 18548: 'St Nazaire', 27–28 March 1942 from the Kriegswissenschaftlicheabteilung.

PG 20537: Großadmiral Dönitz statement on personnel.

PG 24098: Officer selection criteria.

PG 24908: Re-structure of the U-boat organization.

PG 29399: Various training programmes.

PG 30130: KTB Log of the Type IXC, U-130, Routeing Sheet.

PG 30247: KTB des FdU, 28 September 1939.

PG 30248: FdL KTB, 28 September 1939.

PG 30250: KTB entry for 23 October 1939.

PG 30252: BdU KTB entry for 29 November 1939.

PG 30256: BdU KTB entry for 21 January 1940.

PG 30259: BdU KTB entry for 2 March 1940, 'Weserübung'.

PG 30274: BdU KTB entry for 1 October 1940, U-boats.

PG 30275: BdU KTB entry, Conclusions, 20 October 1940.

PG 30284: BdU KTB entry, 6 March 1941. Investigations.

PG 30301: BdU KTB entries, December 1941.

PG 30309B: BdU KTB entry, 25 July 1942.

PG 30310: BdU KTB entries for August 1942.

PG 30311: BdU KTB entries for 1–15 September 1942.

PG 30313: BdU KTB entry, 7 November 1942.

PG 30314: BdU KTB entries for December 1942

PG 30315: BdU KTB entry for 15 January 1943.

PG 30323: BdU KTB entry dated 10 May 1943, 'OR analyses'.

PG 30324: BdU KTB entries 16–31 May 1943.

PG 30324: Signal to all boats in 'Donau' 0836 on 19.5.1943, file copy 545.

PG 30325: BdU KTB entry, 'U-boats as of 1 June 1943'.

PG 30327: 2/Skl /BdU Op. KTB entry for 7 July 1943.

PG 30334: General observations.

PG 30335: BdU KTB entry for 28 November 1943, convoy MKS 31.

PG 30341: BdU KTB entries for February 1944.

PG 30348: BdU KTB entry, 6 June 1944. Gruppe 'Landwirt'.

PG 30352: BdU KTB entry for August 1944.

PG 30355: BdU KTB entry for September 1944.

PG 30902: FdU KTB entry dated 2 October 1939.

PG 31013: Notes on U-boat organization.

PG 31020: Authorities created to deal with various aspects of training and work-up.

PG 31044: Personalakte Dönitz.

PG 31747: Dok. 3470/44, Appendix to 1/Skl KTB, November 1944.

PG 31747: 2445/43, Appendix to 1/Skl KTB – gKdos M-Wehr.

PG 31752: 1/Skl KTB Teil C: 'Anwendung der neuen Elektroboote'.

PG 32011: 1/Skl KTB Teil C Heft IV, 'Ein Jahr U-Bootkriegsfuhrung', 24 August 1940.

PG 32021: KTB Seekriegsleitung 1 Abteilung, Nur durch Offizier, Dönitz's change in title from FdU to BdU and rank of Commodore, 19 September 1939.

PG 32029: 1/Skl KTB Teil A, entries May 1940.

PG 32066: 1/Skl KTB Teil A entry 8.6.1943.

PG 32069: 1/Skl KTB Teil A, entries September 1943.

PG 32065: 1/Skl KTB Teil A, entry for 8.6.1943.

PG 32107: Includes U-47's Torpedoschußmeldung.

PG 32119: 1/Skl KTB Teil B Heft V, Januar –Juni 1943.

PG 32125: 1/Skl KTB Teil C Heft IV, Aircraft used between November and December 1943.

PG 32158: 1/Skl KTB Teil C, entries for February 1943.

PG 32173: 1/Skl KTB Teil C Heft IV, Deployment of U-boats.

PG 32174: 1/Skl KTB Teil C Heft IV, 'Rohstoffmangels und Arbeiterlage auf die Führung des U-bootkrieges', gez. Dönitz, 9 September 1942.

PG 32175: 1/Skl KTB Teil C Heft IV, U-boat War, September 1943.

PG 32419a: BdU U-boats (Akte BdU) Orders and Intentions, ff5.

PG 32652: Vortragsprotokoll, Lagevorträge, 13 Oktober 1944.

PG 33048: 1/Skl /IL KTB, Questions of Co-operation with U-boats, 7 September 1944.

PG 33322: Prof. Cornelius to OKM about Torpedoes, 254.

PG 33322: gKdos, Report on Torpedoes 1914/40, 239.

PG 33324: Torpedowesen: Details of OR Torpedo Effectiveness.

PG 33329: 'Chefsache Band 13, Verschiedenes', SS. 91–6.

PG 33349: Skl Iu Allgemein, General Observations.

PG 33351: 1/Skl KTB, Teil C, Iu. U-boat Orders and Cancellations, 13 August 1943.

PG 33352: U-boat Warfare, 14–20 March 1940.

PG 33390: B.Nr. 110 gKdos, 'Aufschlüßelung weiterer U-bootstonnage'.

PG 33416: Files of Iu Chefsache, Relating to Rockets.

PG 33541: 'Personalbedarf', 13 November 1939.

PG 33945: 'Erstellung einer voraktischen Ausbildungseinheit'.

PG 34398: Operational use of the '*Schnorchel*' in the Front-line Training Group.

PG 39324: BdU KTB entry, 21 May 1943 concerning Danube's boats.

PG 42238: Dok 11214, *FEP* Forschung, Erfindungen und Patentwesen.

PG 43149: Issued contracts, April 1944.

Published primary sources

Air historical branch monographs

Royal Air Force in the Maritime War (1950).

The Origins and Development of Operational Research in the Royal Air Force (HMSO) (1963).

The Rise and Fall of the German Air Force 1933–1945 (1983).

Naval history monographs

Barley, F. and Waters, D. W., *The Defeat of the Enemy Attack on Shipping 1939–1945: A Study of Policy and Operations*, NRS, 137 (Aldershot, 1997).

Corbett, Julian, Sir, *History of the Great War Based on Official Documents: Naval Operations,* Vols I–III (1920–3).

Dönitz, Karl, *Memoirs, Ten Years and Twenty Days* (1959).

Hackmann, Willem, *Seek and Strike* (HMSO) (1984).

Hessler, Günther, *The U-boat War in the Atlantic 1939–45,* Vols I – III, written in 1945–6, ed. C. Withers (HMSO) (1989).

Newbolt, Henry, Sir, *History of the Great War Based on Official Documents: Naval Operations,* Vols IV and V (1928–31).

Official Account of the Battle of the Atlantic (HMSO) (1946).Syrett, David, *The Battle of the Atlantic and Naval Signals Intelligence: U-boat Situations and Trends 1941–45*, Navy Records Society, 139 (Aldershot, 1998).

— *The Battle of the Atlantic and Signals Intelligence: U-boat Tracking Papers 1941–1945,* Navy Records Society, 144 (Aldershot, 2002).

The Führer Conferences on Naval Affairs, trans. A. Martiensen post war and published in Brassey's *Naval Annual* (1948) (1990).

Secondary sources

Monographs (English)

Adams, Thomas A., 'The Control of British Merchant Shipping', in *The Battle of the Atlantic 1939–1945: The 50th Anniversary International Naval Conference,* ed. Stephen Howarth and Derek Law (1994), 158–78.

Auphan, P. and Mordal, J., *The French Navy in World War II* (Annapolis, 1959).

Baker, Richard, *The Terror of Tobermory* (1972).

Barnett, Corelli, *The Audit of War* (1986).

— *Engage the Enemy More Closely* (1991).

Bekker, C., *Hitler's Naval War (Verdammte See),* English translation by F. Ziegler (1974).

Beesly, Patrick, *Very Special Intelligence: The Story of the Admiralty's Operational Intelligence Centre 1939–1945* (1977).

— *Room 40: British Naval Intelligence 1914–18* (1982).

Bird, Keith, *Erich Raeder: Admiral of the Reich* (Annapolis, 2006).

Boog, Horst, 'Luftwaffe Support of the German Navy', in *The Battle of the Atlantic 1939–1945,* ed. Stephen Howarth and Derek Law (1994), 302–22.

Bowen, E. G., *Radar Days* (Bristol, 1987).

Breyer, Siegfried, *The German Aircraft Carrier Graf Zeppelin* (Atglen, Pennsylvania, 1989),

Brown, David, 'Revolution manqé : Technical Change in the Royal Navy at the End of the First World War', in *Warship 1993*, ed. Robert Gardiner (1993), 77–88.

— 'Atlantic Escorts 1939–45', in *The Battle of the Atlantic 1939–1945: The 50th Anniversary International Naval Conference*, ed. Stephen Howarth and Derek Law (1994), 452–75.

— *Nelson to Vanguard: Warship Design and Development 1923–1945*, (2006).

— *Atlantic Escorts* (Barnsley, 2007).

Bruce, J. M., *British Aeroplanes, 1914–18* (1957).

Burns, T. and Stalker, G. M., *The Management of Innovation* (1961).

Chalmers, W. S., *Max Horton and the Western Approaches* (1954).

Chatfield, Lord, *The Navy and Defence* (1942).

Churchill, Winston S., *The Second World War* (6) (1948–53).

— *The Second World War* (6) (Chartwell edn.) (1954).

Cornwell, John, *Hitler's Scientists; Science War and the Devils Pact* (New York, 2003).

Corum, James S., *The Luftwaffe: Creating the Operational Air War 1918–1940* (Kansas, 1999).

Dewar, K. G. B., *The Navy from Within* (1939).

Edwards, Bernard, *Dönitz and the Wolf Packs* (1996).

Franklin, George, *Britain's Anti-submarine Capability 1919–1939* (2003).

Gardner, W. J. R., 'An Allied Perspective', in *The Battle of the Atlantic 1939–1945: The 50th Anniversary International Naval Conference,* ed. Stephen Howarth and Derek Law (1994), 516–37.

— 'The Battle of the Atlantic, 1941 – the First Turning Point?', in *Sea Power: Theory and Practice*, ed. Geoffrey Till (Ilford, 1994), 109–23.

— 'Blackett and the Black Art', in *Patrick Blackett*, ed. Peter Hoare (2003), 126–37.

Gemzell, Carl Axel, *Organization, Conflict and Innovation: A Study of German Naval Strategic Planning, 1888–1940* (Lund 1973).

Gibbs, N. H., *Grand Strategy* (1976), (1931).

Glover, William, 'Manning and Training Allied Navies', in *The Battle of the Atlantic 1939–1945: The 50th Anniversary International Naval Conference*, ed. Stephen Howarth and Derek Law (1994), 188–213.

Goldrick, James, 'Work-up', in *The Battle of the Atlantic 1939–1945: The 50th Anniversary International Naval Conference,* ed. Stephen Howarth and Derek Law (1994), 220–39.

Grove, E. J., *The Future of Sea Power* (1990).

— 'The Modern Views: The Battle and Post-war British Naval Policy', in *The Battle of the Atlantic 1939–1945: The 50th Anniversary International Naval Conference,* ed. Stephen Howarth and Derek Law (1994), 576–83.

Gunston, Bill, 'British 'R' Class', *Submarines in Colour* (Blandford, 1976).

Hague, Arnold, *The Allied Convoy System 1939–1945; It's Organization Defence and Operation* (2000).

Hartcup Guy, *The Effect of Science on the Second World War* (Basingstoke, 2000).

Hendrie, Andrew, *The Cinderella Service, Coastal Command 1939–1945* (Barnsley, 2006).

Henry, D., 'British Submarine Policy 1918–1939', in *Technical Change and British Naval Policy 1860–1939*, ed. Bryan Ranft (1977), 80–107.

Herrick, John, 'Sub-surface Warfare, the History of Division 6', NDRC *Dept. of Defense, Research and Development Board*, Washington DC (January 1951).

Hinsley, F. H. and Stripp, A., *Code Breakers: The Inside Story of Bletchley Park* (Oxford, 1993).

Hinsley, F. H., Thomas, E. E., Ransom, C. F. G. and Knight, R. C., *British Intelligence in the Second World War*, I (1979).

— *British Intelligence in the Second World War*, II (1981).

— *British Intelligence in the Second World War*, III (1984).

Hobbs, David, 'Ship-borne Air Anti-submarine Warfare', in *The Battle of the Atlantic 1939–1945: The 50th Anniversary International Naval Conference*, ed. Stephen Howarth and Derek Law (1994), 388–407.

Hough, Richard, *The Great War At Sea 1914–1918* (New York, 1983).

Howard, Michael, *The Continental Commitment* (1972).

Howse, D., *Radar at Sea* (1993).

Ireland, Bernard, *Battle of the Atlantic* (Barnsley, 2003).

Irving, David, *Göring: A Biography*, www.fpp.co.uk/books/goering (Electronic version 2002).

Isby, D. C. (ed.), *The Luftwaffe and the War at Sea 1939–1945: As Seen by Officers of the Kriegsmarine and Luftwaffe* (2005).

Jellicoe, John, *The Submarine Peril: The Admiralty Policy in 1917* (1934).

Joubert de la Ferté, Philip, *Birds and Fishes* (1960).

Kahn, David, *Seizing the Enigma: The Race to Break the German U-boat Codes 1939–1943* (New York, 2001).

Kennedy, Paul M., 'British "Net Assessment" and the Coming of the Second World War', in *Calculations: Net Assessment and the Coming of World War II*, ed. W. Murray and A. Millett (New York, 1992), 19–59.

Kroge, Harry von, *GEMA; Birthplace of German Radar and Sonar*, trans. and ed. Louis Brown (Bristol, 2000).

Lambert, Andrew, 'Sea Power 1939–1940: Churchill and the Strategic Origins of the Battle of the Atlantic', in *Sea Power: Theory and Practice*, ed. Geoffrey Till (Ilford, 1994), 86–107.

Lanchester, F. W., *Aircraft in Warfare* (1916).

Layman, R. D., *Naval Aviation in the First World War: Its Impact and Influence* (1996).

Lenton, H. T., *German Warships of the Second World War* (1975).

Lewin, Ronald, *Ultra Goes to War* (London, 1978).

Llewellyn-Jones, Malcolm, 'A Clash of Cultures: The Case for Large Convoys', in *Patrick Blackett*, ed. Peter Hoare (2003a), 138–59.

— 'The Pursuit of Realism: British Anti-submarine Tactics and Training to Counter the Fast Submarine, 1944–52', in *The Face of Naval Battle; The Human Experience of Modern War at Sea*, ed. John Reeve and David Stephens (Crows Nest NSW, 2003b), 219–39.

Loewenheim, L., Langley, H. D. and Jonas, Manfred (eds), *Roosevelt and Churchill: Their Secret Wartime Correspondence* (New York, 1975).

Lovell, B., *P. M. S. Blackett: A Biographical Memoir*, (The Royal Society, 1976).

Macintyre, Donald, *U-boat Killer* (1956 and 1999).

— *Battle of the Atlantic* (1961).

Maiolo, Joseph A., *The Royal Navy and Nazi Germany 1933–39: A Study in Appeasement and the Origins of the Second World War* (Basingstoke, 1998).

Marder, Arthur J., 'The Influence of History on Sea Power', *From the Dardanelles to Oran: Studies of the Royal Navy in War and Peace 1915–1940* (1974), 23–63.

McLachlan, Donald, *Room 39: Naval Intelligence in Action 1939–45* (1968).

Meyer, Erwin, *Electro-Acoustics* (1939).

Middlebrook, Martin, *Convoy* (1976).

Milner, Marc, *North Atlantic Run: The Royal Canadian Navy and the Battle for the Convoys* (Toronto, 1985).

— *The Battle of the Atlantic* (Ontario, 2003).

Meigs, M. C., *Slide Rules and Submarines: American Scientists and Subsurface Warfare in World War II* (Washington, 1990).

Messimer, Dwight R., *Find and Destroy: Anti-submarine Warfare in World War 1* (Annapolis, 2001).

Morrison, Samuel E., *History of United States Naval Operations in World War II: Battle of the Atlantic September 1939–May 1943* (1) (1948).

Mulligan, Timothy, *Neither Sharks nor Wolves* (Annapolis, 1999).

Neitzel, Sönke, 'The Deployment of U-boats', in *The Battle of the Atlantic 1939–1945: The 50th Anniversary International Naval Conference,* ed. Stephen Howarth and Derek Law (1994), 276–301.

Niestlé, Axel, 'German Technical and Electronic Development', in *The Battle of the Atlantic 1939–1945: The 50th Anniversary International Naval Conference,* ed. Stephen Howarth and Derek Law (1994), 430–51.

— *German U-boat Losses During World War II* (Annapolis, 1998).

Newbolt, Sir Henry, *Naval Operations*, V (1931).

Owen, David, *Anti-submarine Warfare: An Illustrated History* (Barnsley, 2007).

Padfield, Peter, *Dönitz: The Last Führer* (1984).

— *Men of War* (New York, 1992).

Philbin, Tobias, *The Lure of Neptune* (University of South Carolina Press, 1994).

Preston, Antony, '*V*' & '*W*' *Class Destroyers 1917–45* (1971).

Price, Alfred, *Aircraft versus Submarine, The Evolution of the Anti-Submarine Aircraft 1912-1972* (1973) and (Barnsley, 2004).

Rahn, Werner, 'The Campaign: The German Perspective', in *The Battle of the Atlantic 1939-1945*, ed. Stephen Howarth and Derek Law (1994), 538-53.

— 'German Naval Strategy and Armament 1919-1939', in *Technology and Naval Combat in the Twentieth Century and Beyond*, ed. Philip O'Brien (2001), 109-28.

Ramsay, David, *'Blinker' Hall, Spymaster: The Man Who Brought America into World War I* (Stroud, 2008).

Raynor, D. A., *Escort: The Battle of the Atlantic* (1955),

Rhys-Jones, G., 'The German System: A Staff Perspective', in *The Battle of the Atlantic 1939-1945*, ed. Stephen Howarth and Derek Law (1994), 138-57.

Roper, Trevor H., *Hitler's War Directives 1939-1945* (Edinburgh, 2004).

Rosinski, Herbert, 'German Theories of Sea Warfare', *Brassey's Naval Annual* (1940).

Roskill, Stephen W., *The War at Sea*, 4 parts in three volumes (1954-61).

— *Naval Policy between the Wars: The Period of Anglo-American Antagonism 1919-1929* (1968).

— *Naval Policy between the Wars: The Period of Reluctance 1930-1939* (1976).

— *The Navy at War 1939-1945* (Ware, 1998).

— *Churchill and the Admirals* (Barnsley, 2004).

Rößler, Eberhard, 'U-boat Development and Building', in *The Battle of the Atlantic 1939-1945*, ed. Stephen Howarth and Derek Law (1994), 118-37.

Rowe, A. P., *One Story of Radar* (Cambridge, 1998).

Rust, Eric C., *Naval Officers under Hitler: The Story of Crew 34* (New York, 1991).

Schuster, Carl O., 'German Naval Warfare in WWII', *Strategy & Tactics*, 226 (January/February 2005), 45-6.

Seth, Ronald, *The Fiercest Battle; The Story of North Atlantic Convoy ONS 5, 22nd April-7th May 1943* (1961).

Stern, Robert C., *Type VII U-boats* (1991).

Stille, Mark, *Imperial Japanese Navy Submarines 1941-45* (Oxford, 2007).

Sutcliffe, Paul, 'Operational Research in the Battle of the Atlantic', in *The Battle of the Atlantic 1939-1945*, ed. Stephen Howarth and Derek Law (1994), 418-29.

Tarrant, V. E., *The U-Boat Offensive 1914-45* (1989).

Terraine, John, *The Right of Line* (1985).

— *A Time for Courage: The Royal Air Force in the European War 1939-1945* (New York, 1985).

— *Business in Great Waters* (Ware, 1999).

Terrell, E., *Admiralty Brief: The Story of Inventions That Contributed to Victory in the Battle of the Atlantic* (1958). Till, Geoffrey, 'The Battle of the Atlantic as History', in *The Battle of the Atlantic 1939-1945*, 584-95.

Topp, Erich, 'Manning and Training the U-boat Fleet', in *The Battle of the Atlantic 1939-1945*, 214-19.

von Clausewitz, C., *On War* (Ware, 1997).

von der Porten, Edward, P., *The German Navy in World War Two* (1969).

Waddington, C. H., *O.R. in World War II: Operational Research against the U-boat* (1973).

Waters, D. W., *A Study of the Philosophy and Conduct of Maritime War, 1815–1945* (1957).

Westwood, David, *The U-boat War, The German Submarine Service and the Battle of the Atlantic 1939–45* (2005).

Whitby Michael, 'The Strain of the Bridge: The Second World War Diaries of Commander A. F. C. Layard, DSO, DSC, RN', in *The Face of Naval Battle: The human experience of modern war at sea,* ed. John Reeve and David Stevens (Crows Nest NSW, 2003), 200–18.

Williams, Andrew, *Battle of the Atlantic* (2002).

Williams, Mark, *Captain Gilbert Roberts R. N. and the Anti U-Boat School* (1979).

Wilmott, H. P., 'The Organizations: The Admiralty and the Western Approaches', in *The Battle of the Atlantic 1939–1945: The 50th Anniversary International Naval Conference,* ed. Stephen Howarth and Derek Law (1994), 179–87.

Winterbotham, F. W., *The Ultra Secret* (1974).

Woodman, Richard, *The Real Cruel Sea; The Merchant Navy in the Battle of the Atlantic* (2004).

Zilbert, Edward R., *Albert Speer and the Nazi Ministry of Arms: Economic Institutions and Industrial Production in the German War Economy* (1981).

Zimmerman, D., 'Technology and Tactics', in *The Battle of the Atlantic 1939–1945: The 50th Anniversary International Naval Conference,* ed. Stephen Howarth and Derek Law (1994), 476–89.

— 'Preparations for War', in *Patrick Blackett* ed. Peter Hoare (2003), 110–25.

Monographs (German)

Assmann, Kurt, *Deutsche Seestrategie in Zwei Weltkriegen* (Heidelberg, 1957).

Bendert, H., *Die UB-Boote der Kaiserlichen Marine 1914–1918* (Berlin, 2000).

Brennecke, J., *Haie im Paradies* (Hamburg, 2002).

Busch, F. O., *Das Buch von der Kriegsmarine* (Berlin, 1939).

Busch, R. und Röll, H. J., *U-bootbau auf deutschen Werften* (Cuxhaven, 1994).

— *Der U-bootkrieg 1939 bis 1945: die U-boot Kommandanten* (1) (Hamburg, 1996).

Dönitz, Karl, *Die U-Bootwaffe* (Berlin, 1939).

— *10 Jahre und 20 Tage* (Frankfurt, 1958).

— *40 Fragen an Karl Dönitz* (München, 1980).

Dülffer, J., *Weimar, Hitler und die Marine; Reichspolitik und Flottenbau 1920–1939* (Düsseldorf, 1973).

Gemzell, C. A., *Raeder, Hitler und Skandinavien* (Lund, 1965).

Hümmelchen, G., *Die deutschen Seeflieger 1935–1945* (München, 1976).

Köhl, Fritz, *Vom Original zum Modell: Uboottyp XXI* (Bonn, 2003).

Köhl, F. und Niestlé, A., *U-boottyp VII C* (Koblenz, 1989).

Kube, A., *Pour le mérite und Hakenkreuz: Hermann Göring im Dritten Reich* (München, 1986).

Lohmann, W., und Hildebrand, H. H., *Die deutsche Kriegsmarine 1939–1945* (3) (Bad Nauheim, 1956–64).

Neitzel, Sönke, *Der Einsatz der deutschen Luftwaffe über dem Atlantik und der Nordsee 1939–1945* (Bonn, 1995).

— 'Zum strategischen Misserfolg verdammt?: Die deutsche Luftwaffe in beiden Weltkriegen', in *Erster Weltkrieg-Zweiter Weltkrieg: ein Vergleich*, ed. Bruno Thoß und Hans-Erich Volkmann (Paderborn, 2002), 167–92.

Rahn, Werner, 'Ausbildung zum Marineoffizier zwischen den Weltkriegen', in *Marine Schule Mürwick,* ed. Rahn, (Herford, 1989), ff.143.

Reuter Frank, *Wissenschaftliche Abhandlungen der Arbeitsgemeinschaft für Forschung des Landes Nordrhein-Westfalen,* Bd. 42 (Opladen, 1971).

Rößler, E., *Die torpedos der deutschen U-Boote* (Herford 1984).

Salewski, M., *Die deutsche Seekriegsleitung 1939–45* (3) (München, 1970–5).

Salewski, M., Schottelius, H. und Caspar, G. A., 'Wehrmacht und Nationalsozialismus 1933–1939', in *Handbuch der deutschen Militärgeschichte 1648–1938,* (6) (Freiburg 1964–79), (5).

Sorge, S., *Der Marineoffizier als führer und Erzieher* (Berlin, 1937 und 1943).

Wagner, G., (ed.) *Lagevorträge des Oberbefehlshabers der Kriegsmarine vor Hitler* (München, 1972).

Wegener, Wolfgang, *Die Seestrategie des Weltkrieges* (Berlin, 1929).

Articles

Abrams, J. W., 'Military Applications of Operational Research', *Operations Research*, 5 (3) (June 1957), 434–40.

Aitken, M. and Hage J., 'The Organic Organization and Innovation', *Sociology,* 5 (1) (1971), 63–82.

Anonymous, *The Naval Review,* 20 (November 1932), 635–42.

Balmer, John M. T., 'Comprehending Corporate Identity: Corporate Brand Management and Corporate Marketing', Working Paper No. 06/19, Bradford University, March 2006.

Barley, F. and Waters, D. W., 'The Heel of Achilles', *The Naval Review,* 48 (2) (April 1960), 133–46.

Bellairs, R. M., 'Historical Survey of Trade Defence Since 1914', *Journal of the Royal United Services Institute,* 99 (595) (1954), 359–77.

Bird, Keith W. 'The Origins and Role of German Naval History in the Interwar Period 1918-1939', *Naval War College Review,* 32 (2) (March–April 1979), 52 (January 1993), 143–61.

Callick, E. B., 'VHF Communications at RAE 1947–1942', *Institution of Electrical Engineers International Conference on 100 Years of Radio* (September 1995), 153–60.

Chilton, Air Marshal Sir Edward, RAF Bracknell Paper No. 2, A symposium on the battle of the Atlantic, 21 October 1991.

Crowther, J. G. and Whiddington, R., 'Science at War', *The Naval Review,* 36 (2) (May 1948), 197–200.

Cunningham, W. P., Freeman, Denys and McCloskey, J. F., 'Of Radar and Operations Research: An Appreciation of A. P. Rowe (1898–1976)', *Operations Research,* 32 (4) (July–August 1984), 958–67.

Dawson R. M., The Cabinet Minister and Administration: A. J. Balfour and Sir Edward Carson at the Admiralty, 1915–17, *Canadian Journal of Economics and Political Science,* 9 (1) (February 1943), 1–38, 14–15.

Emme, Eugene M., 'Air Power and National Security', *Annals of the American Academy of Political and Social Science,* 299 (May 1955), 12–24.

Filipowski, Sean R., 'Operation Paukenschlag: An Operational Analysis', *Naval War College,* Newport RI (June 1994).

Fisher, Robert, 'Group Wotan and the Battle for SC 104', *The Mariner's Mirror,* 84 (1) (February 1998), 64–75.

Fortun, M. and Schweber, S. S., 'Scientists and the Legacy of World War II: The Case of Operations Research', *Social Studies of Science,* 23 (4) (November 1993), 595–642.

Franklin, George, 'A Breakdown in Communication: ASDIC in the 1930s', *The Mariners Mirror,* 84 (2) (May 1998), 204–14.

— 'The Origins of the Royal Navy's Vulnerability to Surfaced Night U-boat Attack 1939–40', *The Mariner's Mirror,* 90 (1) (February 2004), 73–84.

Gaul, Walter, 'The Part Played by the German Air Force and the Naval Air Force in the Invasion of Norway', essays by German Officers and Officials on World War II (Wilmington: Scholarly Resources Inc.), n.d., 5.

German, Tony, 'Preserving the Atlantic Lifeline', *Legion Magazine* (May 1998), (no page numbers given).

Goette, Richard, 'Britain and the Delay in Closing the Mid-Atlantic "Air Gap" During the Battle of the Atlantic', *The Northern Mariner,* XV (4) (October 2005), 19–41.

Gretton, P. W., 'Why Don't We Learn from History?', *The Naval Review* 46 (January 1958), 13–25.

Guse, John C., 'Nazi Technical Thought Revisited', *History and Technology,* 26 (1) (2010), 3–33.

Hamilton, C. I., 'The Character and Organization of the Admiralty Operational Intelligence', *War In History* (July 2000), 295–324.

Hansen, Kenneth, 'Raeder versus Wegener: Conflict in German Naval Strategy', *Naval War College Review* Newport RId (Autumn 2005).

Hasslinger, Karl M., 'The U-boat War in the Caribbean: Opportunities Lost', *Naval War College,* Newport RI (March 1996).

Herwig Holger, H., 'Prelude to Weltblitzkrieg: Germany's Naval Policy Toward the United States of America, 1939–41', *The Journal of Modern History*, 43 (4) (December 1971), 649–68.

— 'Generals versus Admirals: The War Aims of the Imperial German Navy 1914–1918', *Central European History* V (September 1972), 208–33.

— 'The Failure of German Sea Power 1914–1945: Mahan, Tirpitz, and Raeder Reconsidered', *International History Review*, 10 (1) (February 1988), 68–105.

Kennedy, P. M., 'The Development of German Naval Operations: Plans against England 1896–1914', *The English Historical Review*, 89 (350) (January 1974), 48–76.

Kraus, Jerome, 'The British Electron Tube and Semi-conductor Industry 1935–62', *Technology and Culture*, 9 (1) (October 1968), 544–61.

Krug, Lt. Cdr A., 'Coordination and Command Relationships between Axis Powers in the Naval War in the Mediterranean 1940–1943', Published Master's Degree in Defence Studies, Dissertation, Canadian Forces College, CSC 31, n.d., 1–91.

Macgregor, David, 'The Use, Misuse, and Non-use of History: The Royal Navy and the Operational Lessons of the First World War', *The Journal of Military History*, 56 (4) (October 1992), 603–16.

Maiolo, Joseph A., 'The Knockout Blow against the Import System: Admiralty Expectations of Nazi Germany's Naval Strategy 1934–39', *Journal of Historical Research*, 72 (178) (June 1999), 202–28.

Marder, Arthur, 'The Influence of History on Sea Power: The Royal Navy and the Lessons of 1914–1918', *Pacific Historical Review*, 41 (4) (November 1972), 413–43.

McCloskey, Joseph F., 'The Beginnings of Operations Research: 1934–1941', *Operations Research*, 35 (1) (1987a), 143–52.

— 'British Operational Research in World War II', *Operations Research*, 35 (3) (1987b), 453–70.

McKercher, B. T. C., 'Our Most Dangerous Enemy: Great Britain's Pre-eminence in the 1930s', *International Historical Revue*, 13 (1991), 751–83.

Milner, Marc, 'The Battle of the Atlantic', *Journal of Strategic Studies*, 13 (1) (1990), 45–66.

Momsen, Bill, 'Code Breaking and Secret Weapons in World War II', Chapter II: 1939–41, http://home.earthlink.net/~nbrass1/1enigma.htm (Internet) *Nautical Brass*, 1993–2007, n.d.

Morris B. S., 'Officer Selection in the British Army 1942–1945', *Occupational Psychology*, XXIII (4) (1949), 219–34.

Neitzel, Sönke, 'Kriegsmarine and Luftwaffe Co-operation in the War against Britain 1939–1945', *War In History*, 10 (2003), 448–63.

Pratt, William V., 'Warfare in the Atlantic', *Foreign Affairs*, 19 (4) (July 1941), 729–36.

Price, Alfred, 'Development of Equipment and Techniques', in *'Seek and Sink'*, RAF Bracknell Paper No 2: 'A Symposium on the Battle of the Atlantic', Sponsored jointly by the Royal Air Force Historical Society and the Royal Air Force Staff College, Bracknell, 21 (October 1991), 49–55.

Raudzens, George, 'War-winning Weapons: The Measurement of Technological Determinism in Military History', *The Journal of Military History*, 54 (4) (October 1990), 403–34.

Redford Duncan, 'The March 1943 Crisis in the Battle of the Atlantic: Myth and Reality', *The Historical Association*, 92 (305) (2007), 64–83.

— 'Inter-and Intra-service Rivalries in the Battle of the Atlantic', *Journal of Strategic Studies*, 32 (6) (December 2009), 899–928.

Rodger, Nicolas, 'The Royal Navy in the Era of the World Wars: Was it Fit for Purpose?', *The Mariner's Mirror*, 97 (1) (February 2011), 272–84.

S. A. S., 'Officer Selection 1945', *The Naval Review*, 78 (3) (July 1990), 259–60.

Scheer, Reinhard, 'Admiral Scheer's Memoirs', in *The War Times Journal* at www.wtj.com.

Schoenfeld, Max, 'Winston Churchill as War Manager: The Battle of the Atlantic Committee 1941', *Military Affairs*, 52 (3) (July 1988), 122–7.

Solandt, Omand, 'Observation, Experiment, and Measurement in Operations Research', *Operations Research Society of America*, 3 (1) (February 1955), 1–14.

Sumida, Jon, 'The Best Laid Plans: The Development of British Battle-fleet Tactics, 1919–42', *International History Review*, XIV (1992), 681–700.

Syrett, David, 'The Battle of the Atlantic: 1943, the Year of Decision', *American Neptune*, (45) 1 (Winter 1985), 46–64.

— 'The Safe and Timely Arrival of Convoy SC-130, 15–25 May 1943', *American Neptune*, 1 (3) (Summer 1990), 219–27.

— 'The Battle for Convoy ONS-154, 26–31 December 1942', *The Northern Mariner*, 7 (2) (April 1997), 41–50.

— 'The Battle for HG 75, 22–29 October 1941', *The Northern Mariner*, 10 (1) (January 1999), 41–51.

Terraine, John, 'Atlantic Victory; 50 Years on', *RUSI Journal*, 138 (5) (1993), 53–9.

Thomas, Edward, in 'Seek and Sink', RAF Bracknell Paper No. 2, A Symposium on the Battle of the Atlantic, 21 October 1991, 38–48.

Thomas, William, 'The Heuristics of War: Scientific Method and the Founders of Operations Research', *British Society for the History of Science*, 40 (2) (June 2007), 251–74.

Tiles, J. E., 'Experimental Evidence vs. Experimental Practice?', *The British Journal for the Philosophy of Science*, 43 (1) (March 1992), 99–109, 99.

Waddington, C. H., Goodeve, Charles and Tomlinson, Rolfe, 'Lord Blackett', *Operational Research Quarterly*, 25 (4) (December 1974), i–viii.

Waters, D. W., 'The Philosophy and Conduct of Maritime War', Part II 1918–45, *Journal of the Royal Naval Scientific Service*, 13 (1958), 183–92.

— 'The Science of Admiralty', *The Naval Review* (October 1963), 395–410; (January 1964), 15–26; (July 1964), 291–309; (October 1964), 423–37.

Williams, E. J., 'Reflections on Operational Research', *Operations Research*, 2 (1954), 441–3.

German articles

Baumann, Egon, 'Die Raketenversuchsstation Toplitzsee 1944–1945', *Marine Rundschau,* 5 (1988), 300–2.

Boog, Horst, 'Das Problem der Selbständigkeit der Luftstreitkräfte in Deutschland 1908–1945', *Militärgeschichtliche Mitteilungen,*1 (1988), 31–60.

Guicking, Dieter, *Erwin Meyer – ein bedeutender deutscher Akustiker Biographische Notizen*, Drittes Physikalisches Institut der Universität Göttingen (Januar 2010).

Rößler, E., 'Die deutsche U-bootausbildung und ihre Vorbereitungen 1925–1945', *Marine Rundschau,* 68 (8) (1971), 453–63.

Salewski, M., 'Das Kriegstagebuch der deutschen Seekriegsleitung im zweiten Weltkrieg', *Marine Rundschau,* 64 (3) (Juni 1967), 137–45.

Syrett, D. und Douglas, W. A. B., 'Die Wende in der Schlacht im Atlantik: Die Schließung des Grönland-Luftlochs 1942–1943', *Marine Rundschau,* 83 (1986), 2–11, 70–3, 147–9.

Theses and dissertations

Abbatiello, J. J., 'British Naval Aviation in the Anti-submarine Campaign 1917–18' (unpublished doctoral thesis, University of London, King's College, 2004).

Buckley, John, 'The Development of RAF Coastal Command Trade Defence Strategy, Policy and Doctrine 1919–1945' (unpublished doctoral thesis, University of Lancaster, 1991).

Carter, Geoffrey H., 'The Rise and Fall of the Portland Naval Base 1845–1995' (unpublished doctoral thesis, University of Exeter, June 1998).

Franklin, D. F., 'British Anti-submarine Tactics 1926–1940' (unpublished master's thesis, University of Glasgow, June 2001).

Gardener, K. E., 'Selection, Training and Career Development of Naval Officers; A Long-term Follow-up, Using Multivariate Techniques' (unpublished doctoral thesis, 1 Graduate Business Centre, City University, London, 1971).

Glover, William, 'Officer Training and the Quest for Operational Efficiency in the Royal Canadian Navy 1939–1945' (unpublished doctoral thesis, University of London, 1998).

Gould, Winston, 'Luftwaffe Maritime Operations in World War II: Thoughts Organization and Technology' (unpublished research report submitted to the Faculty in partial fulfilment of the graduation requirements, Air Command and Staff College, Air University, 2005).

Haslop, Dennis, 'New Product Development and Team Leader Autonomy in Industrial R&D' (unpublished doctoral thesis, Brunel University, 1997).

Koestner, Oberstleutnant Marc S., 'The Luftwaffe's Support of Naval Operations During World War II 1939–1941' (unpublished master's thesis, Canadian Forces College, n.d.).

Krauss, Oliver, 'Rüstung und Rüstungserprobung in der deutschen Marinegeschichte unter besonderer Berücksichtigung der Torpedoversuchsanstalt (TVA)' (unpublished doctoral thesis, Christian-Albrechts-Universität, Kiel, 2006).

Llewellyn-Jones, M., 'The Royal Navy on the Threshold of Modern Anti-submarine Warfare 1944–1949' (unpublished doctoral thesis, University of London, King's College, London, 2004).

Richhardt, Dirk, 'Auswahl und Ausbildung junger Offiziere 1930–1945: zur sozialen Genese des deutschen Offizierkorps' (unpublished doctoral thesis, Universität Marburg, 2002).

Schumacher, Christopher, 'Forschung, Rüstung und Krieg: Formen, Ausmaß und Grenzen des Wissenschaftlereinsatzes für den zweiten Weltkrieg im deutschen Reich' (unpublished doctoral thesis, Ernst-Moritz-Arndt-Universität, Greifswald, 2004).

Skinner, Ian W., 'British Maritime Strategy and Operations in the Western Channel and South-west Approaches 1939–1945' (unpublished doctoral thesis, Exeter University, 1991).

Stilla, Ernst, 'Die Luftwaffe im Kampf um die Luftherrschaft' (unpublished doctoral thesis, Friedrich-Wilhelms-Universität, Bonn, 2005).

Winthrop-Saville, Allison, 'The Development of the U-boat Arm 1919–1935' (unpublished doctoral thesis, University of Washington, 1963).

Index

Page numbers in **bold** refer to charts/figures/tables.

2/Skl 21, 51, 95, 186, 273, 274

a priori 164, 169, 170, 184, 185, 189, 199, 204, 263
  definition of 164
  torpedo failure as an instance 184–5
ACI (Admiralty Convoy Instructions) 129
ACNS (Assistant Chief of Naval Staff) 32, 33, 114
Admiralty pre-war planning 29–31
Air Ministry 41, 71–3, 163, 171, 207, 260
  and the Admiralty 76–8
  failing 258
aircraft 41, 57, 65, 74, 75, 76, 77, 96, 128, 145, 146, 147, 151, 153, 158, 163, 167, 168, 169, 171, 176, 177, 187, 196, 198, 200, 207, 214, 215, 217, 218, 219, 222, 225, 233, 234, 236, 245, 249, 258, 262, 263
  allied 59
    low-flying 238
  American 209, 238
  A/S aircraft 130, 135, 239
  Avenger 235
  British 68, 258
    British Liberator Aircraft 197
    radar-fitted 42, 138
  cameras fitted to 170
  Costal Command aircraft 74–5, 158
  detection of 165
  FAA aircraft 78, 151, 208
  German 68–9
  land-based 76, 215, 217
  long-range 58, 157, 225, 233, 262, 266
    Condor 58, 59
  Luftwaffe aircraft 146
    role of 54, 56
    and the U-boat arm 59, 157
  naval aircraft operations 55–6
  VLR (very long range) aircraft 139, 208, 211
    shore-based 209

Wildcat 235
Alberich (U-boat camouflage) 186, 196, 197, 200, 264, 265
  see also Schnorchel
alliance 208
  Anglo-French 31, 49
  naval 40
American,
  assistance to Britain 35
  -based carrier planes 235
  Destroyers 71
  naval resources 209
Anglo-German Naval Agreement (1935) 18, 29, 83, 86, 165
Anti U-boat Warfare Committee, the 37, 42, 53, 70
anti-submarine,
  course 108
  escort vessels 66, 67
  policy 105
  warfare measures 1, 3, 30, 38, 65, 74, 75, 93, 109, 275
  weapons 76, 112–13
AOC (Air Officer Commanding) 71–2, 74, 207
A/S 3, 39, 79, 94, 105–9, 111, 112, 115, 118, 130, 132, 135, 136, 138, 151, 154, 155, 156, 158, 196, 210, 237, 239, 243, 255, 267
ASDIC (SONAR) 39, 66, 70, 75, 78, 85, 86, 88, 94, 107, 109, 110, 111, 114, 116, 117, 129, 133, 150, 156, 172, 175, 176, 185, 186, 196, 200, 217, 237, 238, 243, 244, 245, 249, 257, 264, 265
  S-Gerät 85
ASE (Admiralty Signals Establishment) 174
ASSB (Allied Anti-submarine Survey Board) 261
ASV 77, 207

ASW (Anti-submarine Warfare) 5, 7, 32,
      33, 41, 53, 77, 78, 99, 105, 106, 112,
      114, 115, 119, 152, 158, 173, 248,
      259, 260, 267
ASW training 105–19, 125, 149, 150, 152,
      261, 267
   A/S ratings training 108–9
   depth charge and attack training 112–13
   officer selection and training 107–8
      training at Portland **108**
   planning for war 109–11
   WA tactical unit 113–19
      Beta Search, the 118
   working up 111–12
ASWORG (Anti-Submarine Warfare
      Operational Research Group)
      169, 263
ATW (Ahead Throwing Weapon) 244, 264
      see also Hedgehog Squid
AUC (Anti-submarine Warfare
      Committee) 13, 70, 256

Baldwin, Stanley 38, 39
Baltic 20–1, 59, 65, 84, 92, 96, 97, 146–8,
      187, 194, 221
Barley, F. 4
   *Defeat of the Enemy Attack on Shipping
      1939–1945: . . . The* (with Water) 4
Barnett, Corelli 30
Battle of the Atlantic *see also* myth of the
      U-boat crisis
   beginning of, the 1
      sinking of *Athenia* and 1
   Churchill's directive 35
   end of, the 1
      withdrawal of U-boats and 1
Battleford 131, 138
Bauer, Flotillenadmiral 51
   see also Rudeltaktik
B-Dienst 5, 16, 17, 23, 24, 33, 52, 57, 61,
      214, 216, 231, 232, 234, 236, 248,
      258, 274
BdU (*Befehlshaber der U-boote*) 4, 12, 17,
      20, 21, 23, 24, 50, 52, 53, 58–60, 71,
      83, 84, 91, 95–7, 99, 118, 125–8,
      130, 132, 139, 146, 149, 155, 157–8,
      175, 184, 185, 187–90, 211, 214–16,
      219–20, 225, 231, 232, 247, 262,
      265, 275
Belgium 31
Benedick (oiler) 213

Bente Maersk (oiler) 213
Beta search 118
Biscay 49, 60, 68, 69, 97, 187
Bismarck 14
Blackburn Kangaroo 41
Blackett, Patrick 164, 165, 169, 170, 171,
      172, 173, 176, 177, 238, 257, 263
Bletchley 33, 126
Blitzkrieg, the 54, 55, 220
Boehm, Admiral 272
bomb 3, 58, 76, 249, 258, 263
      see also weapon
   ASW bomb 77
   smoke bomb 97
Boog, Horst 5
Boot, H. A. H. 166
Bowhill, Air Chief Marshal 74, 75, 77
Brennecke, Jochen 145
   Haie im Paradies 145
British OR 163–5 *see also* German OR
      operational research
      outcomes 3
British training (1943–5) 149–56
   ASW training 150
   continuity training 156
   co-ordinated training 150–3
   submarines as target for training 149
   Zaunkönig, the introduction of 153–6
Bromet, Air Commodore 74
Bruce, S. M. 37
Bundesarchiv Freiburg, the 4
Burwell 129

cabinet 35, 37, 53, 209, 210, 260, 268
CAFO (Confidential Admiralty Fleet
      Orders) 113
camouflage 185–6, 196–7, 200
      see also ASDIC
   Alberich 186, 196, 197, 200, 264, 265
   Schnorchel 147, 157, 196, 200, 236–7,
      239, 240, 247, 248, 265
Canadian,
   escorts 138
   government 138
   RCAF (Royal Canadian Air Force) 209
   RCN (Royal Canadian Navy) 94,
      134, 138
   training for ships 136
   warships 212
CAOR (Chief Advisor on Operational
      Research) 169, 174 *see also* DNOR

Carls, Admiral 15, 60
cavity magnetron, the 3, 166, 167, 177
CB 3, 137, 189, 267, 04050
Chatfield, Admiral 30
Churchill, Winston 1, 35, 40, 42, 67, 68,
    72, 77, 114, 125, 138
cipher 3, 16, 33, 64, 126, 129, 134, 231–3,
    248, 258, 266
CNS (Chief of Naval Staff) 35, 40, 66, 72,
    138 *see also* First Sea Lord
Coastal Command 1, 7, 8, 56, 58,
    60, 71, 73–8, 94, 118, 133, 139,
    149, 151, 158, 169, 171, 175, 177,
    207–9, 237, 239, 262, 263, 267
    see also Western Approaches
    Command
  from 1942 onwards 207–9
  Coastal Command ORS 169–72
  patrols and developments 239
Colpoys, Captain 71
Commerce Warfare 2, 5, 23, 61, 115
    see also guerre de course
committee,
  Anti U-boat Warfare Committee 37, 42,
    53, 70, 76
  Anti-submarine Warfare Committee
    (AUC) 13, 70, 256
  Battle of the Atlantic Committee
    (BAC) 35, 42, 256
  Committee for Imperial Defence
    (CID) 29, 256
  Joint Planning Committee 30
Convoy 1, 2, 5, 11–27, 29–47, 113,
    128–32, 151, 172–3, 209, 218
    see also Convoy SC-130
  convoy protection assets 38–41
  Destroyer crisis, the 38
  flotillas 38–9
Convoy SC-130 212–20, 267
Convoy system, views on 152
convoy warfare, German planning
    for 11–24
  naval organization and its changing
    relationships 13–15
  naval problems and Hitler 11–13
  naval war staff and U-boat
    command 15–17
    Skl 15
    Skl /U 16, 20
    Stab der Marine 15
  U-boat arm 17–22

command and control 20–2
  re-birth of, the 17–20
Corbett, Julian 257
Corvette 69–70, 94, 128, 130, 131–2,
    134, 136, 187, 212, 213
    see also Destroyer
  Battleford 131
  Chilliwack 131
  Flower class 69, 245
  frigates 70
  HMCS *Kitchener* 212
  HMS *Loosestrife* 212
  HMS *Pink* 212
  HMS *Snowflake* 212
  HMS *Sunflower* 212
  Napanee 131
  RCN corvettes 128
CPVA (*Chemisch-Physikalische
    Versuchsanstalt*) 197
Crampton, Christopher 174
Creasy, Captain 115
cruiser 18–19, 30, 31, 42, 70, 89, 187
  Battle cruiser 18
  German 30
  light 19
Cunningham, Admiral 72, 111
CVEs (Carrier Vessel Escorts) 2

Darke, Admiral 155
DCNS (Deputy Chief of Naval Staff) 32
decryption 3, 16, 126, 233, 274
    see also B-Dienst xB-Dienst
Dee, P. I. 166
deployment 50, 52, 96, 105, 130, 147, 149,
    157, 164, 169, 178, 187, 189, 220,
    245, 263, 266
  of Escorts Groups 72, 261
  of U-boats 52, 275
Denning, Lt-Cdr 33
Denniston, Naval Commander 33
Destroyer 18–19, 31, 38–9, 65–7, 69–71,
    78, 94, 106, 108, 128–9, 131–2, 144,
    187, 210, 212, 213, 218, 233
  Burwell 129
  four stacker Destroyers, American 71
  German 94, 144
  HMS *Duncan* 212
  HMS *Viceroy* 132
  HMS *Vidette* 212
  Polish 65
  St Francis 132

St Laurent 128
Type I Hunt class 69
V and W class 66
detection 3, 57, 61, 76, 77, 86, 105, 106,
    109–11, 129, 150, 154, 157, 165–7,
    193, 194, 196, 199, 215, 221, 234–9,
    241–6, 249, 258, 262, 263, 265, 266
of aircraft 165
ASDIC detection 237, 241
of convoys 3, 57, 61, 258
    HE detection 244, 245, 265
    Magnetic Anomaly Detector
    (MAD) 238, 263
    of radar transmissions 194
sono-buoys 238, 245, 249, 263
of submarines 76, 86, 105, 106, 110
of surface vessels 111
of U-boats 77, 157, 166, 236, 241,
    262, 263
underwater detection 194, 221, 242
Division 15–17, 21, 29, 32–4, 39, 40, 52,
    67, 87, 91, 109, 190, 191
Admiralty's Plans and Operations
    Divisions 16
Anti-submarine Division 106, 135
ASW Division 32, 33
Division of Inventions and Patents 191
Military Science Division 274
Naval Air Division 78
Naval Intelligence Division (NID) 15
Naval Plans Division 32, 67
Naval Science Division 149
Ships Manning Division 93
Tactical Division 39, 105
DNOR (Director of Naval Operational
    Research) 169, 172, 174
doctrine 7, 18, 39, 56, 65, 70, 76, 78, 86, 87,
    106, 107, 114, 115, 117, 118, 136,
    147, 152, 170, 255, 260–3, 265, 266
A/S doctrine 118, 136, 152
ASW doctrine 106
RAF doctrine 170
of two escorts per convoy 65
Donau (U-boat group) 214–16, 219,
    220, 222
Dönitz, Admiral 1, 2, 4, 12, 15, 17, 18, 20,
    21, 22, 23, 24, 49, 50, 51, 52, 53, 54,
    57, 59, 60, 61, 73, 83, 84, 85, 88, 89,
    90, 91, 93, 94, 95, 96, 98, 109, 117,
    126, 127, 132, 135, 144, 145, 146,
    147, 148, 157, 173, 175, 184, 185,

    188, 190, 194, 198, 211, 217, 219,
    220, 222, 224, 225, 231, 232, 233,
    234, 235, 239, 240, 242, 244, 247,
    248, 257, 260, 261, 262, 264, 267,
    272, 275
as a tactician 50
Dräger apparatus 88
Duff, Admiral 259
Dunbar-Nasmith, Admiral 65, 66,
    68, 70, 71
Duncan 3, 137, 209, 212, 213, 214, 216,
    217, 219

Emmermann, Kapitänleutnant 149
Empire Union 130
endurance 18, 38, 40–2, 66, 68, 70, 71, 75,
    76, 86, 96–7, 157, 200, 241, 242,
    243, 248, 257–8, 262
Enigma system, the 16, 24, 52, 126, 216,
    231–3, 245, 266, 511
escort(s) 69, 105–23, 133–7, 151, 154–6,
    175, 178, 208, 210, 212, 215, 216,
    262, 263, 267
air escorts 41
anti-escort devices 266
anti-submarine escorts 66, 67
ASDIC-fitted escorts 110
attack strategies on U-boats 175–6
availability of 36, 37, 40, 41, 42, 51, 65,
    257, 260
Carrier Vessel Escorts (CVEs) 2
convoy size and escort efficiency 172–3
endurance 42, 71, 257
escort-training programme 72
Flower class Corvettes as 69, 245
HMCS *Shediac* 130
HMS *Stanley* 116
Itchen 154
long-range escorts 39, 67, 257
refuelling escorts 67, 78, 213, 218,
    255, 257

FAA (Fleet Air Arm) 2
failure,
    of the Admiralty 7, 30, 38, 41, 67
    of Air Ministry 258
    of Churchill's Norwegian campaign 67
    Hitler's failure in co-ordinating
        departments 12, 55, 256
    of the *Luftwaffe* 6, 34
    of operation *Regenbogen* (Rainbow) 14

torpedo failures 49, 184–5, 264
  of the U-boat day attacks 218
Fame 132
FAT *(Flächenabsuchendertorpedo)*
  195, 200
FdL 56, 146
  Fdl Ost 56
  Fdl West 56
FdU (Führer der U-boote) 18, 20, 21, 84,
  95, 275
feedback 2, 5, 8, 13, 17, 23, 37, 87–9, 91,
  96–8, 111, 116–17, 119, 146, 149,
  154, 155, 164, 167–9, 177, 178, 185,
  187, 188, 190, 193–6, 199–201, 249,
  260, 263, 274
  of the attack on *Itchen* 154
  based on operational experience 164
  from experienced commanders 98
  from the field 168
  front-line 116, 117, 119, 200
  for newly trained recruits 98
  practical use of 194–5
  Sunday Soviets to provide 167, 168
  on tests 97
  two way 178
  value of, the 116
FEP (Forschungs, Erfindungs und
  Patentwesen) 21, 165, 168, 172,
  188, 190–5, 198–201, 264, 265
  creation of, the 190–3
Fidelity 128, 132, 133
Fighting Instructions (1939) 42
First Lord 70, 210
First Sea Lord 13, 30, 68, 111, 114,
  210, 242
First World War *see* World War I
Flag Officer 15, 115, 128, 172, 211, 217
Fleet 2, 15, 16, 20, 115, 210–11, 240, 272
  British Battle Fleet 11
  Fleet Building Programme 240
  Home Fleet 210
Fliegerführer Atlantik 58, 146
Fliegerkorps 57, 59, 61
flotilla 92, 93, 95, 96, 98, 146, 148,
  158, 262
Flower class *see* Corvettes
Force de Raid, the 31
France 18, 31, 40, 41, 42, 49, 58, 60, 67,
  69, 71, 78, 97, 106, 107, 148, 257,
  259, 268
Franklin, George 110

Friedeburg, Admiral 20, 52, 83–4, 94, 98,
  143, 144
fuel 50, 51, 66–8, 78, 86, 132, 137, 138,
  200, 234, 235, 245, 248, 255, 265
Führer 2, 6, 12–14, 37, 59, 146, 233, 240,
  247 *see also* Hitler
Führer Conferences, Anglicized 6, 37
  see also Lagevorträge
Funkaufklärung 17
Fürbringer, Werner 88

Gardner, W. J. R. 110, 153
GC&CS (Government Code and
  Cipher School) 3, 6, 33, 215, 218,
  234, 266
General Reconnaissance (GR) 75
German Enigma system *see* Enigma
  system
German Naval Acoustic Torpedo
  (GNAT) 172
German OR 183–201, 264 *see also* British
  OR operational research
  and the development of military
    products 183–4
  post 1942 OR 196–9
    decoys and camouflage 196–7
    radar 198–9
    U-boat rockets 197–8
  pre-1943 OR 184–96
    creation of FEP 190–3
    decoys 185–6
    feedback from meetings,
      use of 194–5
    HUS U-boat 115, 185, 265
    information exchange on OR
      113, 193–4
    institutional and local OR 188–90
    torpedo developments 195–6
    torpedo failures 49, 184–5, 264
    U-boat camouflage *(Alberich)* 186,
      196–7
    weapons and 186–90
German training (1943–5) 143–9
  Elektro U-boats training 148–9
  recruitment drive, the 143–4
  model of recruitment 89
  shortened Commander training 145
  working-up authorities 145–8
Geschwader 233, 262
Glorious (aircraft carrier) 34
Gneisenau 14

Godt, Captain 51, 52, 84, 118, 275
Göring, Herman 14, 19, 54, 55, 56, 61, 146, 233, 262
Göring-Raeder rivalry 55–7
Grace, DTD 39
Graf Zeppelin (carrier) 55
Great Circle 127, 129, 134–5, 137
Gretton, Commander 110, 134, 137, 152, 153, 155, 209, 212, 214, 216, 217, 218
Grey Water Strategy 83–99, 105–19
guerre de course 2, 19, 115, 231, 255

HE Effect 57, 194, 238, 243–5, 249, 265
    see also Hydrophone
Hedgehog, the 237–8, 244, 249, 264
Heer, the 11, 12, 55, 256
Hessler, Commander 50, 52, 58, 91, 155, 275
Heye, Helmuth 18, 19, 49, 50
HF/DF 110, 129, 130, 133, 138, 154, 156, 165, 174–5, 193, 213–16, 218, 219, 231, 263, 266, 267
Hitler, Adolf 2, 4, 6, 11, 12, 13, 14, 15, 18, 19, 22, 23, 24, 29, 37, 42, 51, 53, 54, 55, 57, 61, 114, 115, 126, 128, 145, 146, 148, 185, 186, 211, 233, 234, 240, 242, 247, 256, 260, 262
    differences of opinion with Raeder 14–15
HKU (Höheres Kommando der Unterseebootsausbildung) 87, 99
HMCS *Kitchener* 212, 218
HMCS *Napanee* 128, 131
HMCS *St Laurent* 130, 131, 132, 138
HMS Bruce 165
HMS *Graph* 175
HMS *Loosestrife* 212, 213
HMS *Osprey* 86, 105, 106, 108, 111, 149, 152
HMS *Pink* 212
HMS *St Francis* 132
HMS *Stanley* 116
HMS Sunflower 212
HMS *Tay* 212, 213
HMS *Viceroy* 132
HMS *Vidette* 212, 213, 216
Horton, Admiral 72, 73, 138, 149–50, 151, 152, 154, 155, 158, 210

Hull, Albert W. 198
Hydrophone 85–7 *see also* HE Effect

intelligence 5, 17, 30, 32, 33, 52, 68, 126, 135, 191, 221, 233, 241, 243, 261, 273, 280
inter-service 1, 2, 3, 6, 12, 16, 19, 54–8, 59, 60, 71, 78, 169, 177, 201, 256, 258, 260, 267
    communications 256
    co-operation 2, 3, 54–8, 59, 71, 78, 169, 256, 258, 260
    feedback 201
    OR 3, 193
    relations 16, 177
    rivalry 1, 12, 19, 55, 58, 60, 201, 268
inter-war 256
Italy 41, 70, 158, 255
Itchen 154, 155

Japan 22, 41, 70, 244, 255
Jaumann, J. 196

Keitel, General 12, 19
Kenogami 132
King, Admiral 208
King Edward 130
Knowles, Commander 231
Koch, Commander 222
Krauss, Oliver 187
Kriegsmarine, the 1, 2, 5, 6, 8, 11, 13, 17, 20, 22, 23, 31, 42, 53, 67, 68, 74, 78, 86, 94, 98, 128, 143, 186, 192–3, 221, 225, 239, 240, 255, 256, 258, 259, 263, 264, 265, 266, 268, 273
    courses in 59
    departmental organization chart **192**
    and the *Luftwaffe* 54–8
    organization chart **271**
Kriegswissenschaftlicheabteilung 17, 185, 190, 274
KTB 58, 59, 95, 184, 186, 188, 189, 226
Küpfmüller, Professor 188
Küstenfliegerstaffeln, the 56, 74

Lagevorträge 6, 13, 37, 42, 260, 268
Lambert, Andrew 19, 30, 40, 255
lessons 2, 4, 5, 7, 13, 24, 29, 37, 38, 51, 53, 59, 78, 86, 88, 91, 98, 99, 109, 116, 118, 119, 129, 136, 137, 143, 147,

152, 155, 168, 175, 184, 200, 209,
    226, 232, 241, 255, 259, 260, 262,
    263, 264, 266, 267
  in Convoy Warfare 2, 38, 261
  of inter-service co-operation 59
  learned by *OKM* 201
  learned by the RN 119
  of naval requirements 19
  of SC-104 136
  of tactics and strategy 4, 53, 99, 118,
    143, 260
  of task delegation 24
  of training and procedures 125–32
  from World War I 7, 86, 89, 98, 243
lethality 170, 175, 178
  zone of lethality 170, 178
Llewellyn-Jones, M. 152–3
local OR *see under* German OR
Loewe, Commander 217
Longmore, Air Marshal 73
long-range,
  aircraft 157, 225, 262
  boats 51, 233
  Condor aircraft 58
  escorts 39, 257
  missions 78
  patrols 243
  radar-fitted aircraft 42, 266
  vessels 39
Luftwaffe, the 1, 2, 4, 5, 6, 11, 12, 14, 22, 33,
    34, 78, 89, 91, 145, 146, 147, 151,
    157, 199, 233, 234, 236, 248, 256,
    258, 259, 262, 263, 267, 268, 275
  and the *Kriegsmarine* 54–8
  role in World War II 54
Luftwaffe and the War at Sea 1939–1945 6

Macintyre, Commander 137, 155
MACs (Merchant Aircraft Carriers) 2
Magnetic Anomaly Detector (MAD) 238,
    249, 263 *see also* sono-buoys
Maiolo, Joseph A. 40, 110
Mamba 218
Mansfield, Commodore 71, 137
Marder, Arthur 30, 110
May 1943 207–26
  Coastal Command post 1942 207–9
  Convoy SC-130, the fight for 212–20
    15 May 212–15
    18 May 215–16

18–19 May 216
19 May 216–18
19 to 20 May 218
20 May 219
21 May 219–20
track of **213**
events leading up to 209–11
Melrose Abbey 130
Meyer, Erwin 186
Milner, Marc 4
MND (Marinenachrichtendienst) 16, 17,
    23, 24, 186, 196, 273–4
Mulligan, Timothy 184
myth of the March U-boat crisis, the 3

National Archives Kew, the 5
National Socialism 187, 256
National Socialist leadership 11, 255
National Socialist Party 55
Naval Cypher 283
Naval War Staff 15, 17, 21, 117,
    185, 273–4
  organization chart **273**
Nazism 55, 144
Neitzel, Sönke 5
Newbolt, Henry 257
Nibelung 21, 147, 148, 149, 158, 194, 242
NID (Naval Intelligence Division) 15,
    33, 215
Noble, Admiral 36, 71, 72, 113, 115, 117,
    134, 151–2
North Atlantic, the 1, 23, 36, 53, 54, 65,
    83, 84, 105, 125, 126, 129, 130,
    134, 135, 138, 143, 150, 153, 154,
    156, 157, 158, 169, 173, 176, 210,
    211, 217, 220, 221, 222, 223,
    231–53, 265
  A/S war in May 1943 210
  diversion of U-boats 126
  Grey Water Strategy in 83
  return of the U-boats to 153, 154, 157,
    231–49 *see also individual entry*
  search for convoys 53
  sinkings 36
  U-boats lost in **222–4**
  withdrawal of U-boats from 1, 150, 173,
    220, 247 *see also individual entry*
Northern Spray 212
Norway 12, 21, 40, 41, 49, 58, 64, 67, 69,
    97, 197, 257

_ObdM (Oberbefehlshaber der
Kriegsmarine)_ 6, 12, 13, 15, 16, 17,
21, 23, 24, 51, 56, 57, 60, 188, 192,
193, 240, 247, 262, 268
OIC (Operational Intelligence Centre) 7,
29, 31, 32, 33, 34, 41, 71, 221, 225,
259, 266, 280
  origins of, the 32
  and trade 31–4
    defence of trade, the **31**
  U-boat Tracking Room 32–3
_OKM (Oberkommando der
Kriegsmarine)_ 8, 14, 15, 16, 22, 23,
52, 55, 60, 64, 184, 186, 189–94,
197, 198, 201, 266
OKW (Oberkommando der Wehrmacht) 12
OKW intervention policy 20
ONS-154, convoy 125–39
  battle for, the 128–32
  damages 131
operation _Paukenschlag_ (Drumbeat) 53,
125, 260
operation _Regenbogen_ (Rainbow) 14
operation _Weserübung_ 57
operational research (OR) 2, 3, 7, 8, 52,
118, 147, 163–78, 263, 264, 265, 267
  and analysis of convoys 172–3
  Coastal Command ORS 169–72
  in communications 168–9
  definition of 164
  direction finding research 174–5
  features of 164
  FEP 165, 172
  other naval OR 173–4
  Pascha 147–8
  in radar development 166–8
    Sunday Soviets 166–8
  studies into escort attacks on
    U-boat 175–6
  Sultan 147–8
  the term 'Operational Research' 165–6
ORS 8, 169, 170, 177, 178, 195, 197, 263
Otranto Barrage operations 106

Pascha 147, 148, 265
Pearl Harbour attack, the 22, 116
Peyton-Ward, Commander 58, 74, 75, 76
  _Royal Air Force in the
  Maritime War, The_ 74
PG (Pinched German) 4

Philante 146, 149, 151, 152, 156
planning 11–47, 55, 58, 67, 70, 93, 98, 107,
109–11, 128, 191, 239, 256, 268
Portal, Charles 76
Portland 78, 107, 108, 111, 116, 118,
133, 243
Pound, Admiral 35, 40, 42, 66, 72, 211
Prentice, Commander 136
Prichard, Captain 241, 243
Prien, Lt. 184

radar 3, 8, 77, 133, 198–9, 263
Raeder, Großadmiral 13, 14, 15, 17, 18, 19,
20, 21, 24, 53, 55, 56, 60, 185, 188,
191, 199, 240, 256, 257, 264
  differences of opinion with Hitler 14–15
  resignation 15
RAF (Royal Air Force) 1, 7, 41, 54–6, 71,
73–8, 111, 138, 167, 168, 170, 171,
197, 208, 209, 260
Randall, J. T. 166
Ravenhill, Captain 134
RCN (Royal Canadian Navy) 94, 128, 130,
134, 138, 212
Redford, Duncan 3
Reichsmarine, the 11, 18
return of the U-boats 231–49
  air support and SigInt blackout 233–4
  Coastal Command patrols and
    developments 239
  improved weapons and sensors 237–8
    Hedgehog, the 237–8, 244, 249, 264
    Squid 237–8, 244, 245, 249, 264
  new equipments and tactics 232
  novel detection methods 238
    Magnetic Anomaly Detector
      (MAD) 238, 263
    sono-buoys 238, 245, 249, 263
  operations in inshore waters 236
  refuelling U-boats at sea 234–5
  Schnorchel U-boats 236–7
Rhein, Konteradmiral 191
RNR (Royal Naval Reserves) 109, 218
RNVR (Royal Naval Volunteer
  Reserves) 34, 105, 108, 172
Robb, Air Marshal 71
Roberts, Commander 114, 115, 116, 117,
118, 119, 151
rocket 4, 8, 164, 168, 194, 197, 198,
200, 249

Rodger, Nicholas 19, 30, 40, 255
Rösing, Hans-Rudolf 95
Roskill, Stephen 3, 4, 30, 31, 73
Rößler, Eberhard 51
Rowe, A. P. 165, 166, 167
Rudeltaktik 51, 125, 266
Ruppelt, Oberleutnant 130, 131
Rushbrooke, DNI 33

Scharnhorst 14
Scheer, Admiral 15
Schnee, Commander 149
Schniewind, Admiral 15, 21, 272
Schnorchel *see* under camouflage
Schütze, Captain 95
S/D 105, 108, 109, 149, 156
Seekriegsleitung, the 5, 12, 13, 23
Seelöwe (German invasion) 67
Seraph 172, 245
Shediac 130
SigInt 16, 33, 125, 127, 153, 211, 224, 231, 233, 266, 273, 274
Signals Intelligence Control 17
Skl 13, 15–17, 20, 21, 23, 86, 189, 190
Slatter, Air Marshal 72
Slessor, Air Chief Marshal 208, 239
Snowflake 212, 217
Soekaboemi 130
SONAR 39, 70, 129, 150, 172, 185, 217, 237, 257
sonobuoy 238, 245, 249, 263
    see also Magnetic Anomaly
    Detector
Spanish Civil War, the 32
Speer, Albert 240
Squid 237–8, 244, 245, 249, 264
Staffel 57
Stephenson, Vice Admiral 106, 118, 119
strategy 1, 13, 19–21, 24, 29–31, 40, 50, 53, 60, 76, 83–123, 153, 172, 189, 209, 226, 256, 259, 262, 268
    see also tactical
  A/S strategy 152
  balance between tactics and 15
  commerce warfare strategy 19
  of convoys 3, 74, 237
  defensive 153
  development 3
  Dönitz strategy 53
  escort attack strategies 175–6

Grey Water strategy 83, 105
  naval 17, 30, 31
  oceanic 50
  strategic aims 11
  strategic zone 209
  Wegener's Atlantic strategy 259
Stummel, Konteradmiral 196

tactic(al) 4, 5, 7, 20, 32, 39, 55, 56, 71, 72, 74, 77, 78, 86, 92, 93, 96, 97, 99, 105, 106, 111, 113–19, 125, 129, 133, 134, 136, 138, 146, 149, 150, 151, 152, 154, 156, 158, 163, 170, 208, 220, 221, 241, 245, 260–3, 267
  anti-acoustic tactic 155
  anti GNAT tactics 155
  anti-U-boat tactic 114, 116, 134
  A/S tactic 156
  ASW tactic 99, 151
  Blitzkrieg tactic 54, 55, 220
  courses 115
  doctrine 7, 86, 115, 117, 118, 260
  evasion tactic 233, 245
  exercises 92, 119, 262
  gunnery tactic 260
  lessons 4
  methodology 4
  problems 170, 178
  procedures 99
  Rudeltaktik 51, 125, 266
  solutions 4, 20, 119, 125
  subordination 56
  table 245, 260
  tactical school 5, 7, 72, 78, 116, 117, 154
  teachers 154
  torpedo tactic 154
  training 92, 96, 99, 105, 106, 117, 134, 146, 151, 152, 158, 208, 261, 262, 267
  U-boat tactic 97, 99, 232, 260, 262
TAS (Torpedo and Anti-submarine Warfare) 93
Terraine, John 74
Teufer, Korvettekapitän 190
Third Reich, the 144, 183
Thornton, Lt Cmdr 217
Thring, Captain 34
thrower 112, 113, 217
Tirpitz 14, 256
Topp, Commander 144, 147, 149

Tovey, Admiral 72
tracking 29, 32–4, 110, 129, 130, 134
trade 14, 18, 19, 29, 30–4, 39, 50, 67, 68,
      70, 73, 76, 114, 115, 196, 259
Treaty of Versailles, the 11, 18, 29, 255
Trident 14
Troup, Rear Admiral 33
Type 129, 136, 271
Type 'R' submarine **243**, 264, 265
   specifications **244**
Type XX1 21, 240, 265

U-954 217
UAS 6, 86, 97
U-boat archives (Altenbruch, Germany) 6
U-boat arm, the 5, 17–20, 33, 49, 273
         see also return of the U-boats
            withdrawal of U-boats
   command and control 20–2
   dilemma 261
   and Dönitz 18
   and the *Fliegerführer Atlantik* 58
   and *Fliegerkorps X* 61
   and the *Luftwaffe* 5, 74
   strength of, the 98
   weakness of, the 98–9
   Z-plan, the 18, 19, 21, 23
U-boat bases,
   and local co-operation 58–60
   new opportunities for 49–54
      French ports, availability of 49
   and the problem of inter-service
      co-operation 54–8
      Göring-Raeder rivalry 55–7
      Göring's concept of a homogeneous
         Air Force 56
      Raeder's dislike for a combined
         policy 57
U-boat training 83–99, 261
3 year training proposed by Dönitz 93
   average time in 95–6
   commander training 91–3
      F-Gerät 91–2
   for commissioned rank 89–91
      general naval training course 90
      initial sea time 90
      new entry training 89–90
      second sea time 90–1
   *HKU-Höheres Kommando der
      Unterseebootsausbildung* 87, 99

manpower 83–4, 93–5
   Scheinkrieg, the 94
   personnel requirements for Type VII
      and Type IX U-boats 84–6
   the crew of Type IXC 85
   the crew of Type vii, 85
   Ratings' training, general 93
   Skl U.III 86
   standard courses 87–9
   U-boat defence courses 87
   U-bootabwehrschule (UAS) 86
   working-up 96–8
U-boat war, the,
   British shipping losses 35, **36**
   German perception of 4–5
   start of, the 34–7
U-boats,
   versus A/S forces 2
   Elektro-type U-boats 143, 148–9, 158,
      194–5, 240, 247, 262, 265
   hunt for 66
   HUS U-boat 115, 185
   maintenance of 49
   role of, the 23
   Schnorchel U-boats 147, 236–7,
      247, 265
   support groups 50
U-bootabwehrschule (UAS) 6, 86
Usborne, Vice Admiral 114, 115

VCNS (Vice Chief of Naval Staff) 13, 33
VLR (Very Long Range) 139, 208,
      209, 211, 233, 262, 266, 267
   see also under aircraft

WA *see* Western Approaches Command
Walker, Captain 116, 137, 152, 155
Walter, Professor 185, 194
War Cabinet Anti-U-boat Warfare
      Committee 53
War Office Selection Board (WOSB) 107
Warwick Mk I 41
Waters, D. W. 4
   *Defeat of the Enemy Attack on
      Shipping 1939–1945: . . . , The*
      (with Barley) 4
Watson-Watt, Robert 165, 174
WATU (Western Approaches Tactical
      Unit) 5, 150–1, 154, 155, 156, 157,
      158, 172, 178, 245

weapon(s) 3, 7, 8, 17, 21, 31, 77, 91, 96, 98, 112, 114, 143, 145, 152, 155, 157, 163, 164, 166, 168, 172, 175, 178, 184, 186–9, 190, 212, 217, 221, 222, 237–40, 249, 264, 267, 268
 see also individual entries
 400-lb depth-charge 113
 ASDIC 118, 175
 deck gun 112
 improvements in 237–8
 and OR 186–8
 squid 94, 237–8, 244, 245, 249, 264
 torpedo, acoustic 143, 153–6, 200, 232, 264
Wegener, Wolfgang 14, 50, 60, 259
 Die Seestrategie des Weltkrieges 259
Wehrmacht, the 12, 105
Wehrmacht policy 256
Western Approaches Command 7, 65–79, 132, 258
 Coastal Command 73–8
  role in war 73
  at war 75 8
 at Liverpool, 71–3, 1941–5
 Plymouth Command, the 67–8
 structure of, the **72**
 tactical unit 113–18
Western Isles 151
*WFM (Wißenschaftlicherführungsstab der Marine)*188, 265

Wheeler, Commander 218
Wilhelm II Kaiser 42
Williams, E. J. 165, 166, 190, 238
 see also operational research
Wilmott, H. P. 40
Windeyer, Lt. Commander 128, 129, 130, 131, 132, 133, 134, 135, 136, 137, 138
Winn, Rodger 34
withdrawal of U-boats from the North Atlantic 220–6
 reasons for 222–6
  experience of commanders 225–6
  tonnage war 224–5
World War I 5, 7, 11, 12, 17, 18, 22, 29, 30, 34, 38, 40, 42, 50, 54, 70, 85, 89, 98, 106, 112, 129, 165, 174, 185, 243, 258, 259, 261, 262, 265
World War II 2, 6, 17, 30, 38, 54, 55, 73, 107, 112, 118, 134, 171, 183, 255, 258, 263, 267

xB-Dienst 16, 23, 24, 231, 232, 248, 266

Z Plan 18, 19, 21, 23, 60, 256
Zamalek 213, 216
Zaunkönig, the 153–6, 200, 232, 264
Zenker, Admiral 56
Zeppelin (aircraft carrier) 74

Lightning Source UK Ltd.
Milton Keynes UK
UKHW020641100520
362999UK00003B/60

9 781474 236911